Ouran High School Host Club™

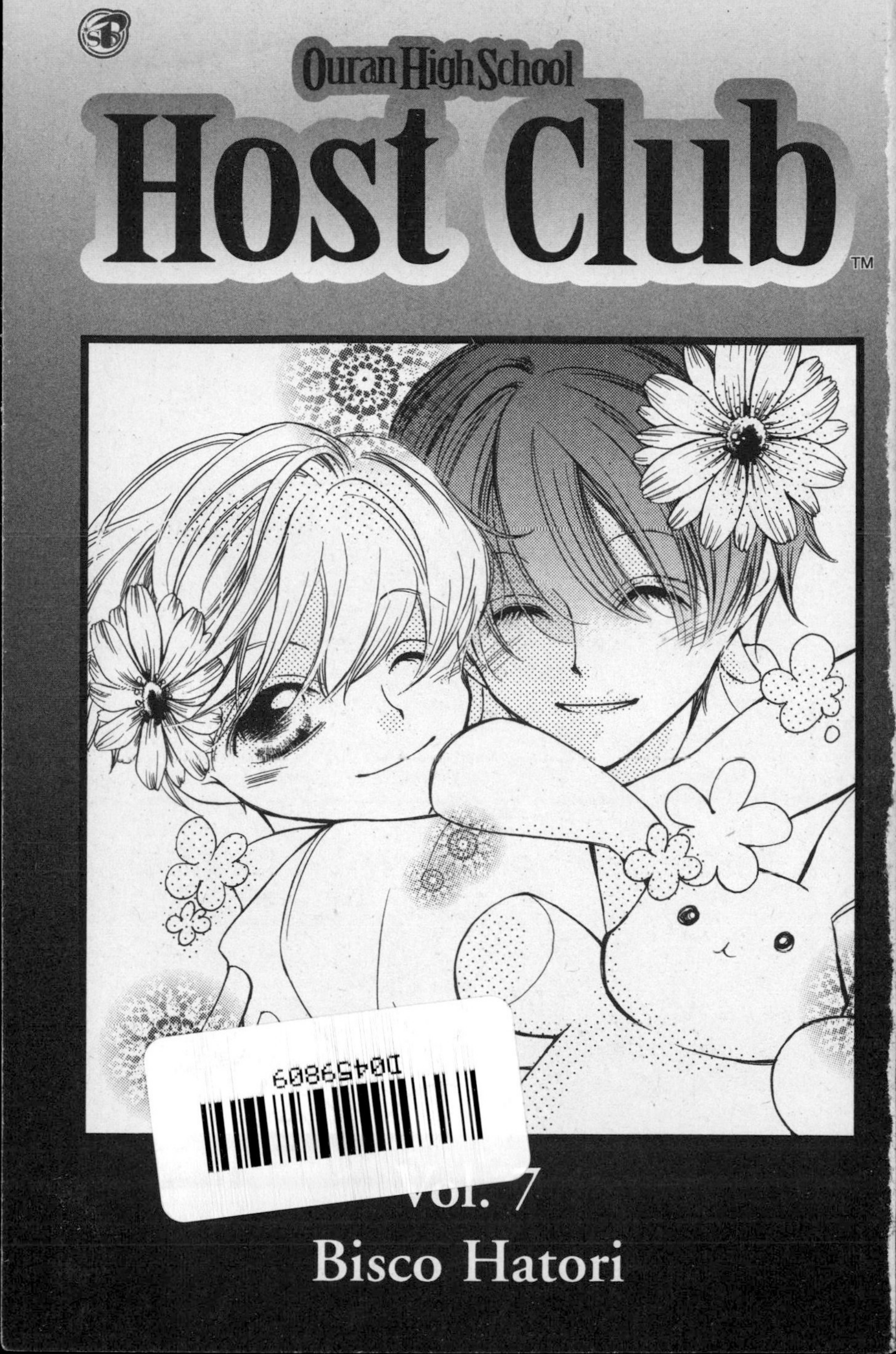

Vol. 7

Bisco Hatori

Ouran High School

Host Club™

Vol. 7

CONTENTS

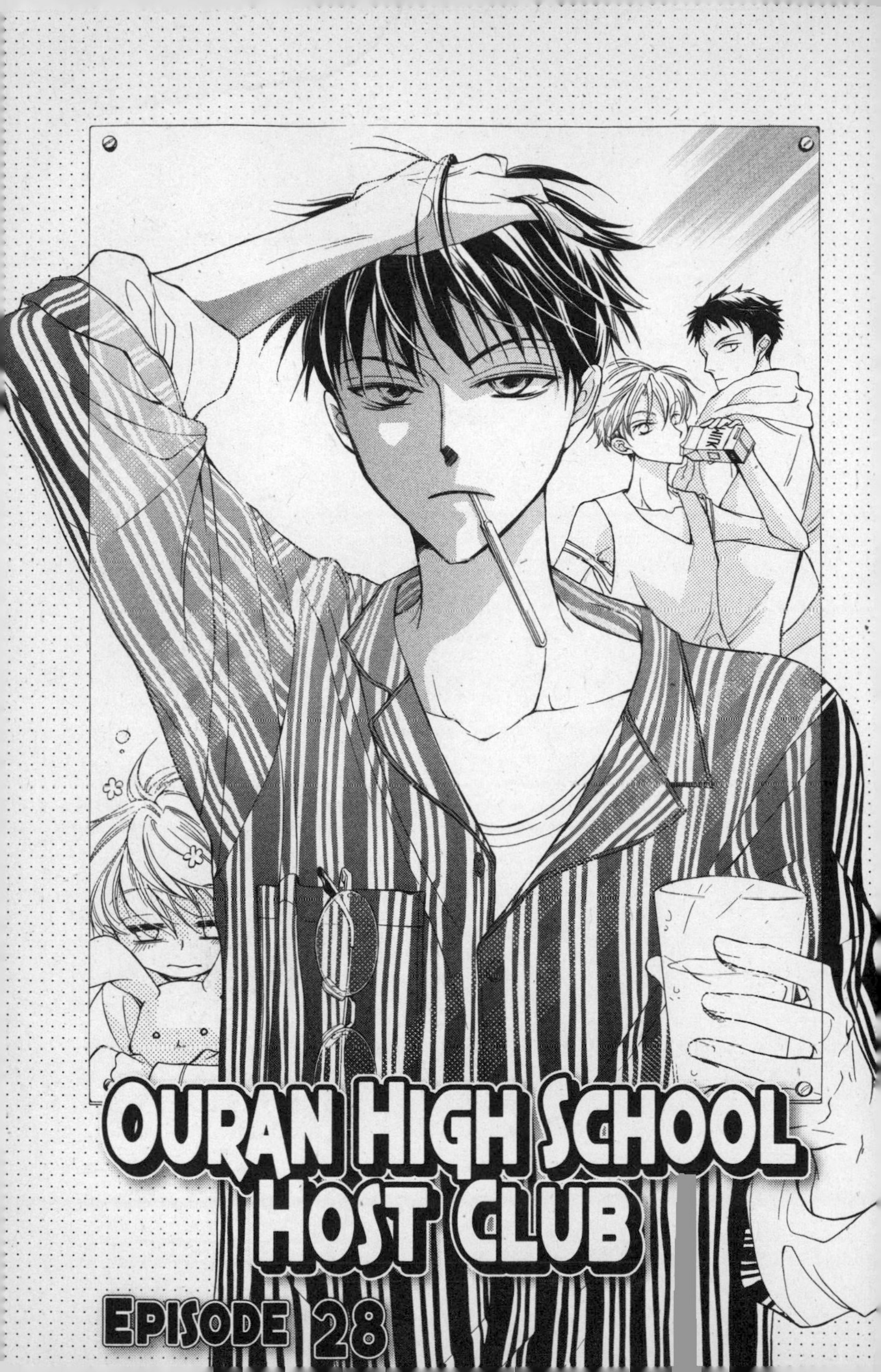
OURAN HIGH SCHOOL
HOST CLUB
EPISODE 28

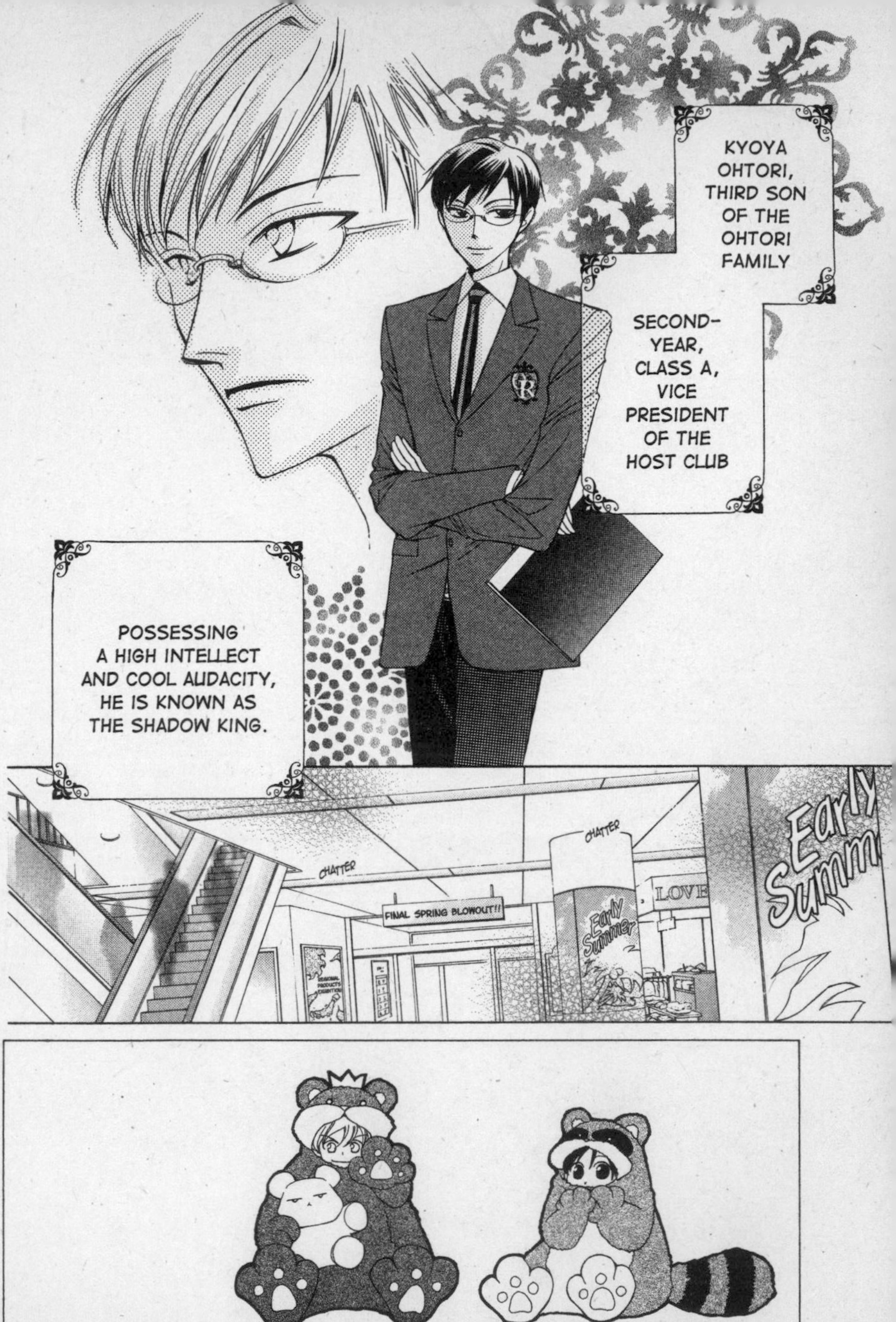
KYOYA OHTORI, THIRD SON OF THE OHTORI FAMILY
SECOND-YEAR, CLASS A, VICE PRESIDENT OF THE HOST CLUB
POSSESSING A HIGH INTELLECT AND COOL AUDACITY, HE IS KNOWN AS THE SHADOW KING.
CHATTER
Early Summer
LOVE
CHATTER
FINAL SPRING BLOWOUT!!

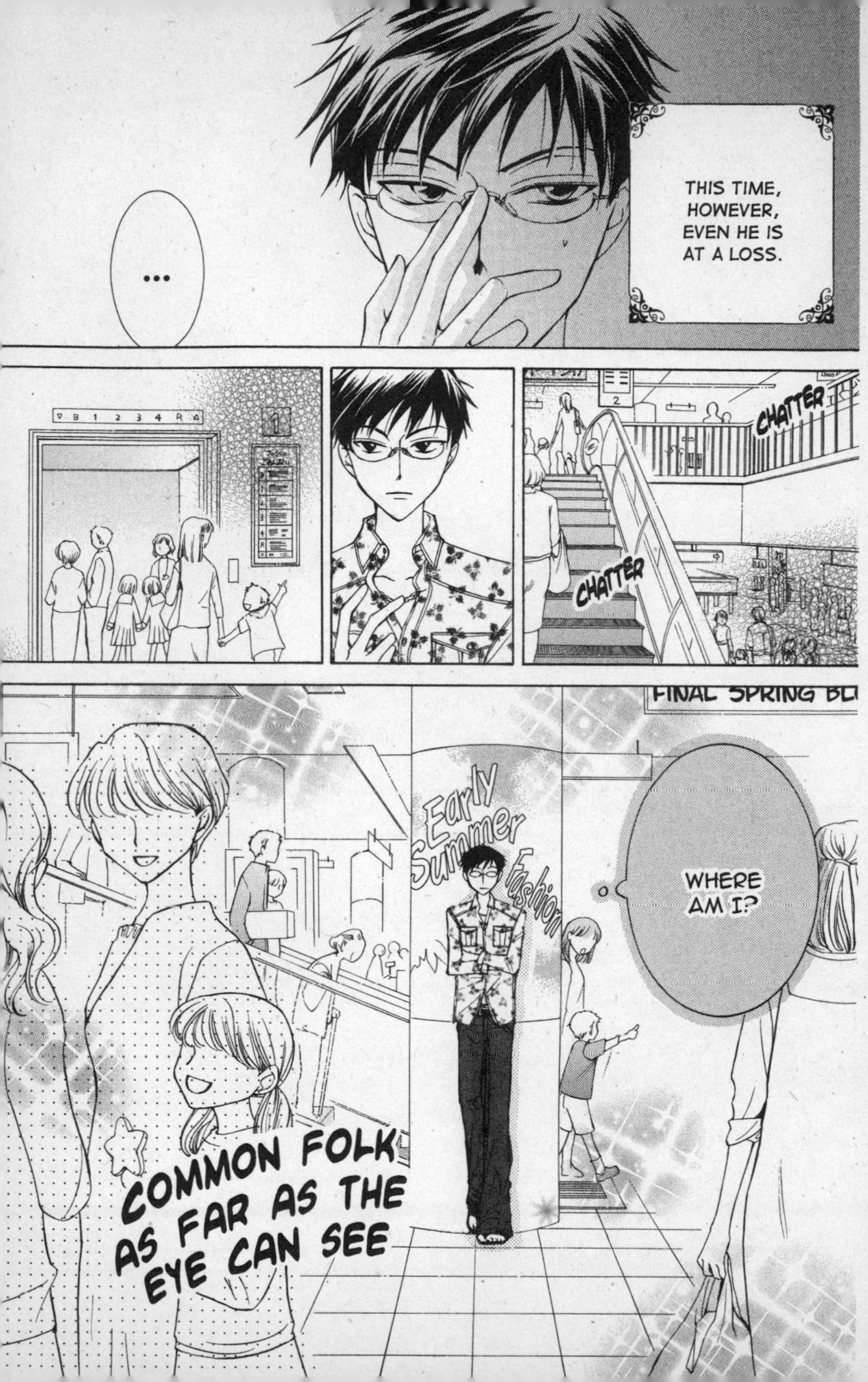
THIS TIME, HOWEVER, EVEN HE IS AT A LOSS.
...
CHATTER
CHATTER
FINAL SPRING
WHERE AM I?
Early Summer Fashion
COMMON FOLK AS FAR AS THE EYE CAN SEE

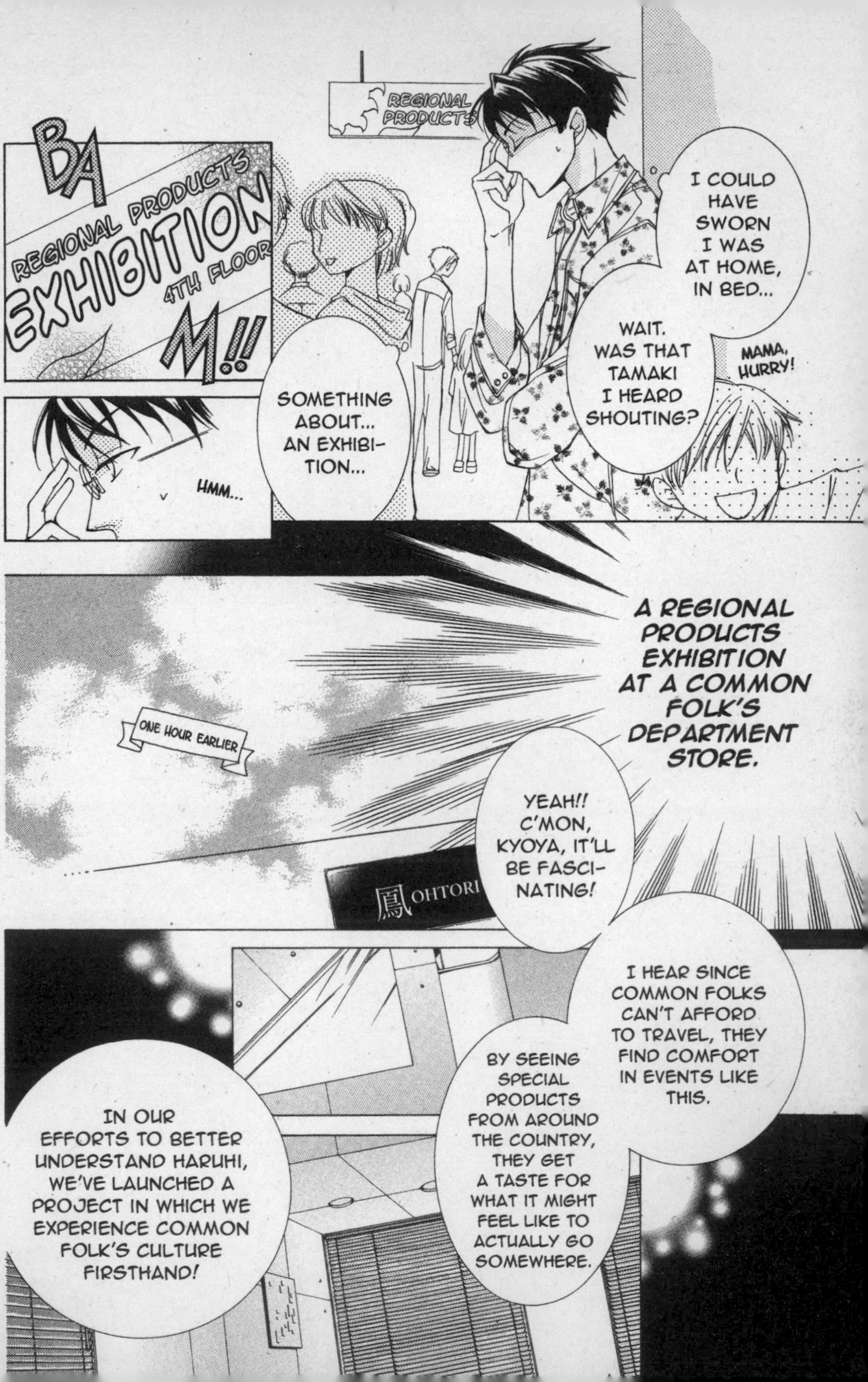
REGIONAL PRODUCTS
I COULD HAVE SWORN I WAS AT HOME, IN BED...
WAIT. WAS THAT TAMAKI I HEARD SHOUTING?
MAMA, HURRY!
SOMETHING ABOUT... AN EXHIBITION...
BA
REGIONAL PRODUCTS EXHIBITION 4TH FLOOR
M!!
HMM...
A REGIONAL PRODUCTS EXHIBITION AT A COMMON FOLK'S DEPARTMENT STORE.
ONE HOUR EARLIER
...
鳳 OHTORI
YEAH!! C'MON, KYOYA, IT'LL BE FASCINATING!
I HEAR SINCE COMMON FOLKS CAN'T AFFORD TO TRAVEL, THEY FIND COMFORT IN EVENTS LIKE THIS.
BY SEEING SPECIAL PRODUCTS FROM AROUND THE COUNTRY, THEY GET A TASTE FOR WHAT IT MIGHT FEEL LIKE TO ACTUALLY GO SOMEWHERE.
IN OUR EFFORTS TO BETTER UNDERSTAND HARUHI, WE'VE LAUNCHED A PROJECT IN WHICH WE EXPERIENCE COMMON FOLK'S CULTURE FIRSTHAND!

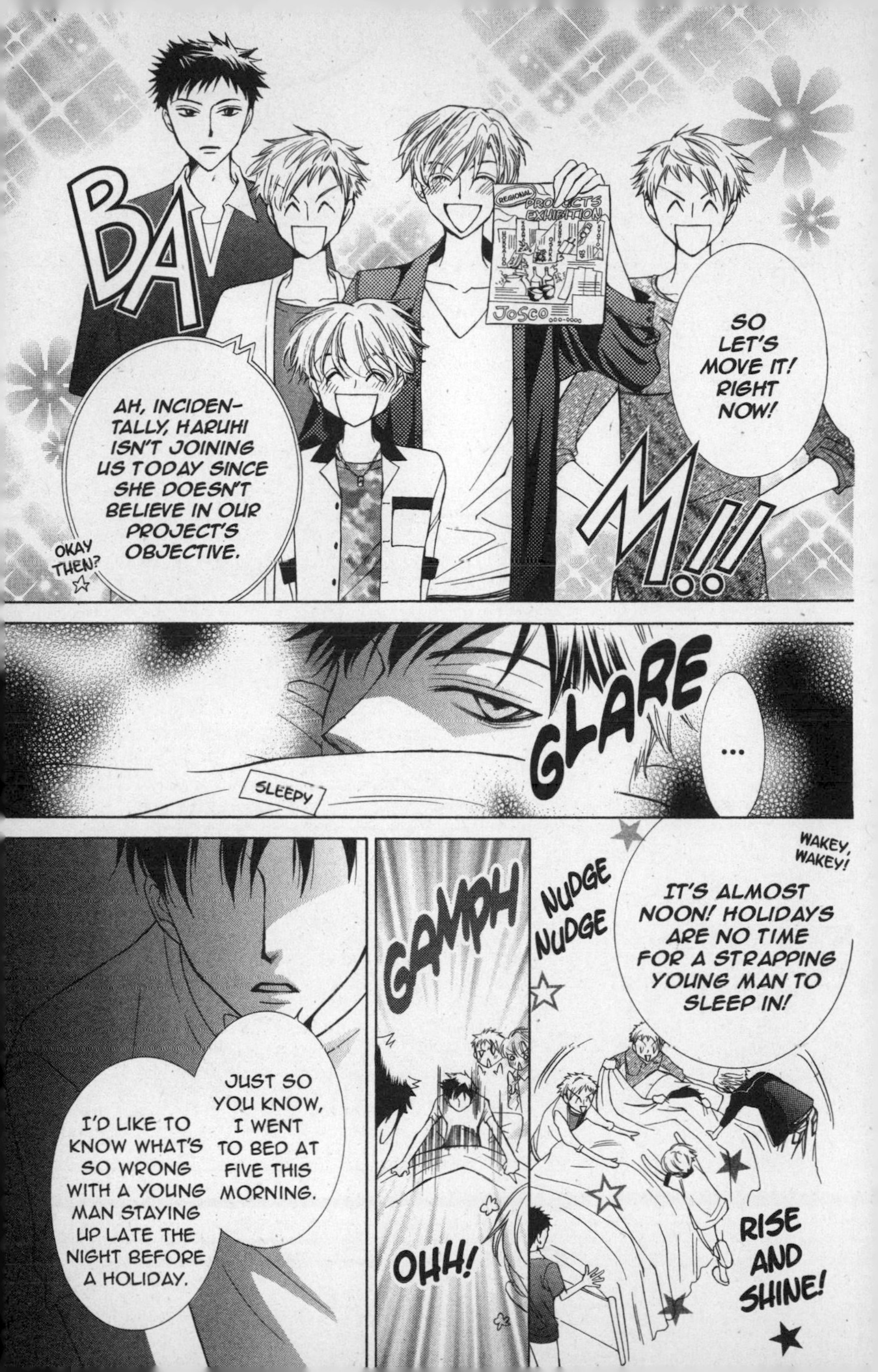
SO LET'S MOVE IT! RIGHT NOW!
BAM!!
REGIONAL
PROJECTS EXHIBITION
JOSCO
AH, INCIDENTALLY, HARUHI ISN'T JOINING US TODAY SINCE SHE DOESN'T BELIEVE IN OUR PROJECT'S OBJECTIVE.
OKAY THEN? ☆
...
GLARE
SLEEPY
WAKEY, WAKEY!
IT'S ALMOST NOON! HOLIDAYS ARE NO TIME FOR A STRAPPING YOUNG MAN TO SLEEP IN!
NUDGE NUDGE
RISE AND SHINE!
CAMPH
OHH!
JUST SO YOU KNOW, I WENT TO BED AT FIVE THIS MORNING.
I'D LIKE TO KNOW WHAT'S SO WRONG WITH A YOUNG MAN STAYING UP LATE THE NIGHT BEFORE A HOLIDAY.

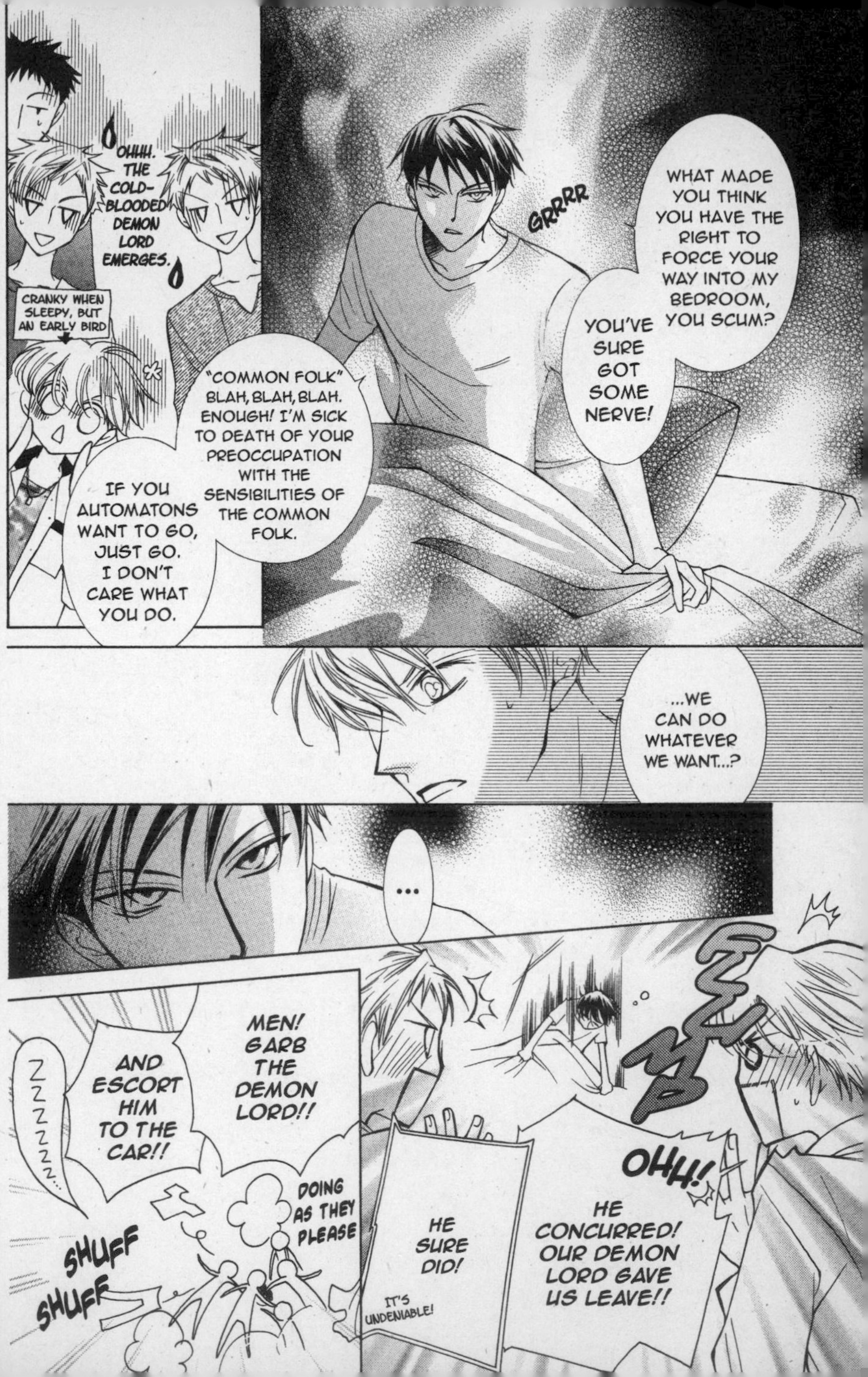
WHAT MADE YOU THINK YOU HAVE THE RIGHT TO FORCE YOUR WAY INTO MY BEDROOM, YOU SCUM?
GRRRR
YOU'VE SURE GOT SOME NERVE!
OHHH. THE COLD-BLOODED DEMON LORD EMERGES.
CRANKY WHEN SLEEPY, BUT AN EARLY BIRD
"COMMON FOLK" BLAH, BLAH, BLAH. ENOUGH! I'M SICK TO DEATH OF YOUR PREOCCUPATION WITH THE SENSIBILITIES OF THE COMMON FOLK.
IF YOU AUTOMATONS WANT TO GO, JUST GO. I DON'T CARE WHAT YOU DO.
...WE CAN DO WHATEVER WE WANT...?
...
OHH!
HE CONCURRED! OUR DEMON LORD GAVE US LEAVE!!
HE SURE DID!
IT'S UNDENIABLE!
MEN! GARB THE DEMON LORD!!
AND ESCORT HIM TO THE CAR!!
ZZZZZZ...
DOING AS THEY PLEASE
SHUFF SHUFF

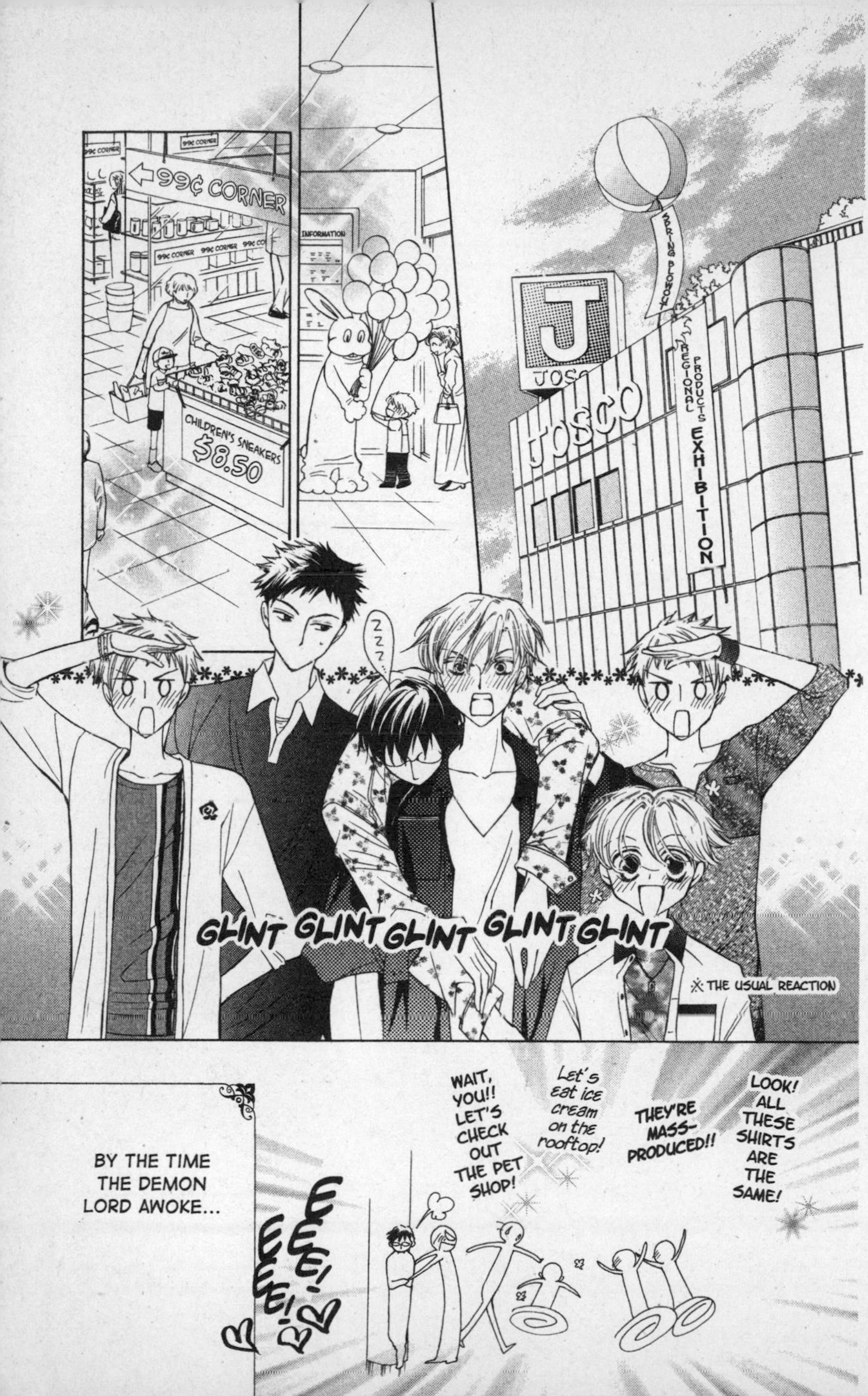

99¢ CORNER
99¢ CORNER
99¢ CORNER 99¢ CORNER
INFORMATION
CHILDREN'S SNEAKERS $8.50
JOSCO
REGIONAL PRODUCTS EXHIBITION
ZZZ...
GLINT GLINT GLINT GLINT GLINT
※ THE USUAL REACTION
LOOK! ALL THESE SHIRTS ARE THE SAME!
THEY'RE MASS-PRODUCED!!
Let's eat ice cream on the rooftop!
WAIT, YOU!! LET'S CHECK OUT THE PET SHOP!
EEEE! EEEE!
BY THE TIME THE DEMON LORD AWOKE...

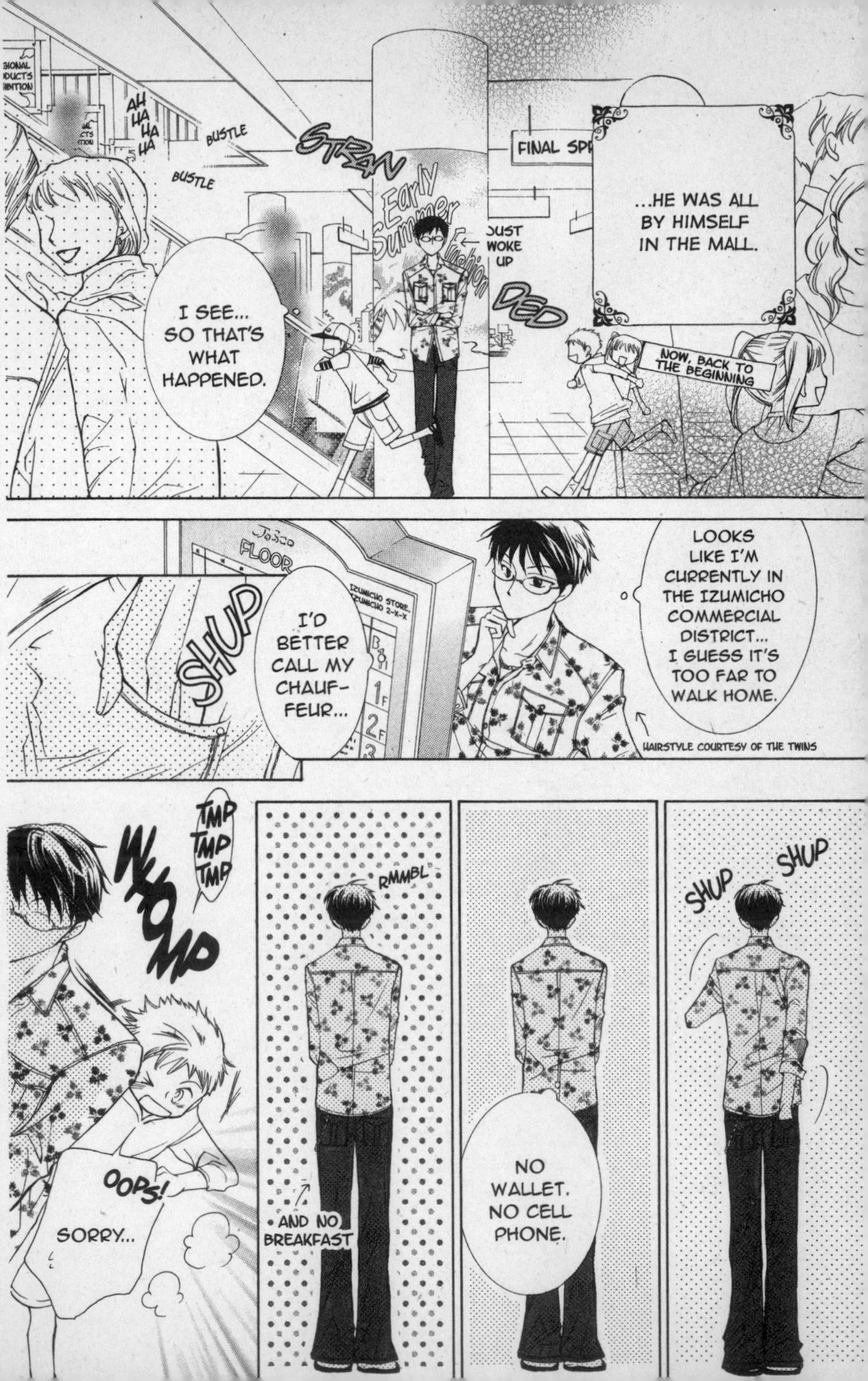
...HE WAS ALL BY HIMSELF IN THE MALL.
NOW, BACK TO THE BEGINNING
DED
JUST WOKE UP
STRAN
Early Summer Fashion
BUSTLE
BUSTLE
AH HA HA HA
I SEE... SO THAT'S WHAT HAPPENED.
LOOKS LIKE I'M CURRENTLY IN THE IZUMICHO COMMERCIAL DISTRICT... I GUESS IT'S TOO FAR TO WALK HOME.
HAIRSTYLE COURTESY OF THE TWINS
FLOOR
I'D BETTER CALL MY CHAUF-FEUR...
SHUP
SHUP
SHUP
NO WALLET. NO CELL PHONE.
RMMBL
AND NO BREAKFAST
TMP TMP TMP
WHOMP
OOPS!
SORRY...

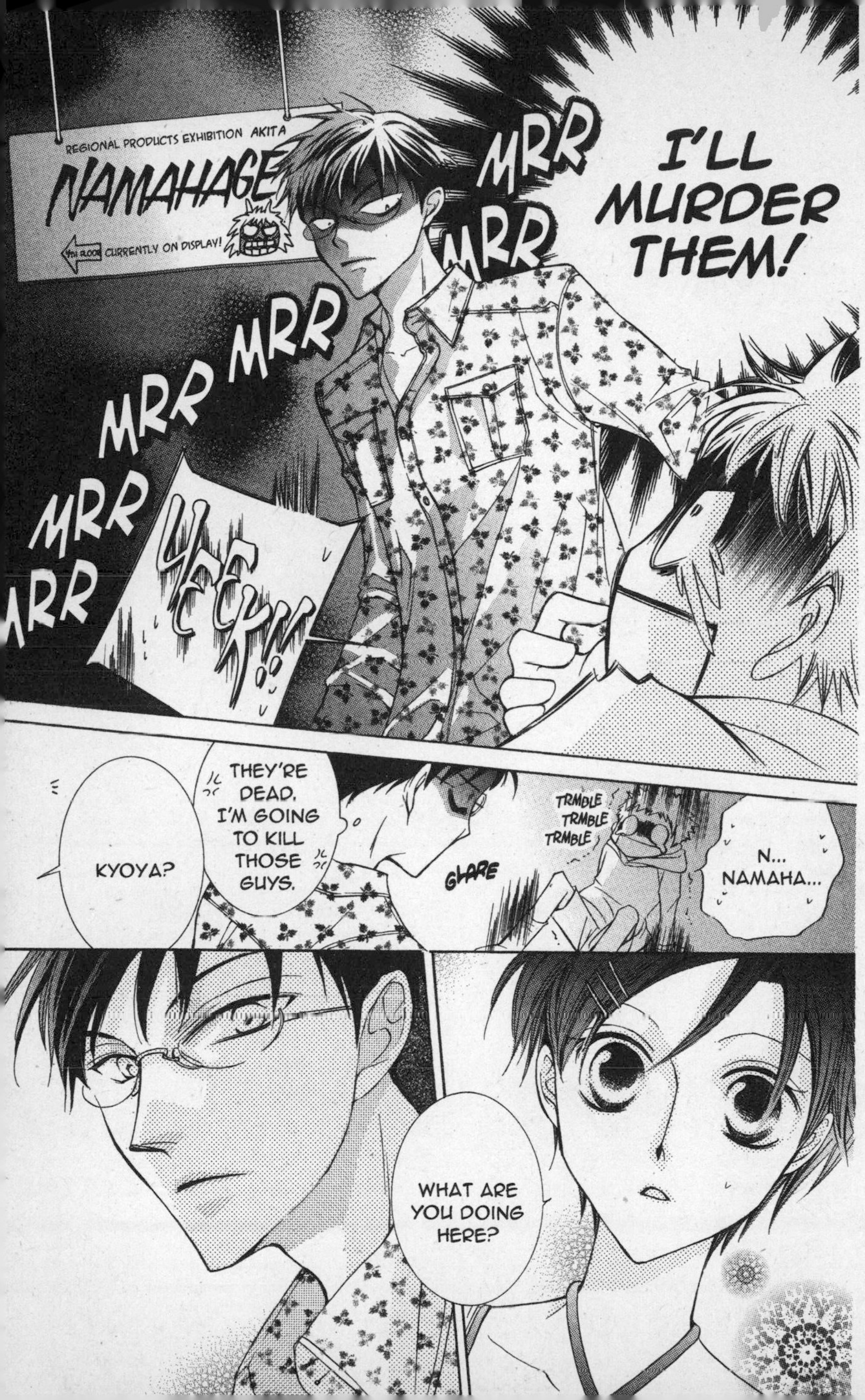

I'LL MURDER THEM!
MRR
MRR
REGIONAL PRODUCTS EXHIBITION AKITA
NAMAHAGE
CURRENTLY ON DISPLAY!
MRR MRR
MRR
MRR
RR
YEEK!!
N... NAMAHA...
TRMBLE TRMBLE TRMBLE
GLARE
THEY'RE DEAD. I'M GOING TO KILL THOSE GUYS.
KYOYA?
WHAT ARE YOU DOING HERE?

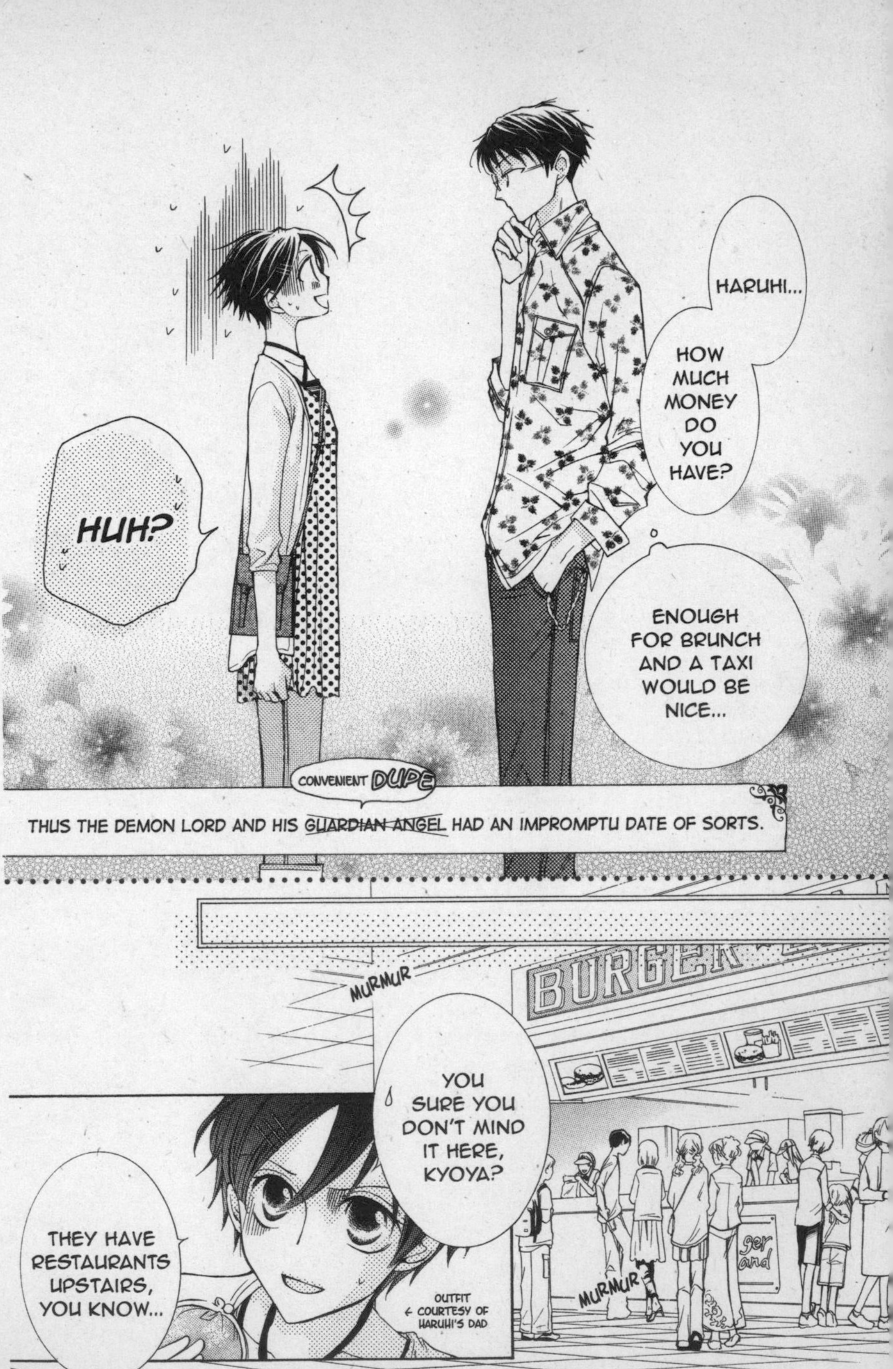
HARUHI...
HOW MUCH MONEY DO YOU HAVE?
HUH?
ENOUGH FOR BRUNCH AND A TAXI WOULD BE NICE...
CONVENIENT DUPE
THUS THE DEMON LORD AND HIS GUARDIAN ANGEL HAD AN IMPROMPTU DATE OF SORTS.
BURGER
MURMUR
YOU SURE YOU DON'T MIND IT HERE, KYOYA?
THEY HAVE RESTAURANTS UPSTAIRS, YOU KNOW...
OUTFIT ← COURTESY OF HARUHI'S DAD
MURMUR

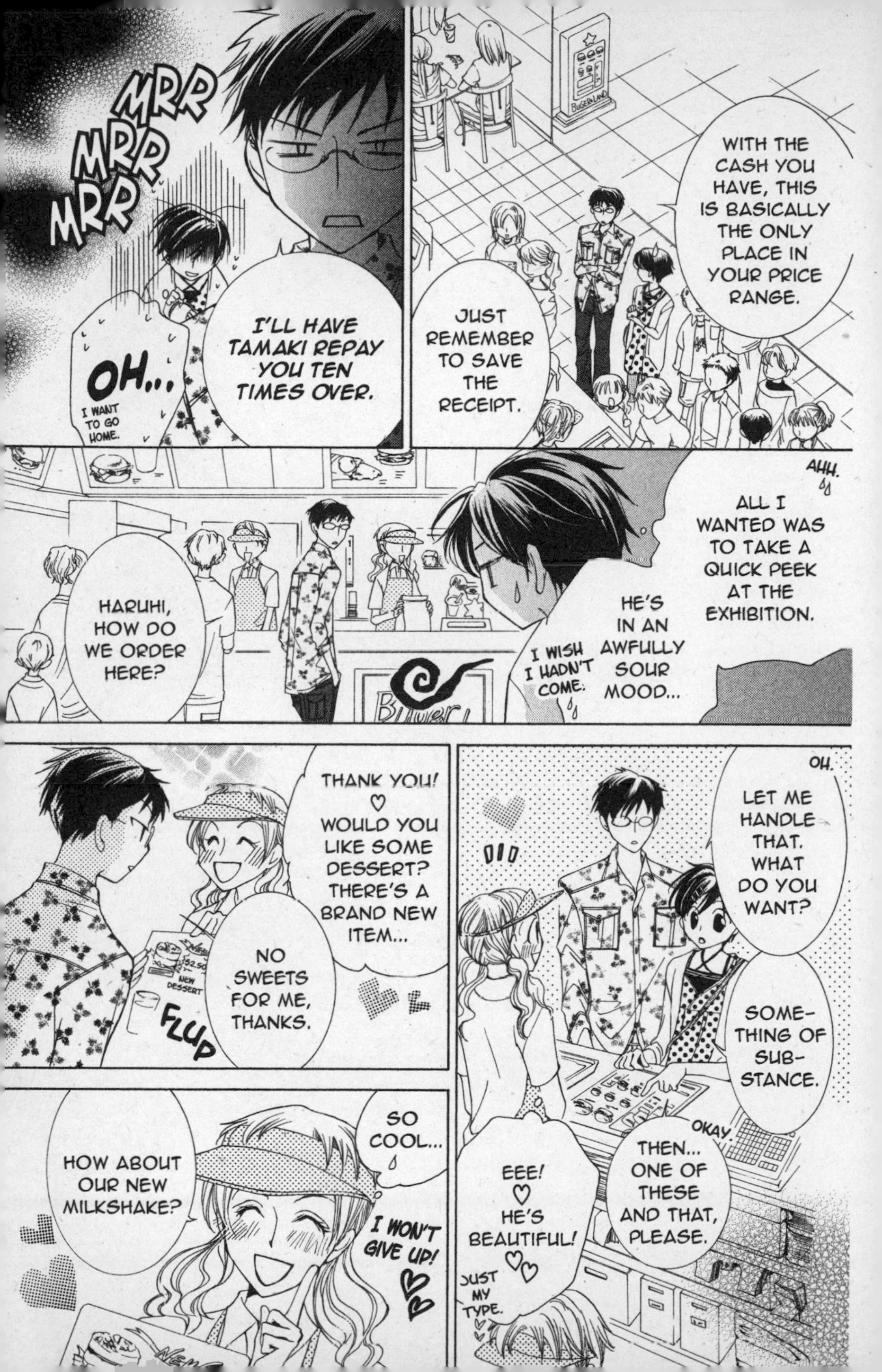
WITH THE CASH YOU HAVE, THIS IS BASICALLY THE ONLY PLACE IN YOUR PRICE RANGE.
JUST REMEMBER TO SAVE THE RECEIPT.
I'LL HAVE TAMAKI REPAY YOU TEN TIMES OVER.
MRR MRR MRR
OH...
I WANT TO GO HOME.
AHH.
ALL I WANTED WAS TO TAKE A QUICK PEEK AT THE EXHIBITION.
HE'S IN AN AWFULLY SOUR MOOD...
I WISH I HADN'T COME.
HARUHI, HOW DO WE ORDER HERE?
OH.
LET ME HANDLE THAT. WHAT DO YOU WANT?
SOMETHING OF SUBSTANCE.
OKAY.
THEN... ONE OF THESE AND THAT, PLEASE.
EEE! ♡ HE'S BEAUTIFUL! ♡♡
JUST MY TYPE.
THANK YOU! ♡ WOULD YOU LIKE SOME DESSERT? THERE'S A BRAND NEW ITEM...
NO SWEETS FOR ME, THANKS.
FLUP
SO COOL...
HOW ABOUT OUR NEW MILKSHAKE?
I WON'T GIVE UP!

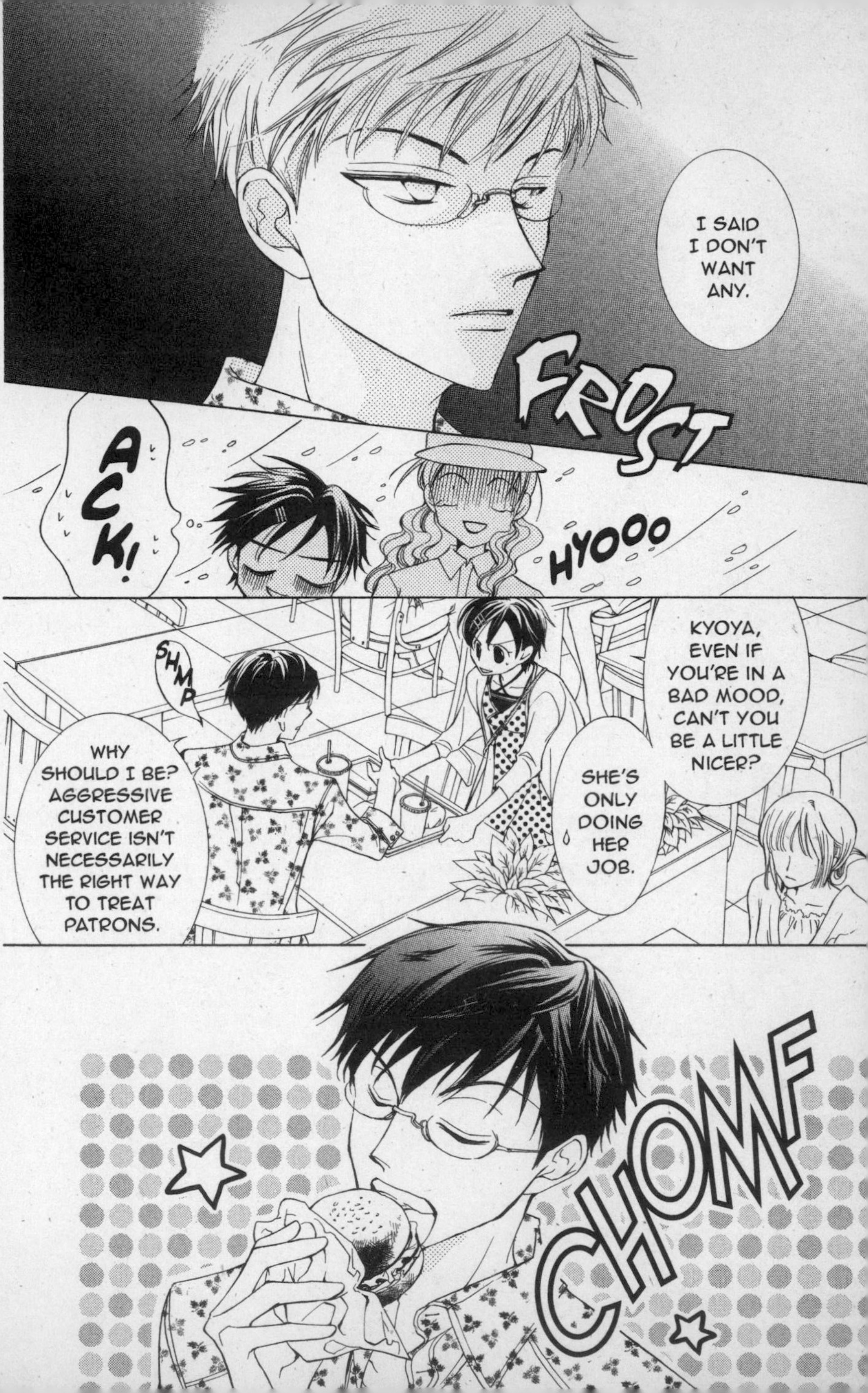
I SAID I DON'T WANT ANY.
FROST
HYOOO
ACK!
KYOYA, EVEN IF YOU'RE IN A BAD MOOD, CAN'T YOU BE A LITTLE NICER?
SHE'S ONLY DOING HER JOB.
SHMP
WHY SHOULD I BE? AGGRESSIVE CUSTOMER SERVICE ISN'T NECESSARILY THE RIGHT WAY TO TREAT PATRONS.
CHOMF

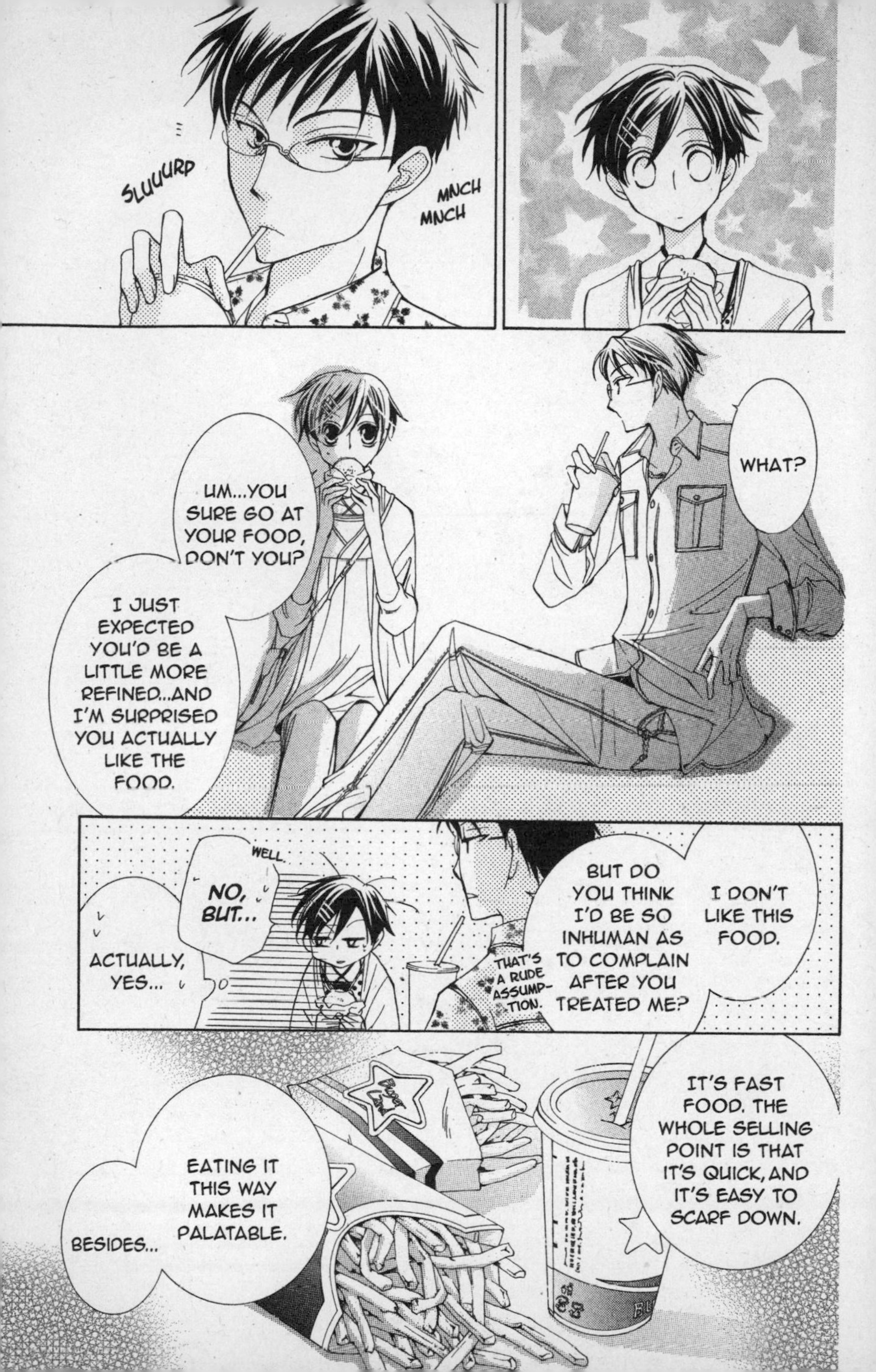
SLUUURP
MNCH MNCH
WHAT?
UM...YOU SURE GO AT YOUR FOOD, DON'T YOU?
I JUST EXPECTED YOU'D BE A LITTLE MORE REFINED...AND I'M SURPRISED YOU ACTUALLY LIKE THE FOOD.
I DON'T LIKE THIS FOOD.
BUT DO YOU THINK I'D BE SO INHUMAN AS TO COMPLAIN AFTER YOU TREATED ME?
THAT'S A RUDE ASSUMPTION.
WELL.
NO, BUT...
ACTUALLY, YES...
IT'S FAST FOOD. THE WHOLE SELLING POINT IS THAT IT'S QUICK, AND IT'S EASY TO SCARF DOWN.
BESIDES...
EATING IT THIS WAY MAKES IT PALATABLE.

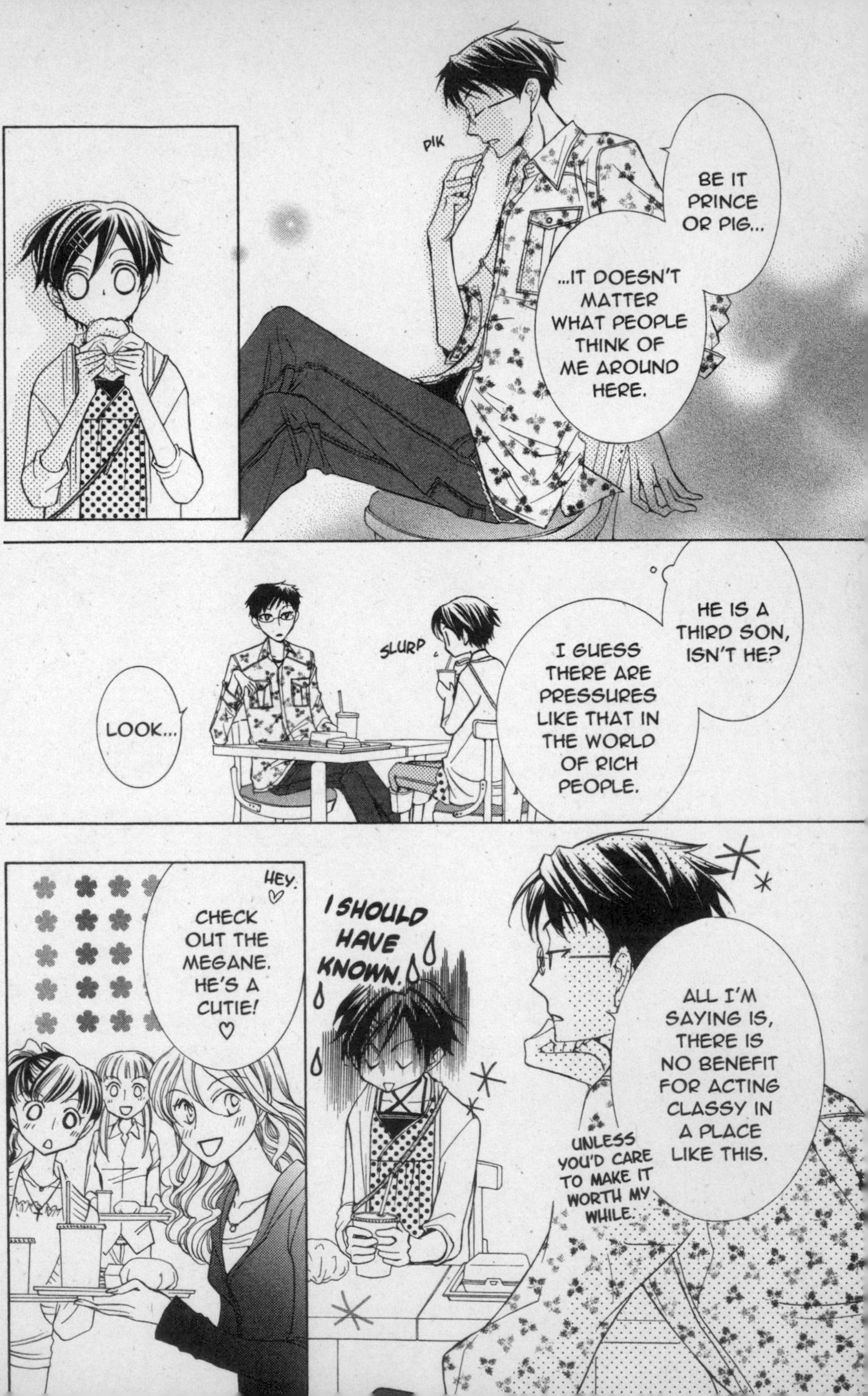
PIK
BE IT PRINCE OR PIG...
...IT DOESN'T MATTER WHAT PEOPLE THINK OF ME AROUND HERE.
HE IS A THIRD SON, ISN'T HE?
I GUESS THERE ARE PRESSURES LIKE THAT IN THE WORLD OF RICH PEOPLE.
SLURP
LOOK...
ALL I'M SAYING IS, THERE IS NO BENEFIT FOR ACTING CLASSY IN A PLACE LIKE THIS.
UNLESS YOU'D CARE TO MAKE IT WORTH MY WHILE.
I SHOULD HAVE KNOWN.
HEY. ♡
CHECK OUT THE MEGANE. HE'S A CUTIE! ♡

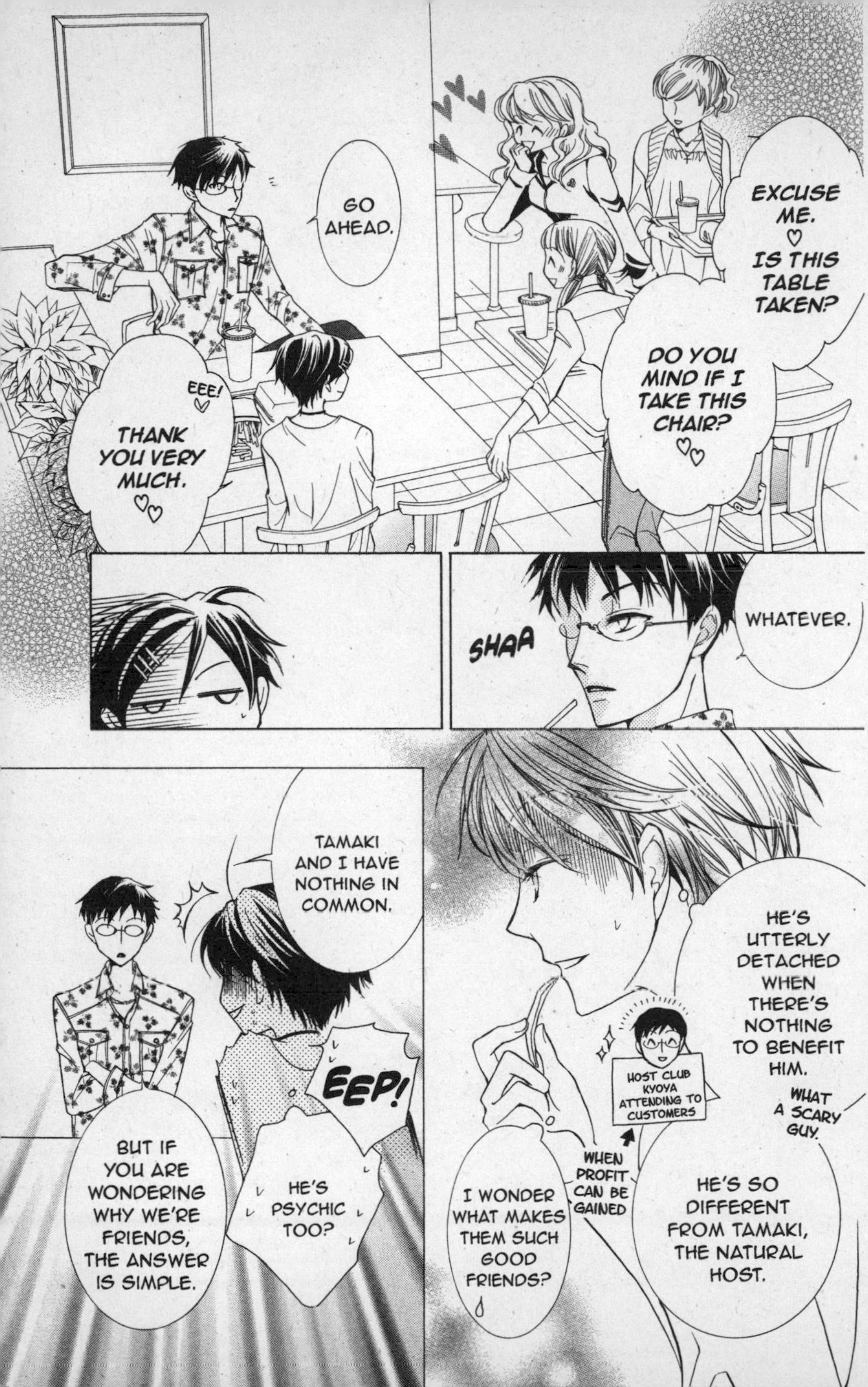
EXCUSE ME. ♡ IS THIS TABLE TAKEN?
DO YOU MIND IF I TAKE THIS CHAIR? ♡♡
GO AHEAD.
EEE! ♡
THANK YOU VERY MUCH. ♡♡
WHATEVER.
SHAA
HE'S UTTERLY DETACHED WHEN THERE'S NOTHING TO BENEFIT HIM.
WHAT A SCARY GUY.
HOST CLUB KYOYA ATTENDING TO CUSTOMERS
WHEN PROFIT CAN BE GAINED
HE'S SO DIFFERENT FROM TAMAKI, THE NATURAL HOST.
I WONDER WHAT MAKES THEM SUCH GOOD FRIENDS?
TAMAKI AND I HAVE NOTHING IN COMMON.
EEP!
HE'S PSYCHIC TOO?
BUT IF YOU ARE WONDERING WHY WE'RE FRIENDS, THE ANSWER IS SIMPLE.

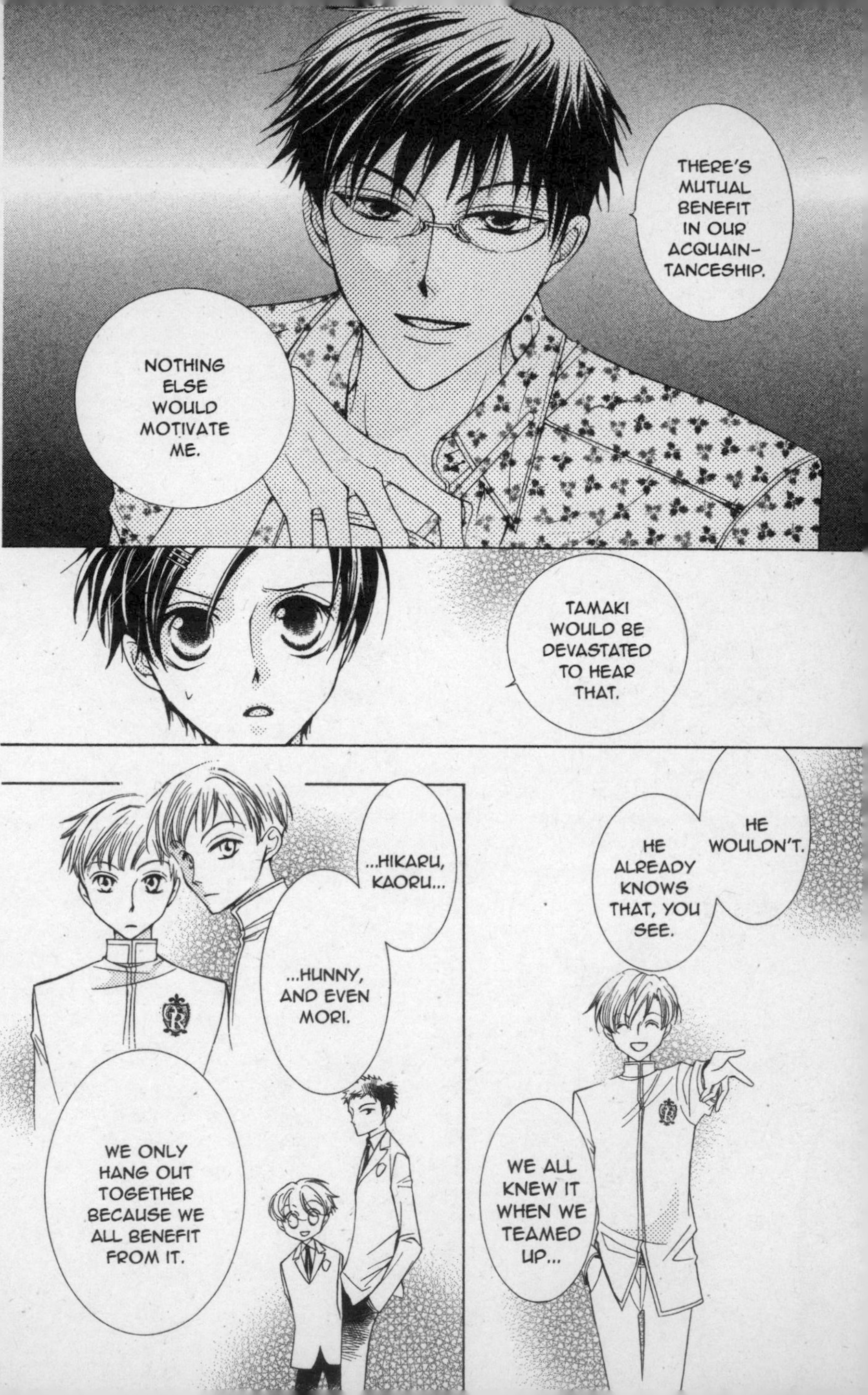
THERE'S MUTUAL BENEFIT IN OUR ACQUAIN-TANCESHIP.
NOTHING ELSE WOULD MOTIVATE ME.
TAMAKI WOULD BE DEVASTATED TO HEAR THAT.
HE WOULDN'T.
HE ALREADY KNOWS THAT, YOU SEE.
WE ALL KNEW IT WHEN WE TEAMED UP...
...HIKARU, KAORU...
...HUNNY, AND EVEN MORI.
WE ONLY HANG OUT TOGETHER BECAUSE WE ALL BENEFIT FROM IT.

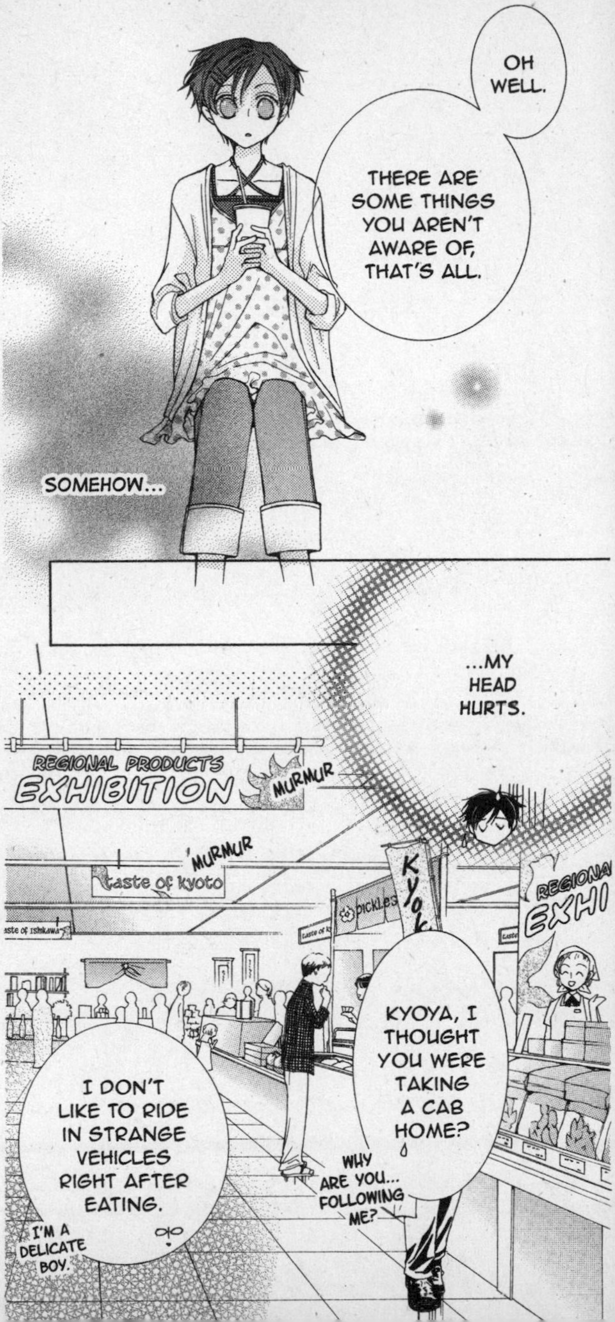
OH WELL.
THERE ARE SOME THINGS YOU AREN'T AWARE OF, THAT'S ALL.
SOMEHOW...
...MY HEAD HURTS.
REGIONAL PRODUCTS EXHIBITION
MURMUR
MURMUR
taste of kyoto
taste of ishikawa
PICKLES
KYOTO
REGIONAL EXHI
KYOYA, I THOUGHT YOU WERE TAKING A CAB HOME?
WHY ARE YOU... FOLLOWING ME?
I DON'T LIKE TO RIDE IN STRANGE VEHICLES RIGHT AFTER EATING.
I'M A DELICATE BOY.

1

✿ HELLO, EVERYONE! HATORI HERE. WE'RE UP TO VOLUME 7!! WAHH!! GYAHH!! EEE!! (I'M FLUSTERED--I NEVER EXPECTED THE SERIES TO GO ON THIS LONG.)

✿ FOR THE FRONT COVER, I MEANT TO DRAW THE TWINS AND HARUHI IN ALLURING CHINESE DRESS. ALAS, I RAN OUT OF IDEAS FOR VOLUME 6, SO I USED THAT THEME THERE. (I THINK KYOYA IS TOO LIMITED IN HIS COSPLAY OPTIONS.)

THEN I CAME UP WITH THE "WESTERN☆" IDEA--BUT AGAIN, I RECENTLY WOUND UP USING IT FOR A COLOR PAGE.

SO THAT'S HOW THIS VOLUME'S COVER CAME ABOUT. NOTHING EVER GOES AS I PLAN OR EXPECT! THEN AGAIN, THAT'S TYPICAL OF *HOST CLUB*, SO ALL IS WELL. YEAH!! (OR SO I TELL MYSELF.)

ANYHOW, LET'S TEAR THROUGH VOLUME 7 WITH ZEST. THANKS FOR STICKING WITH ME!

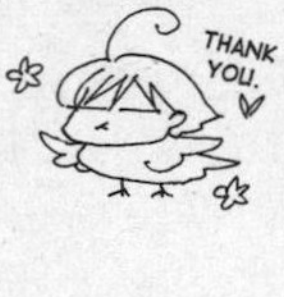
THANK YOU.

※ MY STOMACH HAS BEEN DOING REALLY WELL LATELY. (I USED TO HAVE TERRIBLE STOMACH PROBLEMS.) BUT THE SIDE EFFECT IS I'M NOW GAINING WEIGHT. HMM.

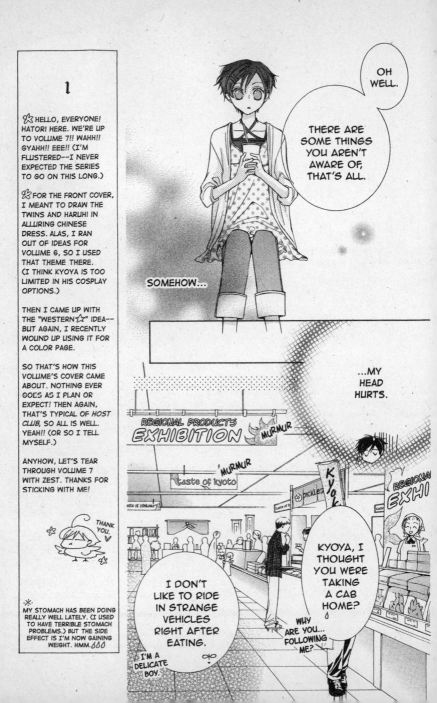

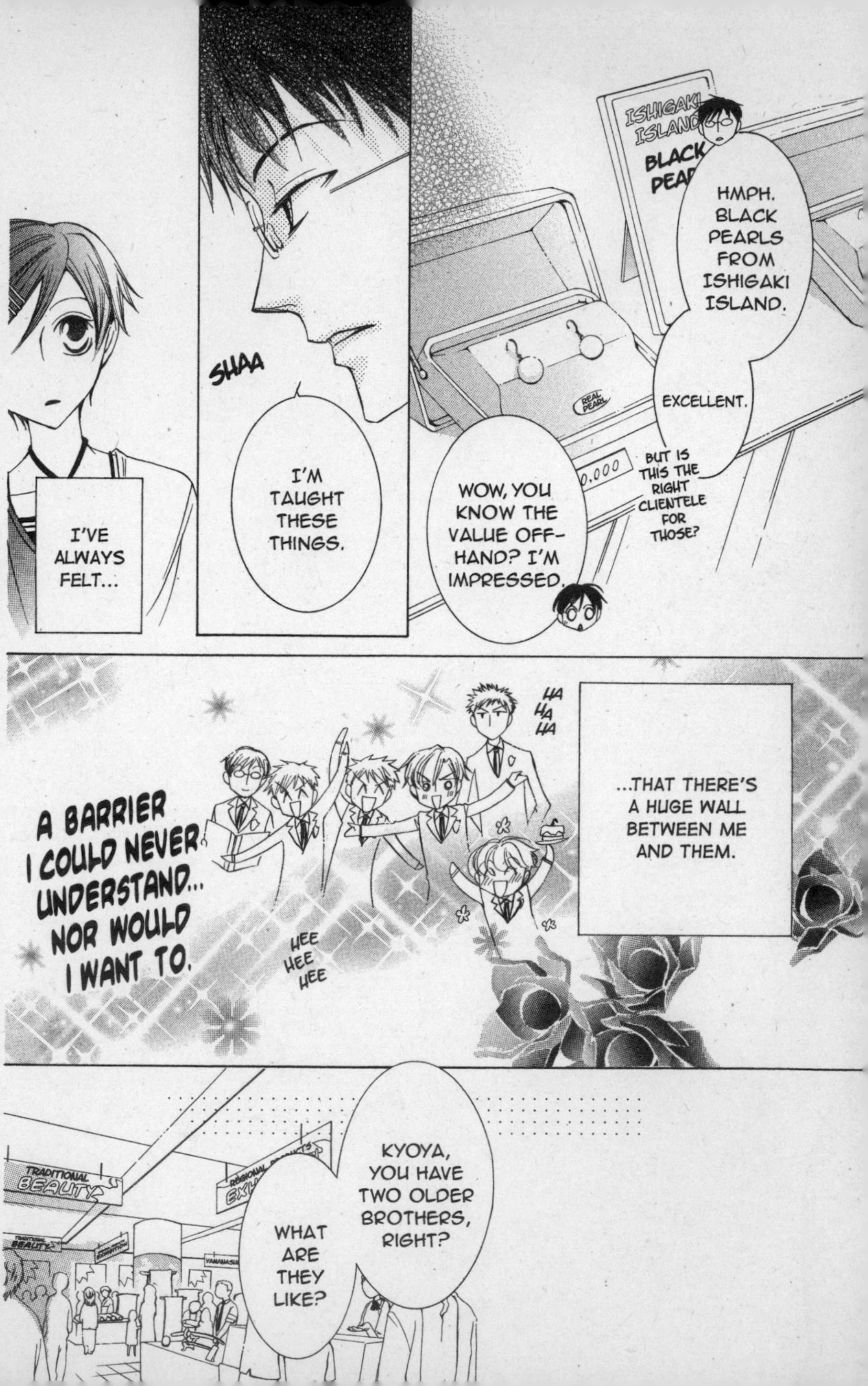
ISHIGAKI ISLAND
BLACK
HMPH. BLACK PEARLS FROM ISHIGAKI ISLAND.
EXCELLENT.
REAL PEARL
BUT IS THIS THE RIGHT CLIENTELE FOR THOSE?
WOW, YOU KNOW THE VALUE OFF-HAND? I'M IMPRESSED.
SHAA
I'M TAUGHT THESE THINGS.
I'VE ALWAYS FELT...
...THAT THERE'S A HUGE WALL BETWEEN ME AND THEM.
HA HA HA
HEE HEE HEE
A BARRIER I COULD NEVER UNDERSTAND... NOR WOULD I WANT TO.
TRADITIONAL BEAUTY
KYOYA, YOU HAVE TWO OLDER BROTHERS, RIGHT?
WHAT ARE THEY LIKE?

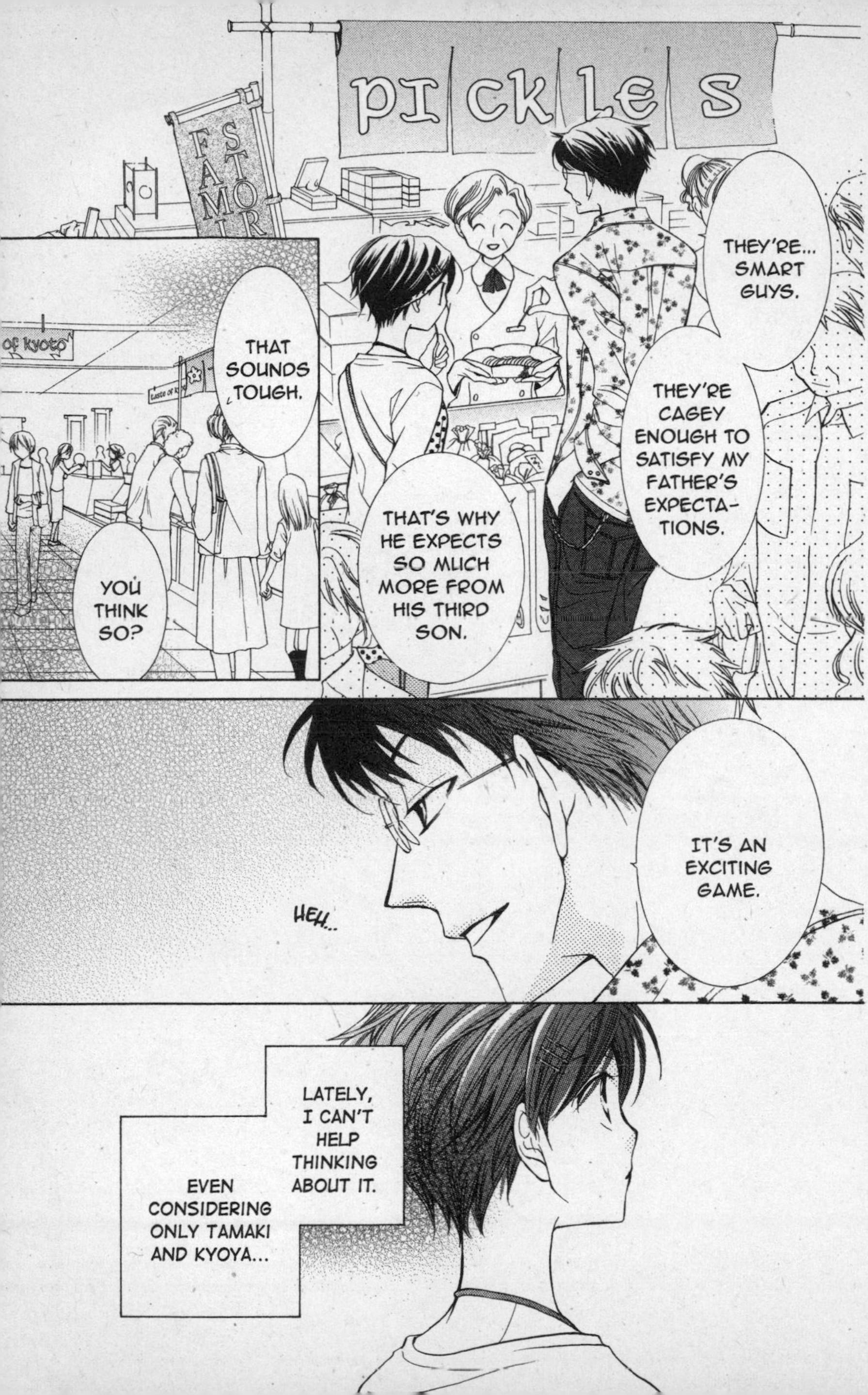
pickles
THEY'RE... SMART GUYS.
THEY'RE CAGEY ENOUGH TO SATISFY MY FATHER'S EXPECTATIONS.
THAT'S WHY HE EXPECTS SO MUCH MORE FROM HIS THIRD SON.
of kyoto
THAT SOUNDS TOUGH.
YOU THINK SO?
IT'S AN EXCITING GAME.
HEH...
LATELY, I CAN'T HELP THINKING ABOUT IT.
EVEN CONSIDERING ONLY TAMAKI AND KYOYA...

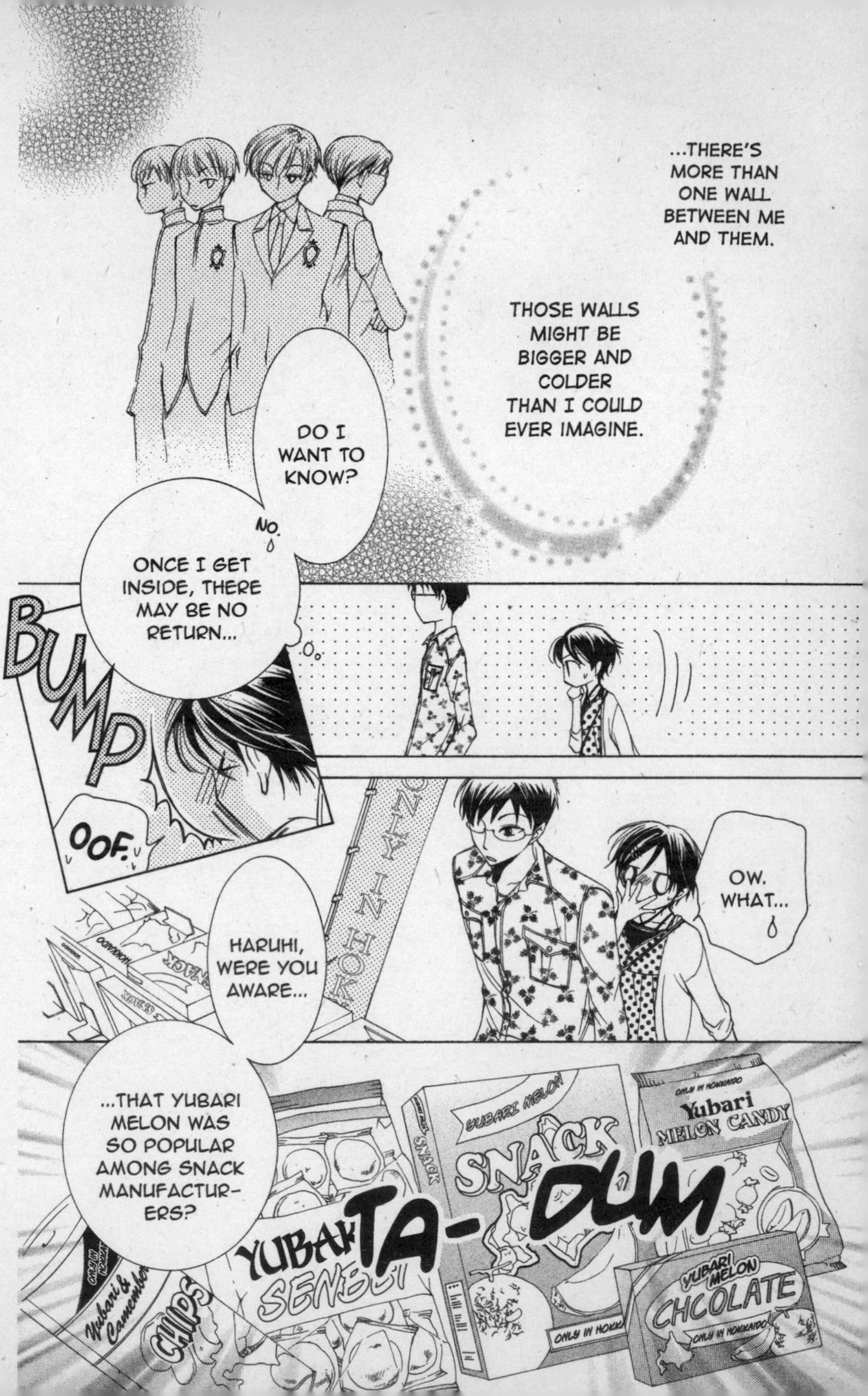
...THERE'S MORE THAN ONE WALL BETWEEN ME AND THEM.
THOSE WALLS MIGHT BE BIGGER AND COLDER THAN I COULD EVER IMAGINE.
DO I WANT TO KNOW?
NO.
ONCE I GET INSIDE, THERE MAY BE NO RETURN...
BUMP
OOF.
ONLY IN HOK
OW. WHAT...
HARUHI, WERE YOU AWARE...
...THAT YUBARI MELON WAS SO POPULAR AMONG SNACK MANUFACTURERS?
ONLY IN HOKKAIDO Yubari MELON CANDY
YUBARI MELON SNACK
ONLY IN HOKKA
YUBARI MELON CHCOLATE
ONLY IN HOKKAIDO
TA-DUM
SENBEI
CHIPS
Yubari & Camembert

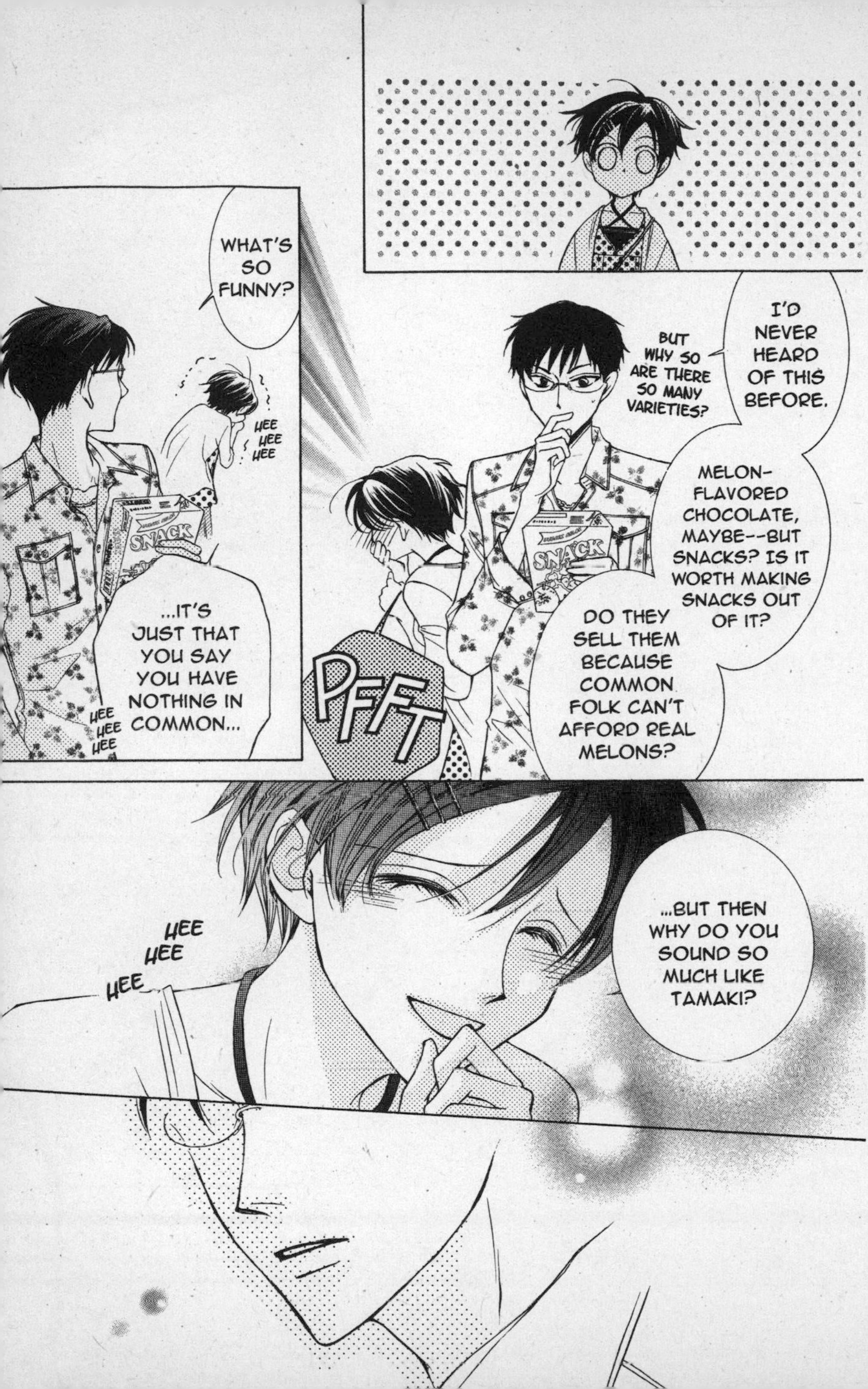
I'D NEVER HEARD OF THIS BEFORE.
BUT WHY SO ARE THERE SO MANY VARIETIES?
MELON-FLAVORED CHOCOLATE, MAYBE--BUT SNACKS? IS IT WORTH MAKING SNACKS OUT OF IT?
DO THEY SELL THEM BECAUSE COMMON FOLK CAN'T AFFORD REAL MELONS?
PFFT
WHAT'S SO FUNNY?
HEE HEE HEE
...IT'S JUST THAT YOU SAY YOU HAVE NOTHING IN COMMON...
HEE HEE HEE
...BUT THEN WHY DO YOU SOUND SO MUCH LIKE TAMAKI?
HEE HEE HEE

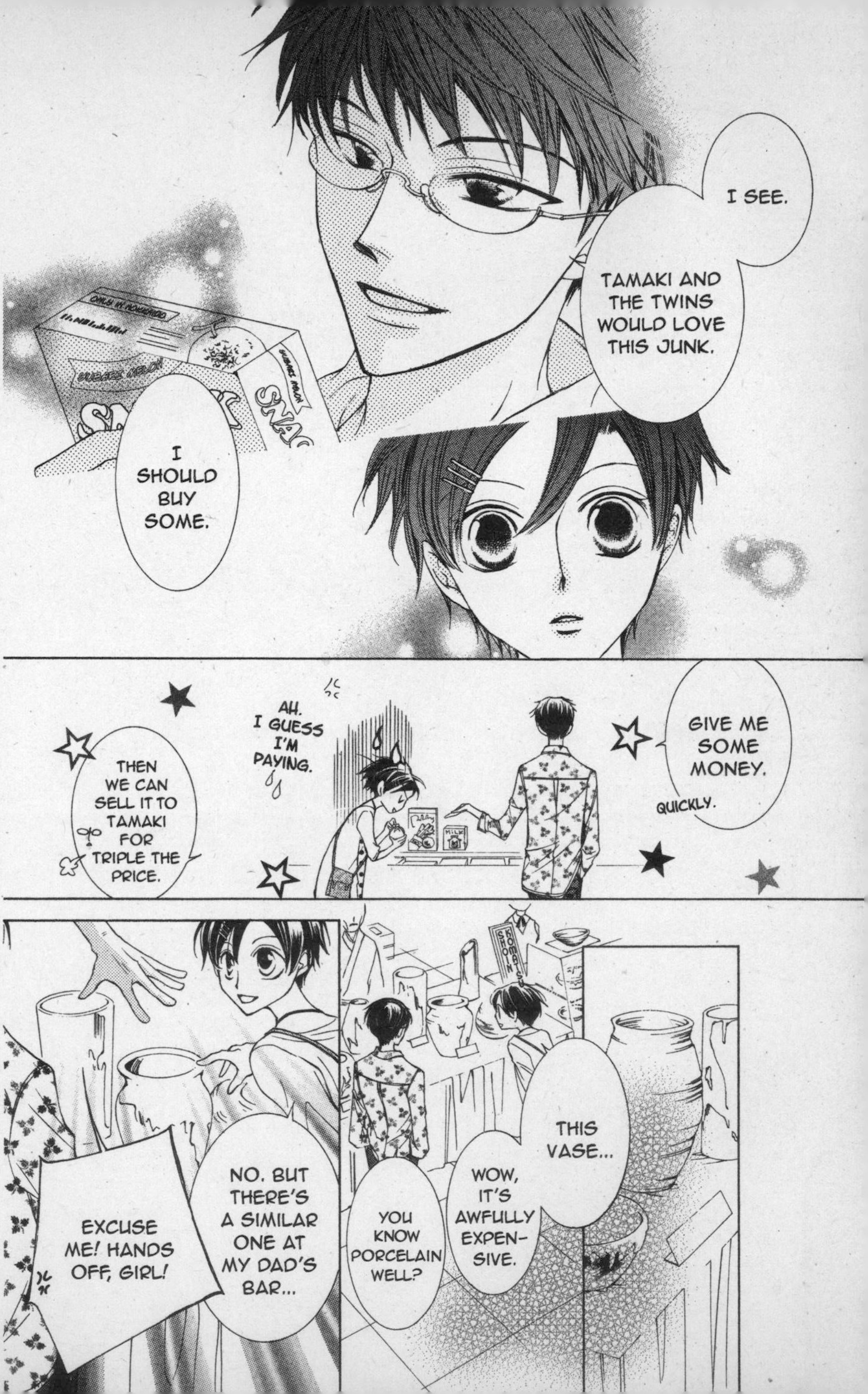
I SEE.
TAMAKI AND THE TWINS WOULD LOVE THIS JUNK.
I SHOULD BUY SOME.
GIVE ME SOME MONEY.
QUICKLY.
AH. I GUESS I'M PAYING.
THEN WE CAN SELL IT TO TAMAKI FOR TRIPLE THE PRICE.
SHOIN KOMATSU
THIS VASE...
WOW, IT'S AWFULLY EXPENSIVE.
YOU KNOW PORCELAIN WELL?
NO. BUT THERE'S A SIMILAR ONE AT MY DAD'S BAR...
EXCUSE ME! HANDS OFF, GIRL!

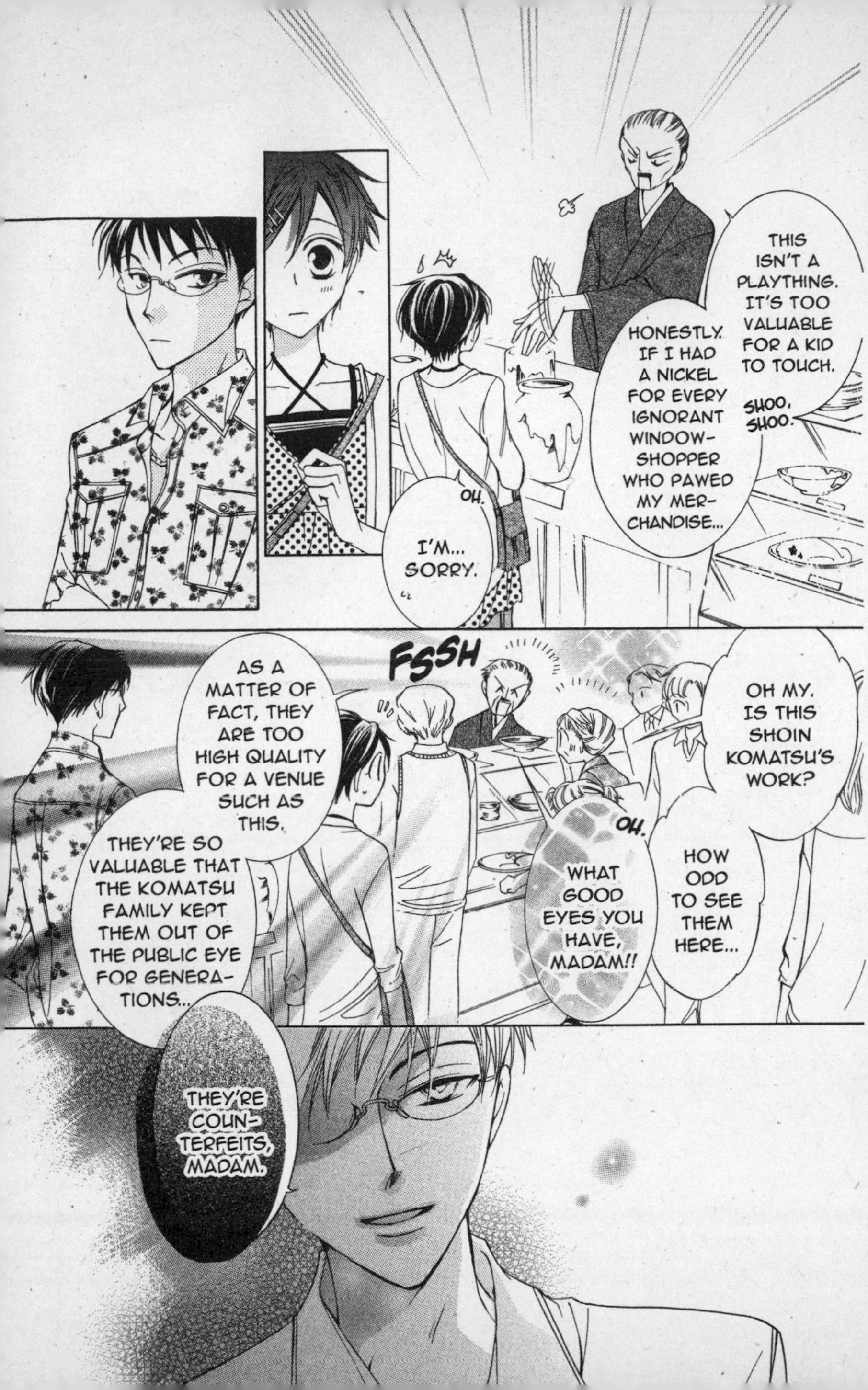
THIS ISN'T A PLAYTHING. IT'S TOO VALUABLE FOR A KID TO TOUCH.
SHOO, SHOO.
HONESTLY. IF I HAD A NICKEL FOR EVERY IGNORANT WINDOW-SHOPPER WHO PAWED MY MER-CHANDISE...
OH.
I'M... SORRY.
OH MY. IS THIS SHOIN KOMATSU'S WORK?
HOW ODD TO SEE THEM HERE...
OH.
WHAT GOOD EYES YOU HAVE, MADAM!!
FSSH
AS A MATTER OF FACT, THEY ARE TOO HIGH QUALITY FOR A VENUE SUCH AS THIS.
THEY'RE SO VALUABLE THAT THE KOMATSU FAMILY KEPT THEM OUT OF THE PUBLIC EYE FOR GENERA-TIONS...
THEY'RE COUN-TERFEITS, MADAM.

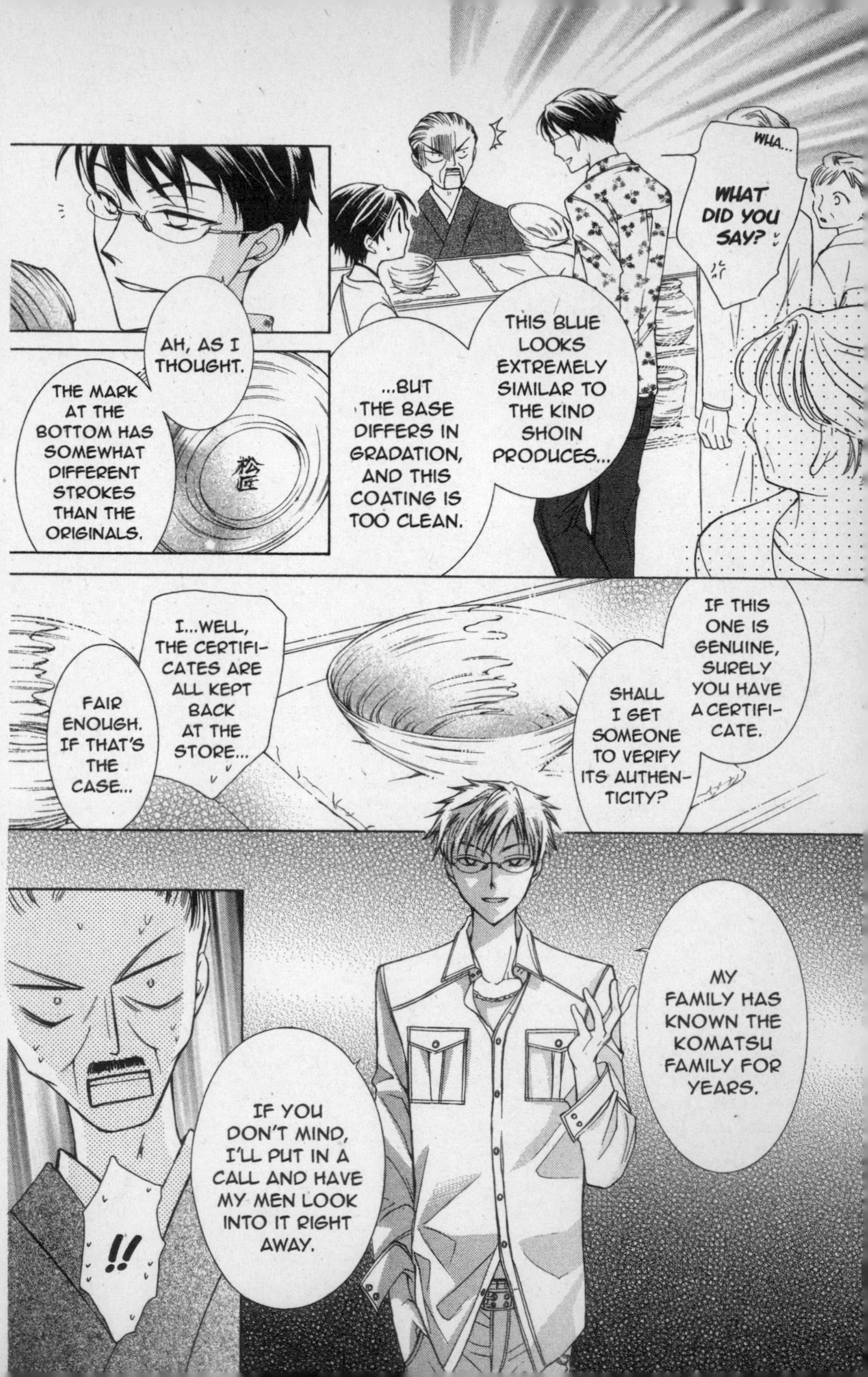
WHA...
WHAT DID YOU SAY?
THIS BLUE LOOKS EXTREMELY SIMILAR TO THE KIND SHOIN PRODUCES...
...BUT THE BASE DIFFERS IN GRADATION, AND THIS COATING IS TOO CLEAN.
AH, AS I THOUGHT.
THE MARK AT THE BOTTOM HAS SOMEWHAT DIFFERENT STROKES THAN THE ORIGINALS.
IF THIS ONE IS GENUINE, SURELY YOU HAVE A CERTIFICATE.
SHALL I GET SOMEONE TO VERIFY ITS AUTHENTICITY?
I...WELL, THE CERTIFICATES ARE ALL KEPT BACK AT THE STORE...
FAIR ENOUGH. IF THAT'S THE CASE...
MY FAMILY HAS KNOWN THE KOMATSU FAMILY FOR YEARS.
IF YOU DON'T MIND, I'LL PUT IN A CALL AND HAVE MY MEN LOOK INTO IT RIGHT AWAY.
!!

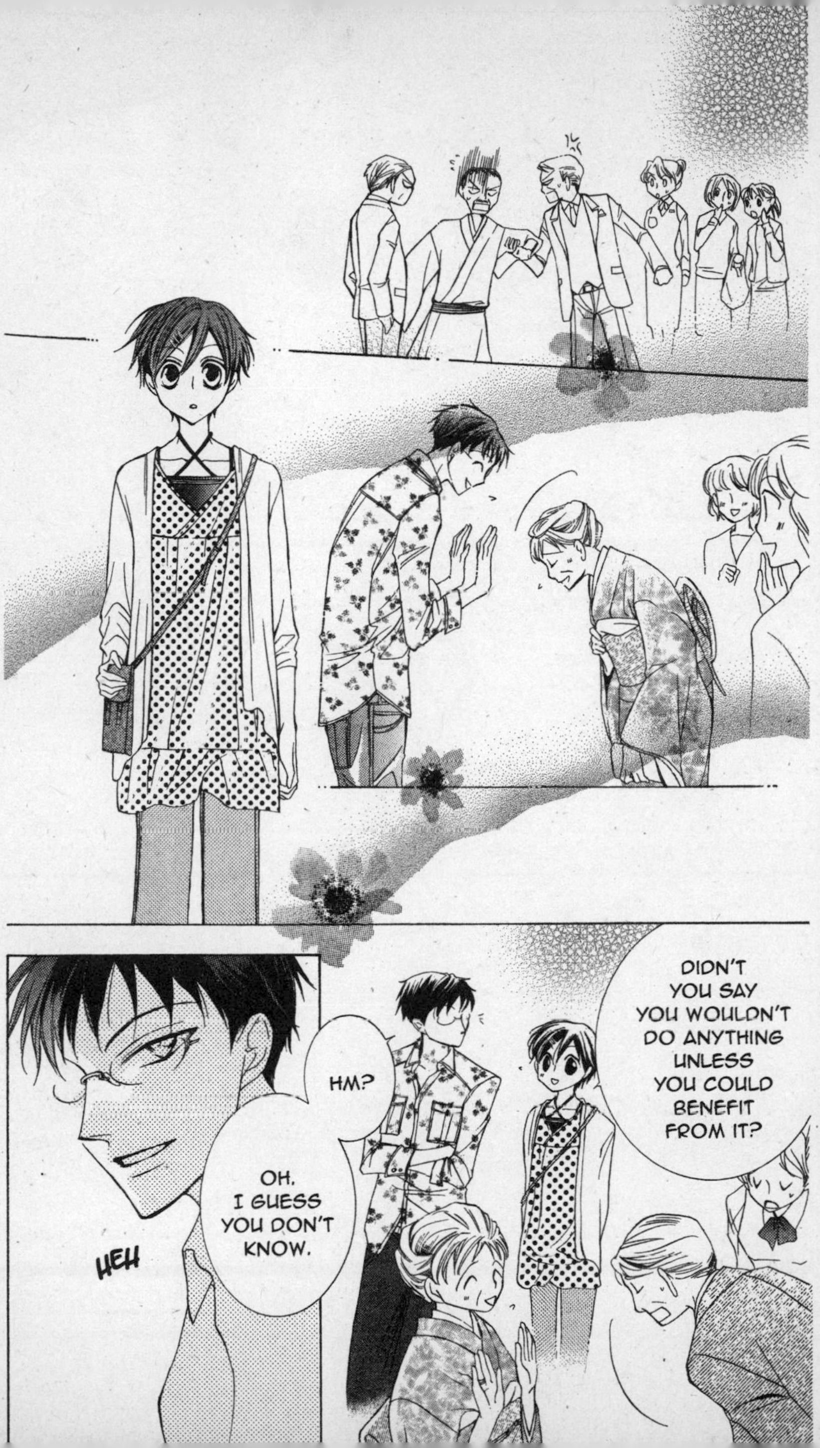
DIDN'T YOU SAY YOU WOULDN'T DO ANYTHING UNLESS YOU COULD BENEFIT FROM IT?
HM?
OH. I GUESS YOU DON'T KNOW.
HEH

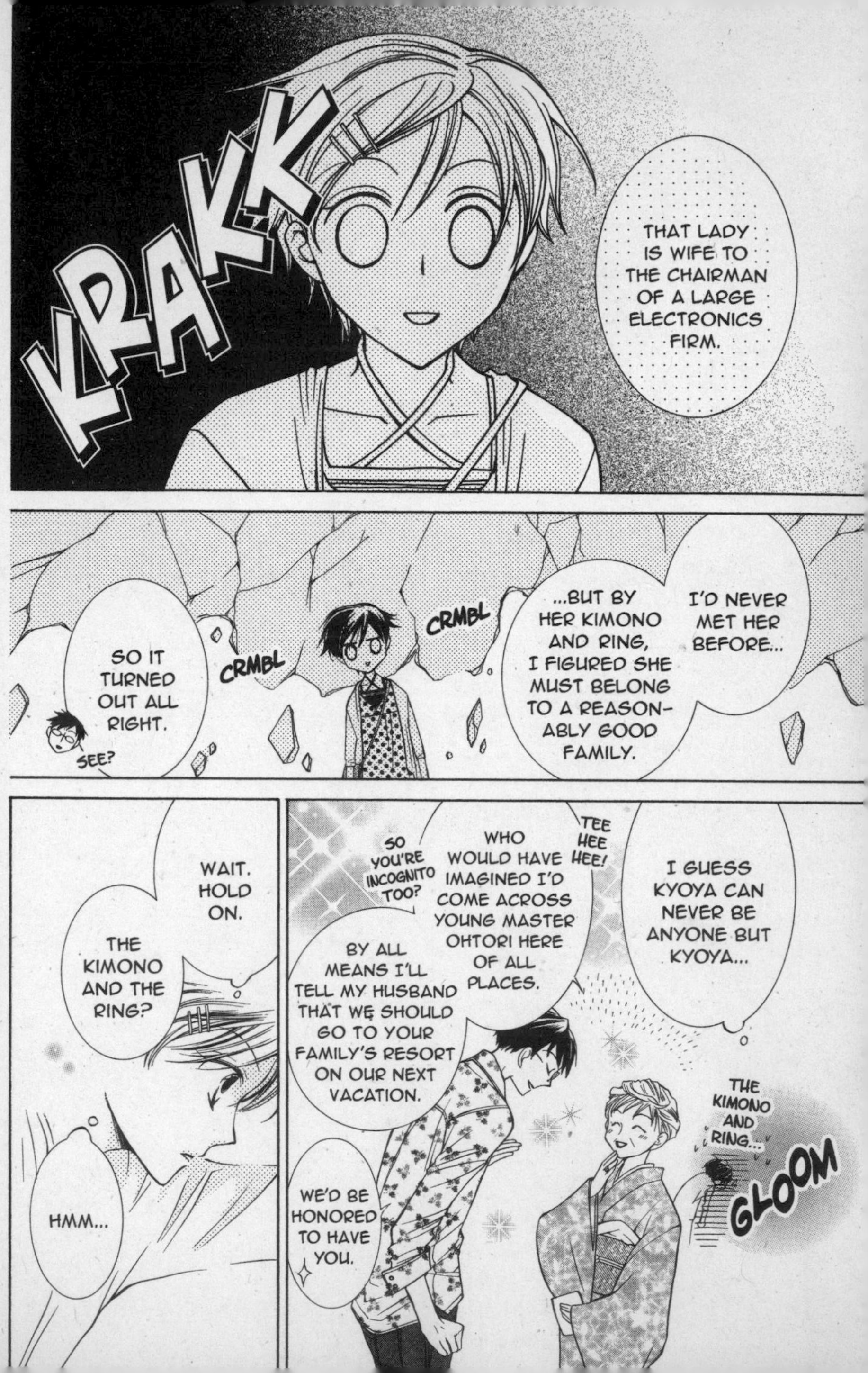
KRAKK
THAT LADY IS WIFE TO THE CHAIRMAN OF A LARGE ELECTRONICS FIRM.
I'D NEVER MET HER BEFORE...
...BUT BY HER KIMONO AND RING, I FIGURED SHE MUST BELONG TO A REASON-ABLY GOOD FAMILY.
CRMBL
CRMBL
SO IT TURNED OUT ALL RIGHT.
SEE?
I GUESS KYOYA CAN NEVER BE ANYONE BUT KYOYA...
TEE HEE HEE!
WHO WOULD HAVE IMAGINED I'D COME ACROSS YOUNG MASTER OHTORI HERE OF ALL PLACES.
SO YOU'RE INCOGNITO TOO?
BY ALL MEANS I'LL TELL MY HUSBAND THAT WE SHOULD GO TO YOUR FAMILY'S RESORT ON OUR NEXT VACATION.
THE KIMONO AND RING...
GLOOM
WE'D BE HONORED TO HAVE YOU.
WAIT. HOLD ON.
THE KIMONO AND THE RING?
HMM...

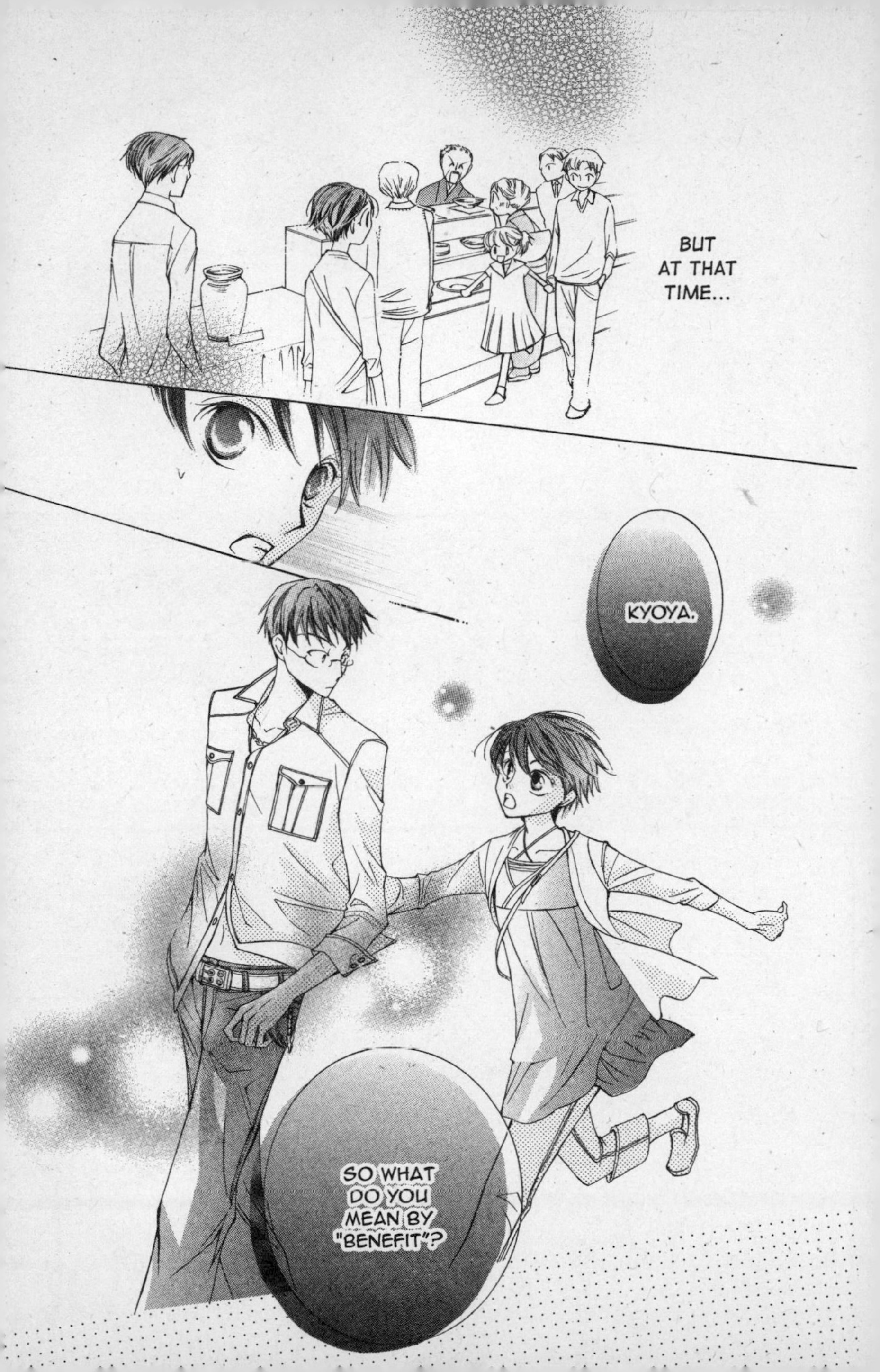
BUT AT THAT TIME...
KYOYA.
SO WHAT DO YOU MEAN BY "BENEFIT"?

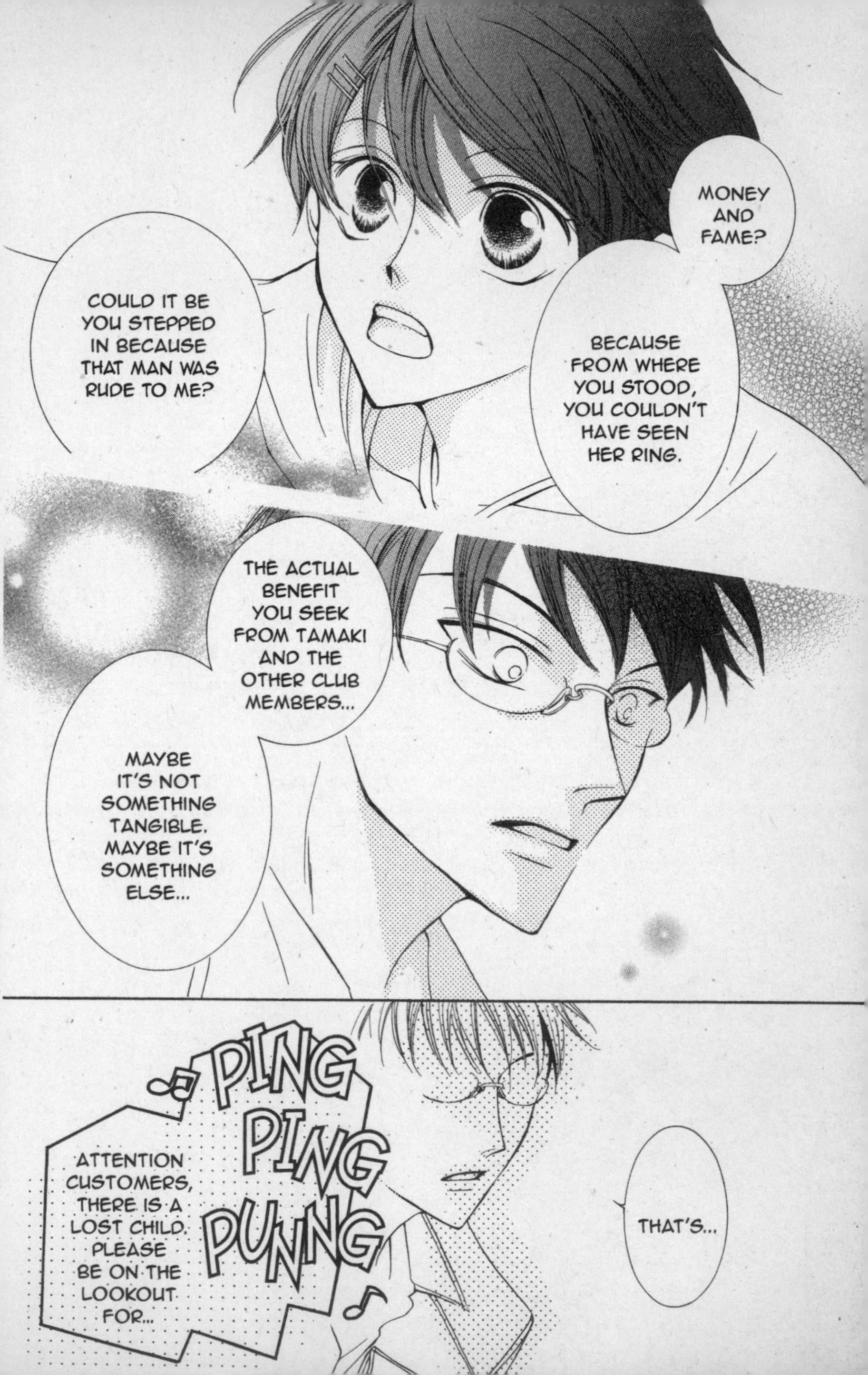
MONEY AND FAME?
BECAUSE FROM WHERE YOU STOOD, YOU COULDN'T HAVE SEEN HER RING.
COULD IT BE YOU STEPPED IN BECAUSE THAT MAN WAS RUDE TO ME?
THE ACTUAL BENEFIT YOU SEEK FROM TAMAKI AND THE OTHER CLUB MEMBERS...
MAYBE IT'S NOT SOMETHING TANGIBLE. MAYBE IT'S SOMETHING ELSE...
THAT'S...
PING PING PUNNG
ATTENTION CUSTOMERS, THERE IS A LOST CHILD. PLEASE BE ON THE LOOKOUT FOR...

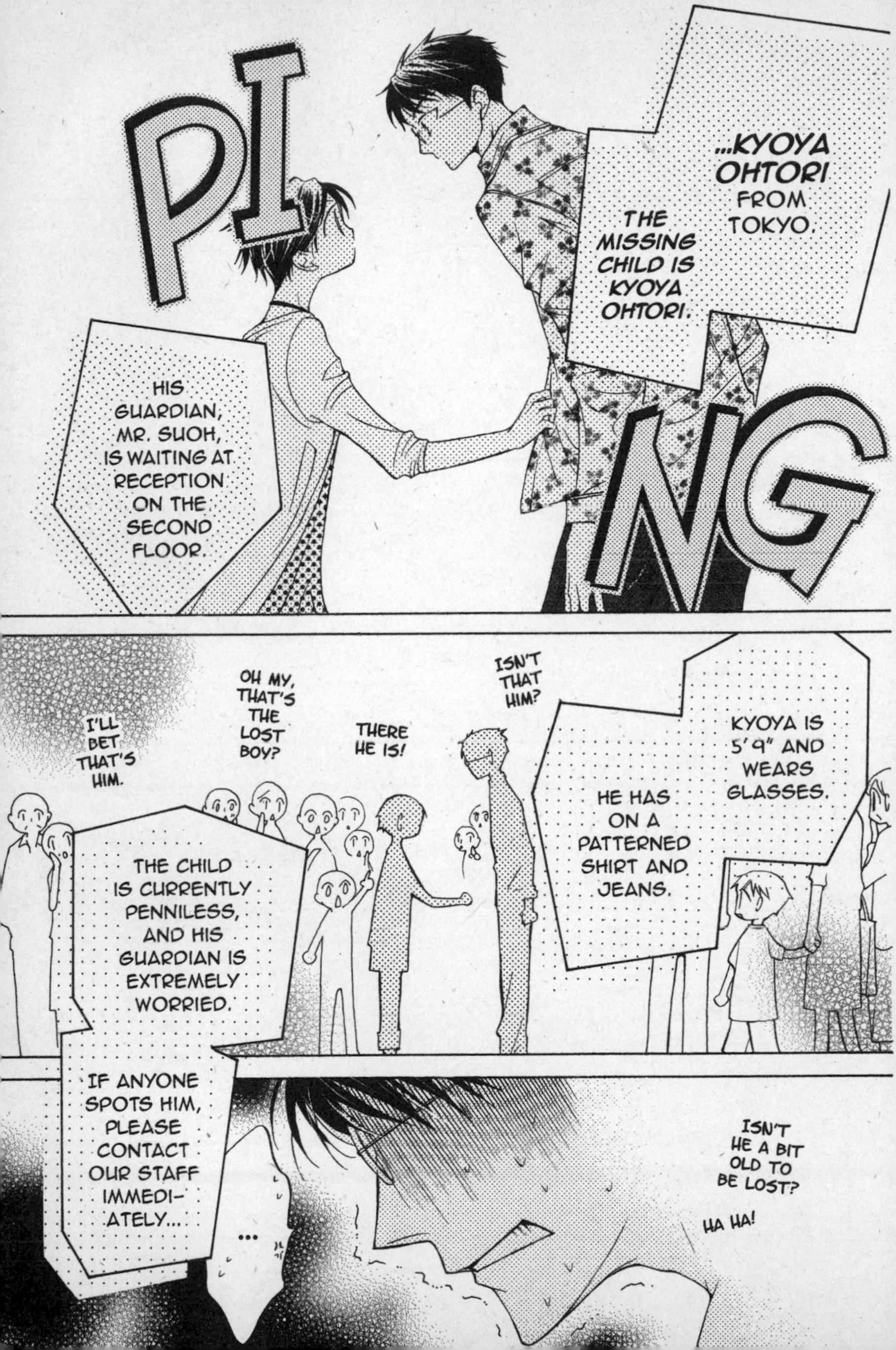
THE MISSING CHILD IS KYOYA OHTORI.
...KYOYA OHTORI FROM TOKYO.
PING
HIS GUARDIAN, MR. SUOH, IS WAITING AT RECEPTION ON THE SECOND FLOOR.
KYOYA IS 5'9" AND WEARS GLASSES.
HE HAS ON A PATTERNED SHIRT AND JEANS.
ISN'T THAT HIM?
THERE HE IS!
OH MY, THAT'S THE LOST BOY?
I'LL BET THAT'S HIM.
THE CHILD IS CURRENTLY PENNILESS, AND HIS GUARDIAN IS EXTREMELY WORRIED.
ISN'T HE A BIT OLD TO BE LOST?
HA HA!
IF ANYONE SPOTS HIM, PLEASE CONTACT OUR STAFF IMMEDI-ATELY...
...

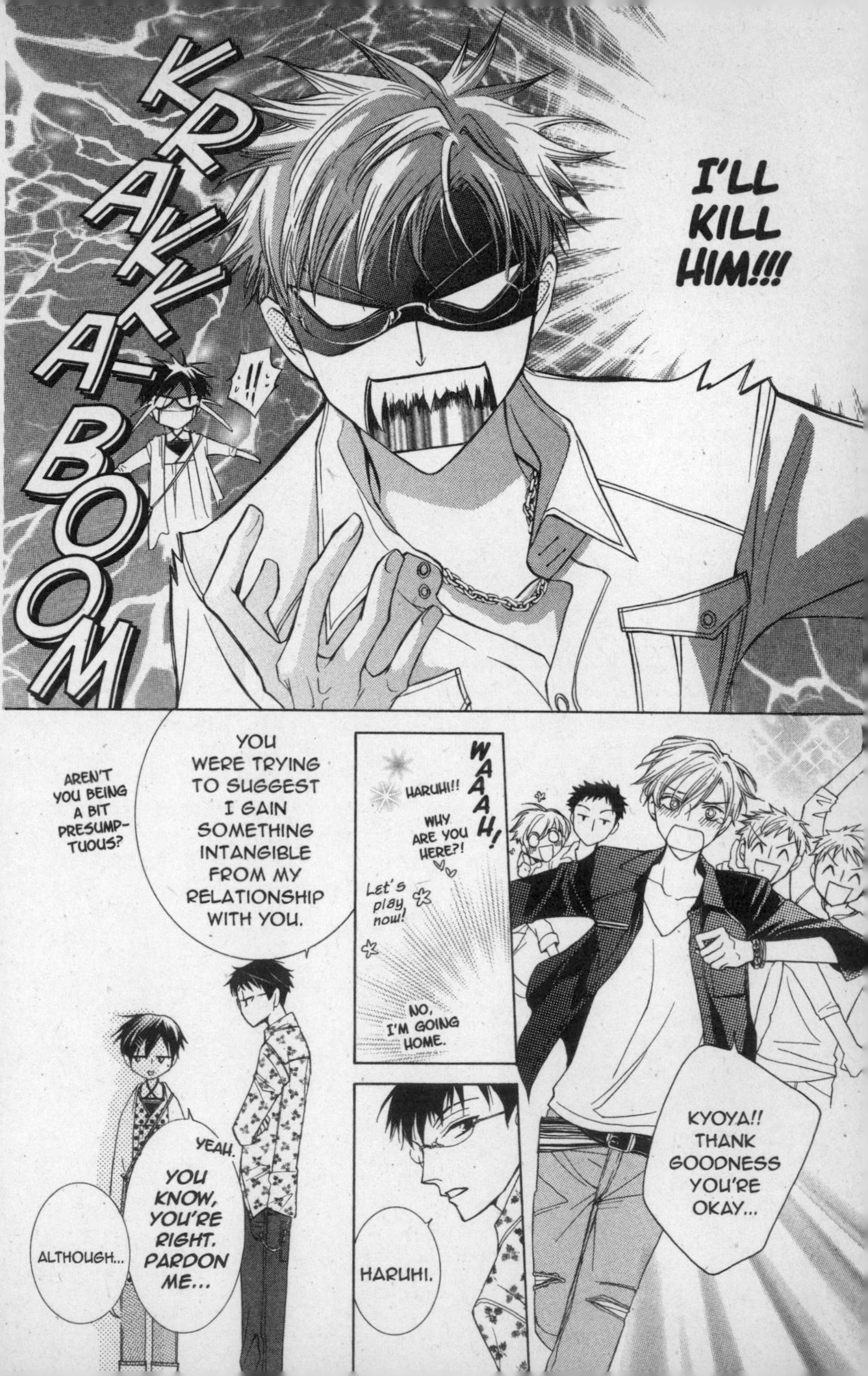
I'LL KILL HIM!!!
KRAKKA-BOOM
!!
KYOYA!! THANK GOODNESS YOU'RE OKAY...
WAAAH!
HARUHI!!
WHY ARE YOU HERE?!
Let's play now!
NO, I'M GOING HOME.
HARUHI.
YOU WERE TRYING TO SUGGEST I GAIN SOMETHING INTANGIBLE FROM MY RELATIONSHIP WITH YOU.
AREN'T YOU BEING A BIT PRESUMP-TUOUS?
YEAH.
YOU KNOW, YOU'RE RIGHT. PARDON ME...
ALTHOUGH...

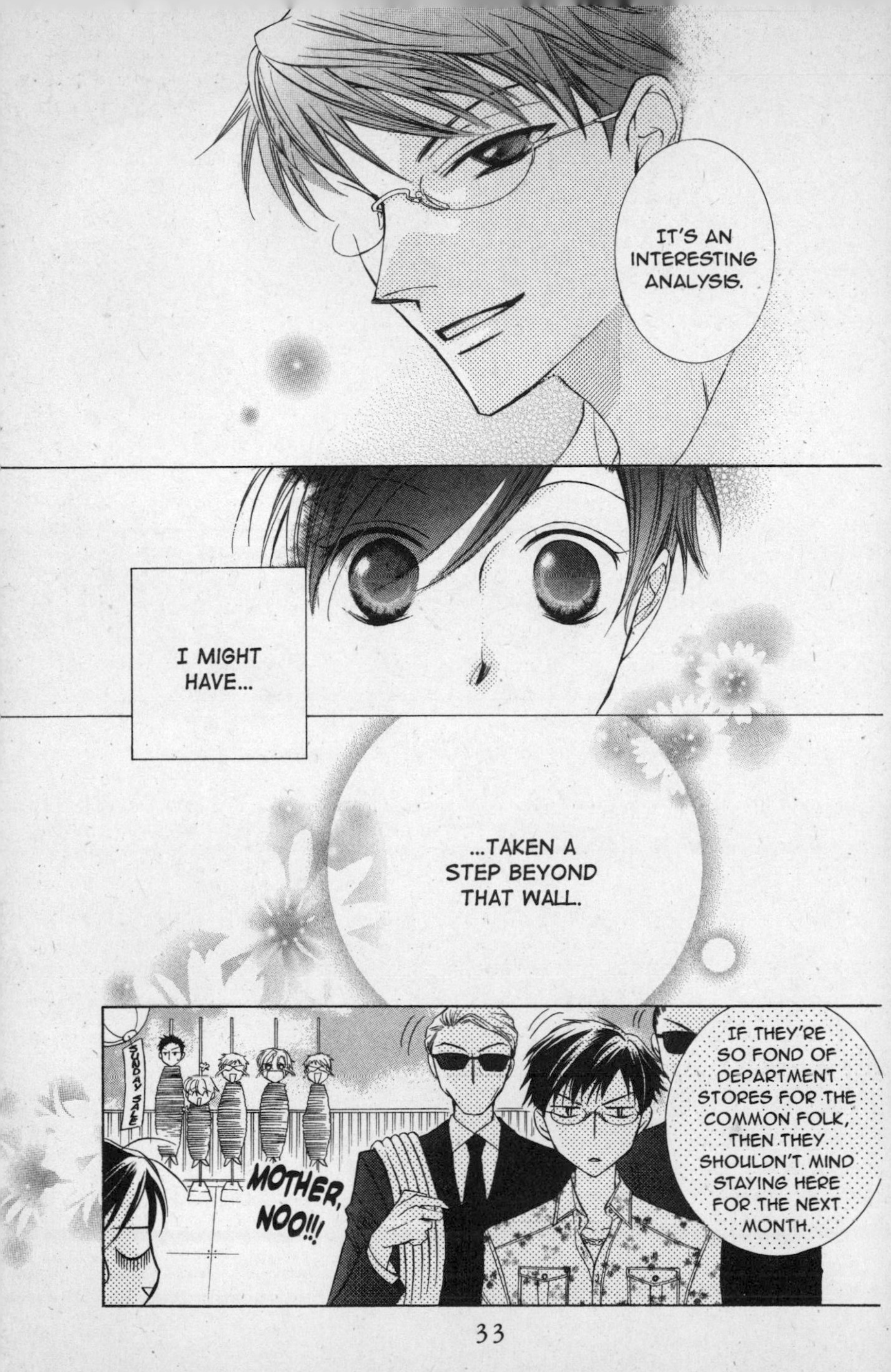
IT'S AN INTERESTING ANALYSIS.
I MIGHT HAVE...
...TAKEN A STEP BEYOND THAT WALL.
IF THEY'RE SO FOND OF DEPARTMENT STORES FOR THE COMMON FOLK, THEN THEY SHOULDN'T MIND STAYING HERE FOR THE NEXT MONTH.
MOTHER, NOO!!!

GUEST ROOM: FAXES ①

SPECIAL THANKS TO
AN TSUKIMIYA

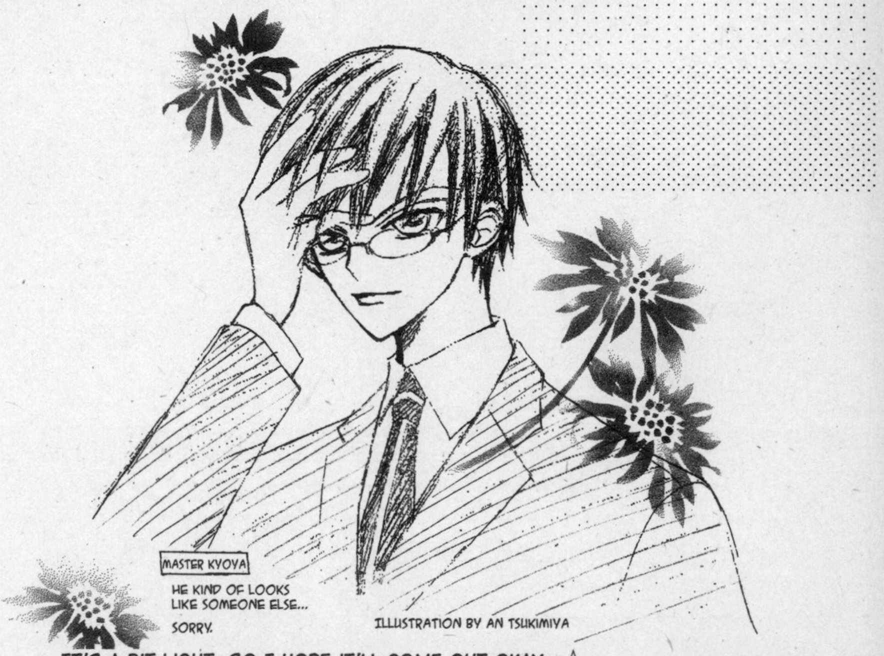
MASTER KYOYA
HE KIND OF LOOKS LIKE SOMEONE ELSE...
SORRY.
ILLUSTRATION BY AN TSUKIMIYA

IT'S A BIT LIGHT, SO I HOPE IT'LL COME OUT OKAY...
THIS IS AN'S OWN KYOYA!! BEAUTIFUL!! INTELLECTUAL!! THANK YOU!!
AN SENDS ME THE MOST WONDERFUL CHRISTMAS AND BIRTHDAY CARDS. WHEN WE CELEBRATE NEW YEAR'S AT HAKUSENSHA, SHE BRINGS TREATS ALL THE WAY FROM HOKKAIDO. TO TOP IT OFF, SHE'S AN INTELLECTUAL KNOCK-OUT WHO KEEPS US ALL ENTERTAINED WITH HER BEAUTIFUL FORM AND FASHION.
AFTER THE PARTY THIS YEAR, WE SPENT ALL NIGHT TALKING IN OUR HOTEL ROOM.
FOR THE PAST FEW YEARS WE'VE HARDLY MET DUE TO SCHEDULING CONFLICTS, BUT LET'S TRY AND GET TOGETHER SOON.♡

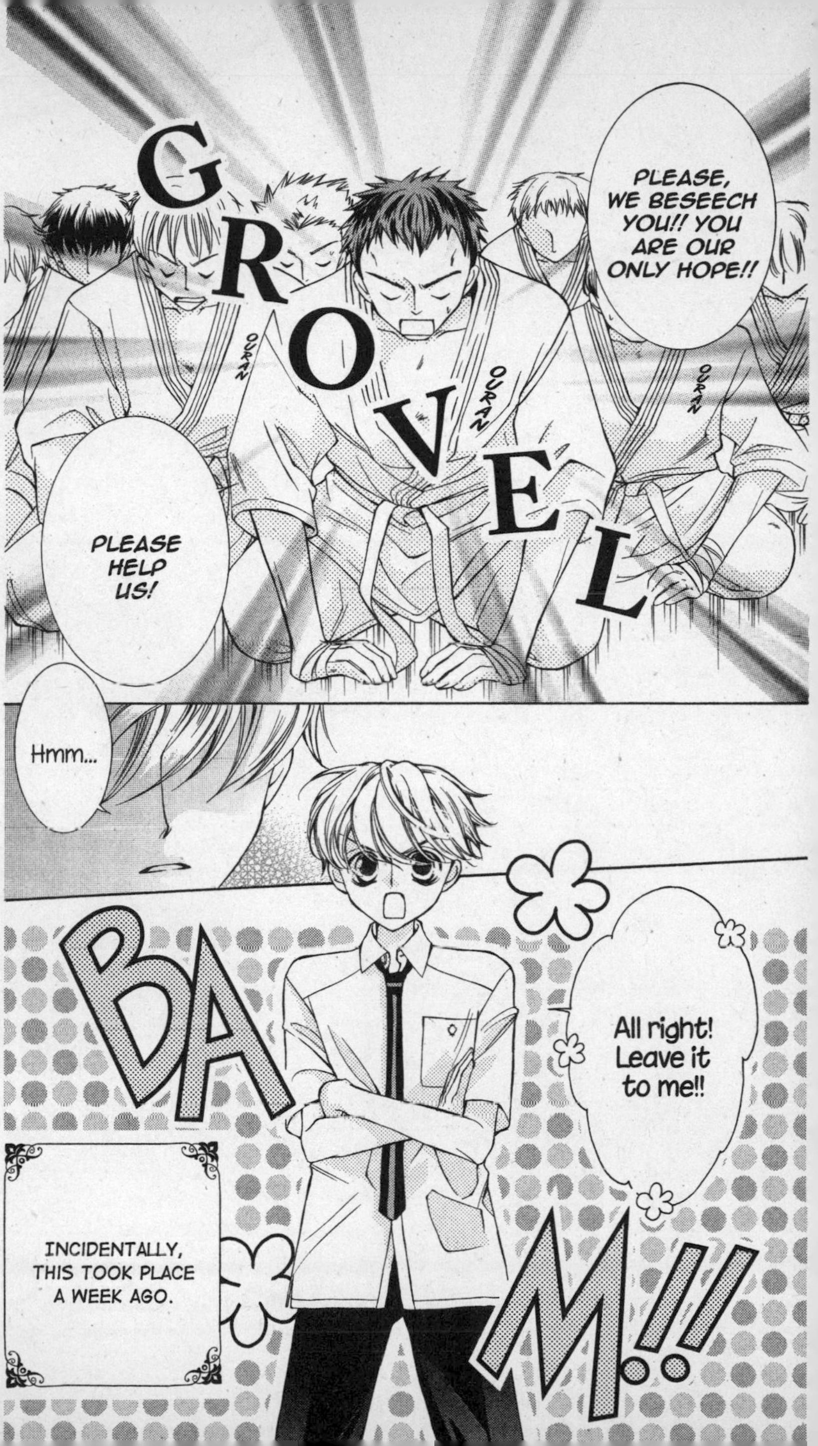
PLEASE, WE BESEECH YOU!! YOU ARE OUR ONLY HOPE!!
OURAN
OURAN
GROVEL
OURAN
PLEASE HELP US!
Hmm...
All right! Leave it to me!!
BAM!!
INCIDENTALLY, THIS TOOK PLACE A WEEK AGO.

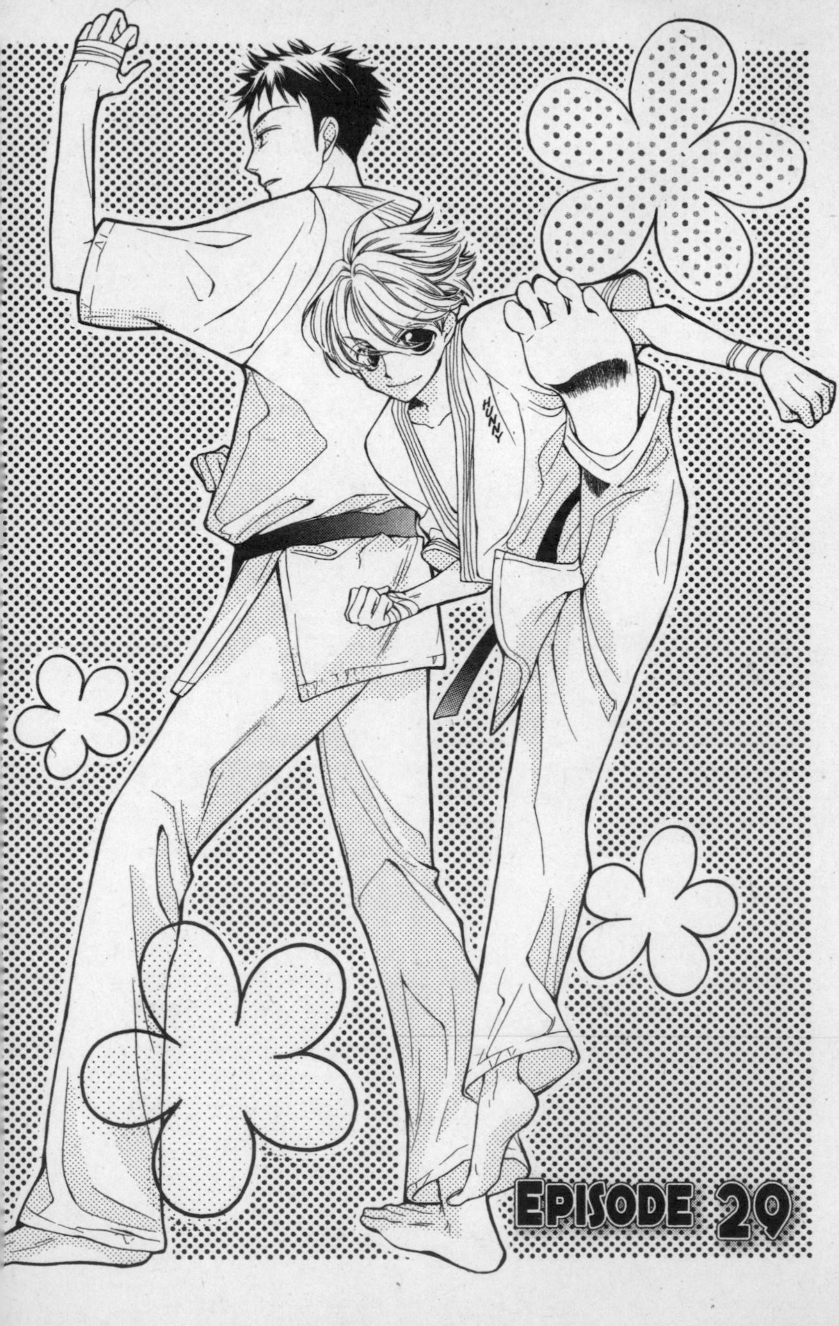
HUNNY
EPISODE 29

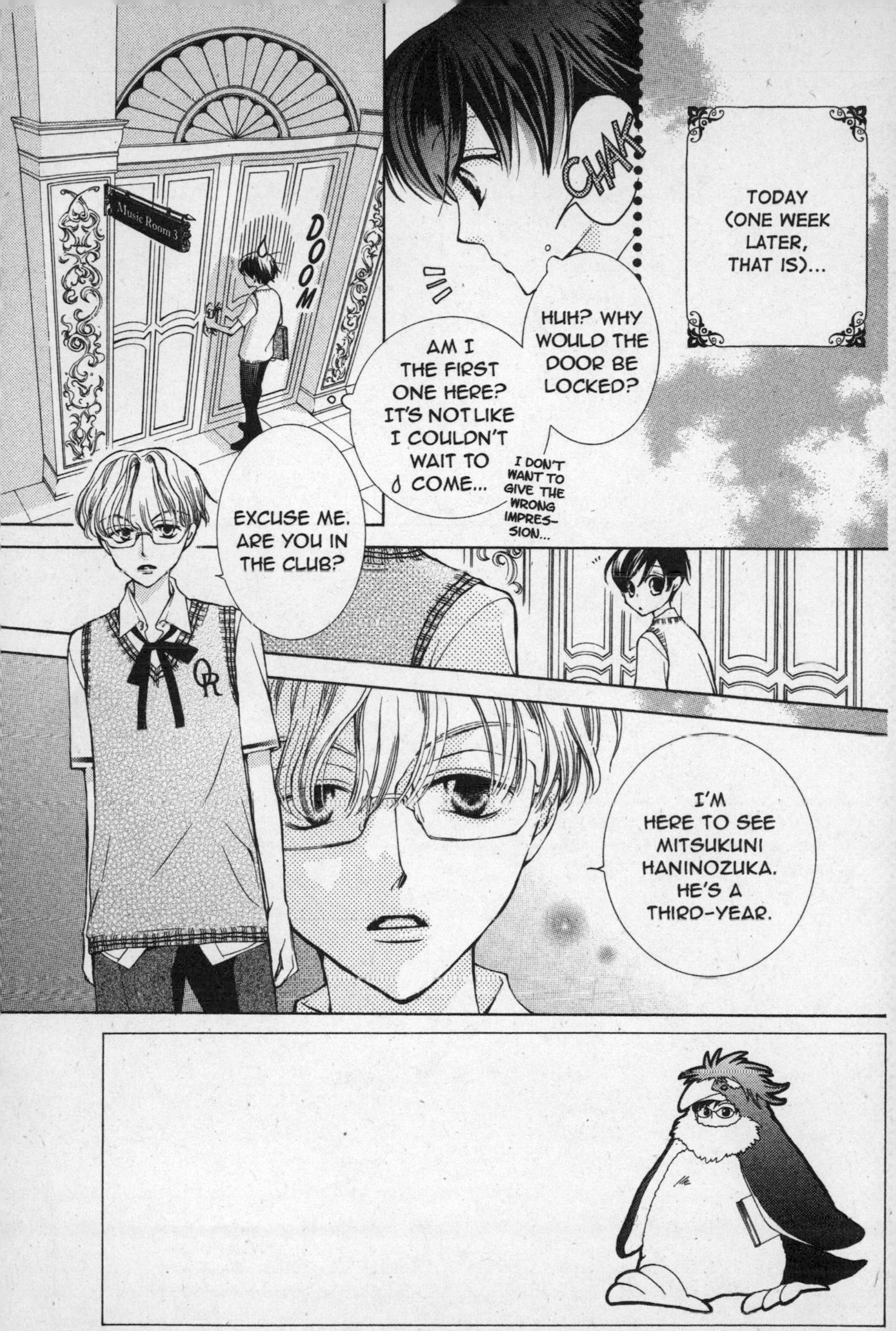
TODAY (ONE WEEK LATER, THAT IS)...
CHAK
HUH? WHY WOULD THE DOOR BE LOCKED?
Music Room 3
DOOM
AM I THE FIRST ONE HERE? IT'S NOT LIKE I COULDN'T WAIT TO COME...
I DON'T WANT TO GIVE THE WRONG IMPRESSION...
EXCUSE ME. ARE YOU IN THE CLUB?
I'M HERE TO SEE MITSUKUNI HANINOZUKA. HE'S A THIRD-YEAR.

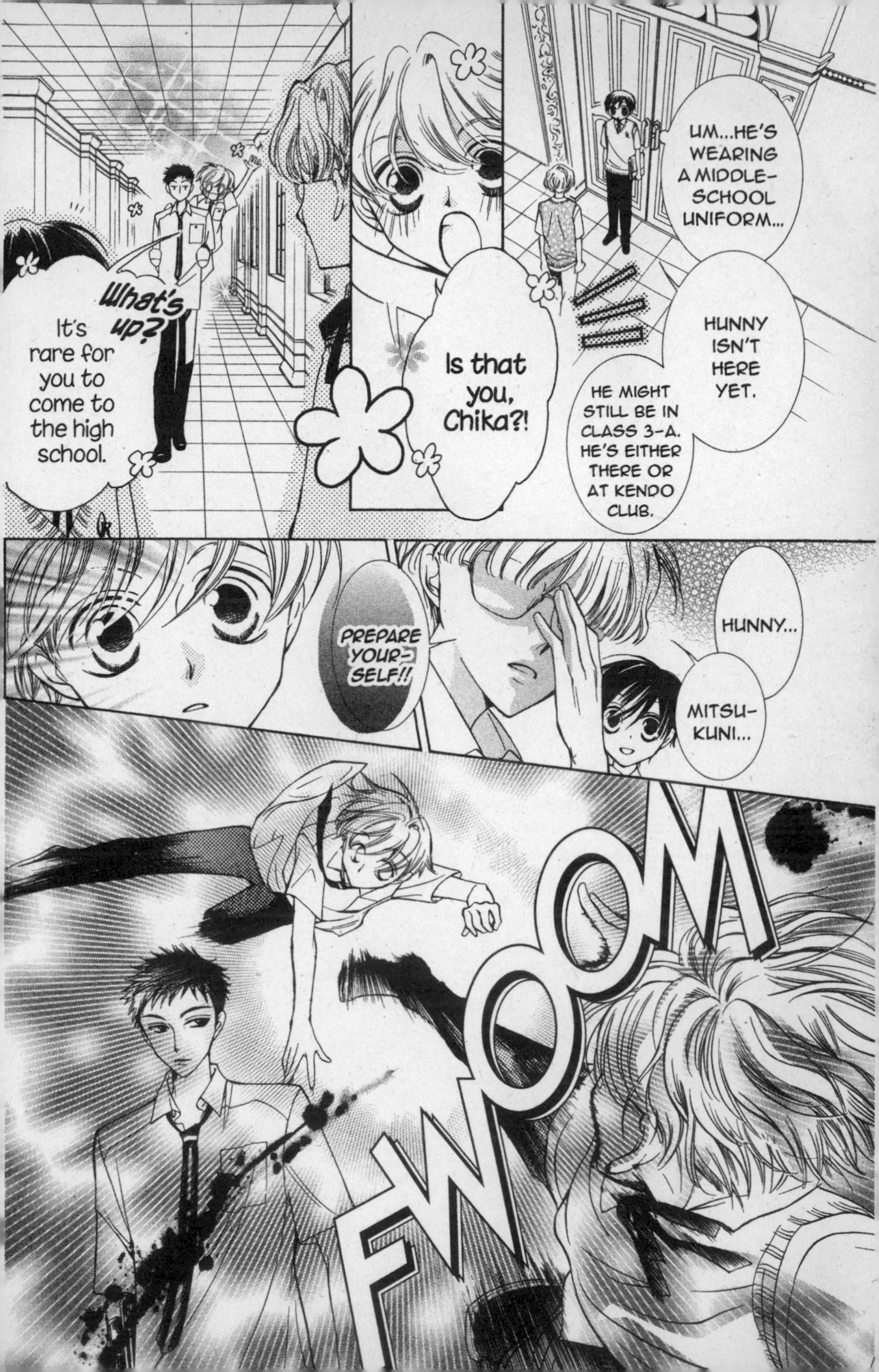
UM...HE'S WEARING A MIDDLE-SCHOOL UNIFORM...
HUNNY ISN'T HERE YET.
HE MIGHT STILL BE IN CLASS 3-A. HE'S EITHER THERE OR AT KENDO CLUB.
Is that you, Chika?!
What's up?
It's rare for you to come to the high school.
HUNNY...
MITSU-KUNI...
PREPARE YOUR-SELF!!
FWOOM

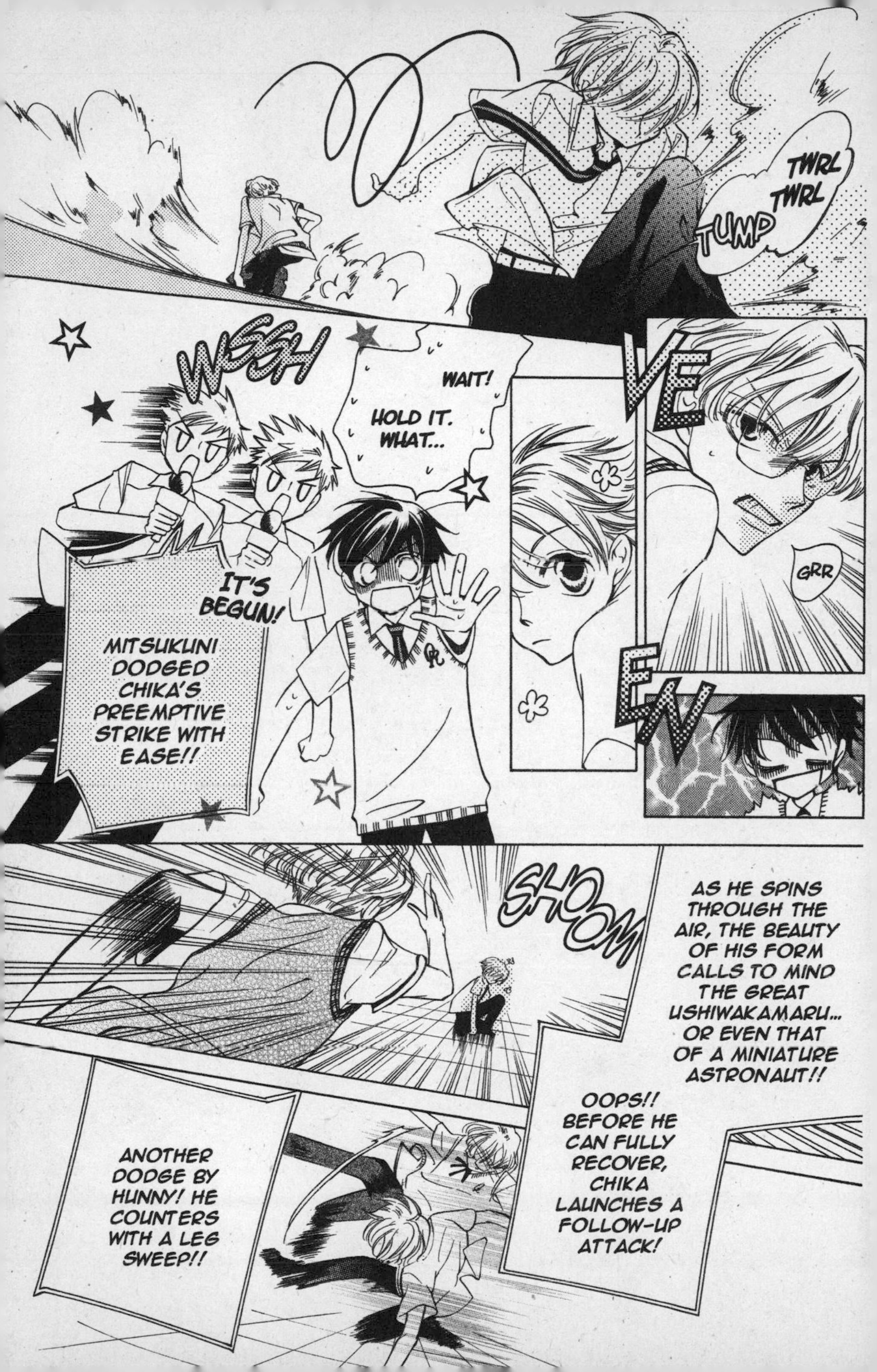
TWRL
TWRL
TUMP
VEEN
GRR
WAIT!
HOLD IT. WHAT...
WISSH
IT'S BEGUN!
MITSUKUNI DODGED CHIKA'S PREEMPTIVE STRIKE WITH EASE!!
SHOOM
AS HE SPINS THROUGH THE AIR, THE BEAUTY OF HIS FORM CALLS TO MIND THE GREAT USHIWAKAMARU... OR EVEN THAT OF A MINIATURE ASTRONAUT!!
OOPS!! BEFORE HE CAN FULLY RECOVER, CHIKA LAUNCHES A FOLLOW-UP ATTACK!
ANOTHER DODGE BY HUNNY! HE COUNTERS WITH A LEG SWEEP!!

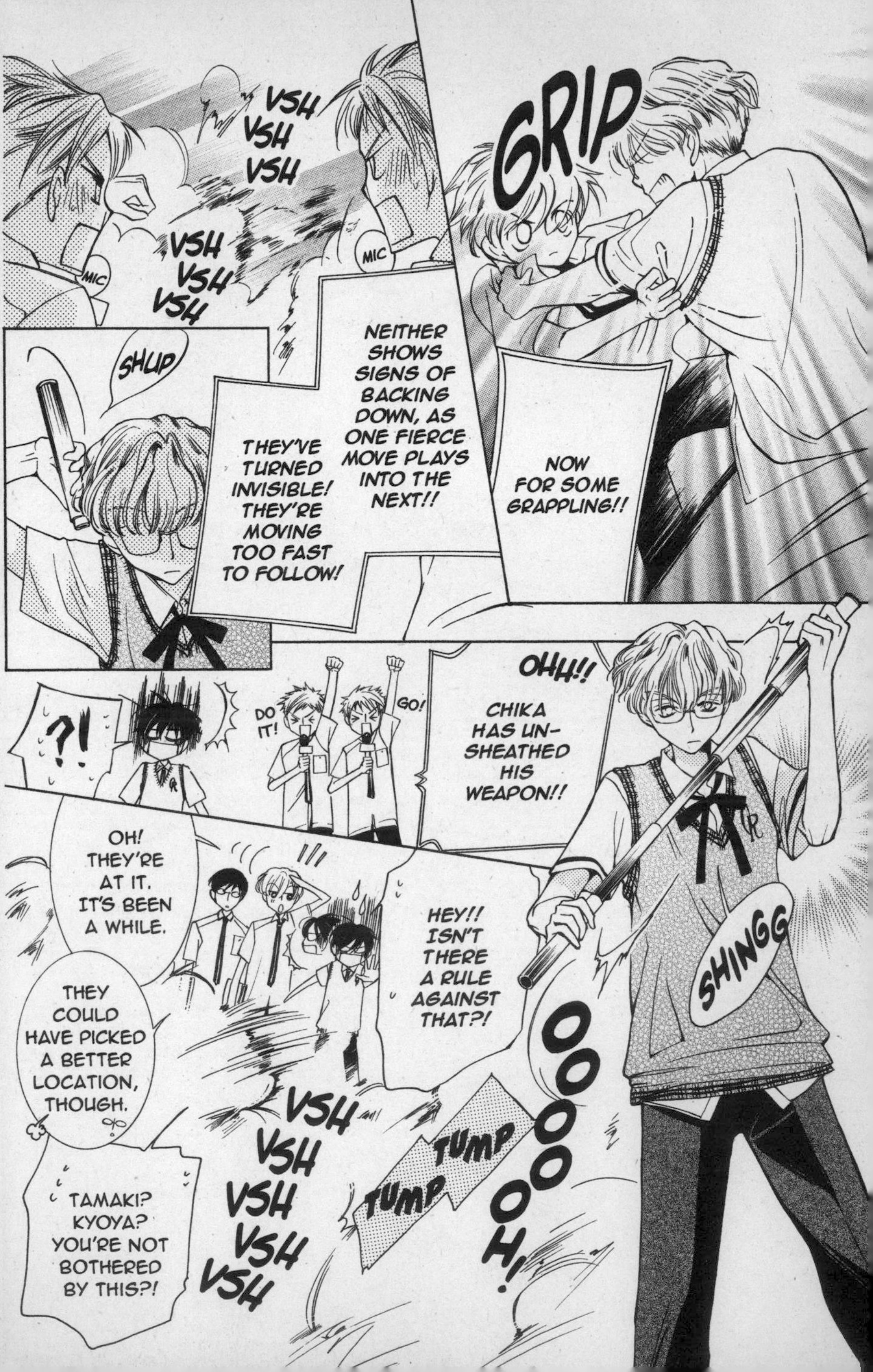
GRIP
NOW FOR SOME GRAPPLING!!
VSH VSH VSH
MIC
MIC
VSH VSH VSH
NEITHER SHOWS SIGNS OF BACKING DOWN, AS ONE FIERCE MOVE PLAYS INTO THE NEXT!!
THEY'VE TURNED INVISIBLE! THEY'RE MOVING TOO FAST TO FOLLOW!
SHUP
OHH!!
CHIKA HAS UN-SHEATHED HIS WEAPON!!
SHINGG
OOOOOOOH!
GO!
DO IT!
?!
HEY!! ISN'T THERE A RULE AGAINST THAT?!
OH! THEY'RE AT IT. IT'S BEEN A WHILE.
THEY COULD HAVE PICKED A BETTER LOCATION, THOUGH.
TUMP TUMP
VSH VSH VSH VSH VSH
TAMAKI? KYOYA? YOU'RE NOT BOTHERED BY THIS?!

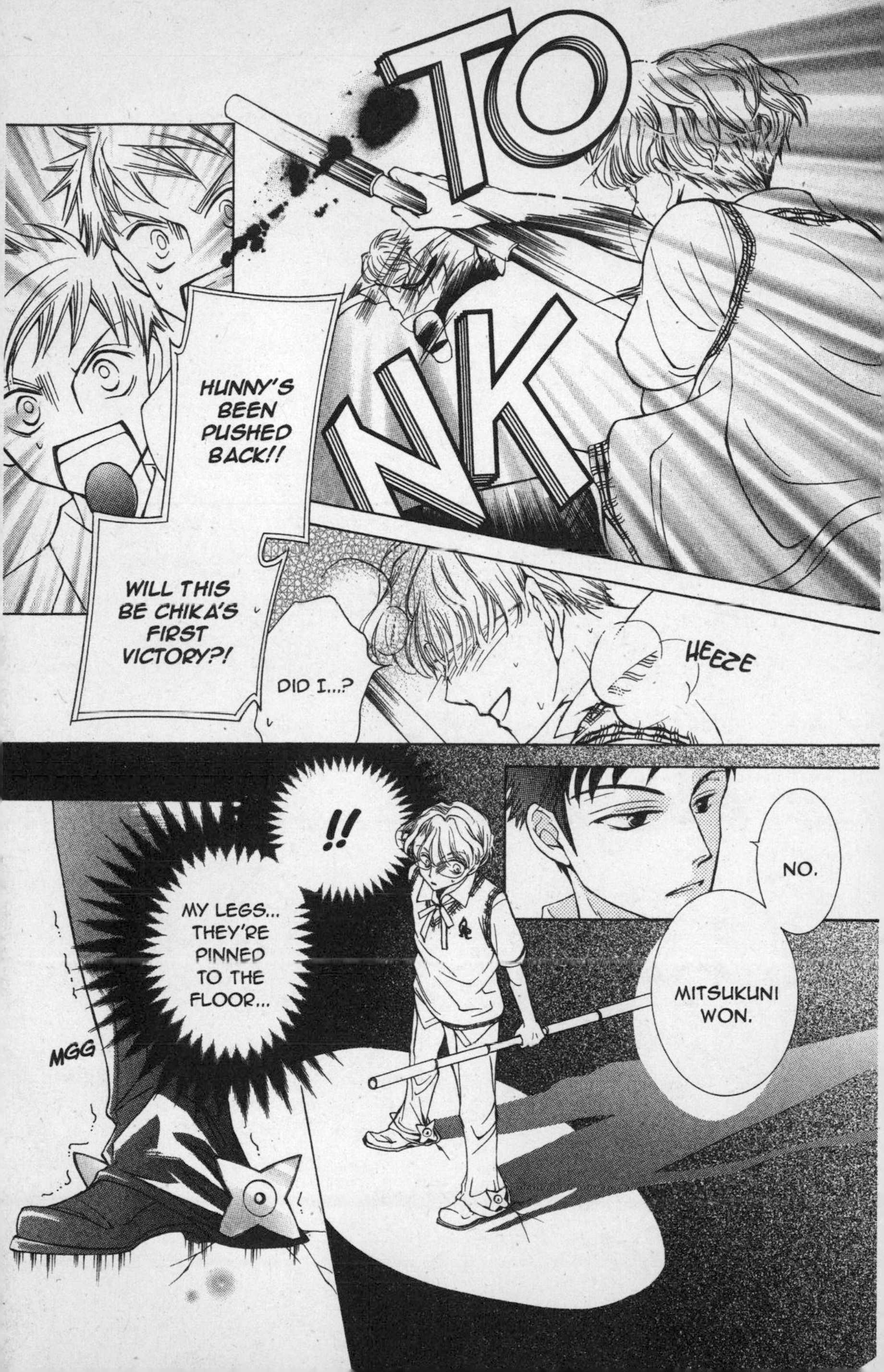
TONK
HUNNY'S BEEN PUSHED BACK!!
WILL THIS BE CHIKA'S FIRST VICTORY?!
HEEZE
DID I...?
NO.
MITSUKUNI WON.
!!
MY LEGS... THEY'RE PINNED TO THE FLOOR...
MGG

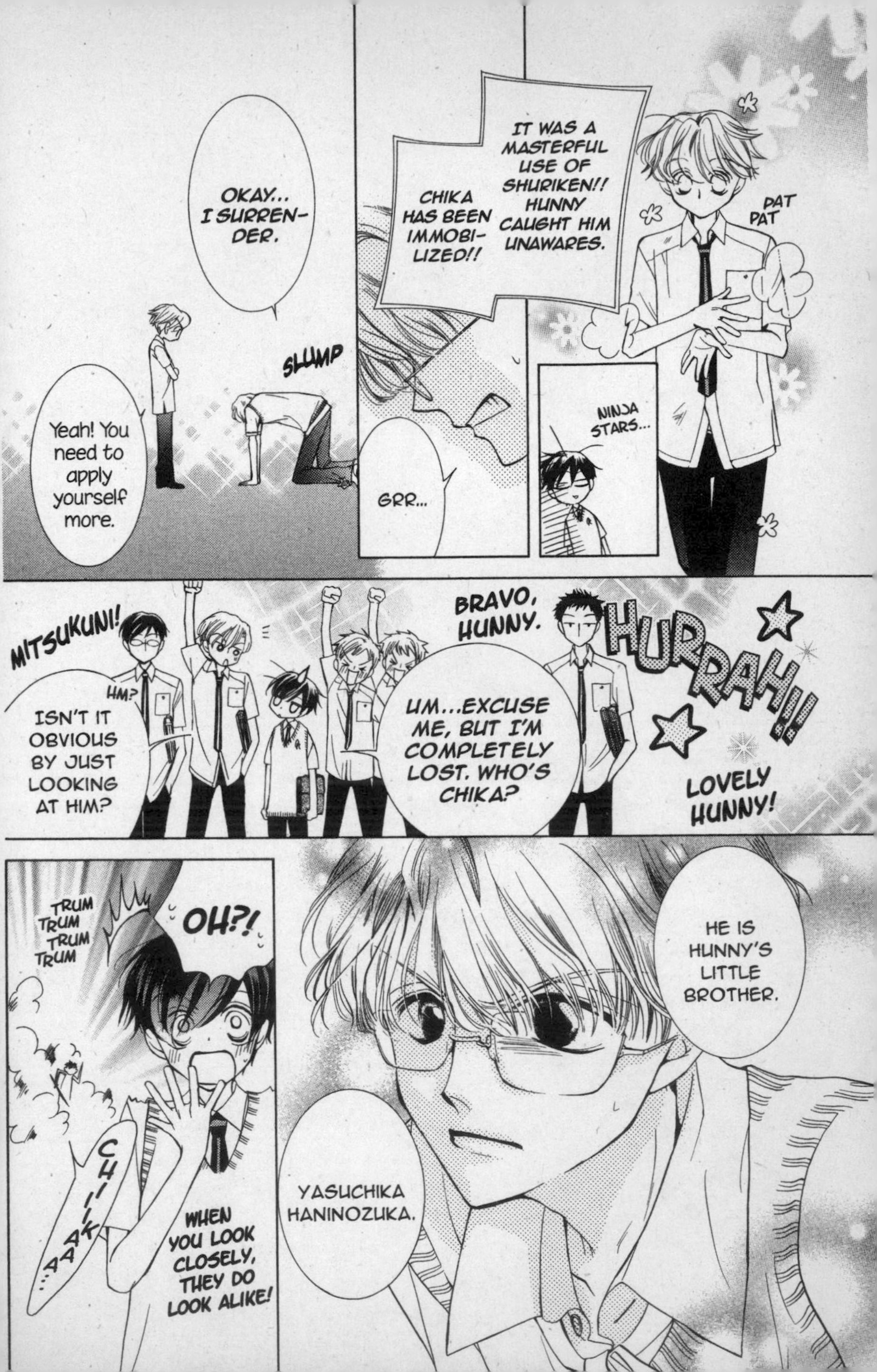
PAT PAT
IT WAS A MASTERFUL USE OF SHURIKEN!! HUNNY CAUGHT HIM UNAWARES.
CHIKA HAS BEEN IMMOBILIZED!!
NINJA STARS...
GRR...
OKAY... I SURRENDER.
SLUMP
Yeah! You need to apply yourself more.
HURRAH!!
LOVELY HUNNY!
BRAVO, HUNNY.
UM...EXCUSE ME, BUT I'M COMPLETELY LOST. WHO'S CHIKA?
MITSUKUNI!
HM?
ISN'T IT OBVIOUS BY JUST LOOKING AT HIM?
HE IS HUNNY'S LITTLE BROTHER.
YASUCHIKA HANINOZUKA.
OH?!
TRUM TRUM TRUM TRUM
CHIIIKAAA...
WHEN YOU LOOK CLOSELY, THEY DO LOOK ALIKE!

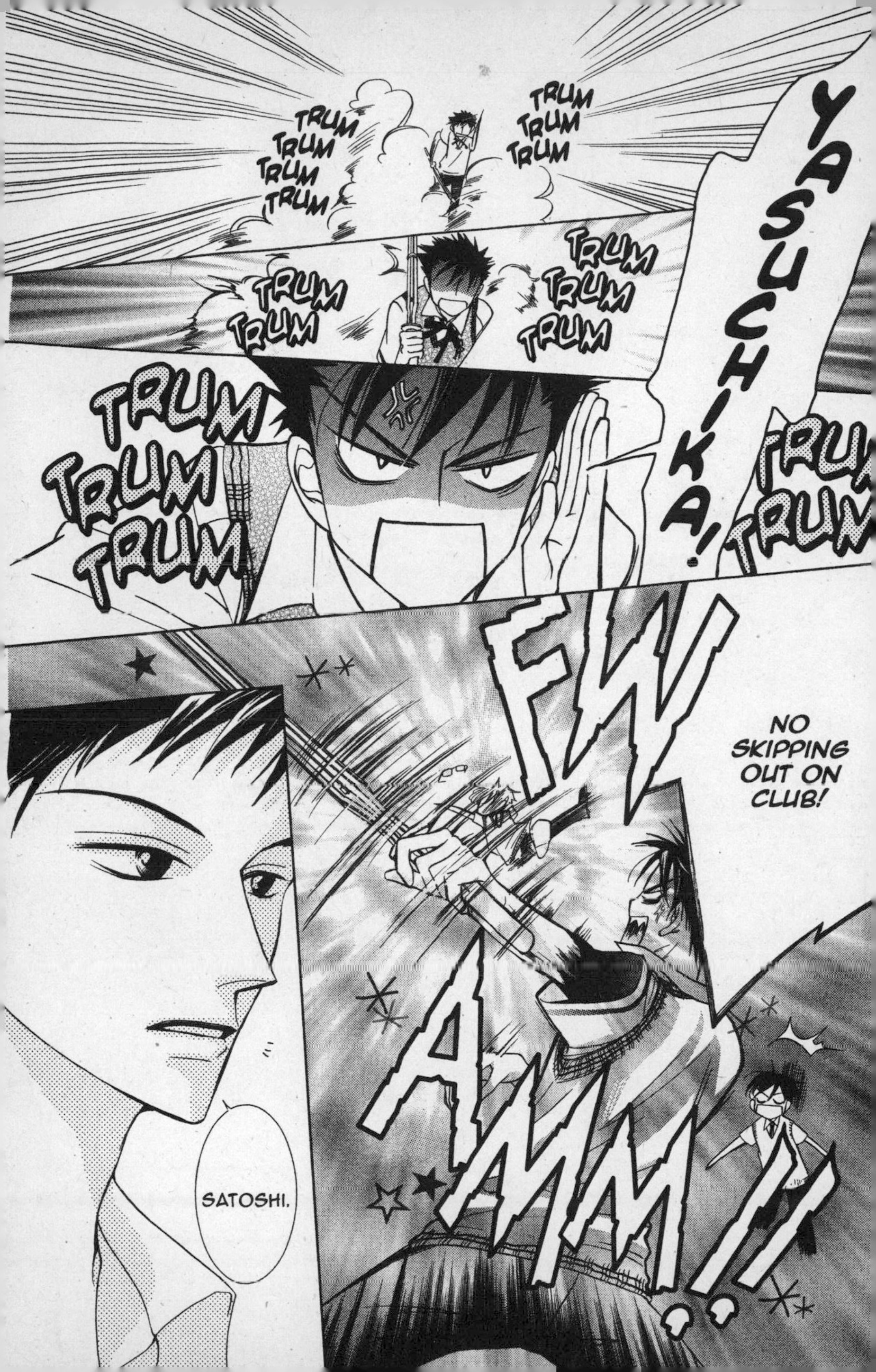
TRUM TRUM TRUM
TRUM TRUM TRUM TRUM
TRUM TRUM TRUM
TRUM TRUM
YASUCHIKA!
TRU TRUM
TRUM TRUM TRUM
NO SKIPPING OUT ON CLUB!
FWAMM!!
SATOSHI.

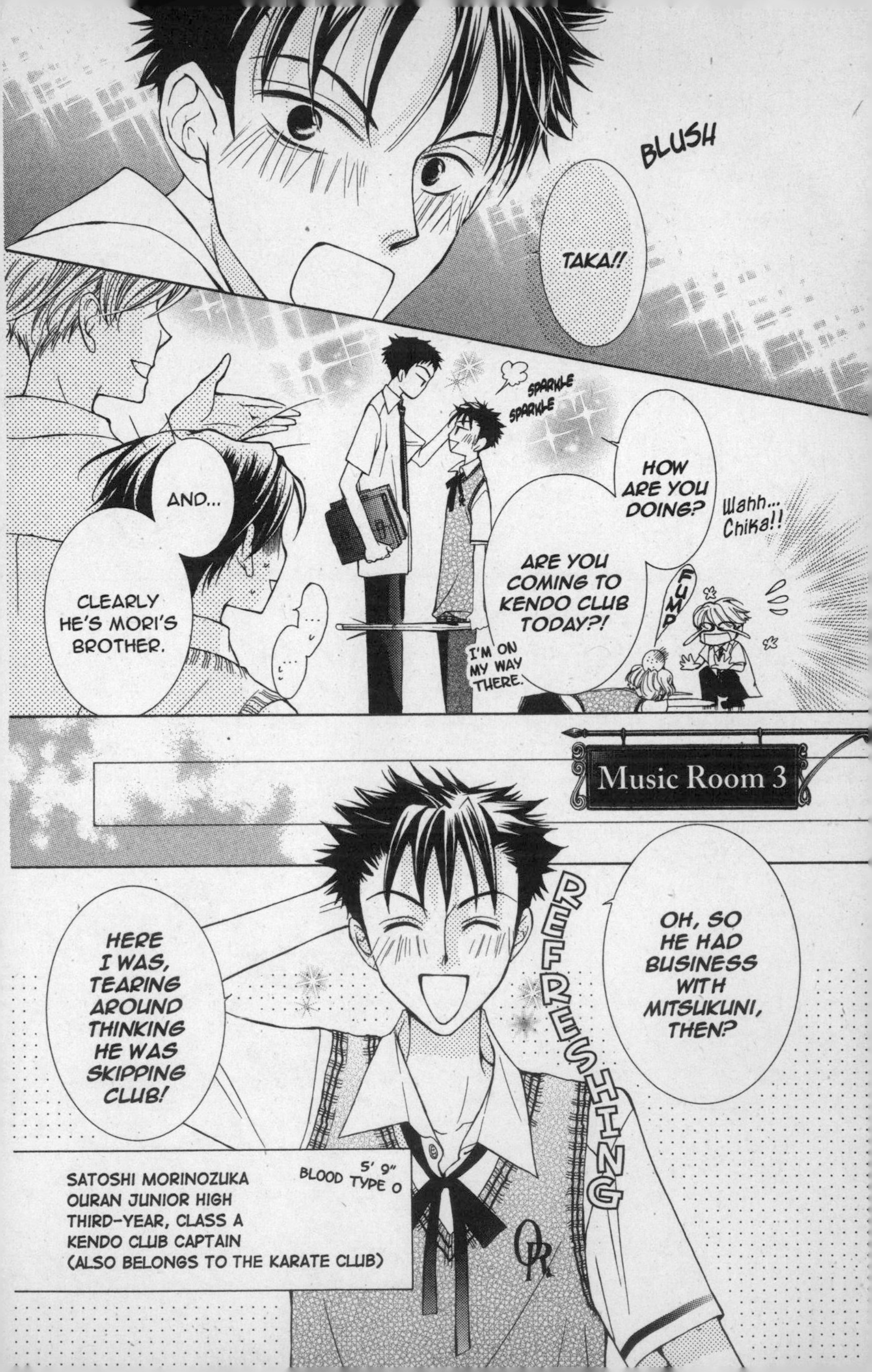
BLUSH
TAKA!!
SPARKLE SPARKLE
HOW ARE YOU DOING?
ARE YOU COMING TO KENDO CLUB TODAY?!
I'M ON MY WAY THERE.
Wahh... Chika!!
FUMP
AND...
CLEARLY HE'S MORI'S BROTHER.
Music Room 3
OH, SO HE HAD BUSINESS WITH MITSUKUNI, THEN?
REFRESHING
HERE I WAS, TEARING AROUND THINKING HE WAS SKIPPING CLUB!
SATOSHI MORINOZUKA
OURAN JUNIOR HIGH
THIRD-YEAR, CLASS A
KENDO CLUB CAPTAIN
(ALSO BELONGS TO THE KARATE CLUB)
5' 9"
BLOOD TYPE O

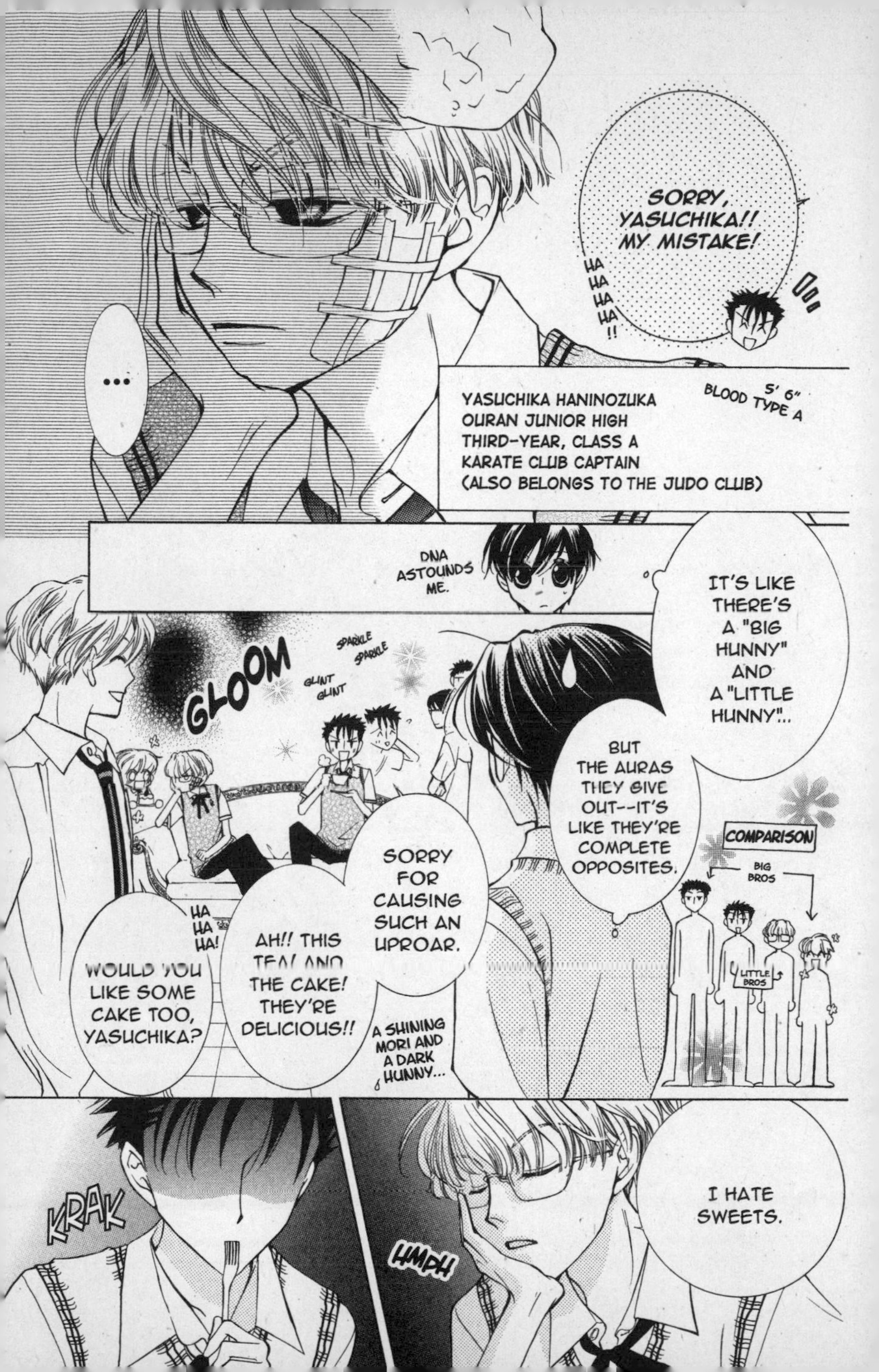
SORRY, YASUCHIKA!! MY MISTAKE!
HA HA HA HA!!
YASUCHIKA HANINOZUKA
OURAN JUNIOR HIGH
THIRD-YEAR, CLASS A
KARATE CLUB CAPTAIN
(ALSO BELONGS TO THE JUDO CLUB)
5' 6"
BLOOD TYPE A
...
IT'S LIKE THERE'S A "BIG HUNNY" AND A "LITTLE HUNNY"...
DNA ASTOUNDS ME.
BUT THE AURAS THEY GIVE OUT--IT'S LIKE THEY'RE COMPLETE OPPOSITES.
COMPARISON
BIG BROS
LITTLE BROS
SPARKLE SPARKLE
GLINT GLINT
GLOOM
SORRY FOR CAUSING SUCH AN UPROAR.
A SHINING MORI AND A DARK HUNNY...
AH!! THIS TEA AND THE CAKE! THEY'RE DELICIOUS!!
HA HA HA!
WOULD YOU LIKE SOME CAKE TOO, YASUCHIKA?
I HATE SWEETS.
HMPH
KRAK

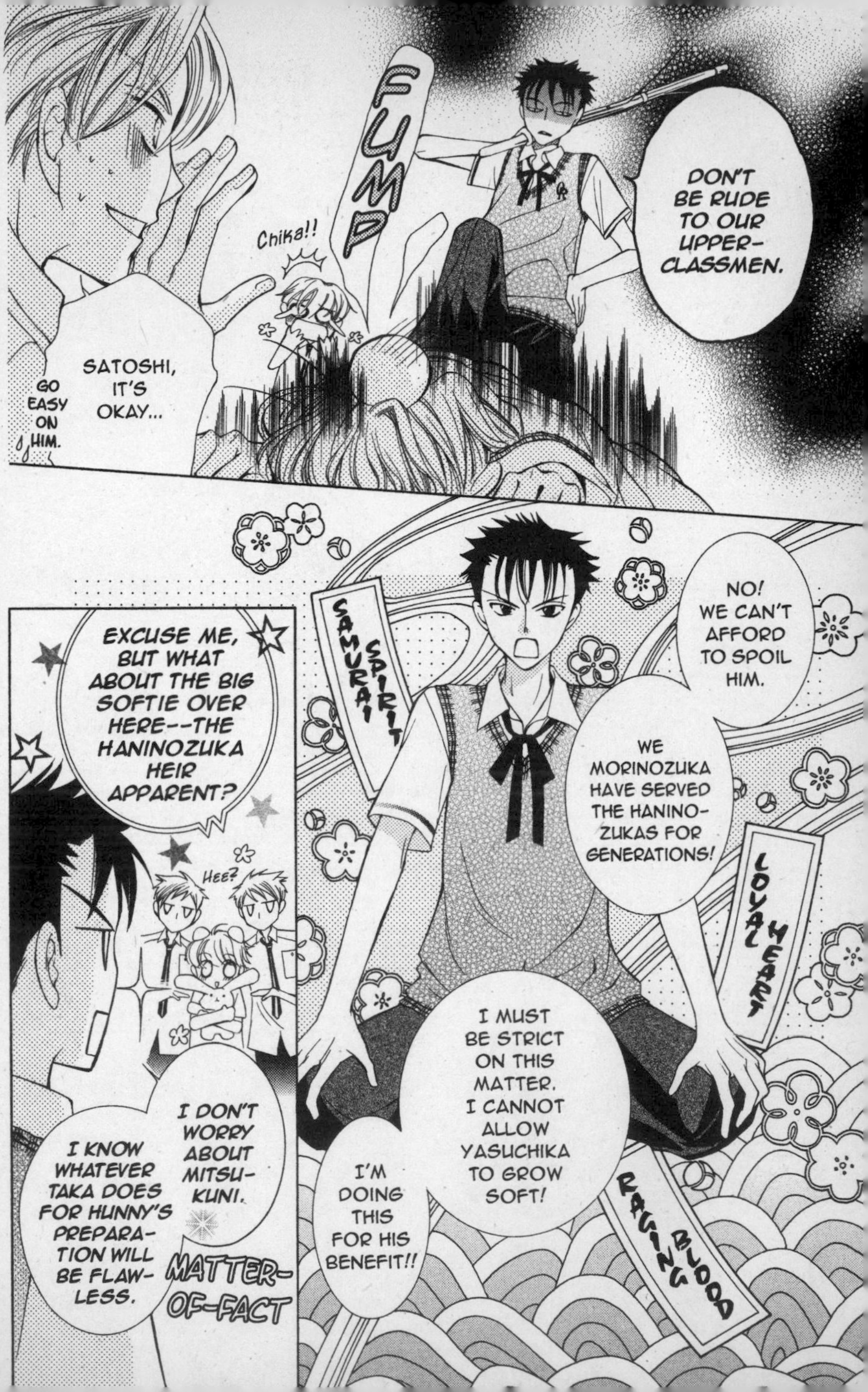
DON'T BE RUDE TO OUR UPPER-CLASSMEN.
FUMP
Chika!!
SATOSHI, IT'S OKAY...
GO EASY ON HIM.
NO! WE CAN'T AFFORD TO SPOIL HIM.
SAMURAI SPIRIT
WE MORINOZUKA HAVE SERVED THE HANINO-ZUKAS FOR GENERATIONS!
LOYAL HEART
I MUST BE STRICT ON THIS MATTER. I CANNOT ALLOW YASUCHIKA TO GROW SOFT!
I'M DOING THIS FOR HIS BENEFIT!!
RAGING BLOOD
EXCUSE ME, BUT WHAT ABOUT THE BIG SOFTIE OVER HERE--THE HANINOZUKA HEIR APPARENT?
HEE?
I DON'T WORRY ABOUT MITSU-KUNI.
I KNOW WHATEVER TAKA DOES FOR HUNNY'S PREPARA-TION WILL BE FLAW-LESS.
MATTER-OF-FACT

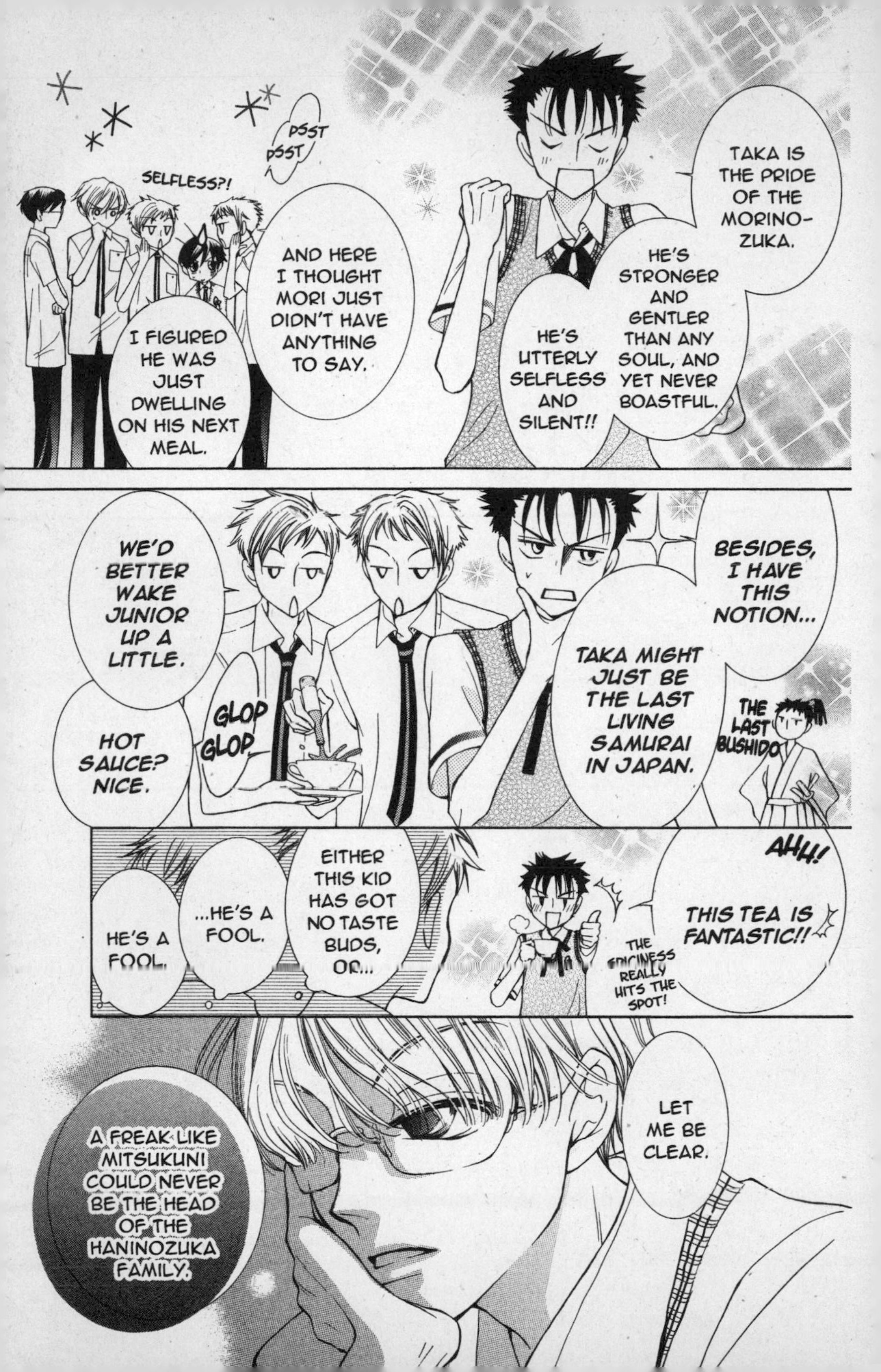
TAKA IS THE PRIDE OF THE MORINO-ZUKA.
HE'S STRONGER AND GENTLER THAN ANY SOUL, AND YET NEVER BOASTFUL.
HE'S UTTERLY SELFLESS AND SILENT!!
PSST PSST
AND HERE I THOUGHT MORI JUST DIDN'T HAVE ANYTHING TO SAY.
SELFLESS?!
I FIGURED HE WAS JUST DWELLING ON HIS NEXT MEAL.
BESIDES, I HAVE THIS NOTION...
TAKA MIGHT JUST BE THE LAST LIVING SAMURAI IN JAPAN.
THE LAST BUSHIDO
WE'D BETTER WAKE JUNIOR UP A LITTLE.
GLOP GLOP
HOT SAUCE? NICE.
AHH!
THIS TEA IS FANTASTIC!!
THE SPICINESS REALLY HITS THE SPOT!
EITHER THIS KID HAS GOT NO TASTE BUDS, OR...
...HE'S A FOOL.
HE'S A FOOL.
LET ME BE CLEAR.
A FREAK LIKE MITSUKUNI COULD NEVER BE THE HEAD OF THE HANINOZUKA FAMILY.

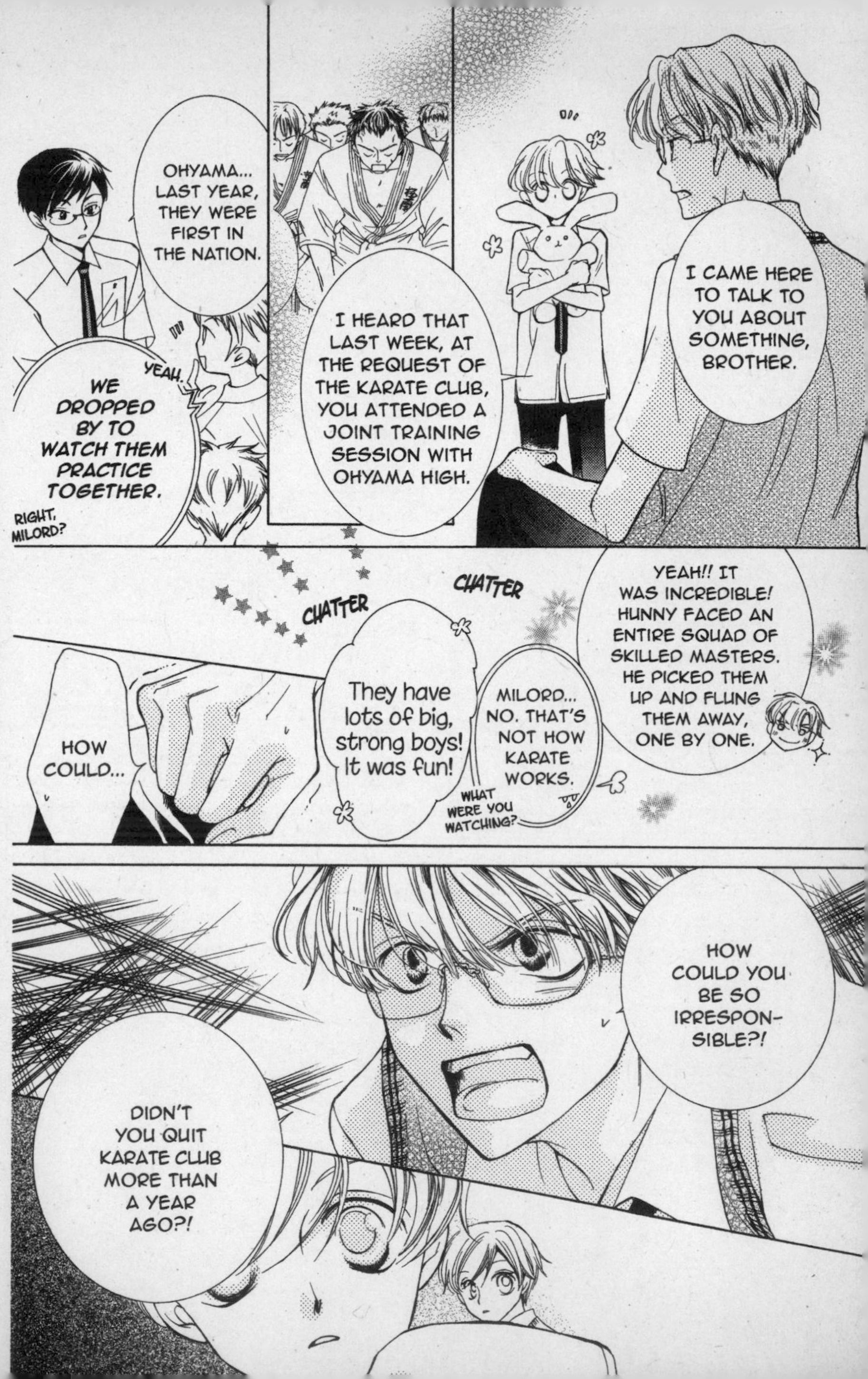
I CAME HERE TO TALK TO YOU ABOUT SOMETHING, BROTHER.
I HEARD THAT LAST WEEK, AT THE REQUEST OF THE KARATE CLUB, YOU ATTENDED A JOINT TRAINING SESSION WITH OHYAMA HIGH.
OHYAMA... LAST YEAR, THEY WERE FIRST IN THE NATION.
YEAH.
WE DROPPED BY TO WATCH THEM PRACTICE TOGETHER.
RIGHT, MILORD?
YEAH!! IT WAS INCREDIBLE! HUNNY FACED AN ENTIRE SQUAD OF SKILLED MASTERS. HE PICKED THEM UP AND FLUNG THEM AWAY, ONE BY ONE.
CHATTER
MILORD... NO. THAT'S NOT HOW KARATE WORKS.
WHAT WERE YOU WATCHING?
They have lots of big, strong boys! It was fun!
CHATTER
HOW COULD...
HOW COULD YOU BE SO IRRESPON-SIBLE?!
DIDN'T YOU QUIT KARATE CLUB MORE THAN A YEAR AGO?!

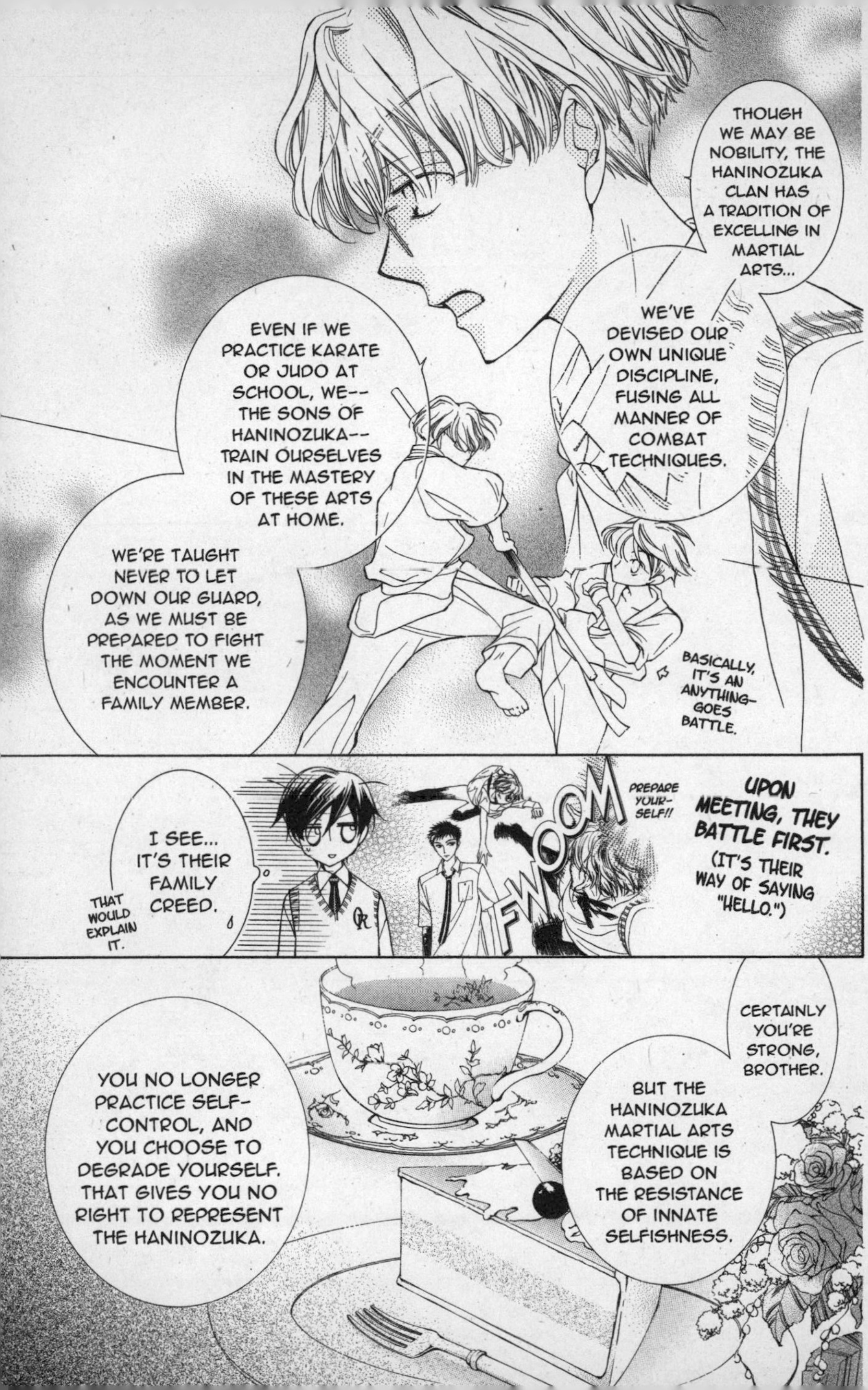
THOUGH WE MAY BE NOBILITY, THE HANINOZUKA CLAN HAS A TRADITION OF EXCELLING IN MARTIAL ARTS...
WE'VE DEVISED OUR OWN UNIQUE DISCIPLINE, FUSING ALL MANNER OF COMBAT TECHNIQUES.
EVEN IF WE PRACTICE KARATE OR JUDO AT SCHOOL, WE-- THE SONS OF HANINOZUKA-- TRAIN OURSELVES IN THE MASTERY OF THESE ARTS AT HOME.
WE'RE TAUGHT NEVER TO LET DOWN OUR GUARD, AS WE MUST BE PREPARED TO FIGHT THE MOMENT WE ENCOUNTER A FAMILY MEMBER.
BASICALLY, IT'S AN ANYTHING-GOES BATTLE.
UPON MEETING, THEY BATTLE FIRST.
(IT'S THEIR WAY OF SAYING "HELLO.")
PREPARE YOURSELF!!
FWOOM
I SEE... IT'S THEIR FAMILY CREED.
THAT WOULD EXPLAIN IT.
CERTAINLY YOU'RE STRONG, BROTHER.
BUT THE HANINOZUKA MARTIAL ARTS TECHNIQUE IS BASED ON THE RESISTANCE OF INNATE SELFISHNESS.
YOU NO LONGER PRACTICE SELF-CONTROL, AND YOU CHOOSE TO DEGRADE YOURSELF. THAT GIVES YOU NO RIGHT TO REPRESENT THE HANINOZUKA.

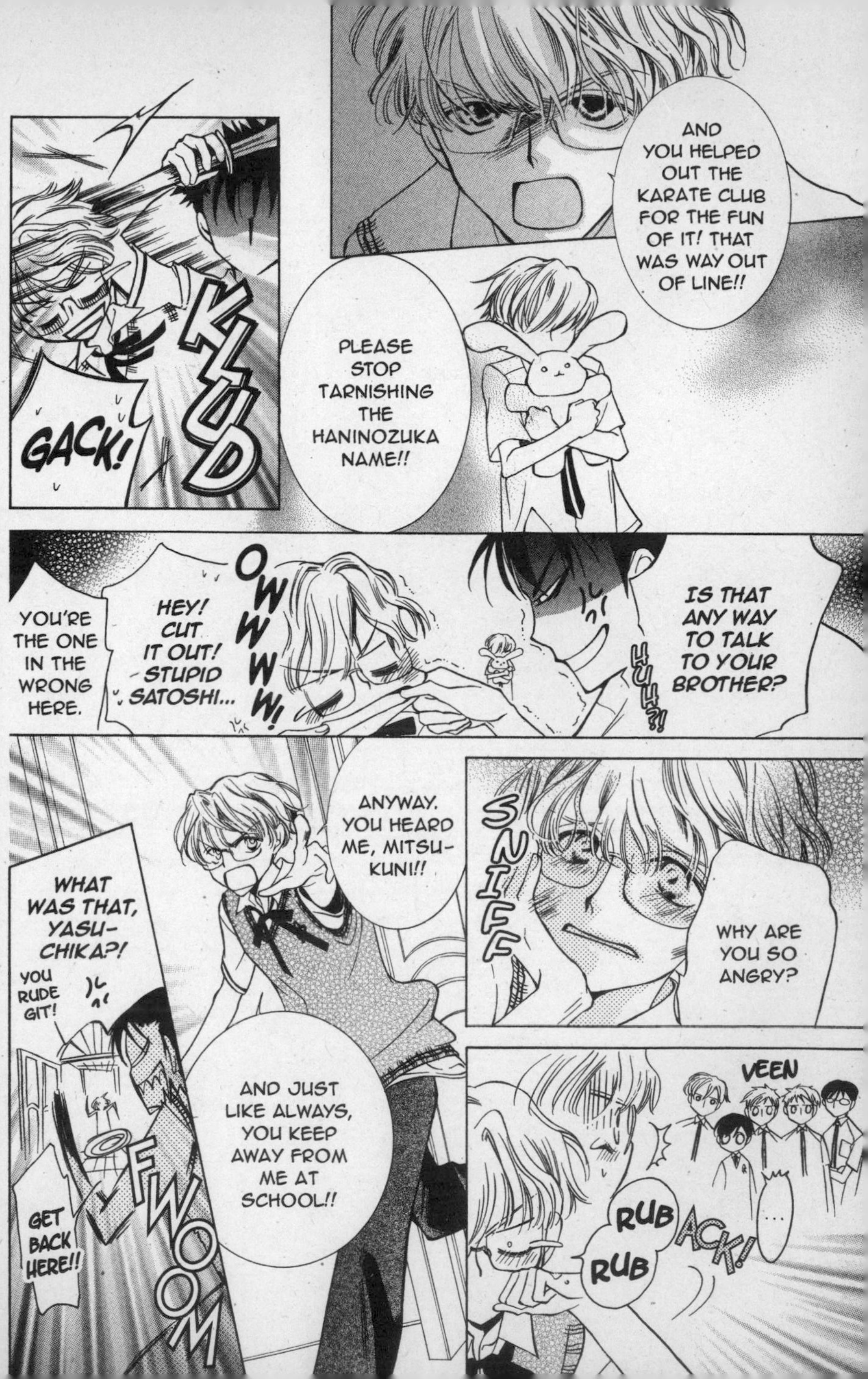
AND YOU HELPED OUT THE KARATE CLUB FOR THE FUN OF IT! THAT WAS WAY OUT OF LINE!!
PLEASE STOP TARNISHING THE HANINOZUKA NAME!!
KLUD
GACK!
IS THAT ANY WAY TO TALK TO YOUR BROTHER?
HUH?!
OWWWWW!
HEY! CUT IT OUT! STUPID SATOSHI...
YOU'RE THE ONE IN THE WRONG HERE.
WHY ARE YOU SO ANGRY?
SNIFF
VEEN
...
ACK!
RUB
RUB
ANYWAY. YOU HEARD ME, MITSU-KUNI!!
AND JUST LIKE ALWAYS, YOU KEEP AWAY FROM ME AT SCHOOL!!
WHAT WAS THAT, YASU-CHIKA?!
YOU RUDE GIT!
FWOOM
GET BACK HERE!!

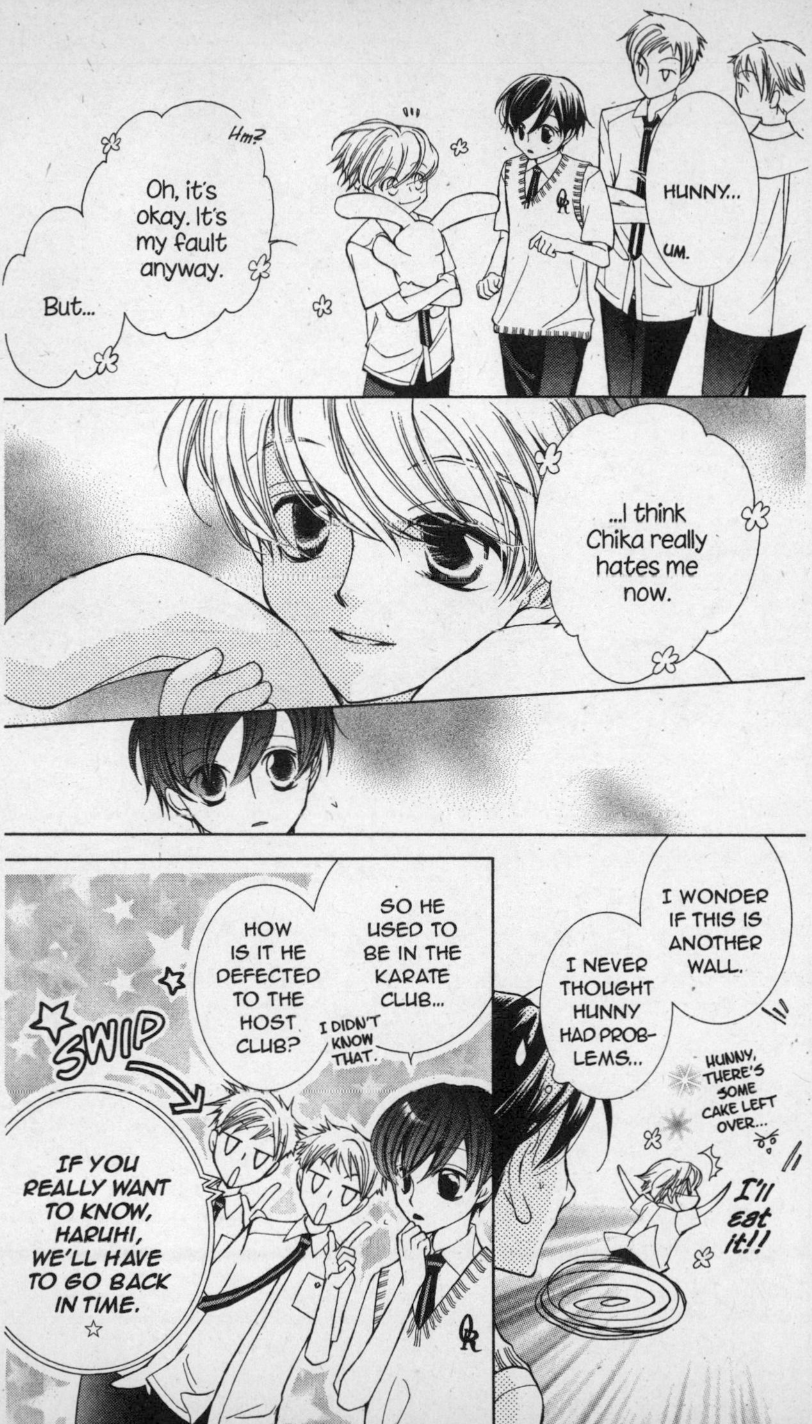
HUNNY...
UM.
Hm?
Oh, it's okay. It's my fault anyway.
But...
...I think Chika really hates me now.
I WONDER IF THIS IS ANOTHER WALL.
I NEVER THOUGHT HUNNY HAD PROB-LEMS...
HUNNY, THERE'S SOME CAKE LEFT OVER...
I'll eat it!!
SO HE USED TO BE IN THE KARATE CLUB...
HOW IS IT HE DEFECTED TO THE HOST CLUB?
I DIDN'T KNOW THAT.
SWIP
IF YOU REALLY WANT TO KNOW, HARUHI, WE'LL HAVE TO GO BACK IN TIME.

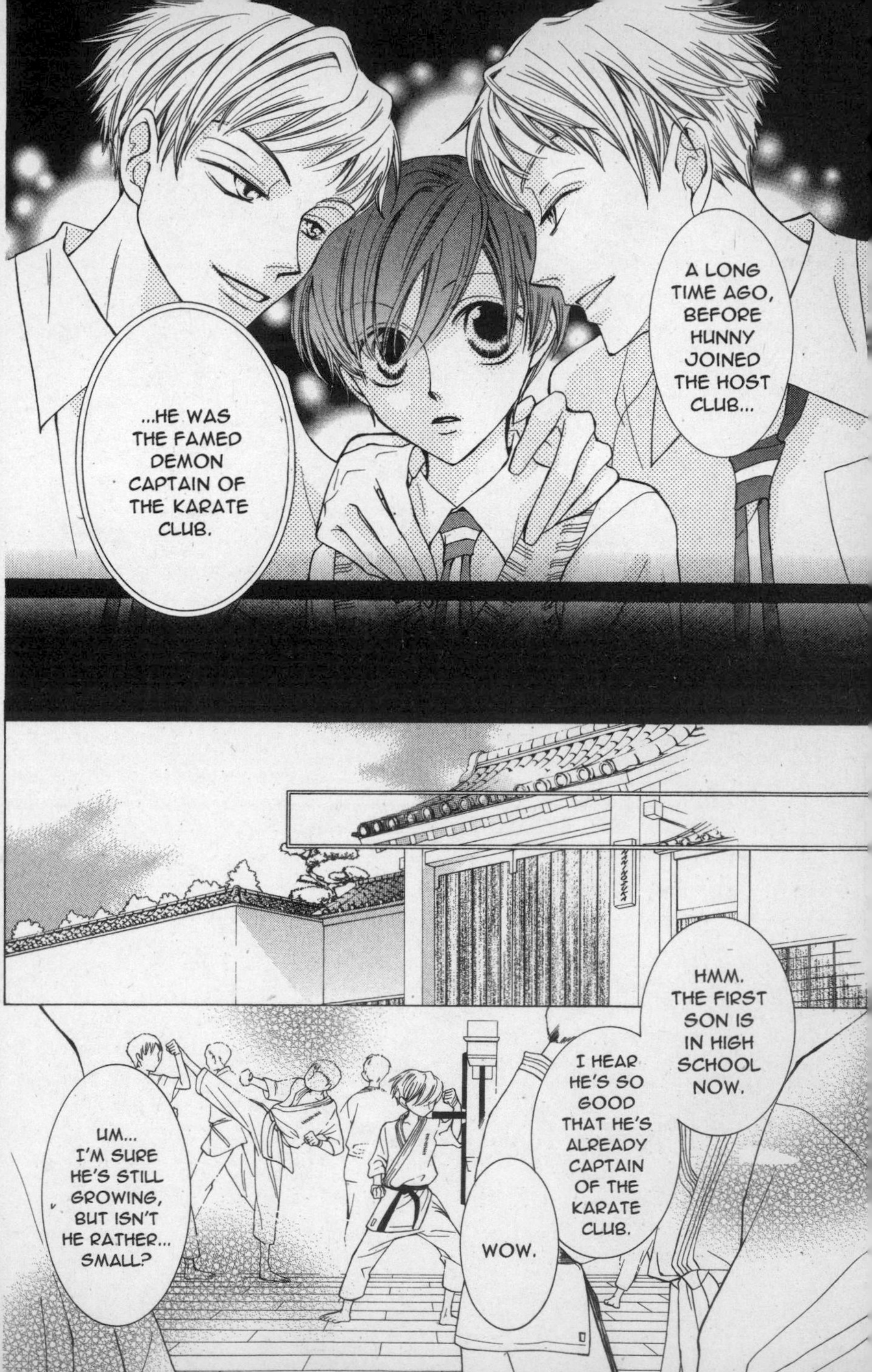
A LONG TIME AGO, BEFORE HUNNY JOINED THE HOST CLUB...
...HE WAS THE FAMED DEMON CAPTAIN OF THE KARATE CLUB.
HMM. THE FIRST SON IS IN HIGH SCHOOL NOW.
I HEAR HE'S SO GOOD THAT HE'S ALREADY CAPTAIN OF THE KARATE CLUB.
WOW.
UM... I'M SURE HE'S STILL GROWING, BUT ISN'T HE RATHER... SMALL?

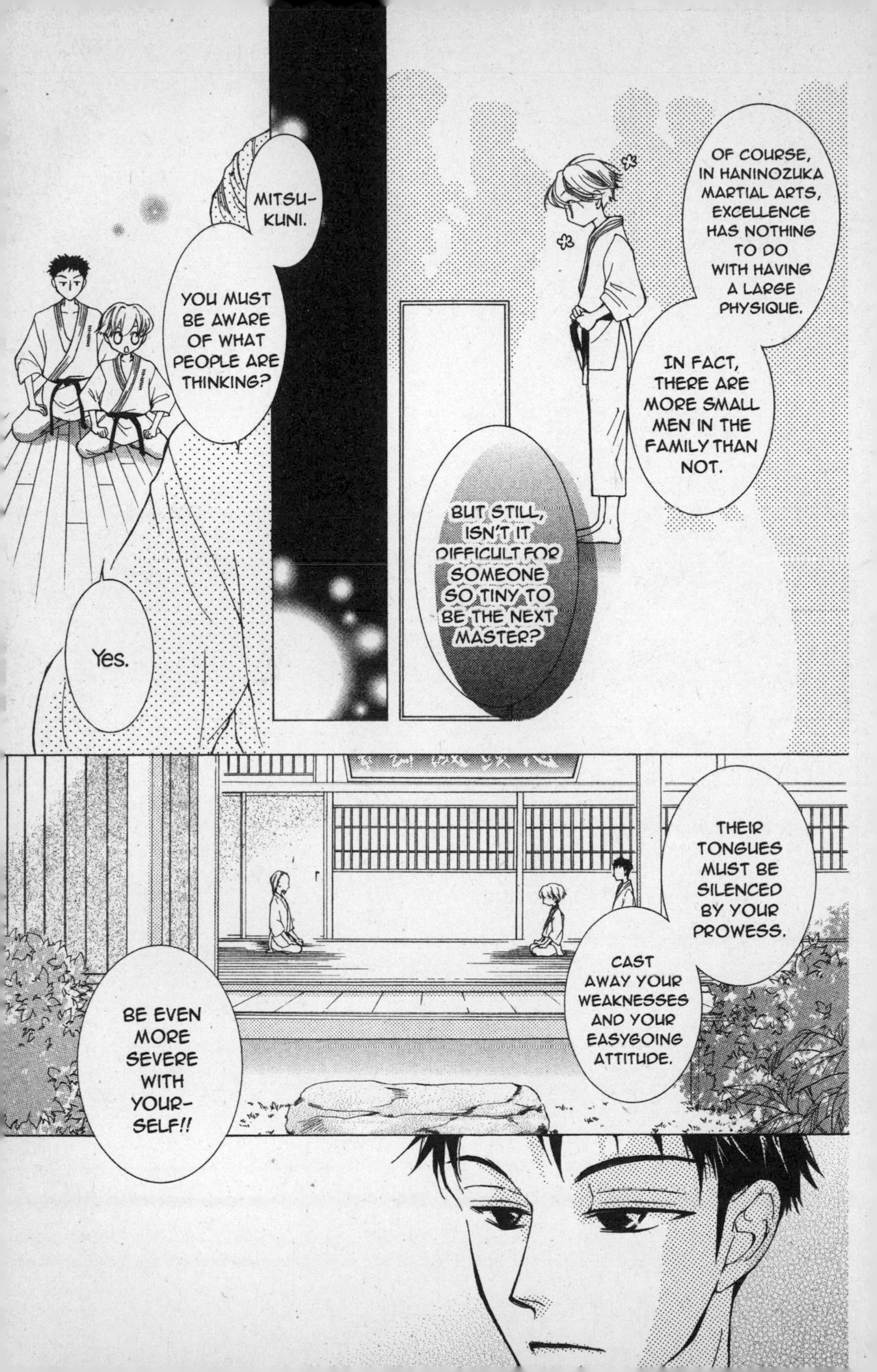
OF COURSE, IN HANINOZUKA MARTIAL ARTS, EXCELLENCE HAS NOTHING TO DO WITH HAVING A LARGE PHYSIQUE.
IN FACT, THERE ARE MORE SMALL MEN IN THE FAMILY THAN NOT.
BUT STILL, ISN'T IT DIFFICULT FOR SOMEONE SO TINY TO BE THE NEXT MASTER?
MITSU-KUNI.
YOU MUST BE AWARE OF WHAT PEOPLE ARE THINKING?
Yes.
THEIR TONGUES MUST BE SILENCED BY YOUR PROWESS.
CAST AWAY YOUR WEAKNESSES AND YOUR EASYGOING ATTITUDE.
BE EVEN MORE SEVERE WITH YOUR-SELF!!

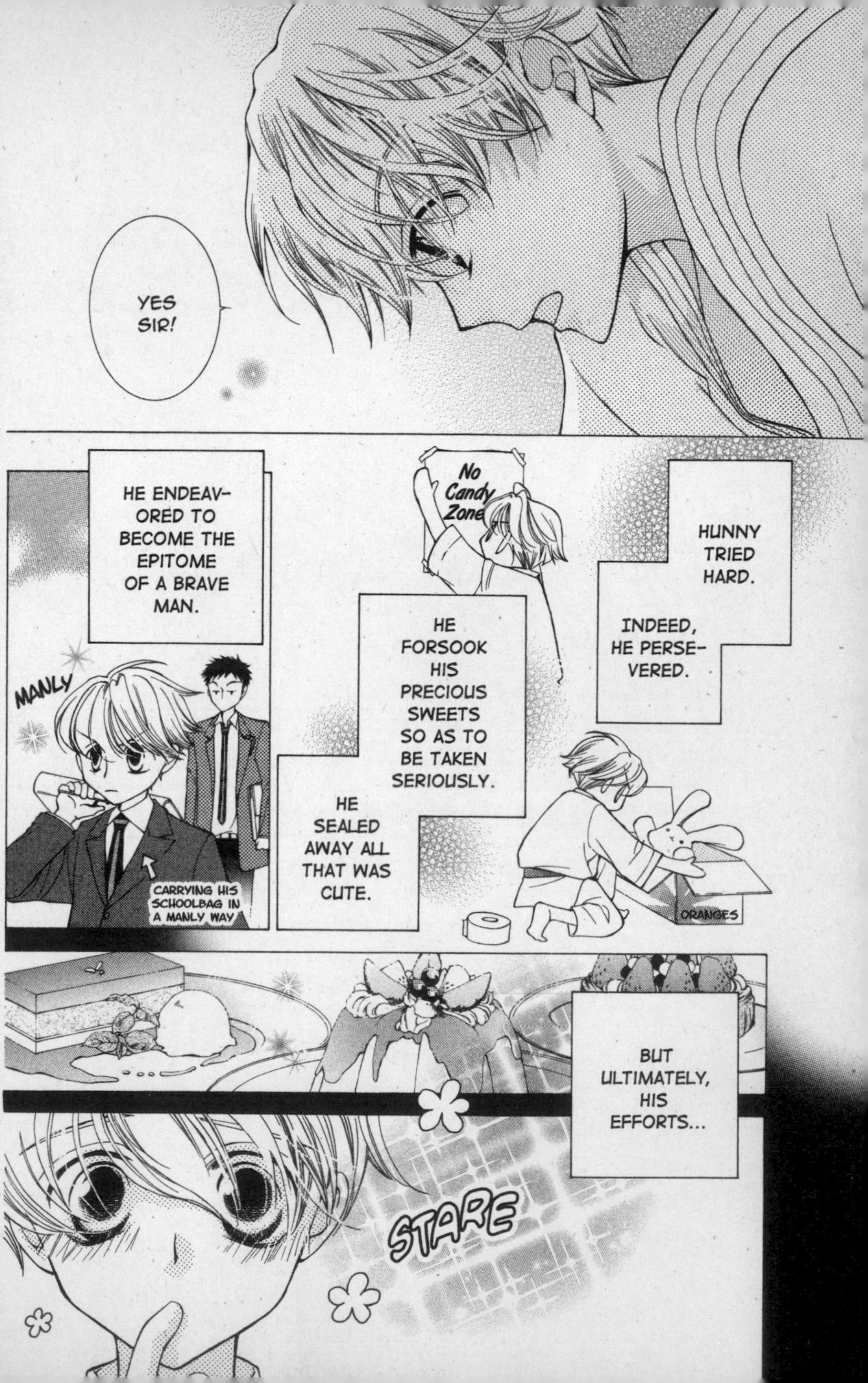
YES SIR!
HUNNY TRIED HARD.
INDEED, HE PERSE-VERED.
No Candy Zone
HE FORSOOK HIS PRECIOUS SWEETS SO AS TO BE TAKEN SERIOUSLY.
HE SEALED AWAY ALL THAT WAS CUTE.
ORANGES
HE ENDEAV-ORED TO BECOME THE EPITOME OF A BRAVE MAN.
MANLY
CARRYING HIS SCHOOLBAG IN A MANLY WAY
BUT ULTIMATELY, HIS EFFORTS...
STARE

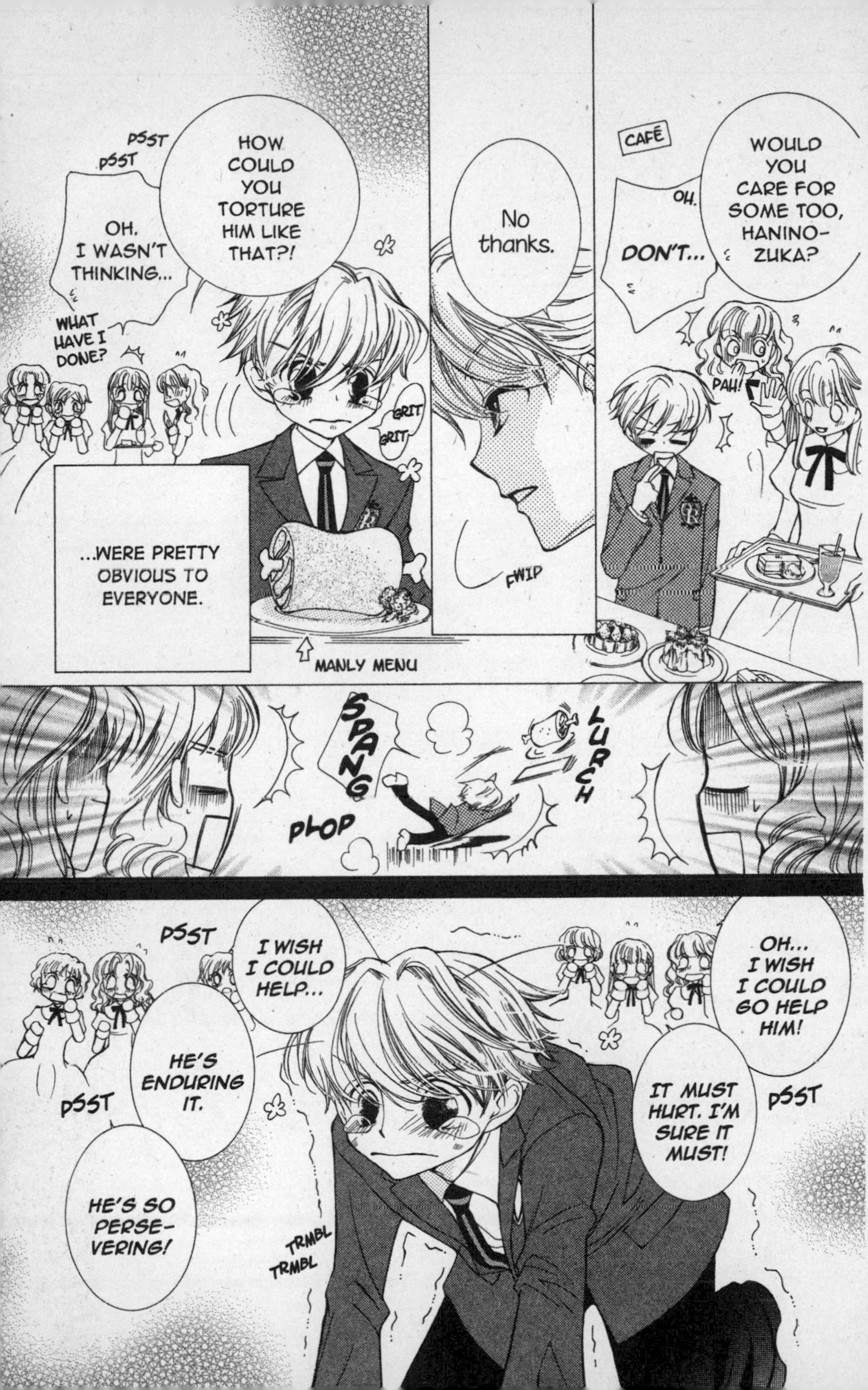
CAFÉ
WOULD YOU CARE FOR SOME TOO, HANINO-ZUKA?
OH. DON'T...
PAH!
No thanks.
FWIP
HOW COULD YOU TORTURE HIM LIKE THAT?!
PSST PSST
OH. I WASN'T THINKING...
WHAT HAVE I DONE?
GRIT GRIT
...WERE PRETTY OBVIOUS TO EVERYONE.
MANLY MENU
LURCH
SPANG
PLOP
OH... I WISH I COULD GO HELP HIM!
PSST
IT MUST HURT. I'M SURE IT MUST!
I WISH I COULD HELP...
PSST
HE'S ENDURING IT.
PSST
HE'S SO PERSEVERING!
TRMBL TRMBL

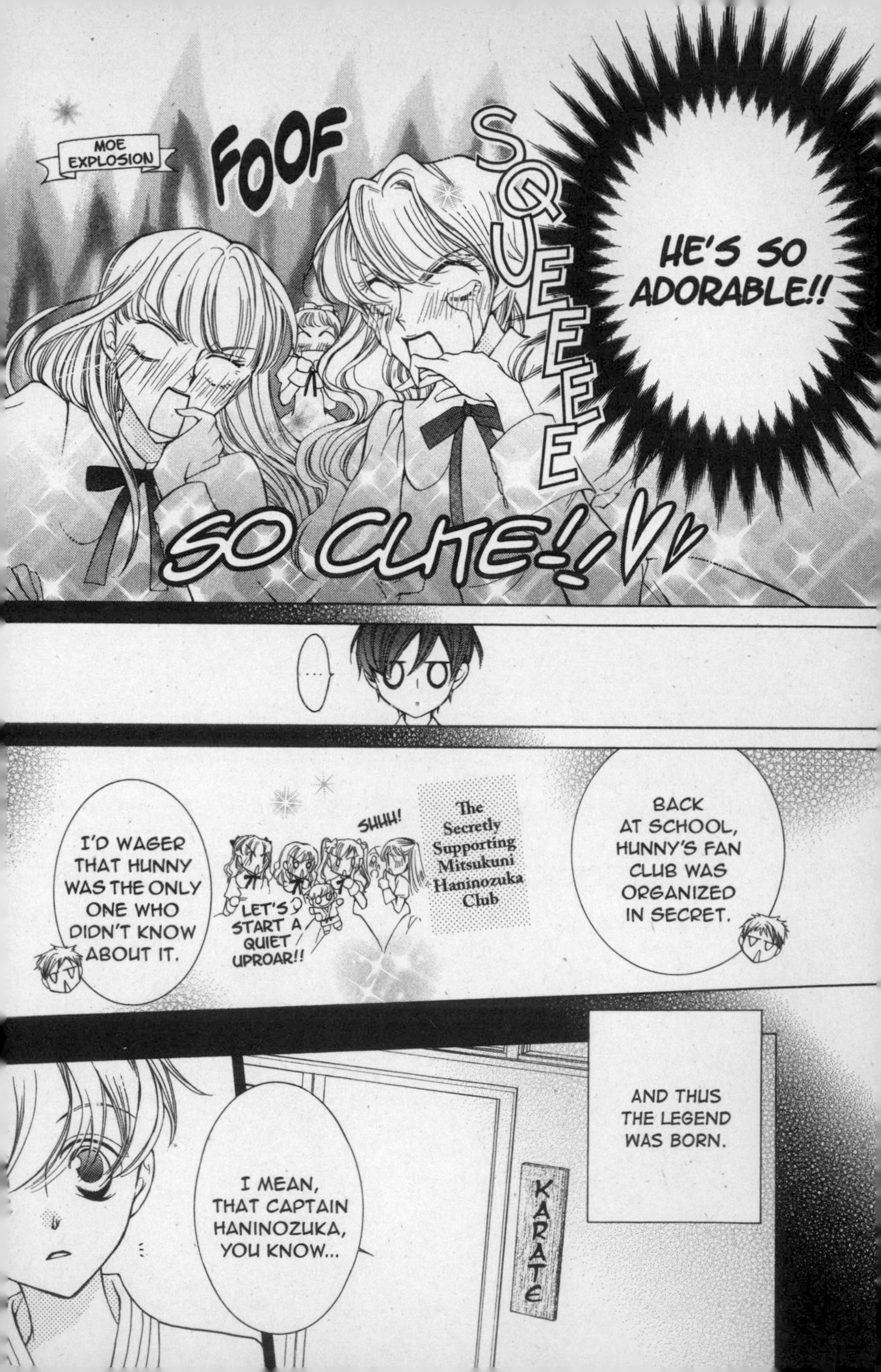
HE'S SO ADORABLE!!
SQUEEEEE
FOOF
MOE EXPLOSION
SO CUTE!!
.....
BACK AT SCHOOL, HUNNY'S FAN CLUB WAS ORGANIZED IN SECRET.
The Secretly Supporting Mitsukuni Haninozuka Club
SHHH!
LET'S START A QUIET UPROAR!!
I'D WAGER THAT HUNNY WAS THE ONLY ONE WHO DIDN'T KNOW ABOUT IT.
AND THUS THE LEGEND WAS BORN.
KARATE
I MEAN, THAT CAPTAIN HANINOZUKA, YOU KNOW...

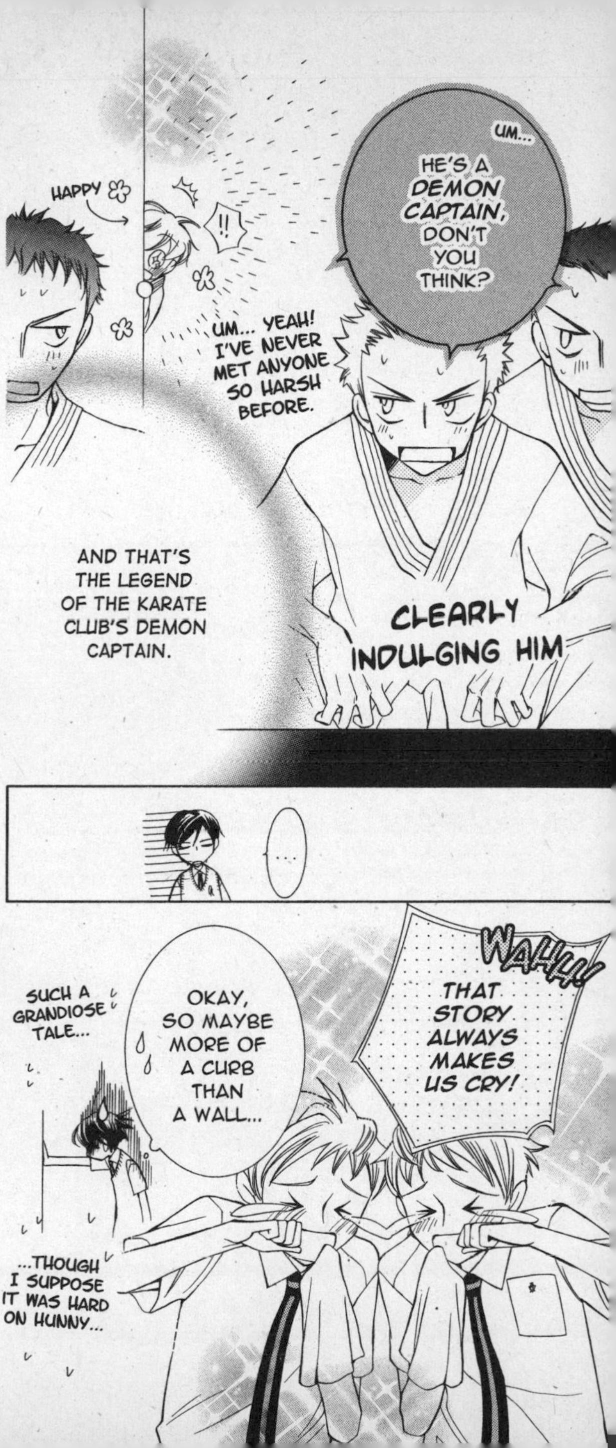
UM...
HE'S A DEMON CAPTAIN, DON'T YOU THINK?
UM... YEAH! I'VE NEVER MET ANYONE SO HARSH BEFORE.
!!
HAPPY
CLEARLY INDULGING HIM
AND THAT'S THE LEGEND OF THE KARATE CLUB'S DEMON CAPTAIN.
...
WAHH!
THAT STORY ALWAYS MAKES US CRY!
OKAY, SO MAYBE MORE OF A CURB THAN A WALL...
SUCH A GRANDIOSE TALE...
...THOUGH I SUPPOSE IT WAS HARD ON HUNNY...

2

✿ I JUST REMEMBERED SOMETHING! I RECEIVED A LETTER THAT HAD: "I SEE YOU USED THE WORD "OTEMAMI" IN VOLUME 6. I DON'T SUPPOSE YOU WATCH --?"

↑ A RECENT TV DRAMA

UM. ACTUALLY, "OTEMAMI" IS A FAD WORD THAT WAS POPULAR BACK WHEN I WAS IN ELEMENTARY SCHOOL! I BET THE SHOW'S SCRIPTWRITER HAD A TWINGE OF NOSTALGIA AND USED THE OLD TERM. YOU KNOW, I DON'T EVEN KNOW IF THE WORD WAS NEW BACK THEN. IT COULD'VE BEEN AROUND MUCH LONGER. WHATEVER THE CASE MAY BE, I GUESS LINGUISTIC TRENDS DO COME IN CYCLES LIKE THIS.

✿ INCIDENTALLY, THE CURRENT VOGUE IN LETTER-WRITING SEEMS TO BE JOTTING

H/K

AT THE BEGINNING OF A NEW PARAGRAPH WHEN SHOWING A CHANGE IN TOPIC.

DO YOU KNOW WHAT IT MEANS? YOU CAN FIND THE ANSWER IN THE NEXT COLUMN!

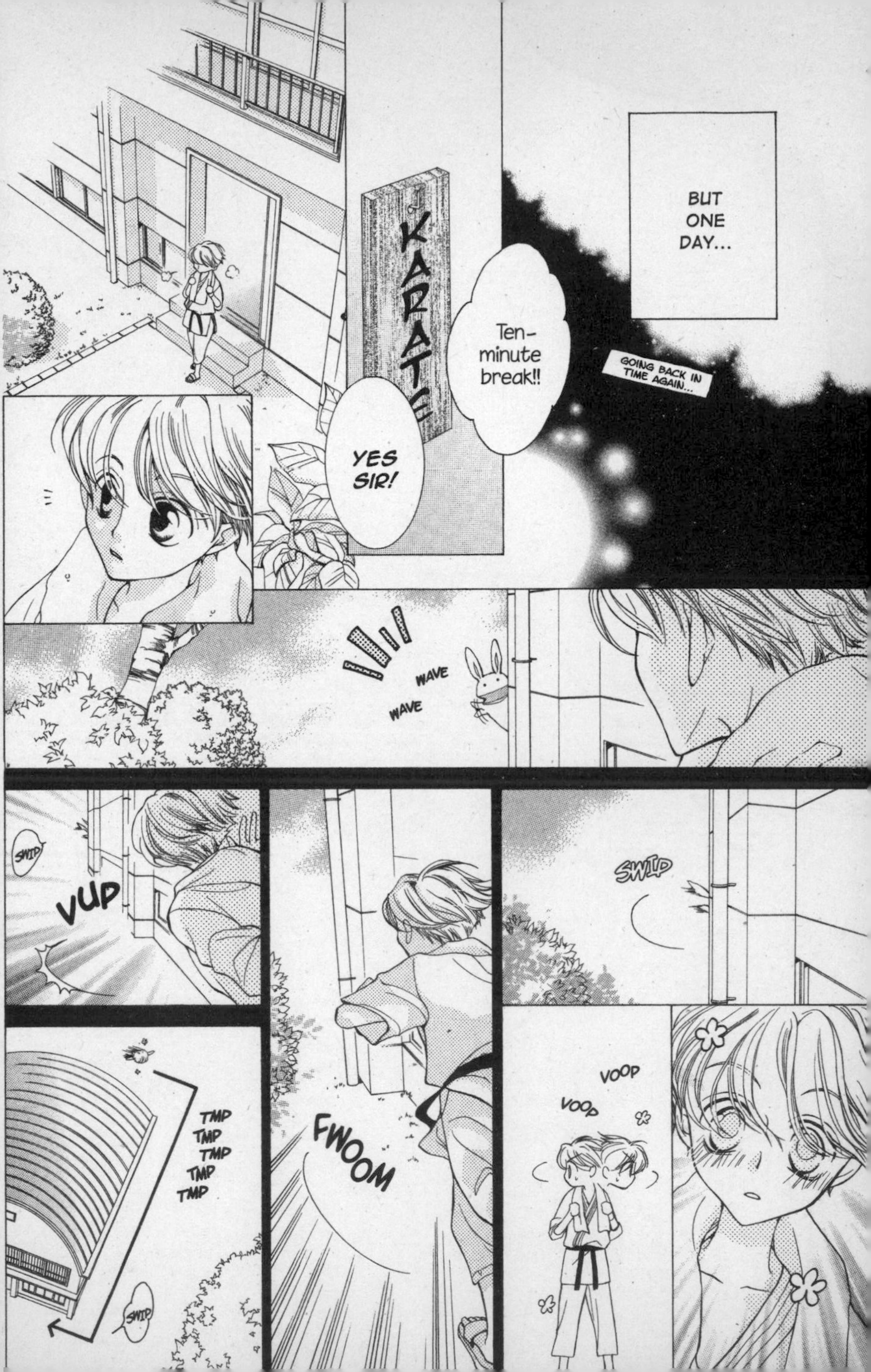

BUT ONE DAY...
GOING BACK IN TIME AGAIN...
Ten-minute break!!
YES SIR!
WAVE
WAVE
SWIP
VOOP
VOOP
FWOOM
SWIP
VUP
TMP
TMP
TMP
TMP
TMP
SWIP

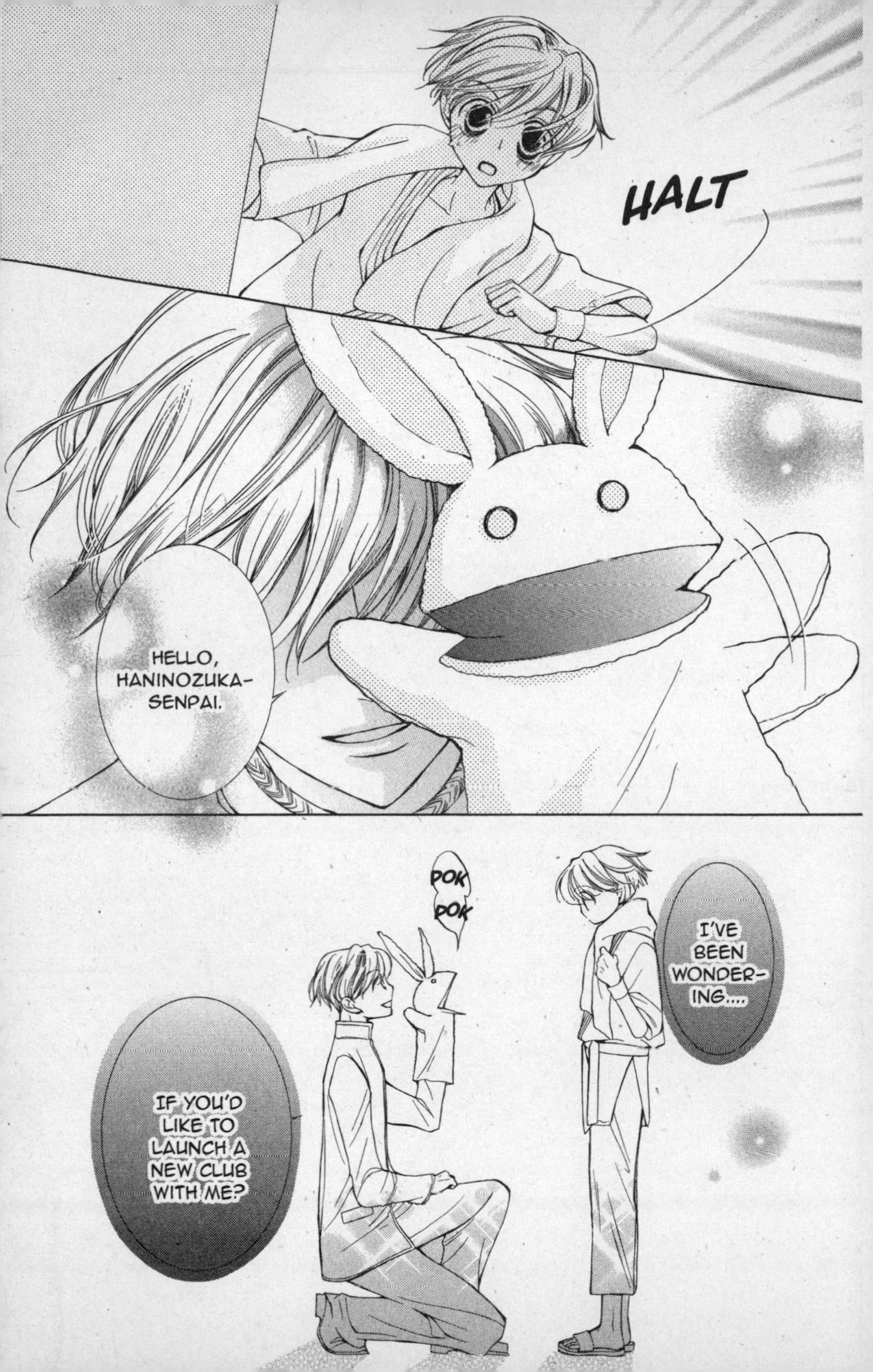
HALT
HELLO, HANINOZUKA-SENPAI.
I'VE BEEN WONDERING....
POK POK
IF YOU'D LIKE TO LAUNCH A NEW CLUB WITH ME?

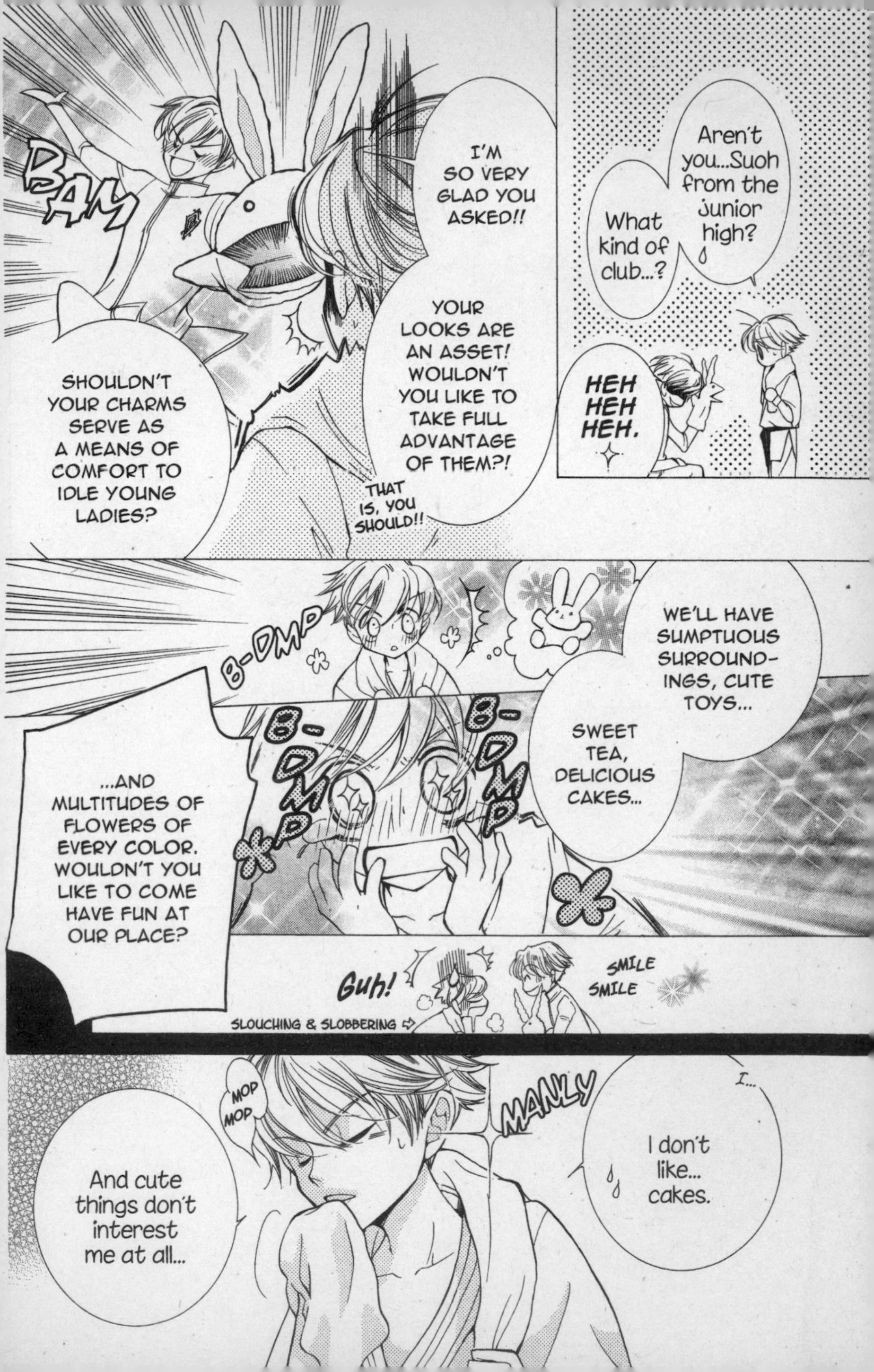
Aren't you...Suoh from the junior high?
What kind of club...?
HEH HEH HEH.
I'M SO VERY GLAD YOU ASKED!!
YOUR LOOKS ARE AN ASSET! WOULDN'T YOU LIKE TO TAKE FULL ADVANTAGE OF THEM?!
THAT IS, YOU SHOULD!!
BAM
SHOULDN'T YOUR CHARMS SERVE AS A MEANS OF COMFORT TO IDLE YOUNG LADIES?
WE'LL HAVE SUMPTUOUS SURROUNDINGS, CUTE TOYS...
B-DMP
SWEET TEA, DELICIOUS CAKES...
B-DMP
B-DMP
...AND MULTITUDES OF FLOWERS OF EVERY COLOR. WOULDN'T YOU LIKE TO COME HAVE FUN AT OUR PLACE?
SMILE SMILE
Guh!
SLOUCHING & SLOBBERING
I...
I don't like... cakes.
MANLY
MOP MOP
And cute things don't interest me at all...

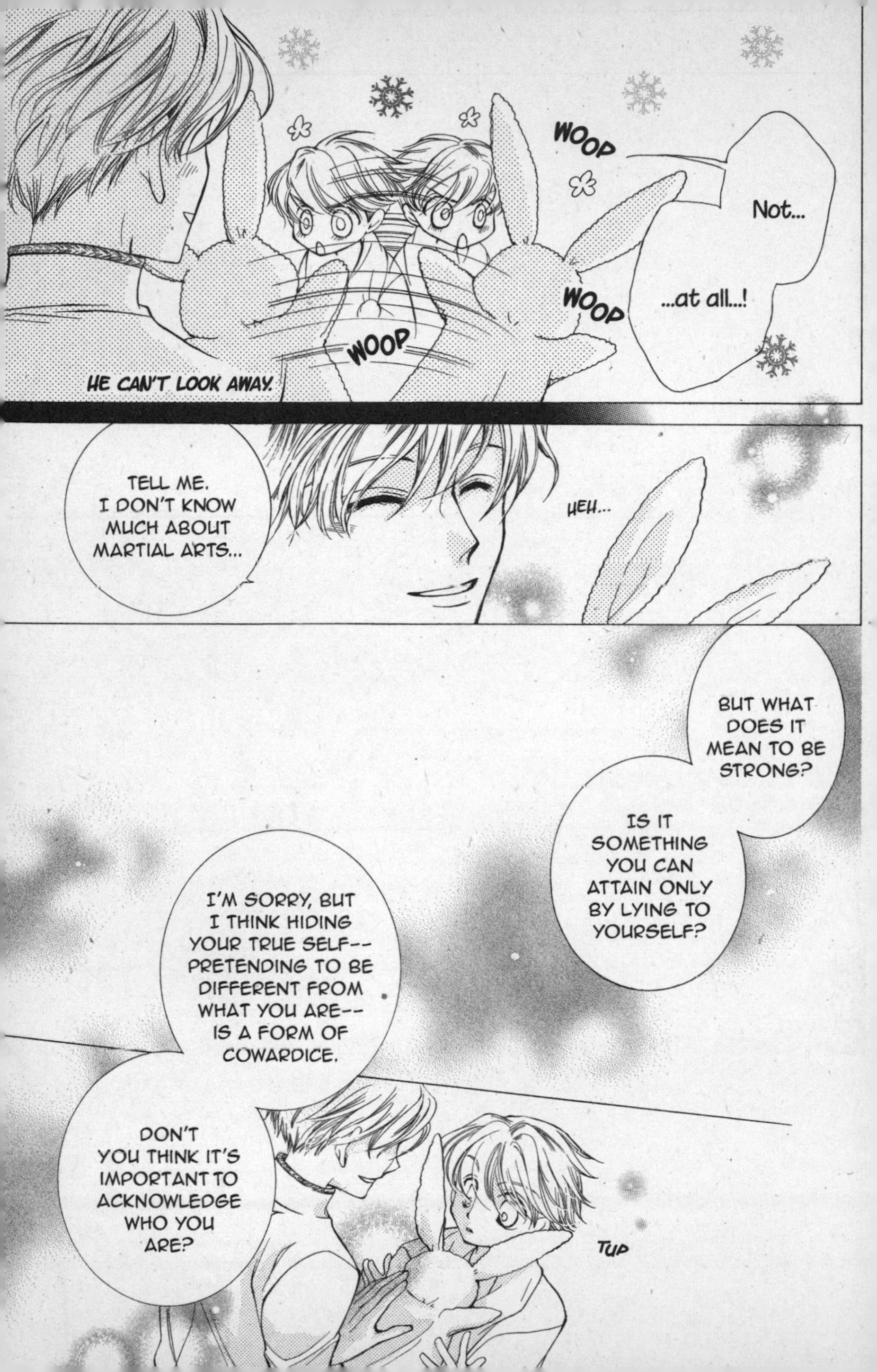
WOOP
Not...
...at all...!
WOOP
WOOP
HE CAN'T LOOK AWAY.
HEH...
TELL ME. I DON'T KNOW MUCH ABOUT MARTIAL ARTS...
BUT WHAT DOES IT MEAN TO BE STRONG?
IS IT SOMETHING YOU CAN ATTAIN ONLY BY LYING TO YOURSELF?
I'M SORRY, BUT I THINK HIDING YOUR TRUE SELF-- PRETENDING TO BE DIFFERENT FROM WHAT YOU ARE-- IS A FORM OF COWARDICE.
TUP
DON'T YOU THINK IT'S IMPORTANT TO ACKNOWLEDGE WHO YOU ARE?

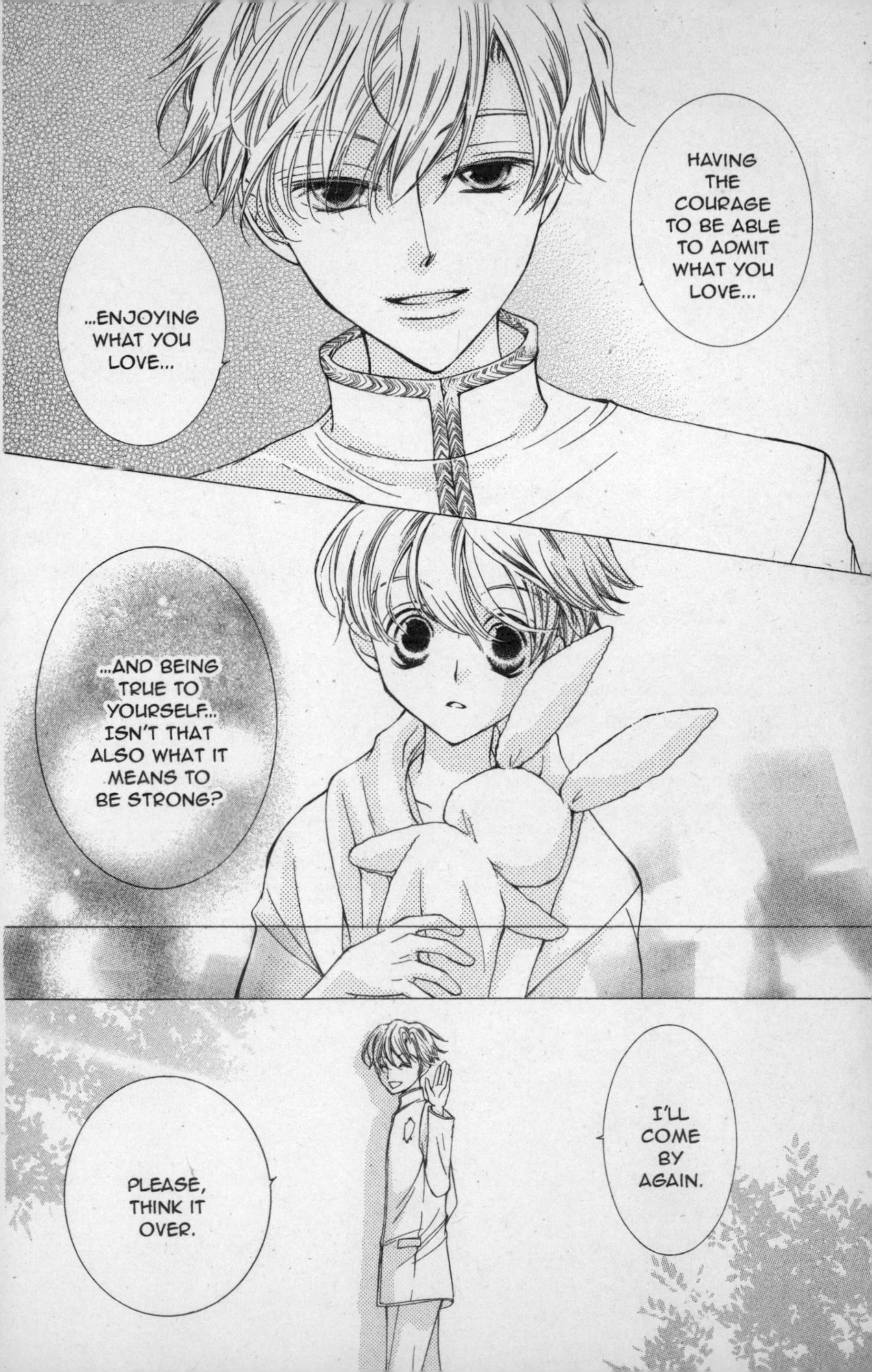
HAVING THE COURAGE TO BE ABLE TO ADMIT WHAT YOU LOVE...
...ENJOYING WHAT YOU LOVE...
...AND BEING TRUE TO YOURSELF... ISN'T THAT ALSO WHAT IT MEANS TO BE STRONG?
I'LL COME BY AGAIN.
PLEASE, THINK IT OVER.

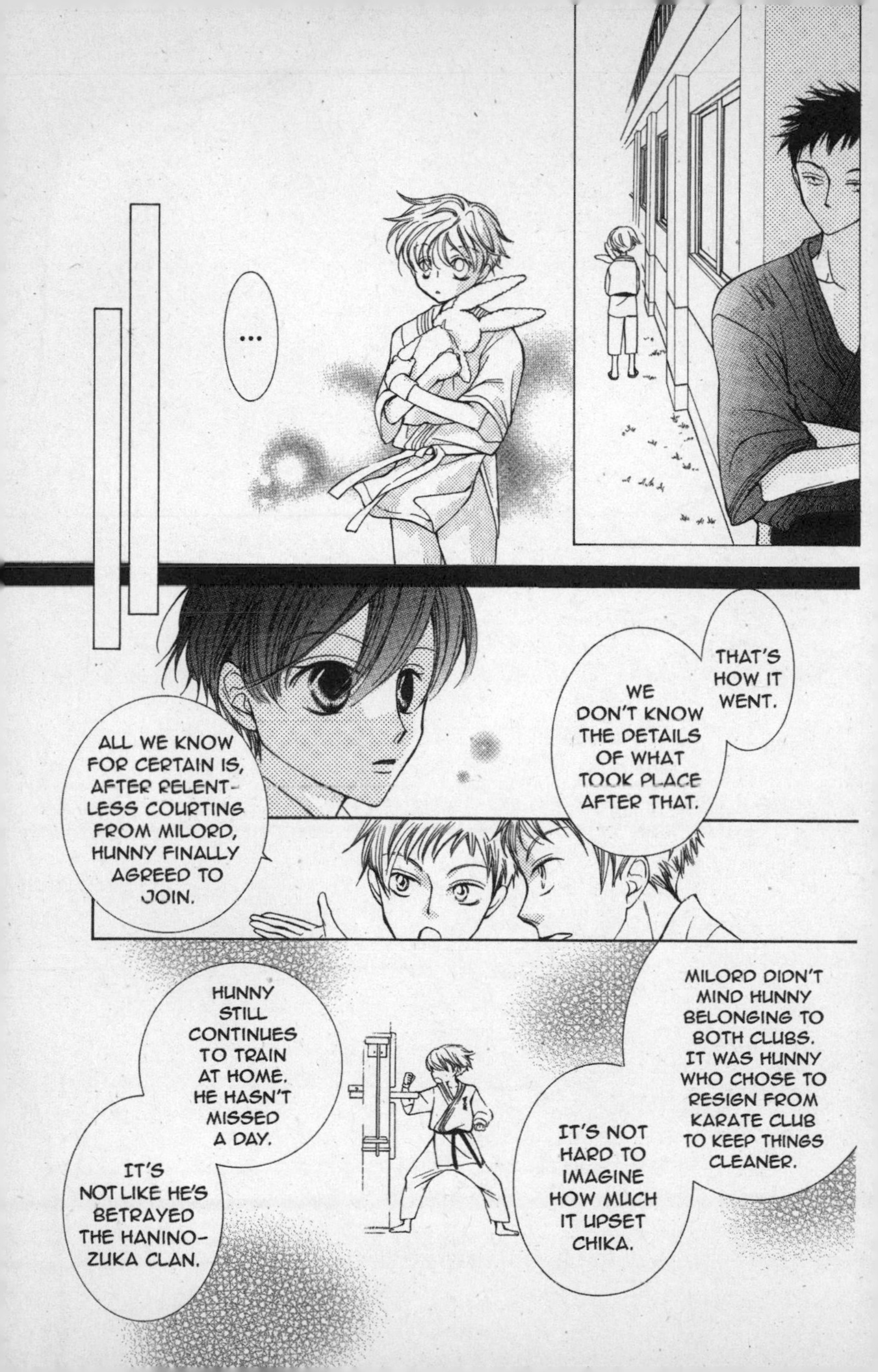
...
THAT'S HOW IT WENT.
WE DON'T KNOW THE DETAILS OF WHAT TOOK PLACE AFTER THAT.
ALL WE KNOW FOR CERTAIN IS, AFTER RELENT-LESS COURTING FROM MILORD, HUNNY FINALLY AGREED TO JOIN.
MILORD DIDN'T MIND HUNNY BELONGING TO BOTH CLUBS. IT WAS HUNNY WHO CHOSE TO RESIGN FROM KARATE CLUB TO KEEP THINGS CLEANER.
IT'S NOT HARD TO IMAGINE HOW MUCH IT UPSET CHIKA.
HUNNY STILL CONTINUES TO TRAIN AT HOME. HE HASN'T MISSED A DAY.
IT'S NOT LIKE HE'S BETRAYED THE HANINO-ZUKA CLAN.

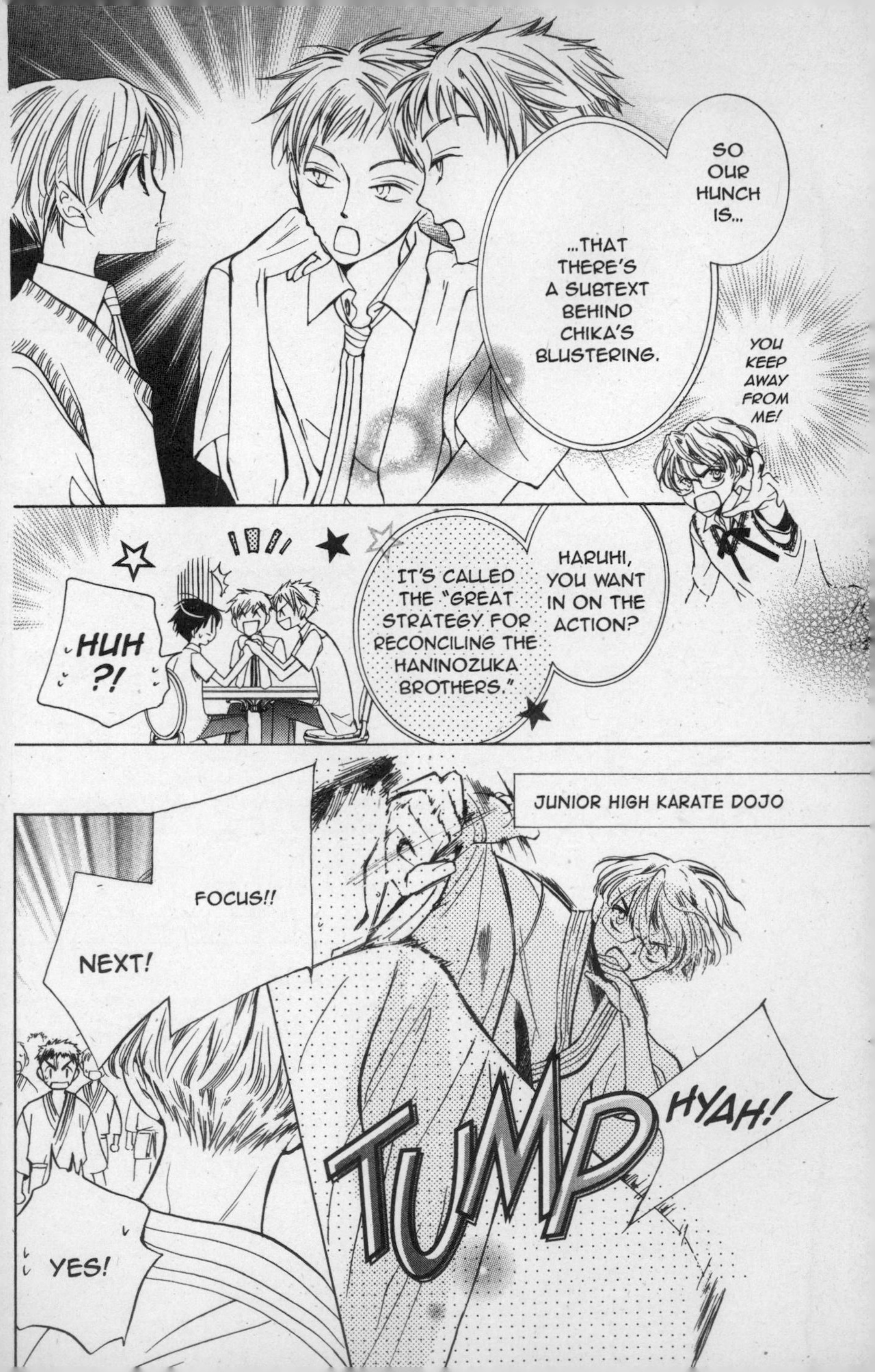
SO OUR HUNCH IS...
...THAT THERE'S A SUBTEXT BEHIND CHIKA'S BLUSTERING.
YOU KEEP AWAY FROM ME!
HARUHI, YOU WANT IN ON THE ACTION?
IT'S CALLED THE "GREAT STRATEGY FOR RECONCILING THE HANINOZUKA BROTHERS."
HUH ?!
JUNIOR HIGH KARATE DOJO
HYAH!
TUMP
FOCUS!!
NEXT!
YES!

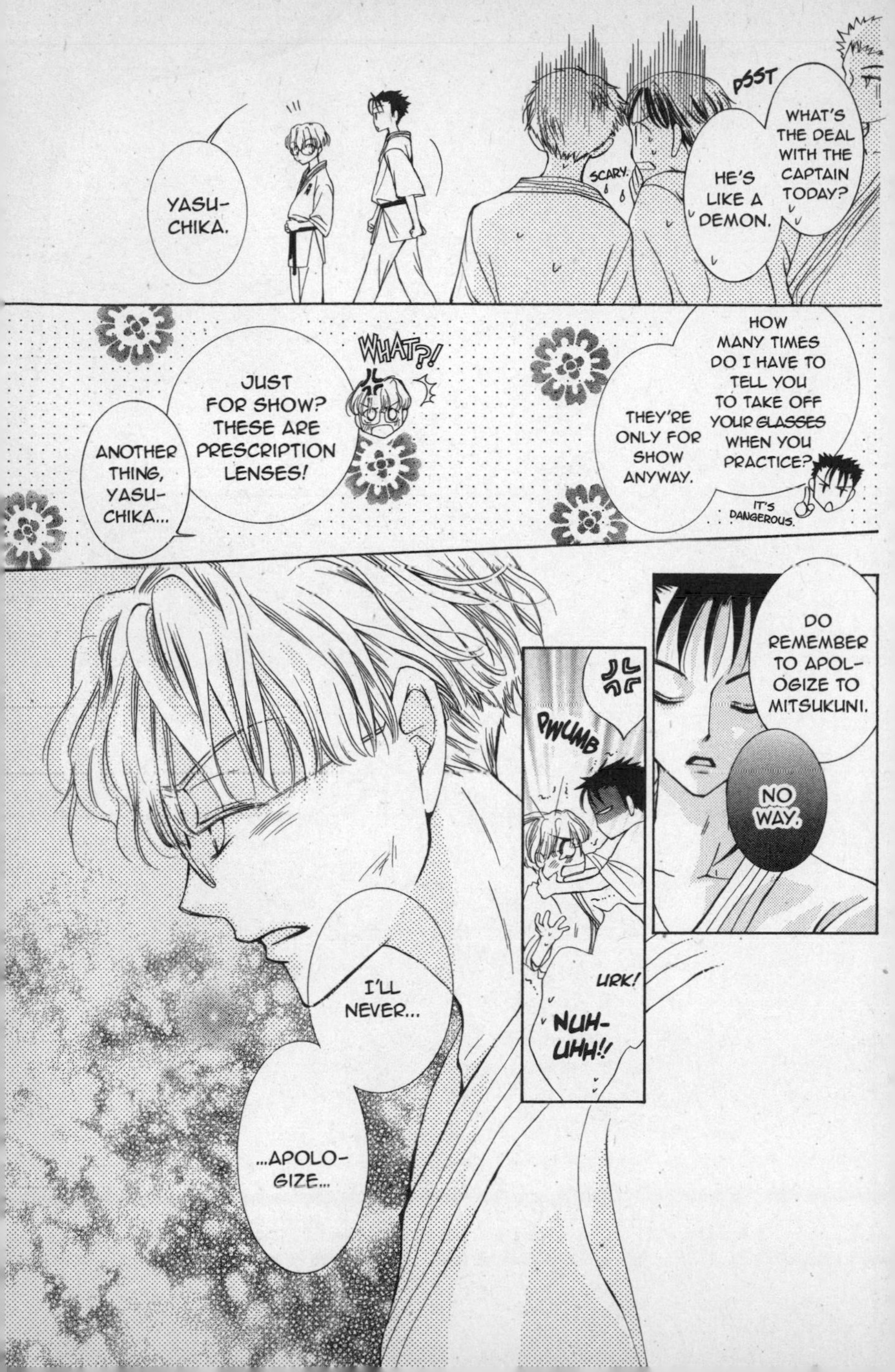
PSST
WHAT'S THE DEAL WITH THE CAPTAIN TODAY?
HE'S LIKE A DEMON.
SCARY.
YASU-CHIKA.
HOW MANY TIMES DO I HAVE TO TELL YOU TO TAKE OFF YOUR GLASSES WHEN YOU PRACTICE?
IT'S DANGEROUS.
THEY'RE ONLY FOR SHOW ANYWAY.
WHAT?!
JUST FOR SHOW? THESE ARE PRESCRIPTION LENSES!
ANOTHER THING, YASU-CHIKA...
DO REMEMBER TO APOLO-GIZE TO MITSUKUNI.
NO WAY.
PWUMB
URK!
NUH-UHH!!
I'LL NEVER...
...APOLO-GIZE...

GUEST ROOM: FAXES ②

SPECIAL THANKS TO
MEKA TANAKA!
(FOR THE SECOND TIME!!)

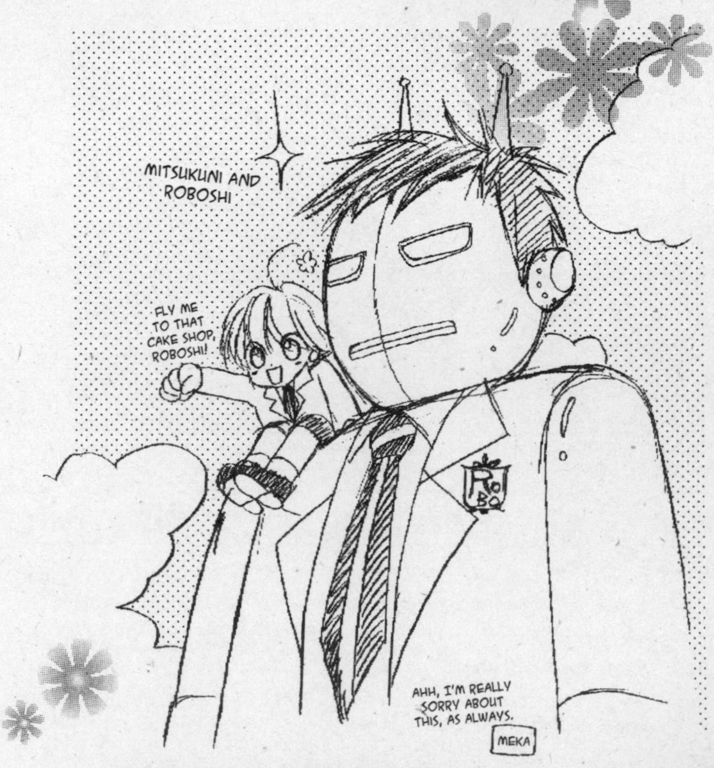
MITSUKUNI AND ROBOSHI
FLY ME TO THAT CAKE SHOP, ROBOSHI!
ROBO
AHH, I'M REALLY SORRY ABOUT THIS, AS ALWAYS.
MEKA

RETURNING HOME FROM A MEETING ONE DAY,
I FOUND THIS FAX WAITING TO RELAX ME.
I WONDER WHAT MEKA TANAKA THINKS MORI IS... AND HUNNY LOOKS SO CUTE... OH, IT'S TERRIBLE! IT MAKES ME WANT TO PUNCH HER. (THAT'S A COMPLIMENT.)
OH!! THE SCHOOL BADGE SAYS "ROBO" (LAUGH). I'D LOVE TO DRAW A SHORT 4-PANEL STRIP USING THIS CONCEPT. OR RATHER, I'D LOVE FOR HER TO DRAW ONE. FOR THIS,
I'LL TAKE HER OUT TO A NEW RESTAURANT IN TAKADANOBABA CALLED SUGAKIYA RAMEN!! THANKS!!

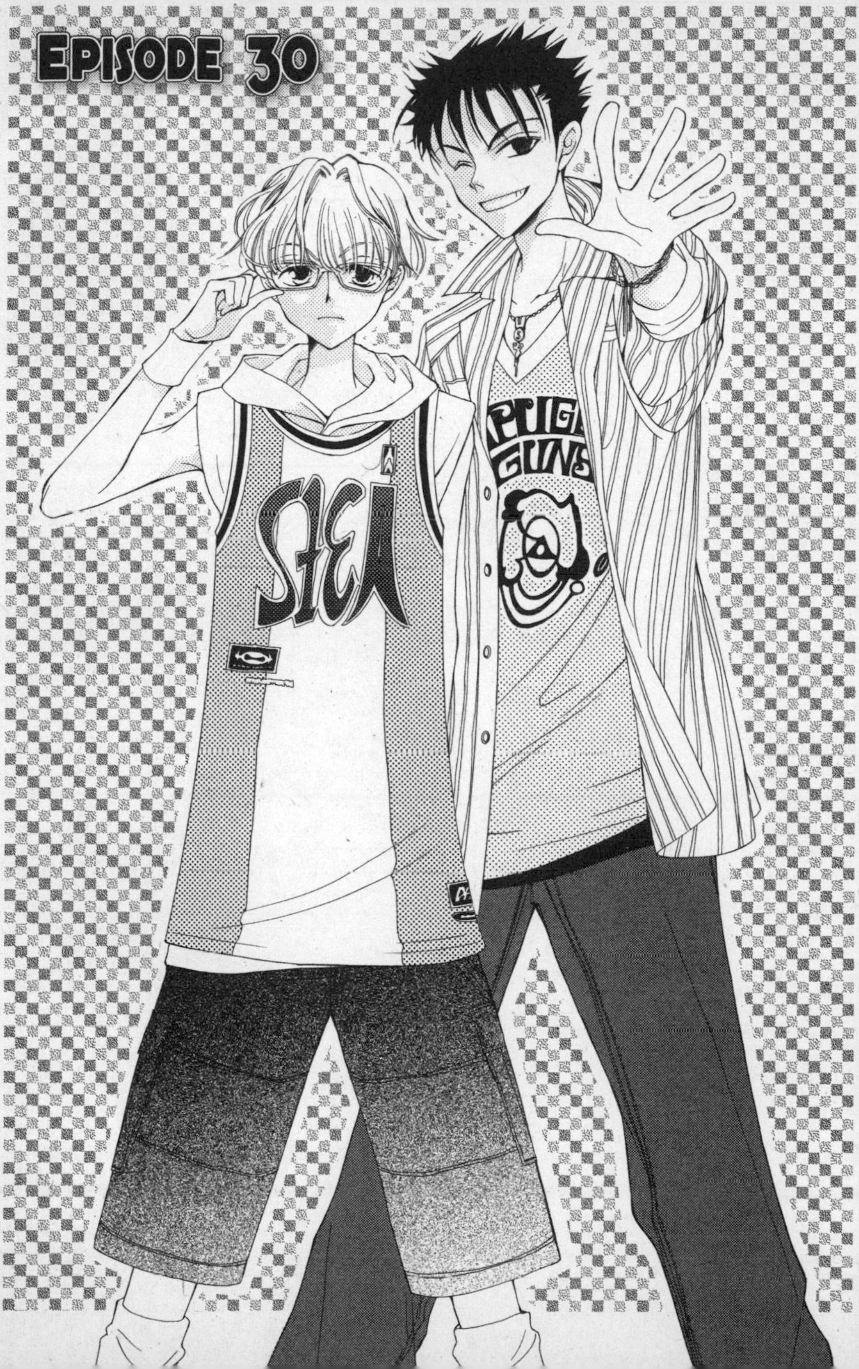
EPISODE 30

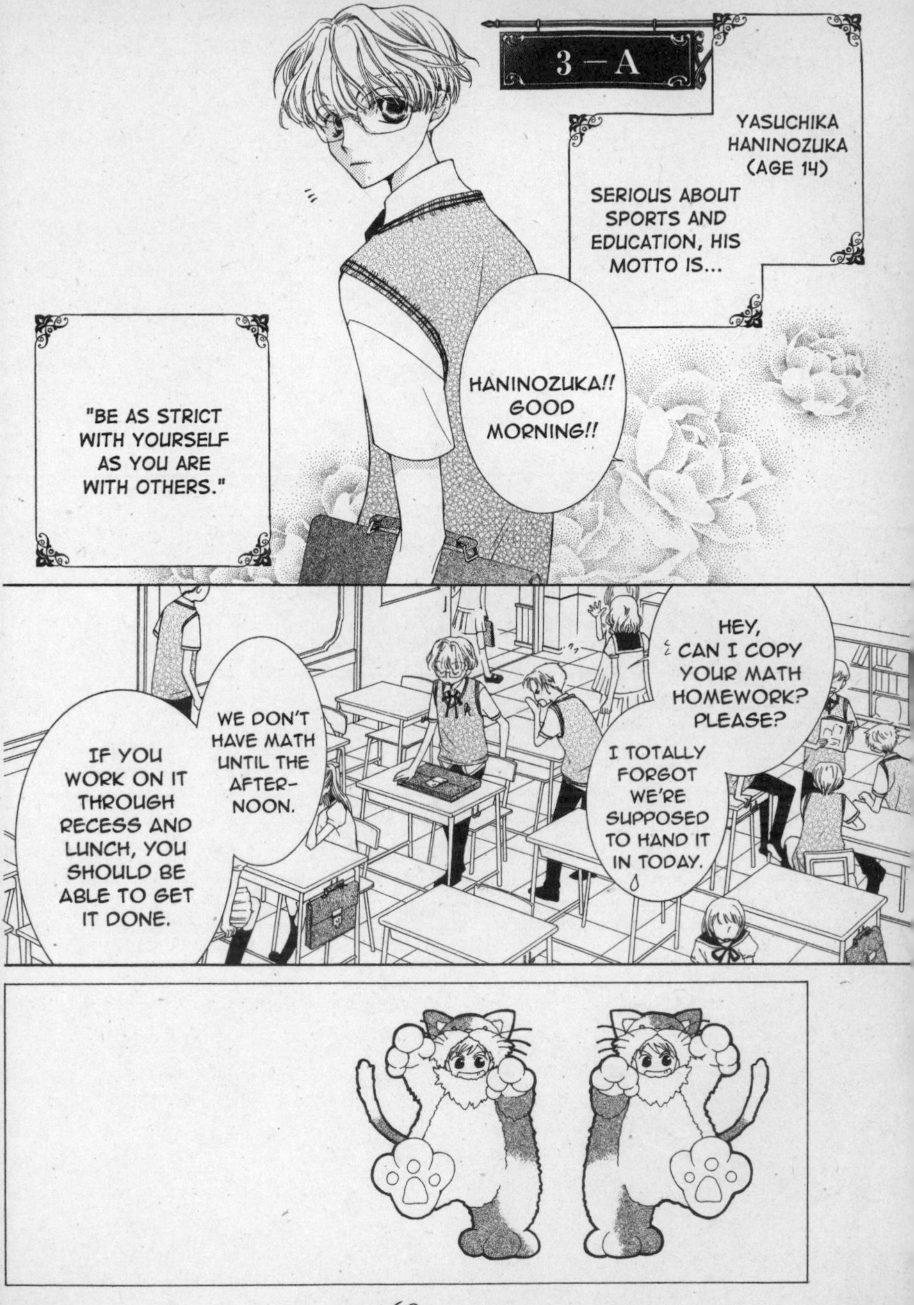
3-A
YASUCHIKA HANINOZUKA (AGE 14)
SERIOUS ABOUT SPORTS AND EDUCATION, HIS MOTTO IS...
HANINOZUKA!! GOOD MORNING!!
"BE AS STRICT WITH YOURSELF AS YOU ARE WITH OTHERS."
HEY, CAN I COPY YOUR MATH HOMEWORK? PLEASE?
I TOTALLY FORGOT WE'RE SUPPOSED TO HAND IT IN TODAY.
WE DON'T HAVE MATH UNTIL THE AFTER-NOON.
IF YOU WORK ON IT THROUGH RECESS AND LUNCH, YOU SHOULD BE ABLE TO GET IT DONE.

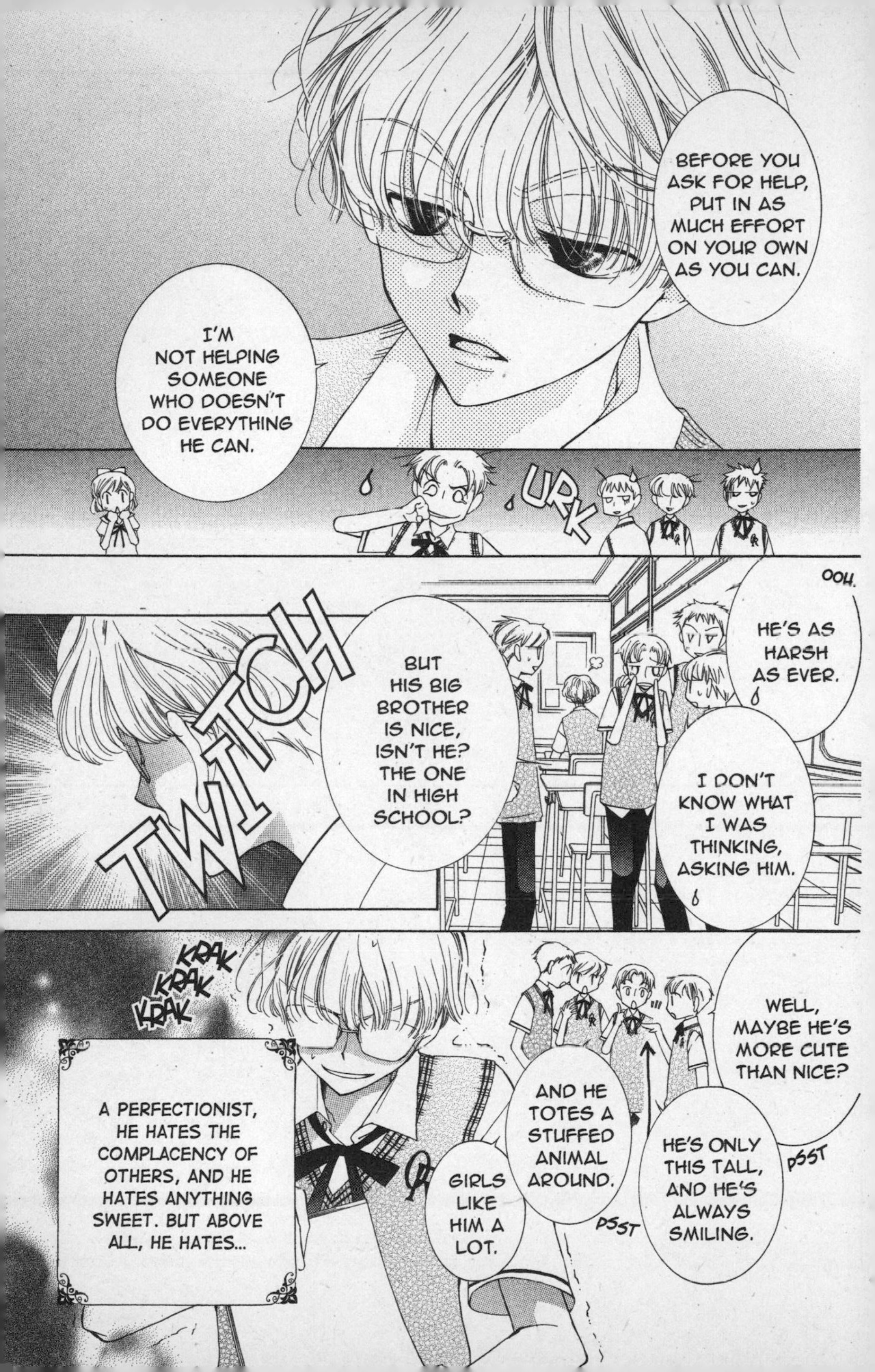
BEFORE YOU ASK FOR HELP, PUT IN AS MUCH EFFORT ON YOUR OWN AS YOU CAN.
I'M NOT HELPING SOMEONE WHO DOESN'T DO EVERYTHING HE CAN.
URK
OOH.
HE'S AS HARSH AS EVER.
I DON'T KNOW WHAT I WAS THINKING, ASKING HIM.
BUT HIS BIG BROTHER IS NICE, ISN'T HE? THE ONE IN HIGH SCHOOL?
TWITCH
WELL, MAYBE HE'S MORE CUTE THAN NICE?
PSST
HE'S ONLY THIS TALL, AND HE'S ALWAYS SMILING.
AND HE TOTES A STUFFED ANIMAL AROUND.
PSST
GIRLS LIKE HIM A LOT.
KRAK KRAK KRAK
A PERFECTIONIST, HE HATES THE COMPLACENCY OF OTHERS, AND HE HATES ANYTHING SWEET. BUT ABOVE ALL, HE HATES...

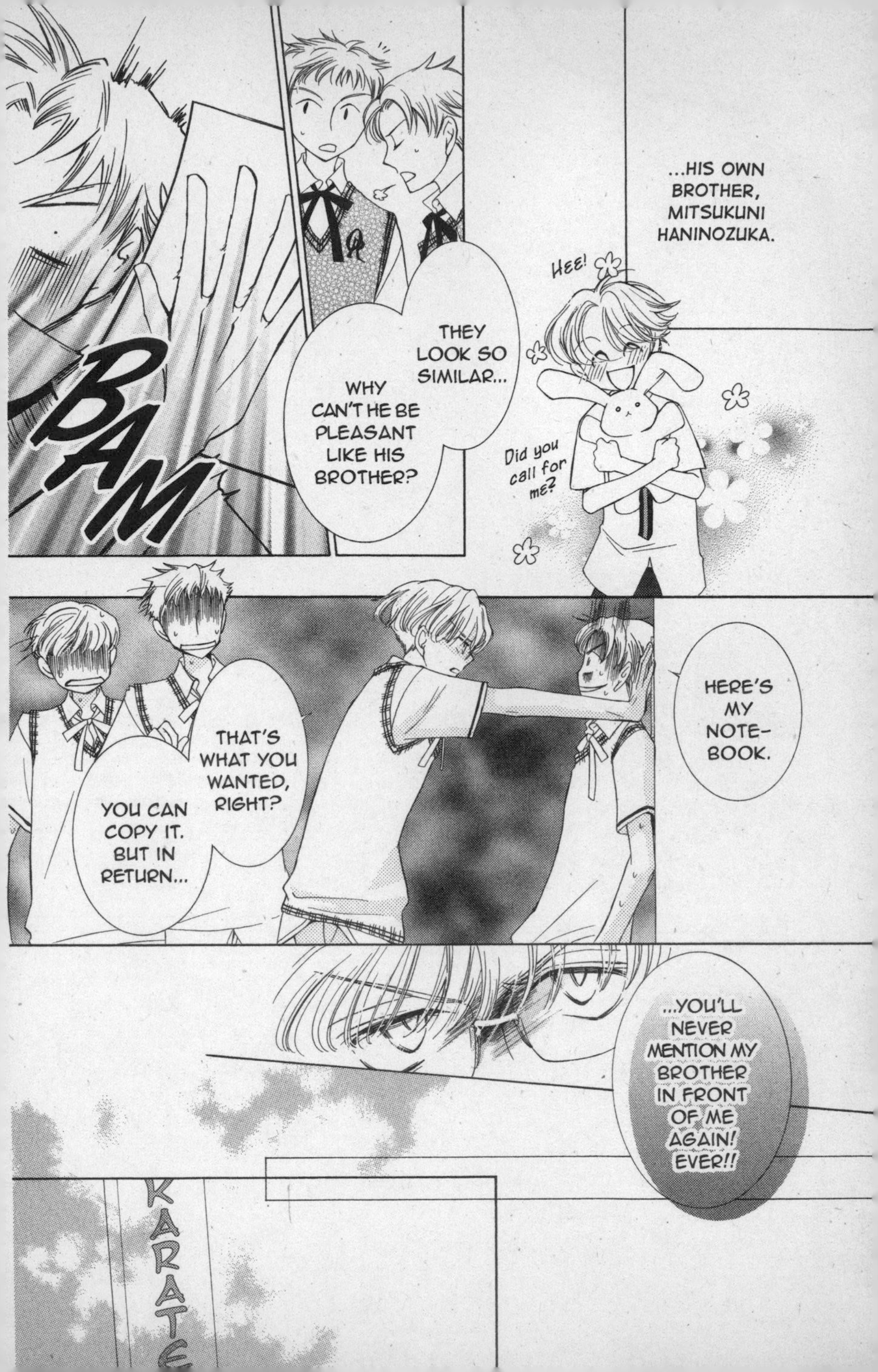
...HIS OWN BROTHER, MITSUKUNI HANINOZUKA.
HEE!
Did you call for me?
THEY LOOK SO SIMILAR...
WHY CAN'T HE BE PLEASANT LIKE HIS BROTHER?
BAM
HERE'S MY NOTE-BOOK.
THAT'S WHAT YOU WANTED, RIGHT?
YOU CAN COPY IT. BUT IN RETURN...
...YOU'LL NEVER MENTION MY BROTHER IN FRONT OF ME AGAIN! EVER!!
KARATE

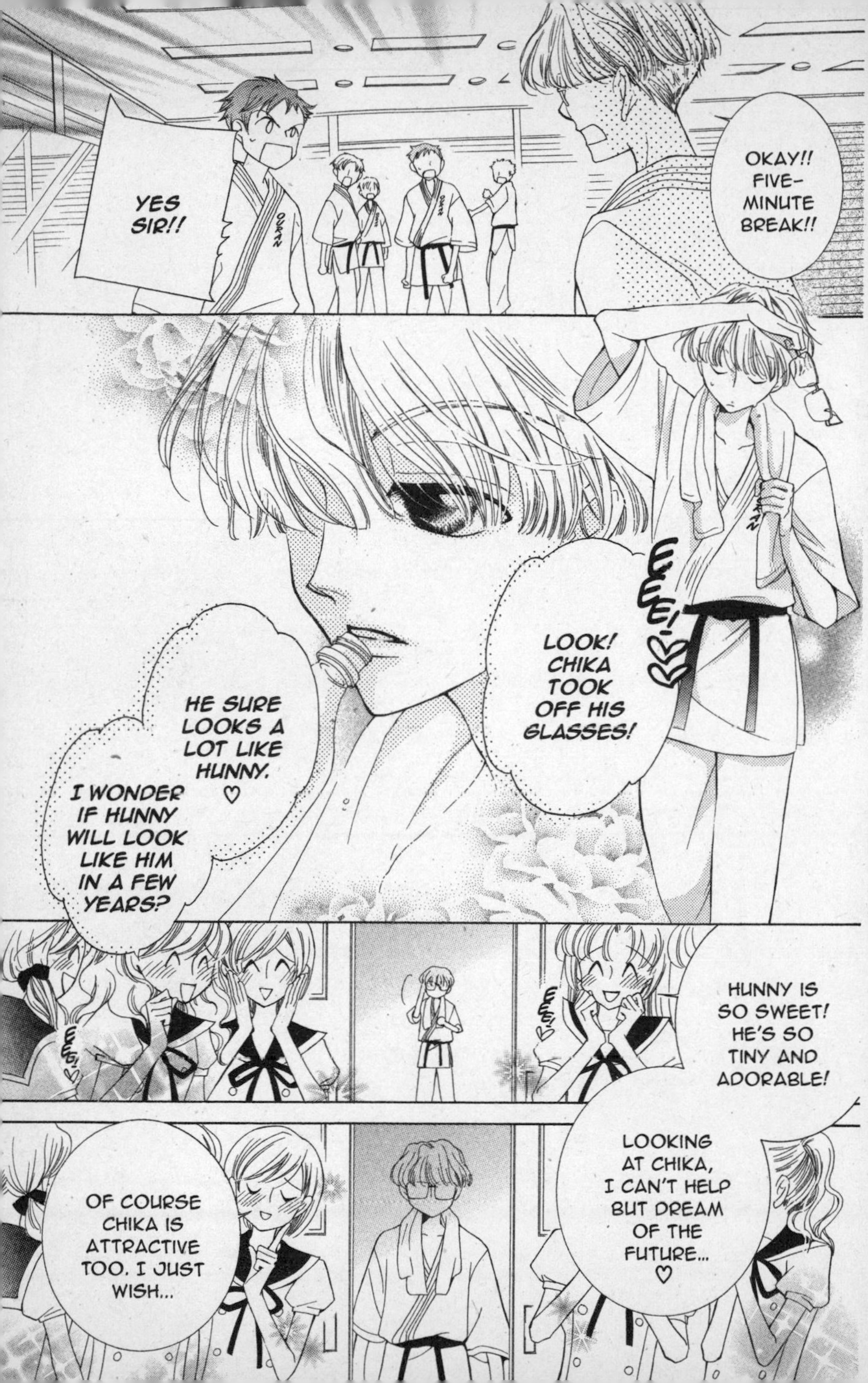
OKAY!! FIVE-MINUTE BREAK!!
YES SIR!!
EEE!
LOOK! CHIKA TOOK OFF HIS GLASSES!
HE SURE LOOKS A LOT LIKE HUNNY. ♡
I WONDER IF HUNNY WILL LOOK LIKE HIM IN A FEW YEARS?
EEE!
HUNNY IS SO SWEET! HE'S SO TINY AND ADORABLE!
EEE!
LOOKING AT CHIKA, I CAN'T HELP BUT DREAM OF THE FUTURE... ♡
OF COURSE CHIKA IS ATTRACTIVE TOO. I JUST WISH...

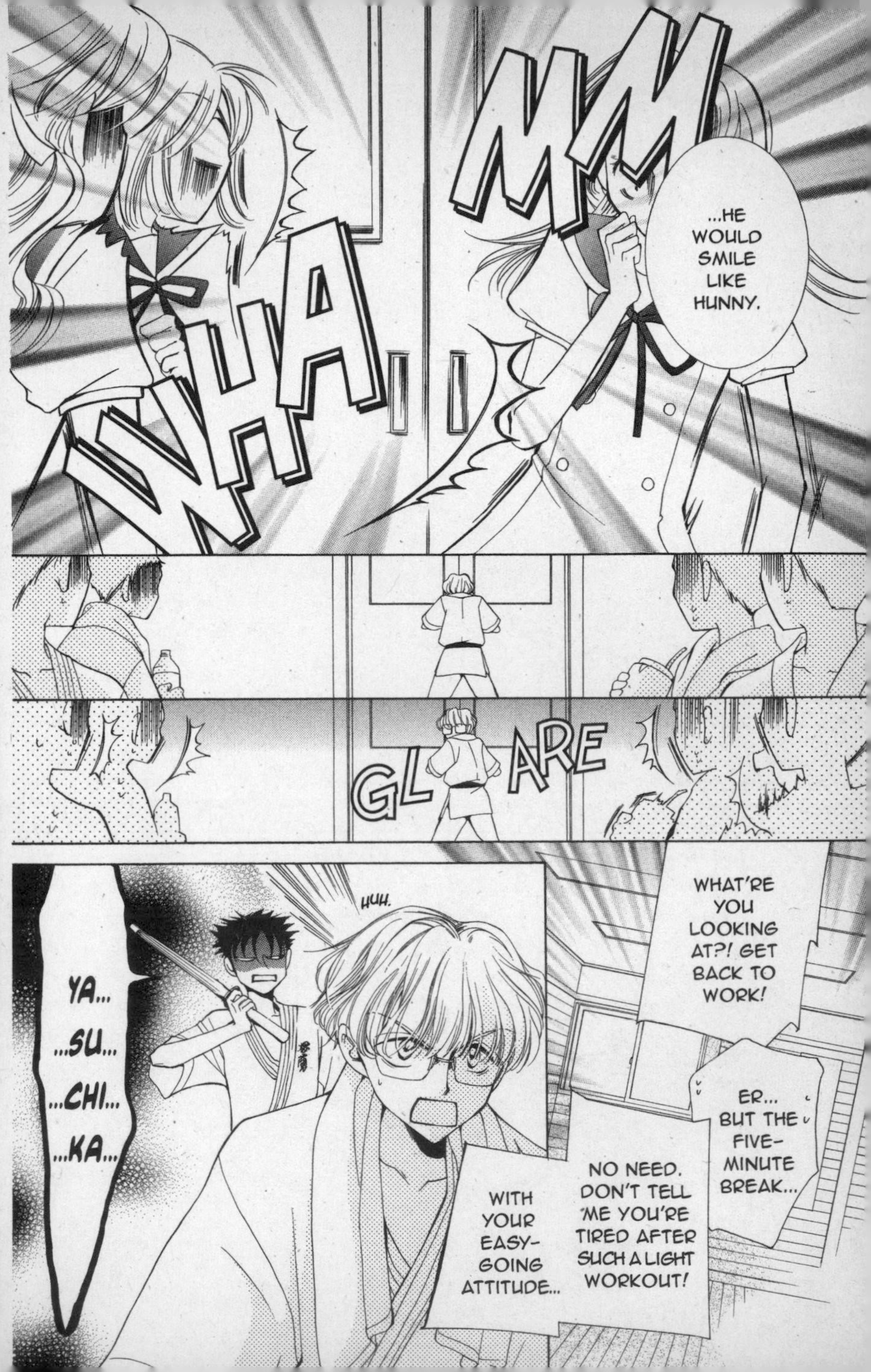
...HE WOULD SMILE LIKE HUNNY.
MM
WHA
GLARE
WHAT'RE YOU LOOKING AT?! GET BACK TO WORK!
HUH.
ER... BUT THE FIVE-MINUTE BREAK...
NO NEED. DON'T TELL ME YOU'RE TIRED AFTER SUCH A LIGHT WORKOUT!
WITH YOUR EASY-GOING ATTITUDE...
YA... ...SU... ...CHI... ...KA...

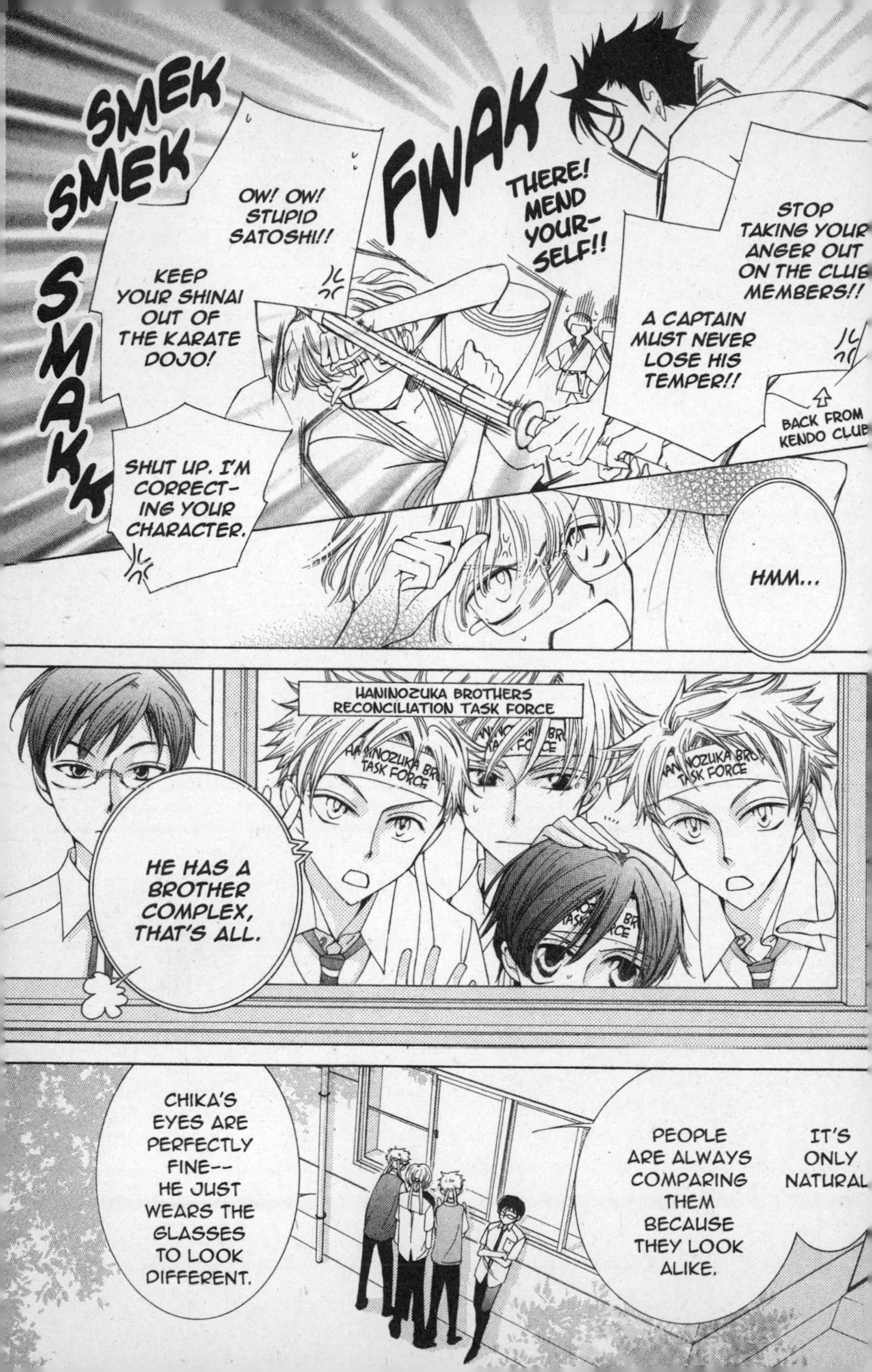
STOP TAKING YOUR ANGER OUT ON THE CLUB MEMBERS!!
A CAPTAIN MUST NEVER LOSE HIS TEMPER!!
BACK FROM KENDO CLUB
THERE! MEND YOUR-SELF!!
FWAK
OW! OW! STUPID SATOSHI!!
SMEK SMEK
KEEP YOUR SHINAI OUT OF THE KARATE DOJO!
SMAKK
SHUT UP. I'M CORRECT-ING YOUR CHARACTER.
HMM...
HANINOZUKA BROTHERS RECONCILIATION TASK FORCE
HE HAS A BROTHER COMPLEX, THAT'S ALL.
IT'S ONLY NATURAL
PEOPLE ARE ALWAYS COMPARING THEM BECAUSE THEY LOOK ALIKE.
CHIKA'S EYES ARE PERFECTLY FINE-- HE JUST WEARS THE GLASSES TO LOOK DIFFERENT.

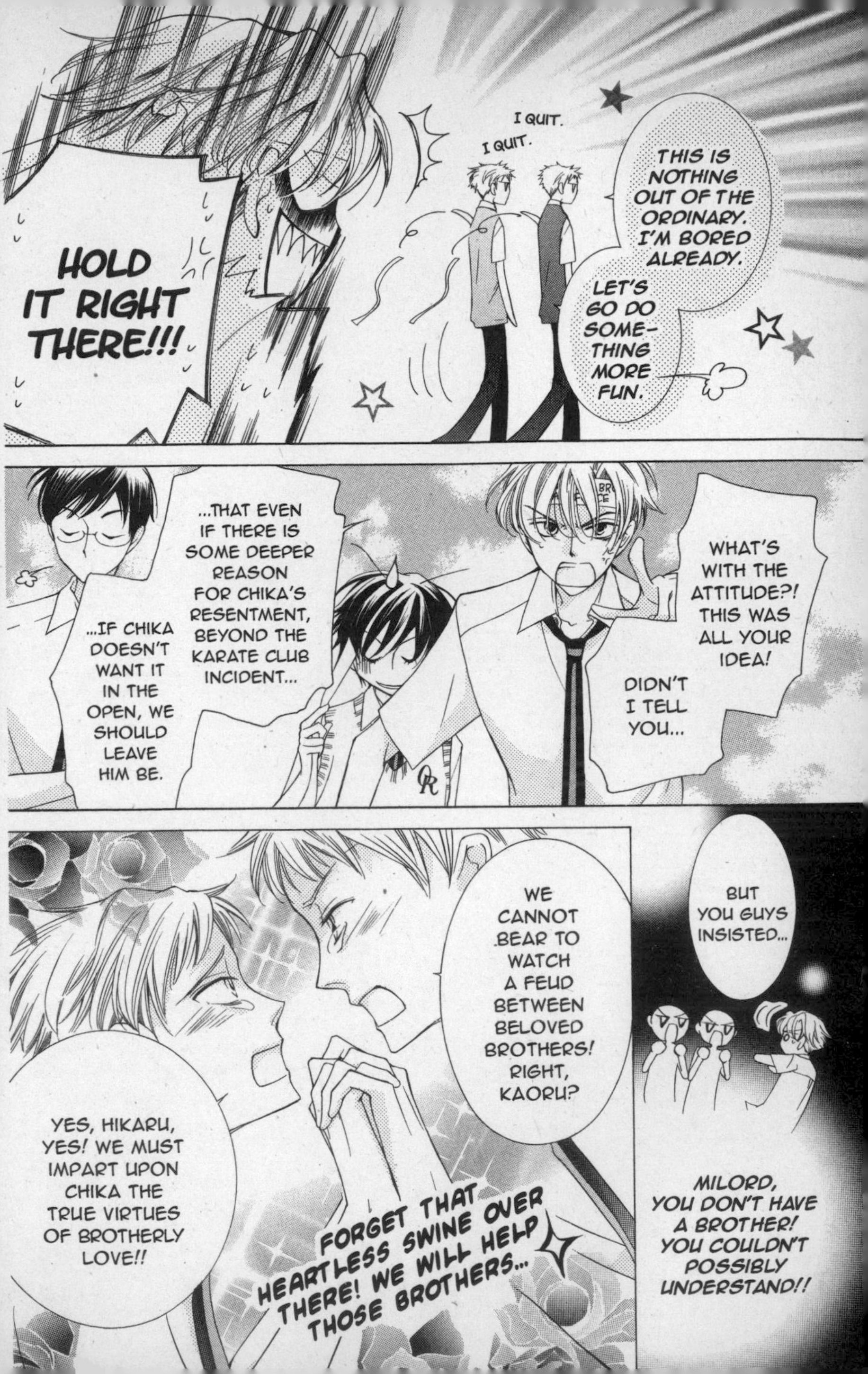

I QUIT.
I QUIT.
THIS IS NOTHING OUT OF THE ORDINARY. I'M BORED ALREADY.
LET'S GO DO SOME-THING MORE FUN.
HOLD IT RIGHT THERE!!!
WHAT'S WITH THE ATTITUDE?! THIS WAS ALL YOUR IDEA!
DIDN'T I TELL YOU...
...THAT EVEN IF THERE IS SOME DEEPER REASON FOR CHIKA'S RESENTMENT, BEYOND THE KARATE CLUB INCIDENT...
...IF CHIKA DOESN'T WANT IT IN THE OPEN, WE SHOULD LEAVE HIM BE.
BUT YOU GUYS INSISTED...
MILORD, YOU DON'T HAVE A BROTHER! YOU COULDN'T POSSIBLY UNDERSTAND!!
WE CANNOT BEAR TO WATCH A FEUD BETWEEN BELOVED BROTHERS! RIGHT, KAORU?
YES, HIKARU, YES! WE MUST IMPART UPON CHIKA THE TRUE VIRTUES OF BROTHERLY LOVE!!
FORGET THAT HEARTLESS SWINE OVER THERE! WE WILL HELP THOSE BROTHERS...

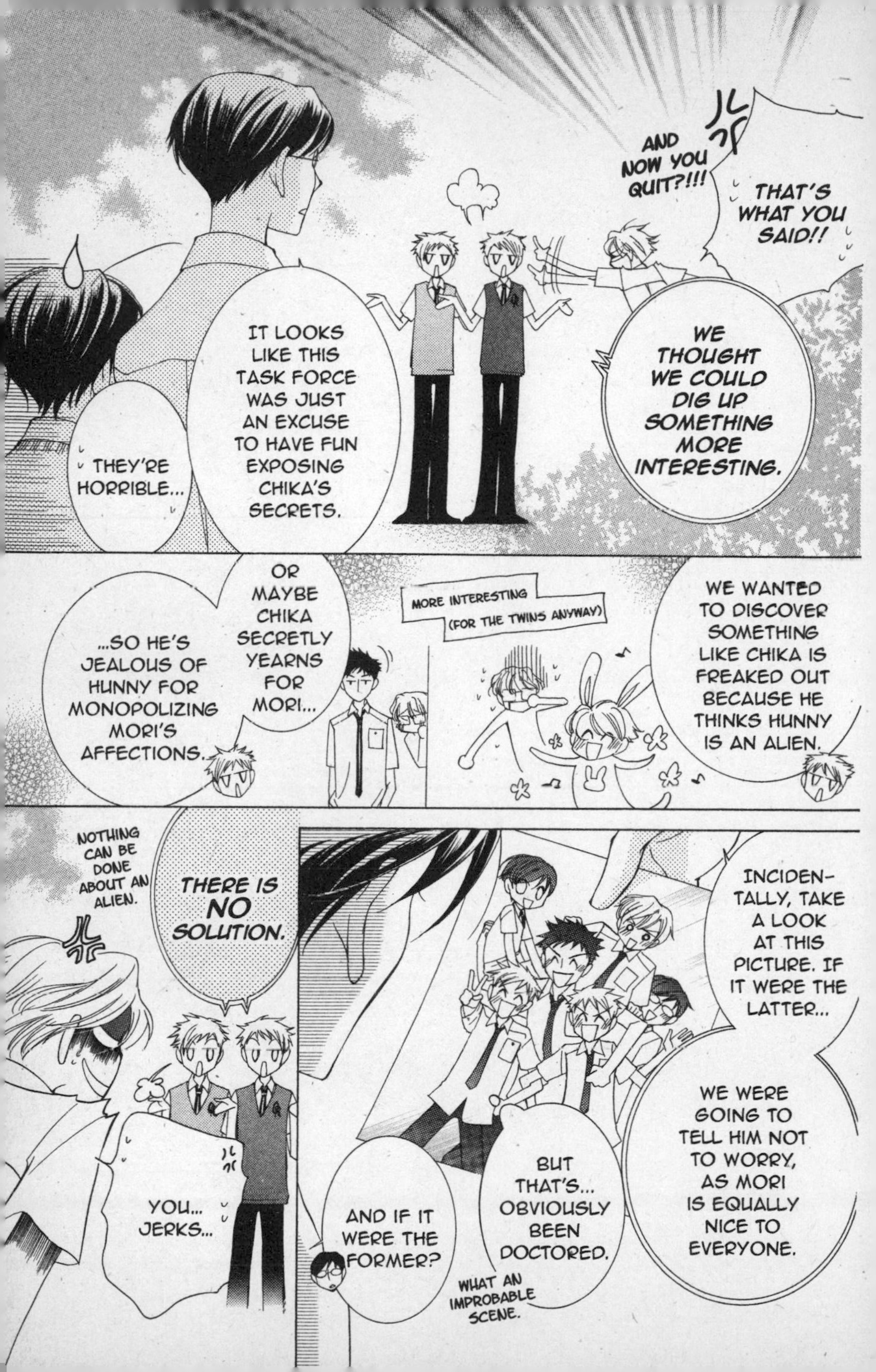
AND NOW YOU QUIT?!!!
THAT'S WHAT YOU SAID!!
WE THOUGHT WE COULD DIG UP SOMETHING MORE INTERESTING.
IT LOOKS LIKE THIS TASK FORCE WAS JUST AN EXCUSE TO HAVE FUN EXPOSING CHIKA'S SECRETS.
THEY'RE HORRIBLE...
WE WANTED TO DISCOVER SOMETHING LIKE CHIKA IS FREAKED OUT BECAUSE HE THINKS HUNNY IS AN ALIEN.
MORE INTERESTING
(FOR THE TWINS ANYWAY)
OR MAYBE CHIKA SECRETLY YEARNS FOR MORI...
...SO HE'S JEALOUS OF HUNNY FOR MONOPOLIZING MORI'S AFFECTIONS.
INCIDENTALLY, TAKE A LOOK AT THIS PICTURE. IF IT WERE THE LATTER...
WE WERE GOING TO TELL HIM NOT TO WORRY, AS MORI IS EQUALLY NICE TO EVERYONE.
BUT THAT'S... OBVIOUSLY BEEN DOCTORED.
AND IF IT WERE THE FORMER?
WHAT AN IMPROBABLE SCENE.
THERE IS NO SOLUTION.
NOTHING CAN BE DONE ABOUT AN ALIEN.
YOU... JERKS...

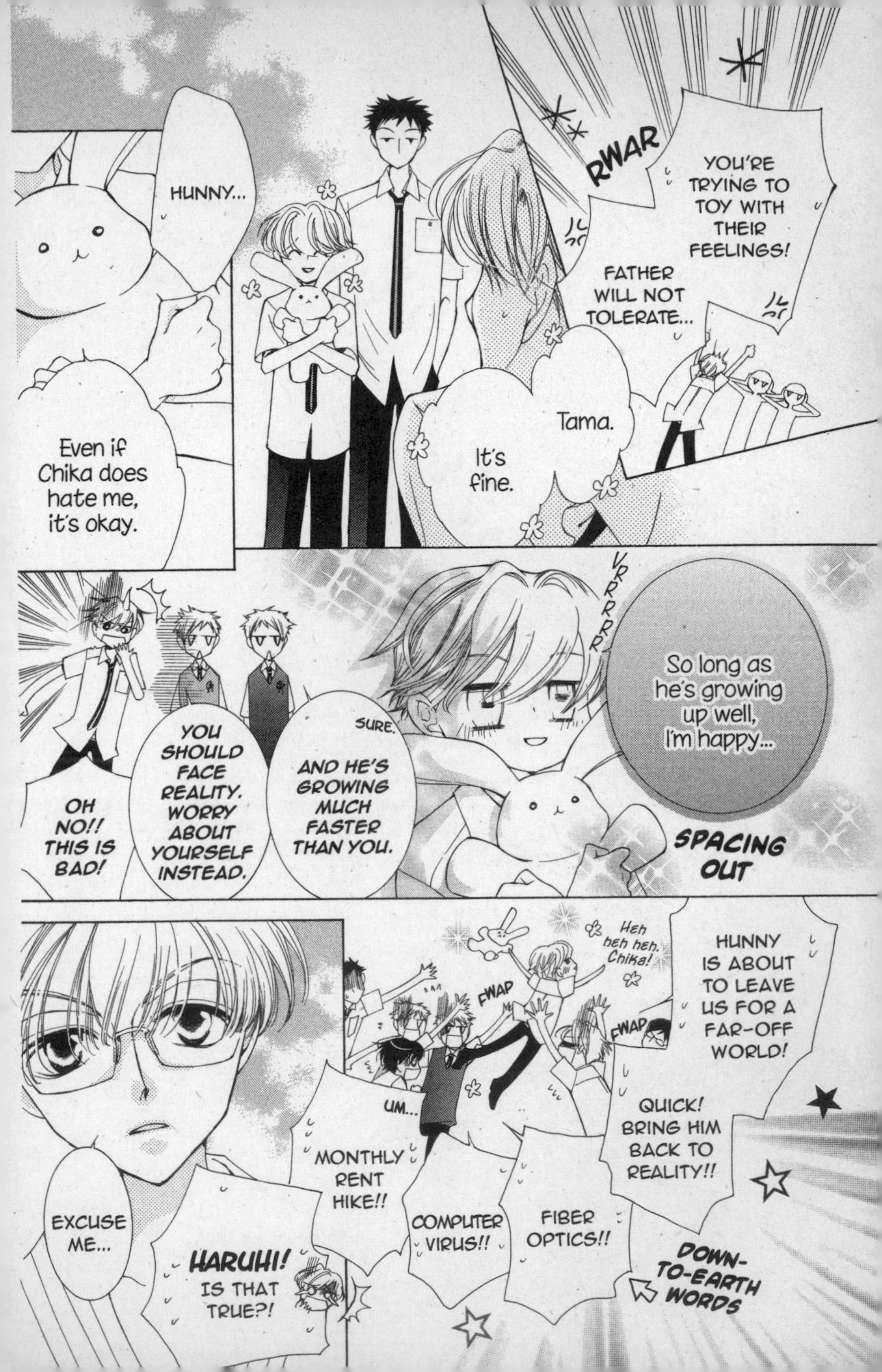
RWAR
YOU'RE TRYING TO TOY WITH THEIR FEELINGS!
FATHER WILL NOT TOLERATE...
Tama.
It's fine.
HUNNY...
Even if Chika does hate me, it's okay.
VRRRRR
So long as he's growing up well, I'm happy...
SPACING OUT
SURE.
AND HE'S GROWING MUCH FASTER THAN YOU.
YOU SHOULD FACE REALITY. WORRY ABOUT YOURSELF INSTEAD.
OH NO!! THIS IS BAD!
HUNNY IS ABOUT TO LEAVE US FOR A FAR-OFF WORLD!
Heh heh heh. Chika!
FWAP
FWAP
QUICK! BRING HIM BACK TO REALITY!!
FIBER OPTICS!!
COMPUTER VIRUS!!
UM...
MONTHLY RENT HIKE!!
DOWN-TO-EARTH WORDS
HARUHI! IS THAT TRUE?!
EXCUSE ME...

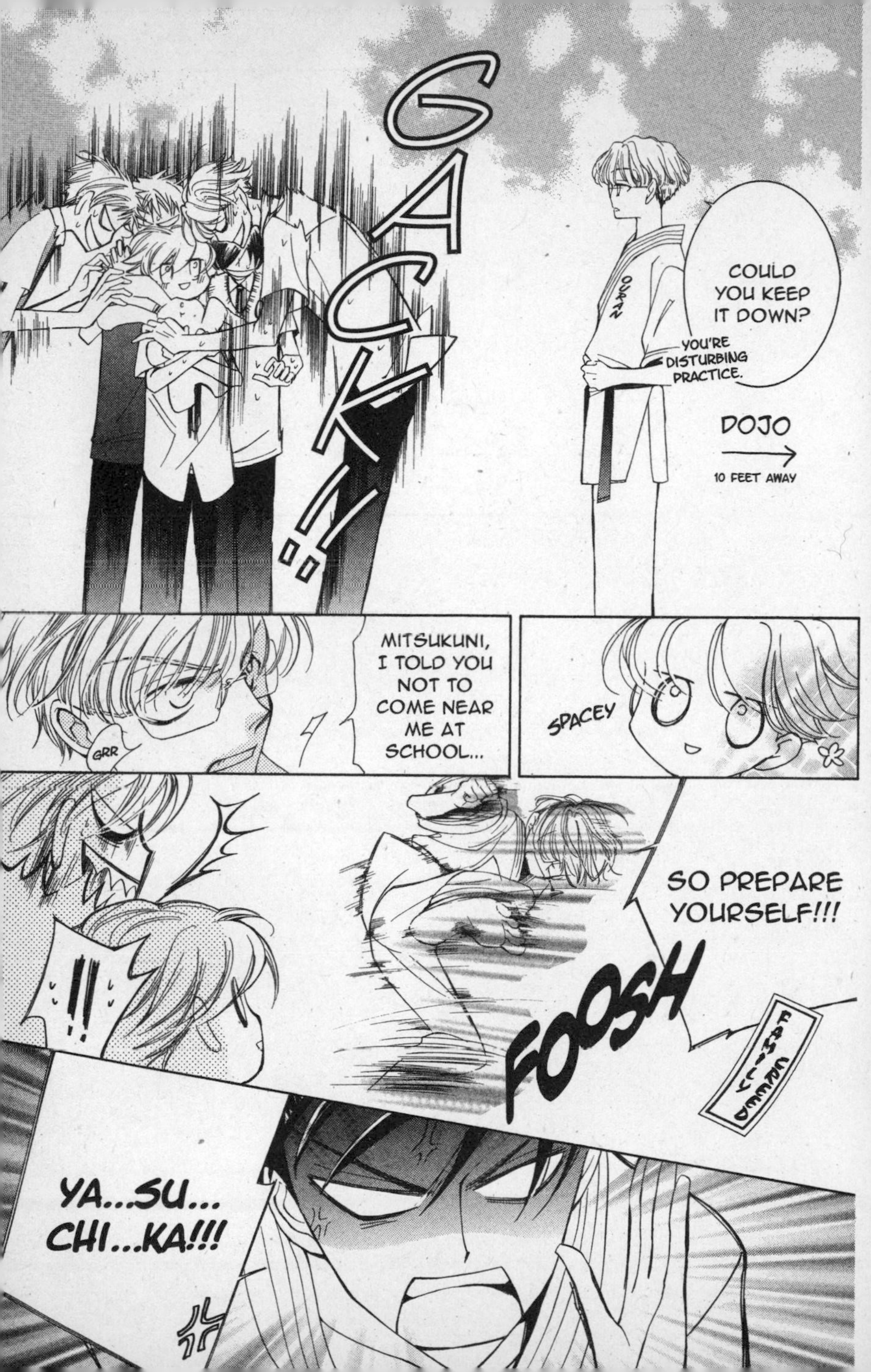
OURAN
COULD YOU KEEP IT DOWN?
YOU'RE DISTURBING PRACTICE.
DOJO
10 FEET AWAY
GACK!!
SPACEY
MITSUKUNI, I TOLD YOU NOT TO COME NEAR ME AT SCHOOL...
GRR
SO PREPARE YOURSELF!!!
FAMILY CREED
FOOSH
!!
YA...SU...CHI...KA!!!

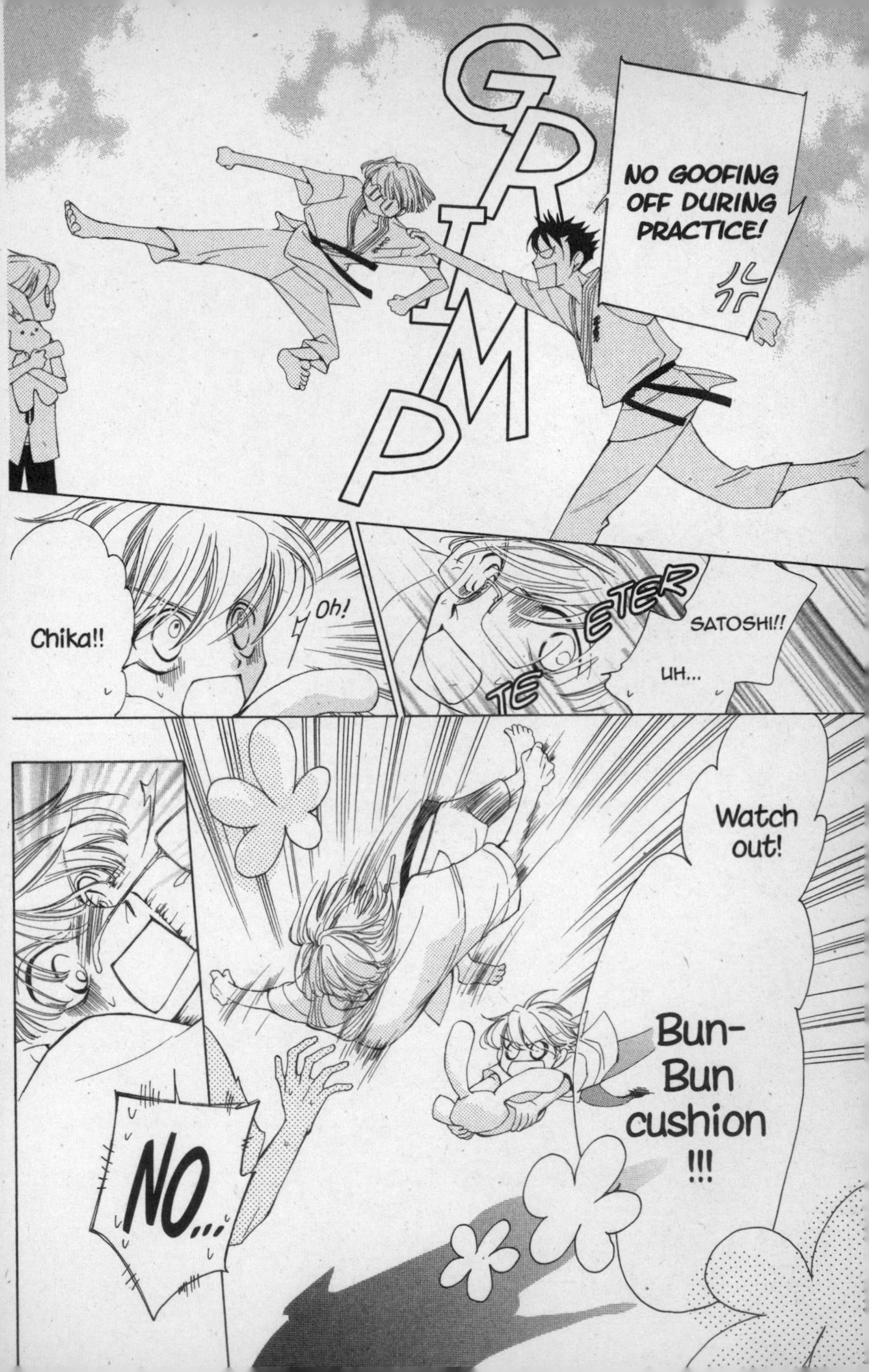
NO GOOFING OFF DURING PRACTICE!
GRIMP
SATOSHI!!
TETETER
UH...
Oh!
Chika!!
Watch out!
Bun-Bun cushion !!!
NO...

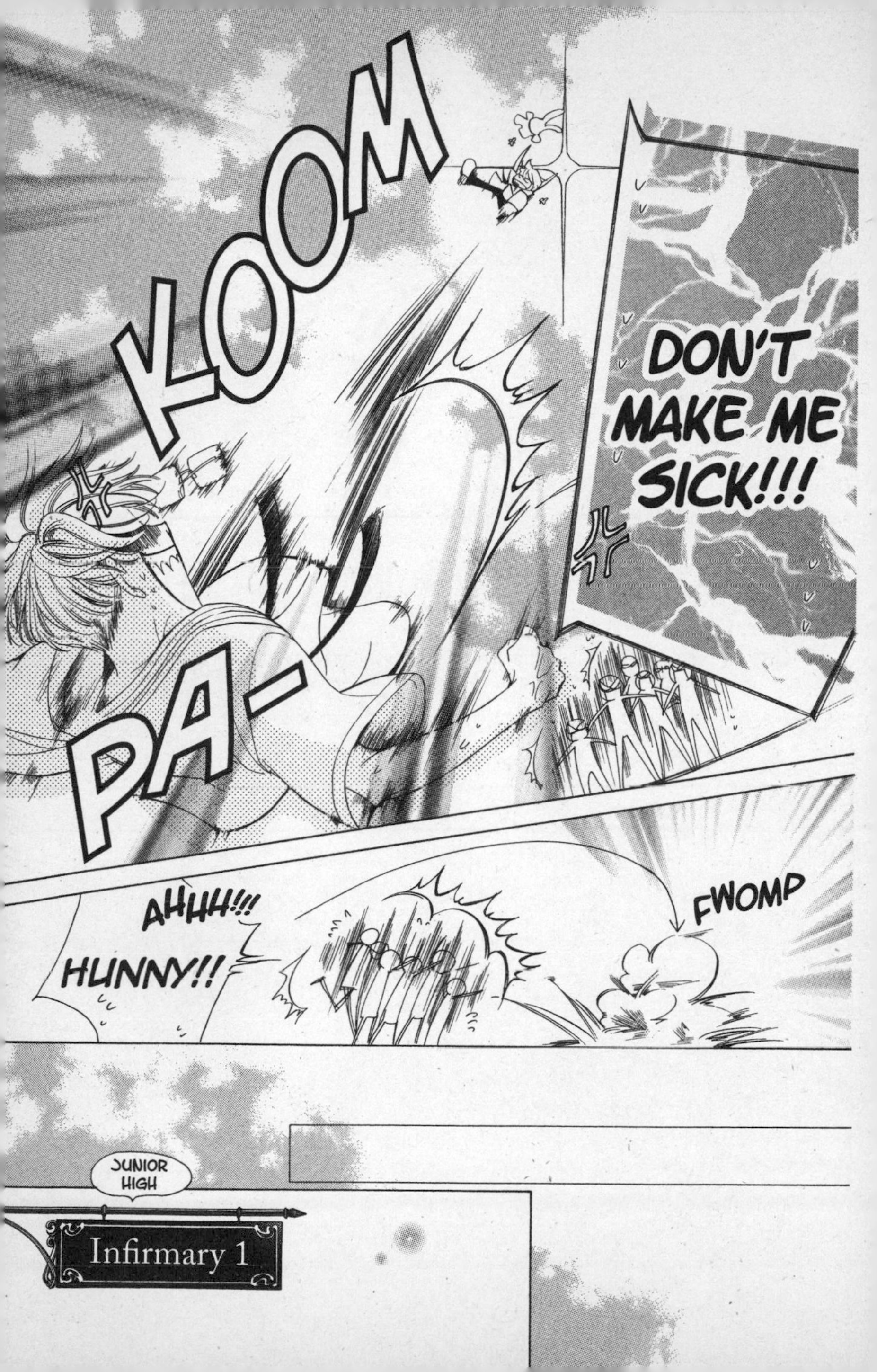
DON'T MAKE ME SICK!!!
PA-
KOOM
FWOMP
AHHH!!!
HUNNY!!
JUNIOR HIGH
Infirmary 1

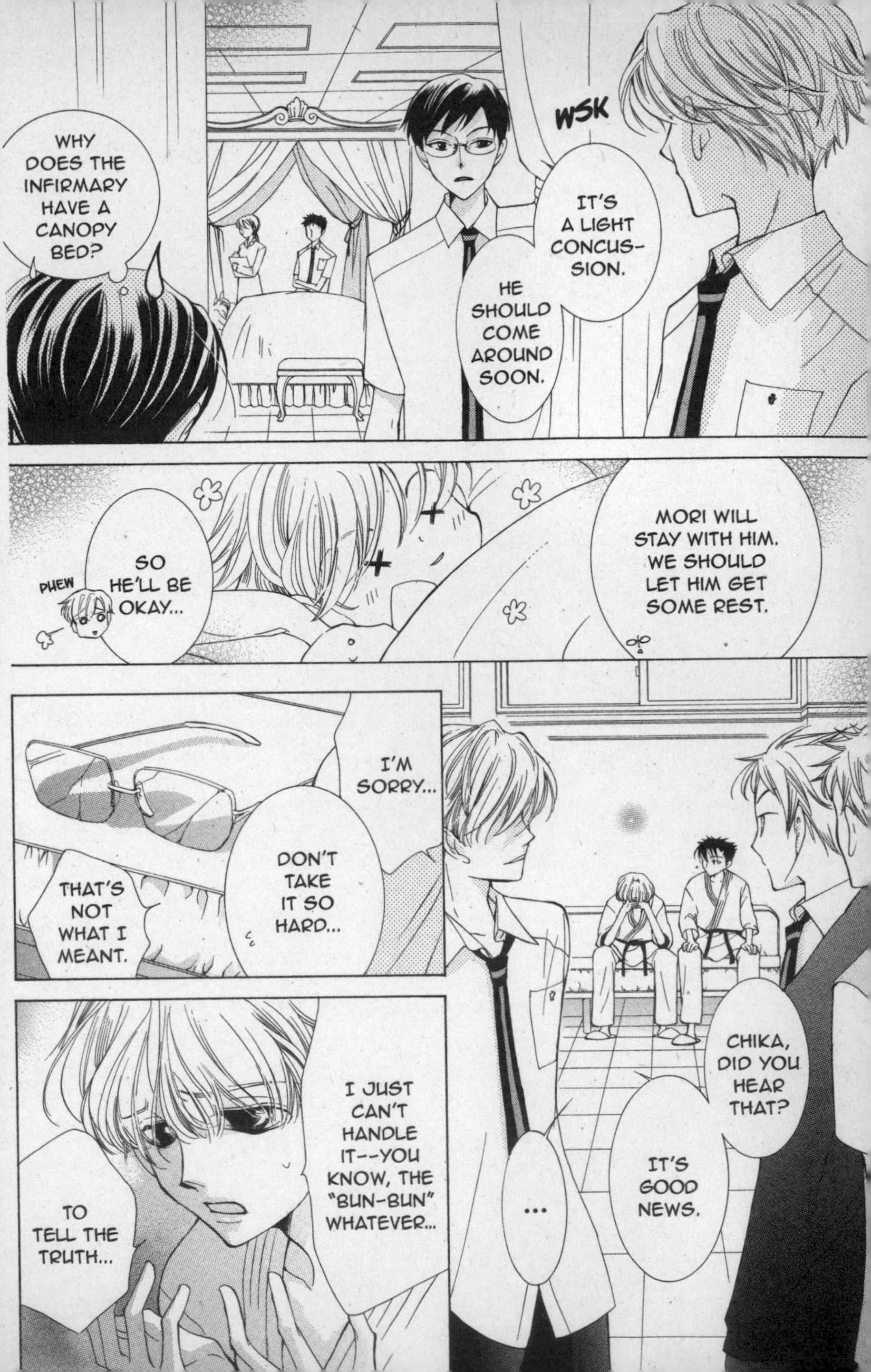
WSK
IT'S A LIGHT CONCUSSION.
HE SHOULD COME AROUND SOON.
WHY DOES THE INFIRMARY HAVE A CANOPY BED?
MORI WILL STAY WITH HIM. WE SHOULD LET HIM GET SOME REST.
PHEW
SO HE'LL BE OKAY...
CHIKA, DID YOU HEAR THAT?
IT'S GOOD NEWS.
...
I'M SORRY...
DON'T TAKE IT SO HARD...
THAT'S NOT WHAT I MEANT.
I JUST CAN'T HANDLE IT--YOU KNOW, THE "BUN-BUN" WHATEVER...
TO TELL THE TRUTH...

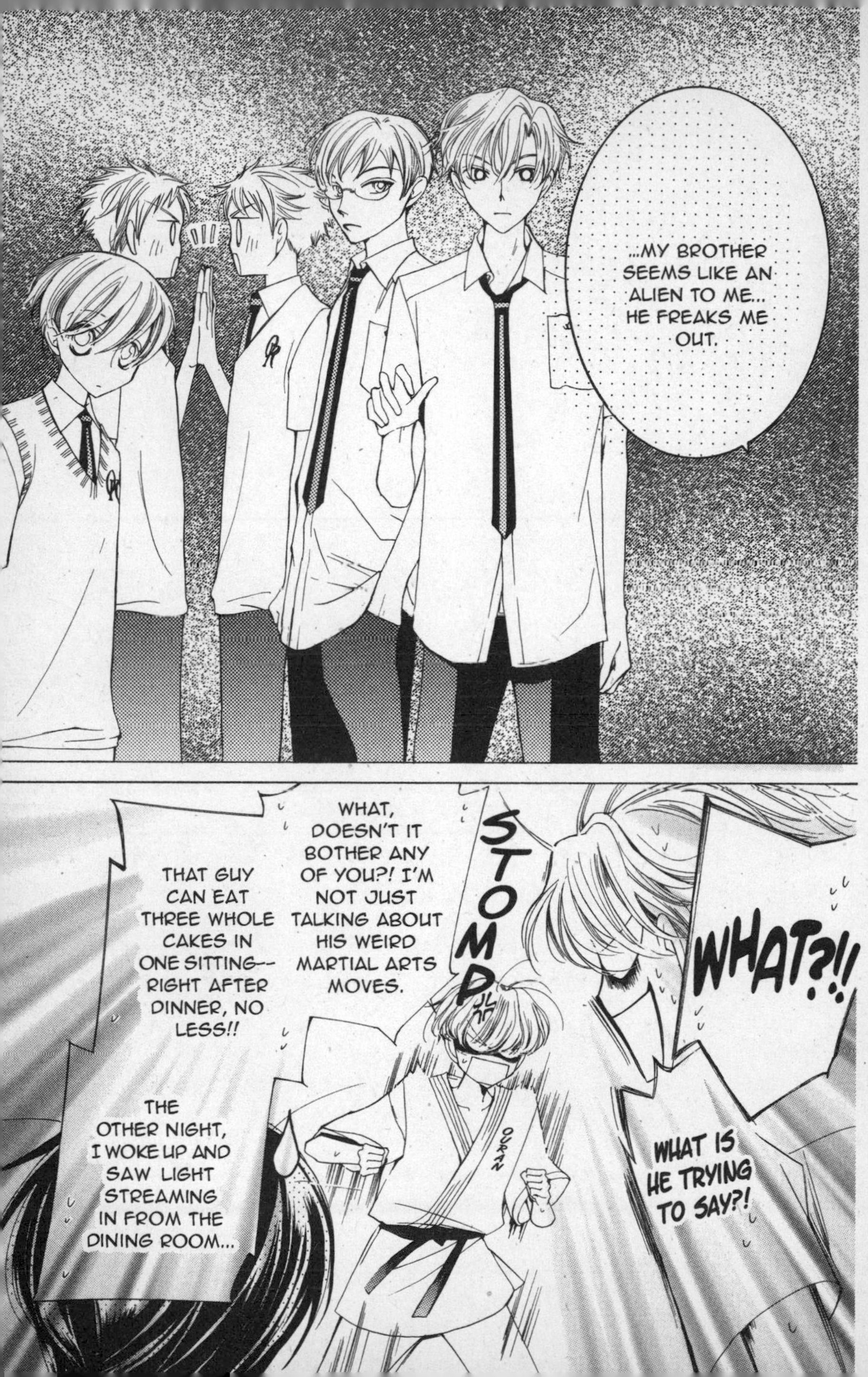
...MY BROTHER SEEMS LIKE AN ALIEN TO ME... HE FREAKS ME OUT.
WHAT?!!
STOMP
WHAT, DOESN'T IT BOTHER ANY OF YOU?! I'M NOT JUST TALKING ABOUT HIS WEIRD MARTIAL ARTS MOVES.
THAT GUY CAN EAT THREE WHOLE CAKES IN ONE SITTING--RIGHT AFTER DINNER, NO LESS!!
WHAT IS HE TRYING TO SAY?!
OURAN
THE OTHER NIGHT, I WOKE UP AND SAW LIGHT STREAMING IN FROM THE DINING ROOM...

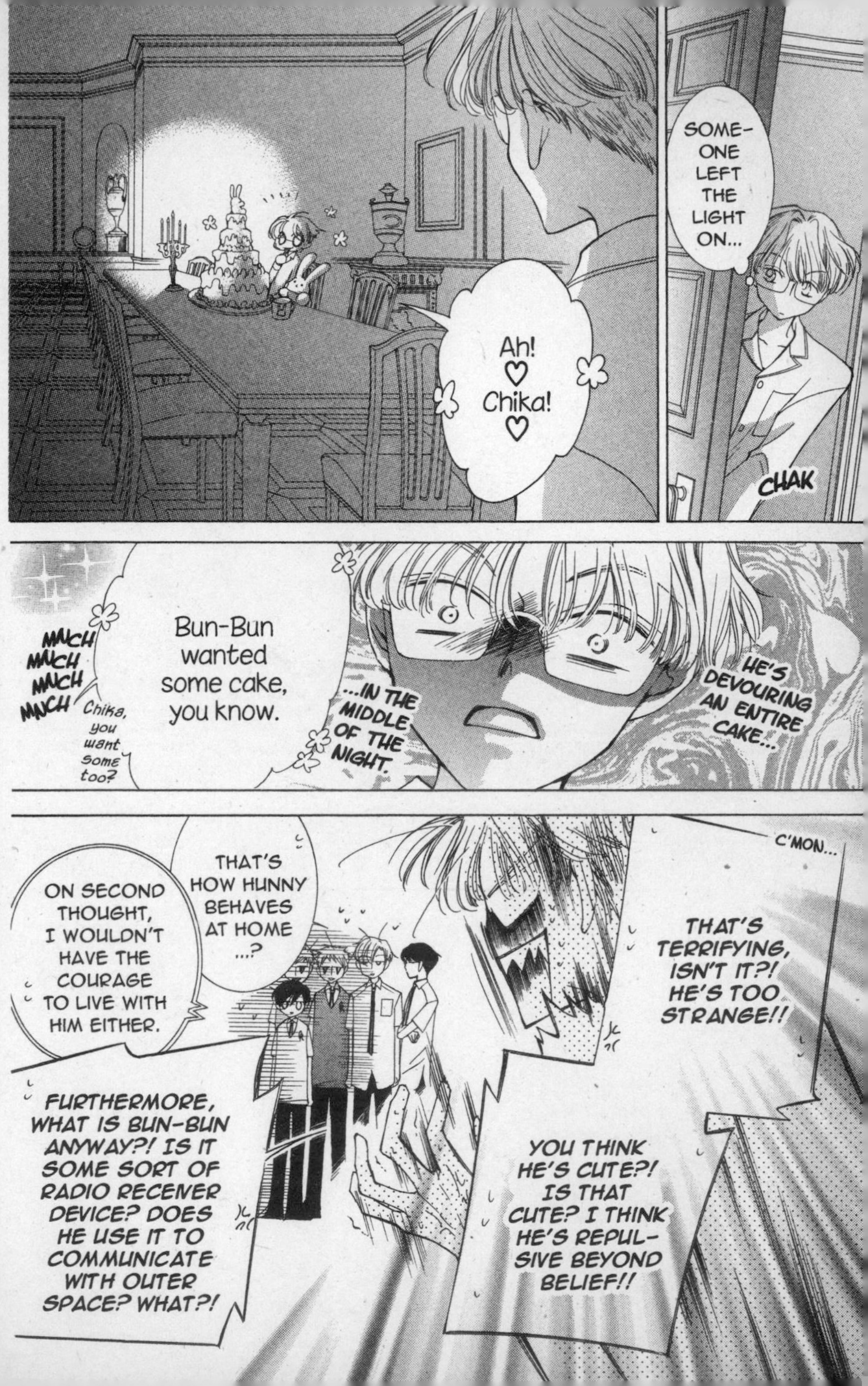

SOME-ONE LEFT THE LIGHT ON...
CHAK
Ah! ♡ Chika! ♡
HE'S DEVOURING AN ENTIRE CAKE...
...IN THE MIDDLE OF THE NIGHT.
Bun-Bun wanted some cake, you know.
Chika, you want some too?
MUNCH MUNCH MUNCH MUNCH
C'MON...
THAT'S TERRIFYING, ISN'T IT?! HE'S TOO STRANGE!!
YOU THINK HE'S CUTE?! IS THAT CUTE? I THINK HE'S REPUL-SIVE BEYOND BELIEF!!
FURTHERMORE, WHAT IS BUN-BUN ANYWAY?! IS IT SOME SORT OF RADIO RECEIVER DEVICE? DOES HE USE IT TO COMMUNICATE WITH OUTER SPACE? WHAT?!
THAT'S HOW HUNNY BEHAVES AT HOME ...?
ON SECOND THOUGHT, I WOULDN'T HAVE THE COURAGE TO LIVE WITH HIM EITHER.

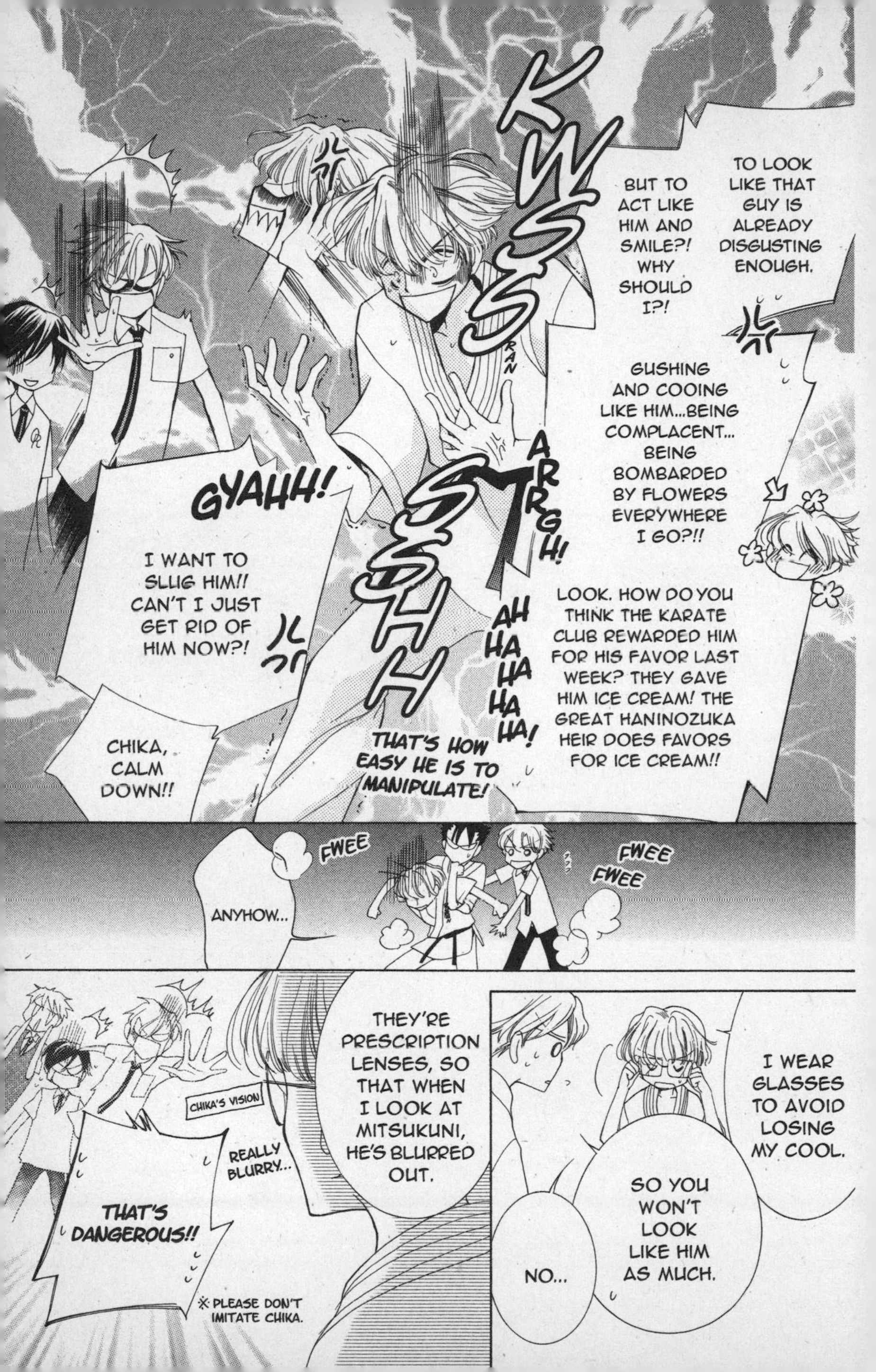
TO LOOK LIKE THAT GUY IS ALREADY DISGUSTING ENOUGH.
BUT TO ACT LIKE HIM AND SMILE?! WHY SHOULD I?!
KWSSS
RAN
GUSHING AND COOING LIKE HIM...BEING COMPLACENT... BEING BOMBARDED BY FLOWERS EVERYWHERE I GO?!!
LOOK. HOW DO YOU THINK THE KARATE CLUB REWARDED HIM FOR HIS FAVOR LAST WEEK? THEY GAVE HIM ICE CREAM! THE GREAT HANINOZUKA HEIR DOES FAVORS FOR ICE CREAM!!
ARRGH!
SSHHH
AH HA HA HA HA!
THAT'S HOW EASY HE IS TO MANIPULATE!
GYAHH!
I WANT TO SLUG HIM!! CAN'T I JUST GET RID OF HIM NOW?!
CHIKA, CALM DOWN!!
FWEE FWEE
FWEE
ANYHOW...
I WEAR GLASSES TO AVOID LOSING MY COOL.
SO YOU WON'T LOOK LIKE HIM AS MUCH.
NO...
THEY'RE PRESCRIPTION LENSES, SO THAT WHEN I LOOK AT MITSUKUNI, HE'S BLURRED OUT.
REALLY BLURRY...
CHIKA'S VISION
THAT'S DANGEROUS!!
※PLEASE DON'T IMITATE CHIKA.

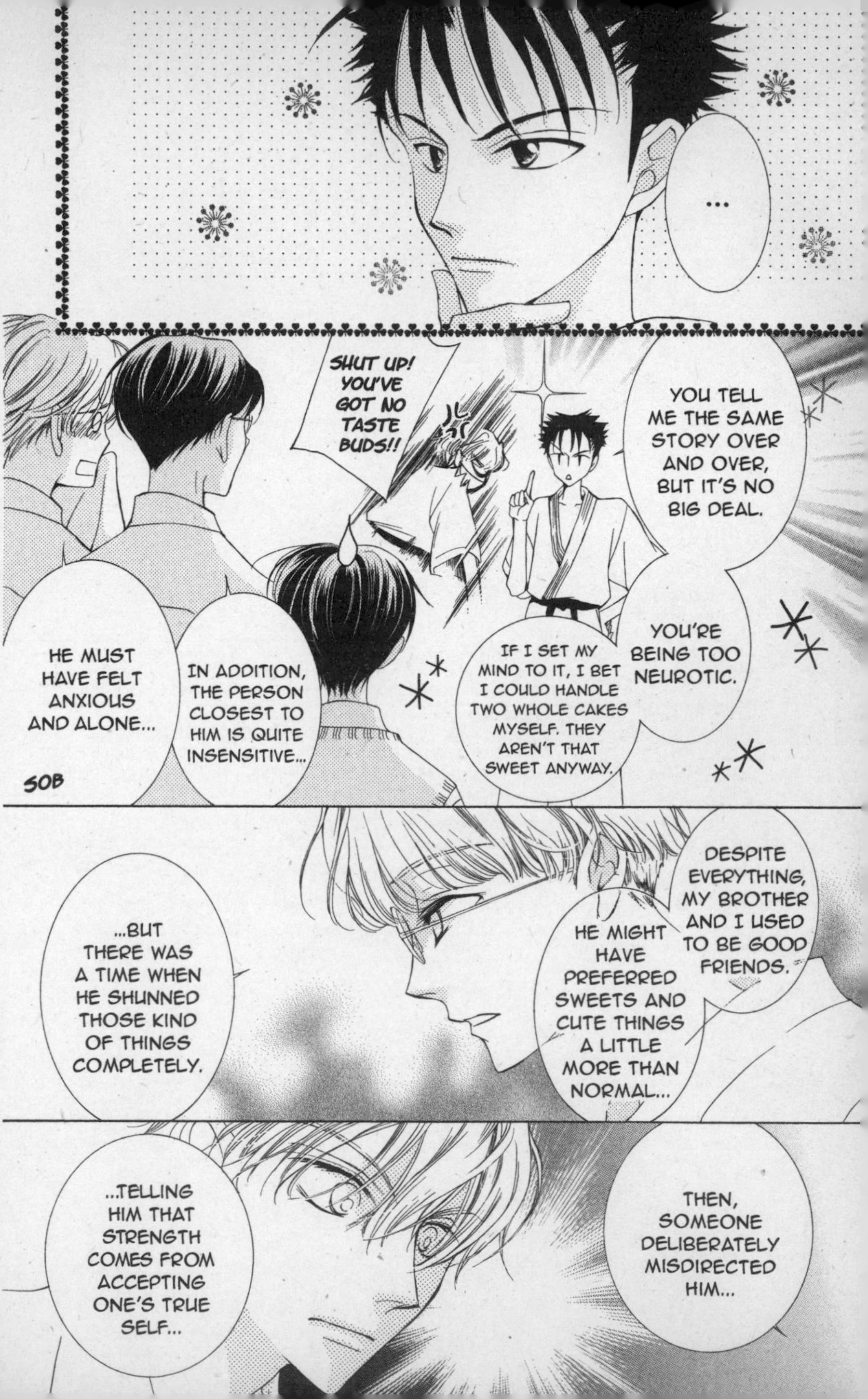
...
YOU TELL ME THE SAME STORY OVER AND OVER, BUT IT'S NO BIG DEAL.
YOU'RE BEING TOO NEUROTIC.
IF I SET MY MIND TO IT, I BET I COULD HANDLE TWO WHOLE CAKES MYSELF. THEY AREN'T THAT SWEET ANYWAY.
SHUT UP! YOU'VE GOT NO TASTE BUDS!!
IN ADDITION, THE PERSON CLOSEST TO HIM IS QUITE INSENSITIVE...
HE MUST HAVE FELT ANXIOUS AND ALONE...
SOB
DESPITE EVERYTHING, MY BROTHER AND I USED TO BE GOOD FRIENDS.
HE MIGHT HAVE PREFERRED SWEETS AND CUTE THINGS A LITTLE MORE THAN NORMAL...
...BUT THERE WAS A TIME WHEN HE SHUNNED THOSE KIND OF THINGS COMPLETELY.
THEN, SOMEONE DELIBERATELY MISDIRECTED HIM...
...TELLING HIM THAT STRENGTH COMES FROM ACCEPTING ONE'S TRUE SELF...

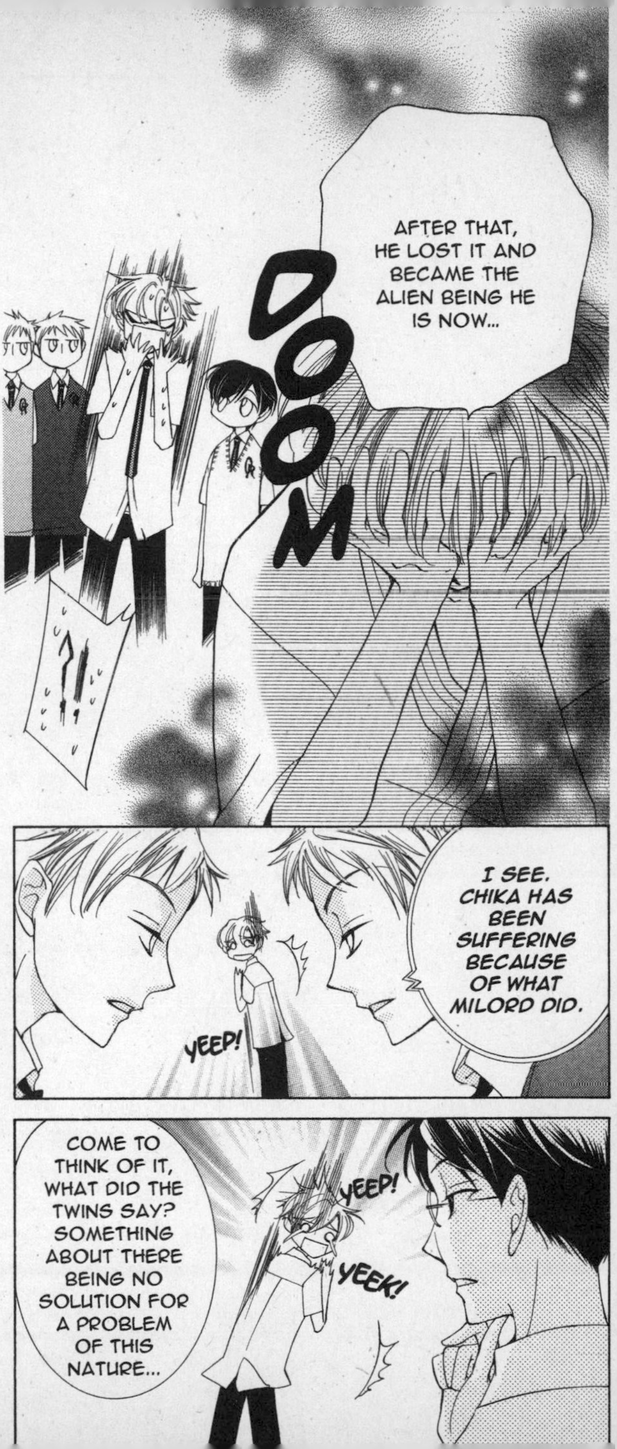
AFTER THAT, HE LOST IT AND BECAME THE ALIEN BEING HE IS NOW...
DOOOM
I SEE. CHIKA HAS BEEN SUFFERING BECAUSE OF WHAT MILORD DID.
YEEP!
YEEP!
YEEK!
COME TO THINK OF IT, WHAT DID THE TWINS SAY? SOMETHING ABOUT THERE BEING NO SOLUTION FOR A PROBLEM OF THIS NATURE...

3

✿NOW FOR THE ANSWER... H/K = *HANASHI WA KAWATTE* ["BY THE WAY"] APPARENTLY, THAT'S THE MEANING.
IT'S INCREDIBLE. WHO CAME UP WITH IT?
I'M SO SORRY.
EARLY ON, I HAD NO IDEA WHAT IT MEANT.
I EVENTUALLY LEARNED IT ONLY AFTER SOMEONE INCLUDED AN EXPLANATION OF IT IN ONE OF THE LETTERS I RECEIVED. THANK YOU!!

ALSO:
HARUHI C = HARUHI-CHAN
HUNNY SP = HUNNY-SENPAI
MORI SP = MORI-SENPAI
...AND SO ON. FOR A WHILE I THOUGHT MAYBE IT MEANT "HUNNY SPECIAL" AND "MORI SPECIAL"???
AH WELL. I GOT IT NOW!! OKAY!!

BUT ABBREVIATIONS LIKE THIS CAN BE HARD FOR OLDER PEOPLE TO INTERPRET--AT LEAST ANYONE OLDER THAN MY GENERATION. SO WHEN YOU WRITE LETTERS TO YOUR TEACHERS, UNCLES, AUNTS, ETC., IT'S PROBABLY BETTER IF YOU AVOID THOSE ABBREVIATIONS ALTOGETHER.☆ LET'S HOPE YOU'LL HEED MY COUNSEL!!

※BUT AS FOR ME, I DEFINITELY WANT TO LEARN WHAT'S IN VOGUE AMONG STUDENTS, SO WHEN YOU WRITE ME, FEEL FREE TO INCLUDE AS MANY AS YOU WANT (LAUGH).

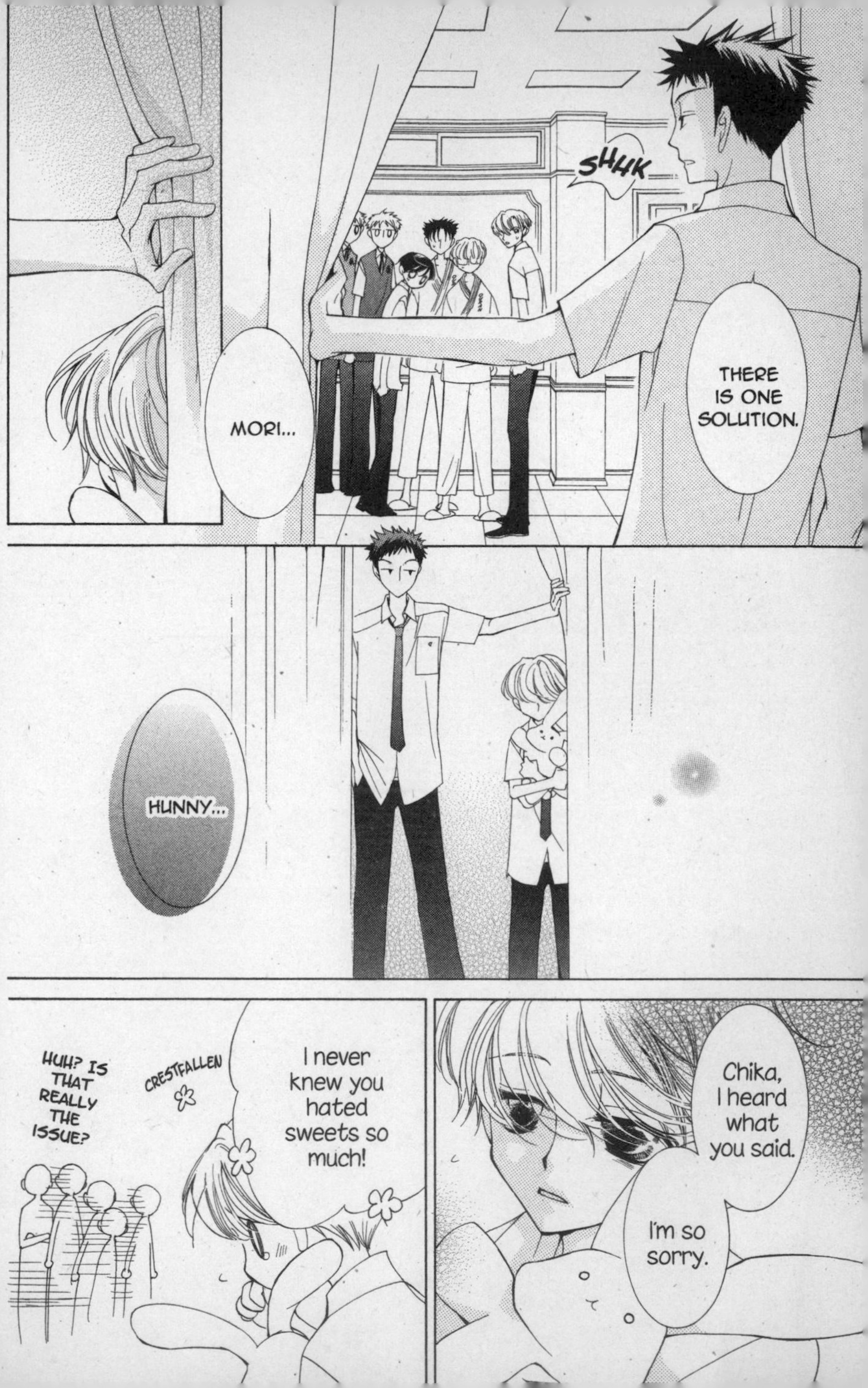
SHHK
THERE IS ONE SOLUTION.
MORI...
HUNNY...
Chika, I heard what you said.
I'm so sorry.
I never knew you hated sweets so much!
CRESTFALLEN
HUH? IS THAT REALLY THE ISSUE?

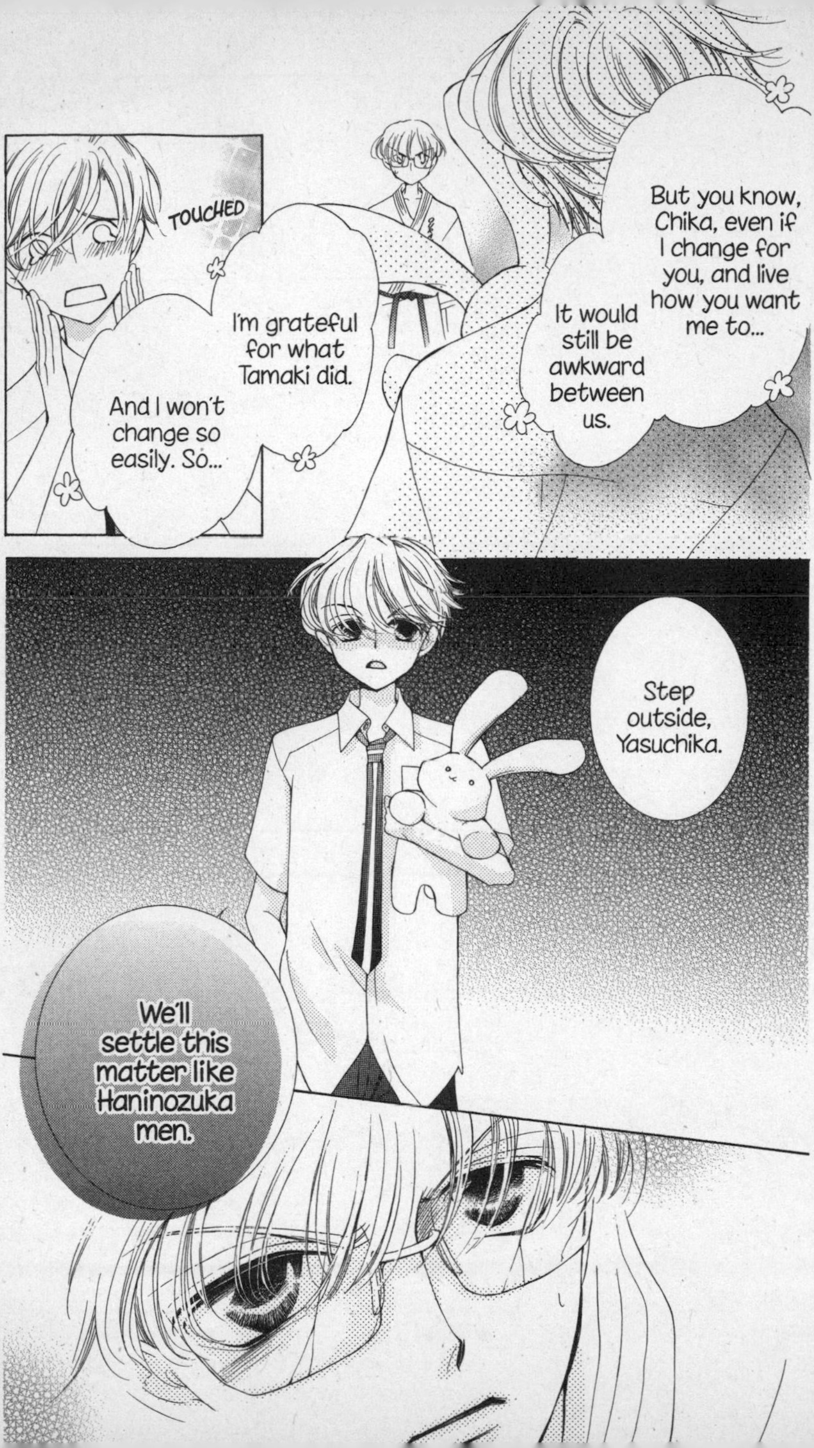
But you know, Chika, even if I change for you, and live how you want me to...
It would still be awkward between us.
I'm grateful for what Tamaki did.
TOUCHED
And I won't change so easily. So...
Step outside, Yasuchika.
We'll settle this matter like Haninozuka men.

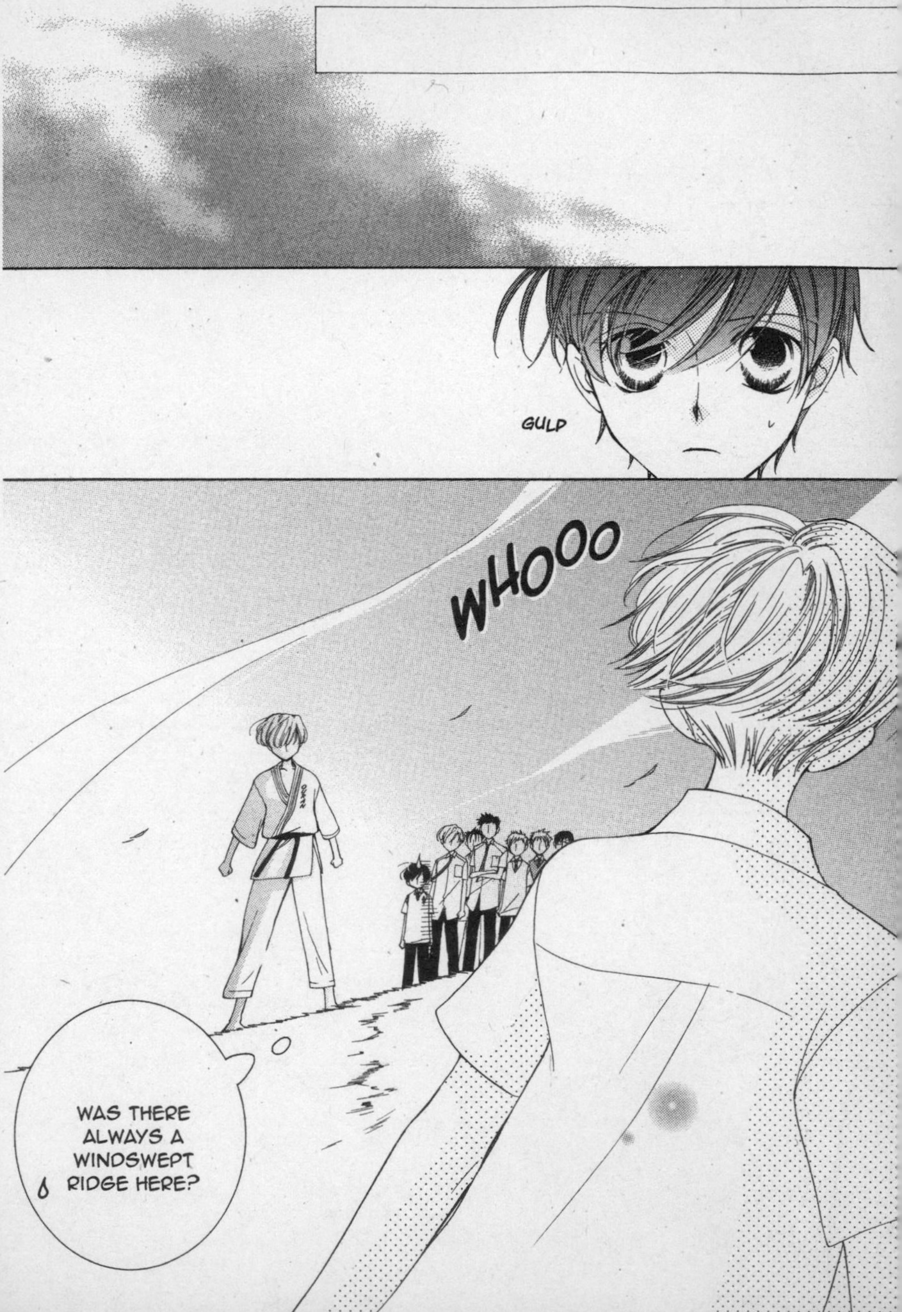
GULP
WHOOO
WAS THERE ALWAYS A WINDSWEPT RIDGE HERE?

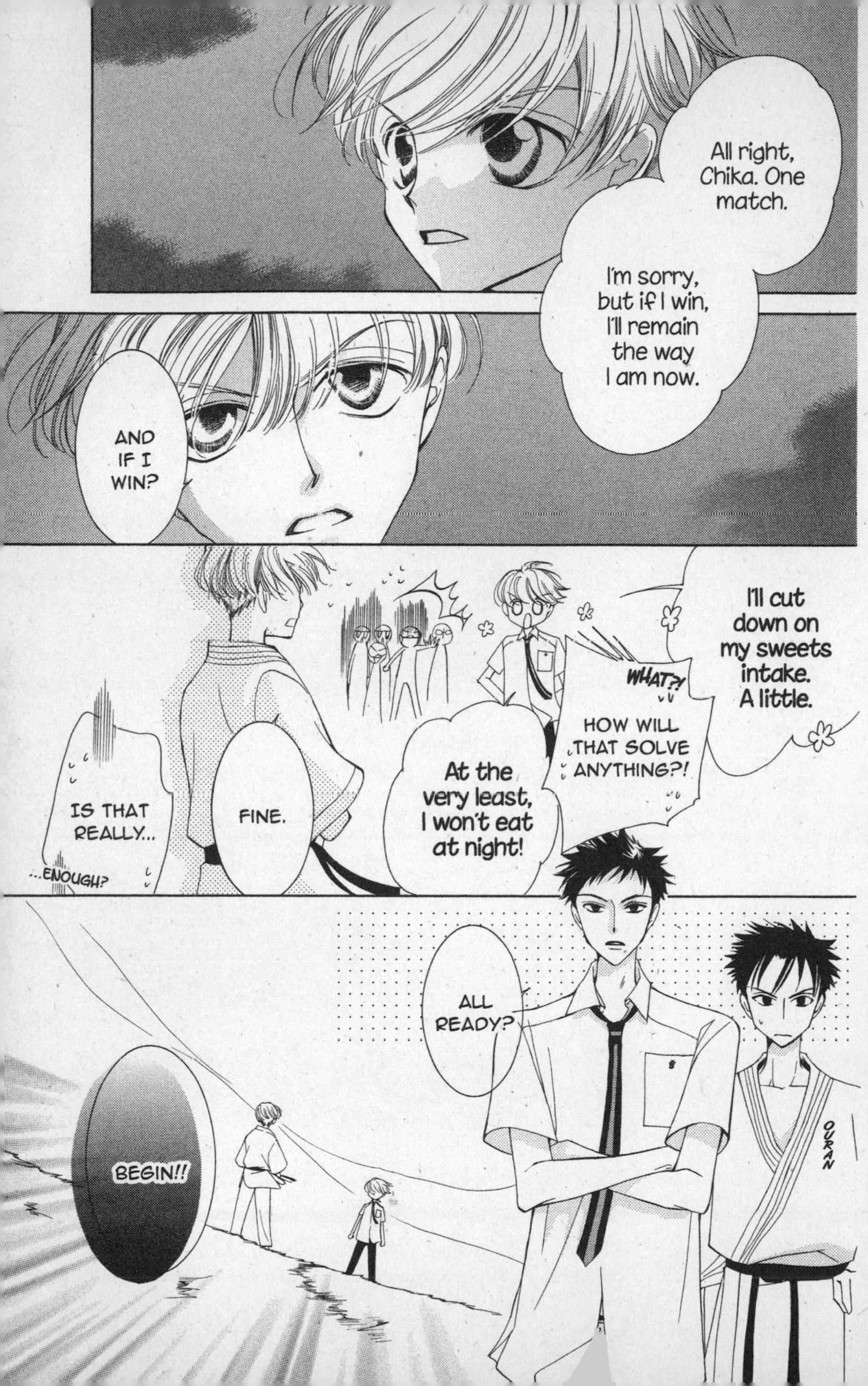
All right, Chika. One match.
I'm sorry, but if I win, I'll remain the way I am now.
AND IF I WIN?
I'll cut down on my sweets intake. A little.
WHAT?!
HOW WILL THAT SOLVE ANYTHING?!
At the very least, I won't eat at night!
FINE.
IS THAT REALLY...
...ENOUGH?
ALL READY?
OURAN
BEGIN!!

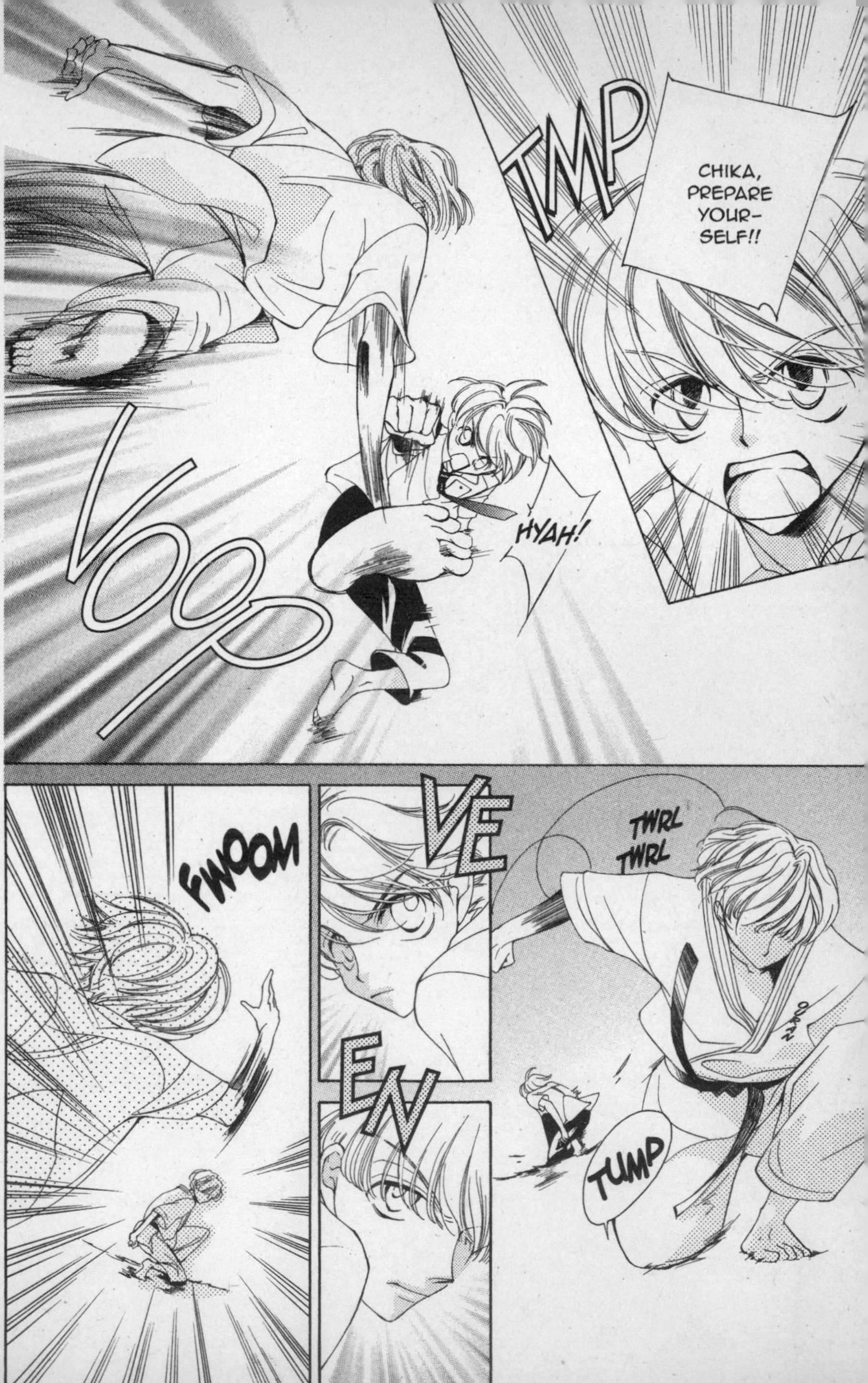
TMP
CHIKA, PREPARE YOUR-SELF!!
HYAH!
VOOP
TWRL TWRL
OURAN
TUMP
VE
EN
FWOOM

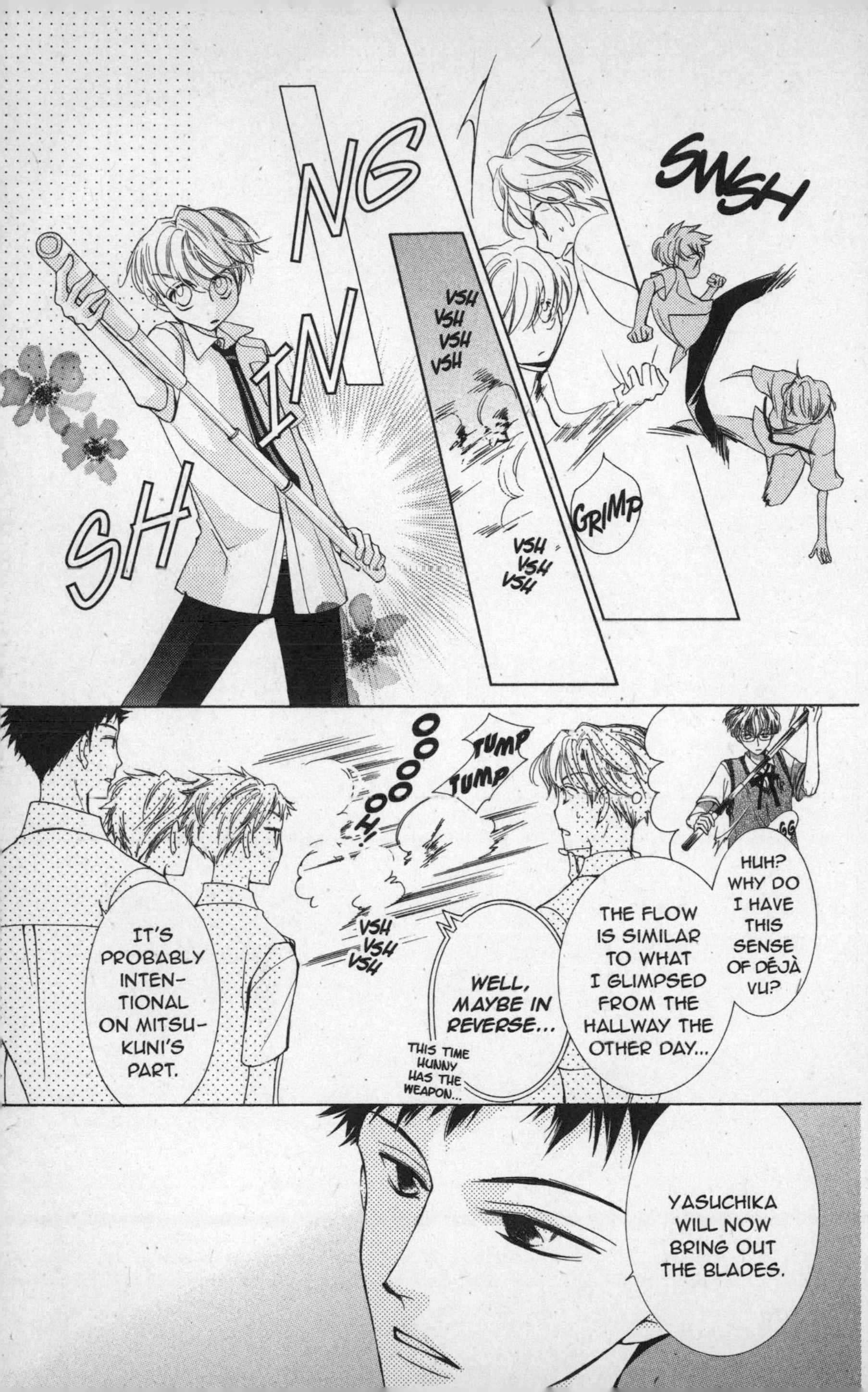
SWSH
GRIMP
VSH
VSH
VSH
VSH
VSH
VSH
VSH
SHING
HUH? WHY DO I HAVE THIS SENSE OF DÉJÀ VU?
GG
THE FLOW IS SIMILAR TO WHAT I GLIMPSED FROM THE HALLWAY THE OTHER DAY...
TUMP
TUMP
OOOOOOH!
WELL, MAYBE IN REVERSE...
THIS TIME HUNNY HAS THE WEAPON...
VSH
VSH
VSH
IT'S PROBABLY INTEN-TIONAL ON MITSU-KUNI'S PART.
YASUCHIKA WILL NOW BRING OUT THE BLADES.

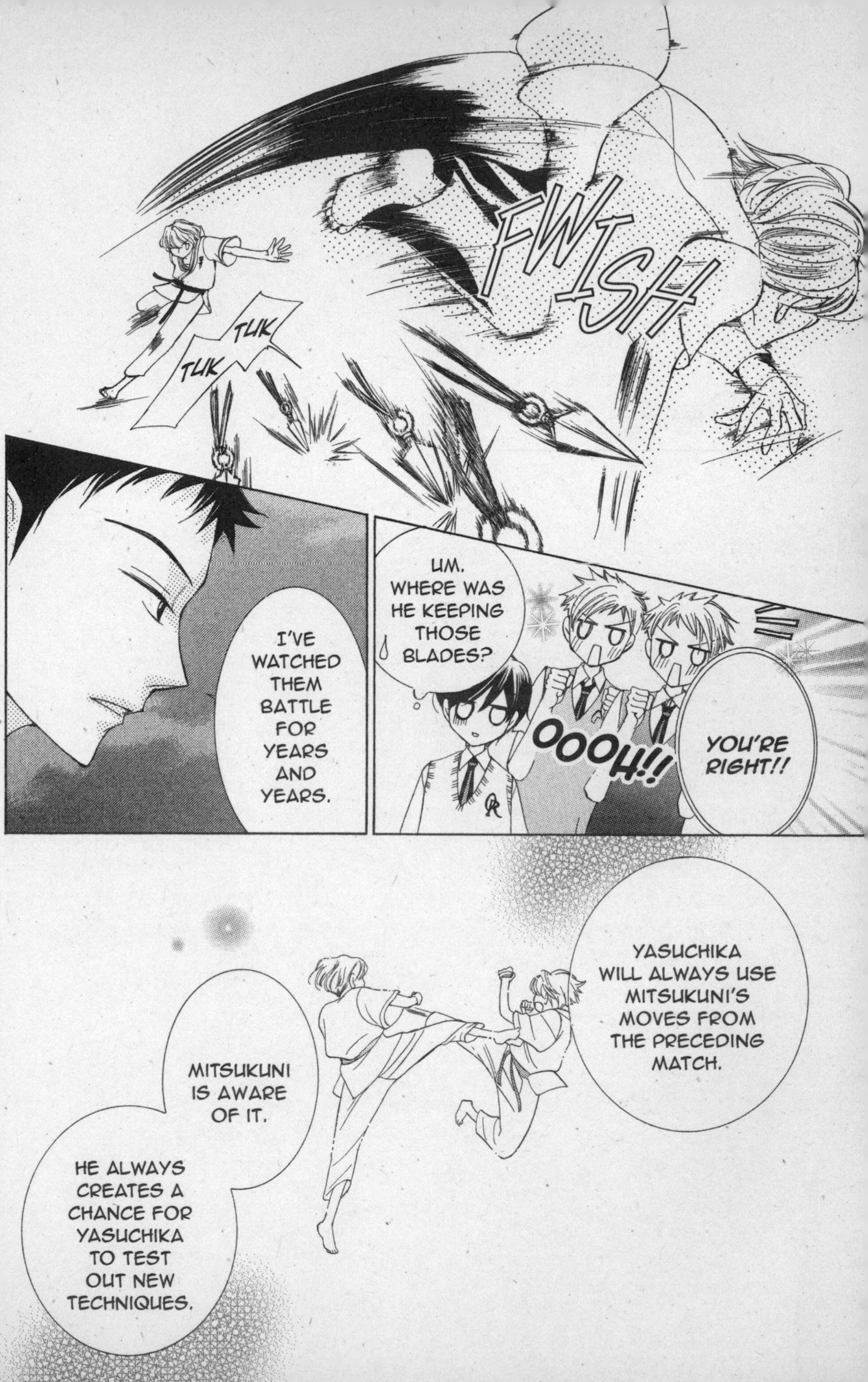
FWISH
TUK
TUK
UM. WHERE WAS HE KEEPING THOSE BLADES?
YOU'RE RIGHT!!
OOOH!!
I'VE WATCHED THEM BATTLE FOR YEARS AND YEARS.
YASUCHIKA WILL ALWAYS USE MITSUKUNI'S MOVES FROM THE PRECEDING MATCH.
MITSUKUNI IS AWARE OF IT.
HE ALWAYS CREATES A CHANCE FOR YASUCHIKA TO TEST OUT NEW TECHNIQUES.

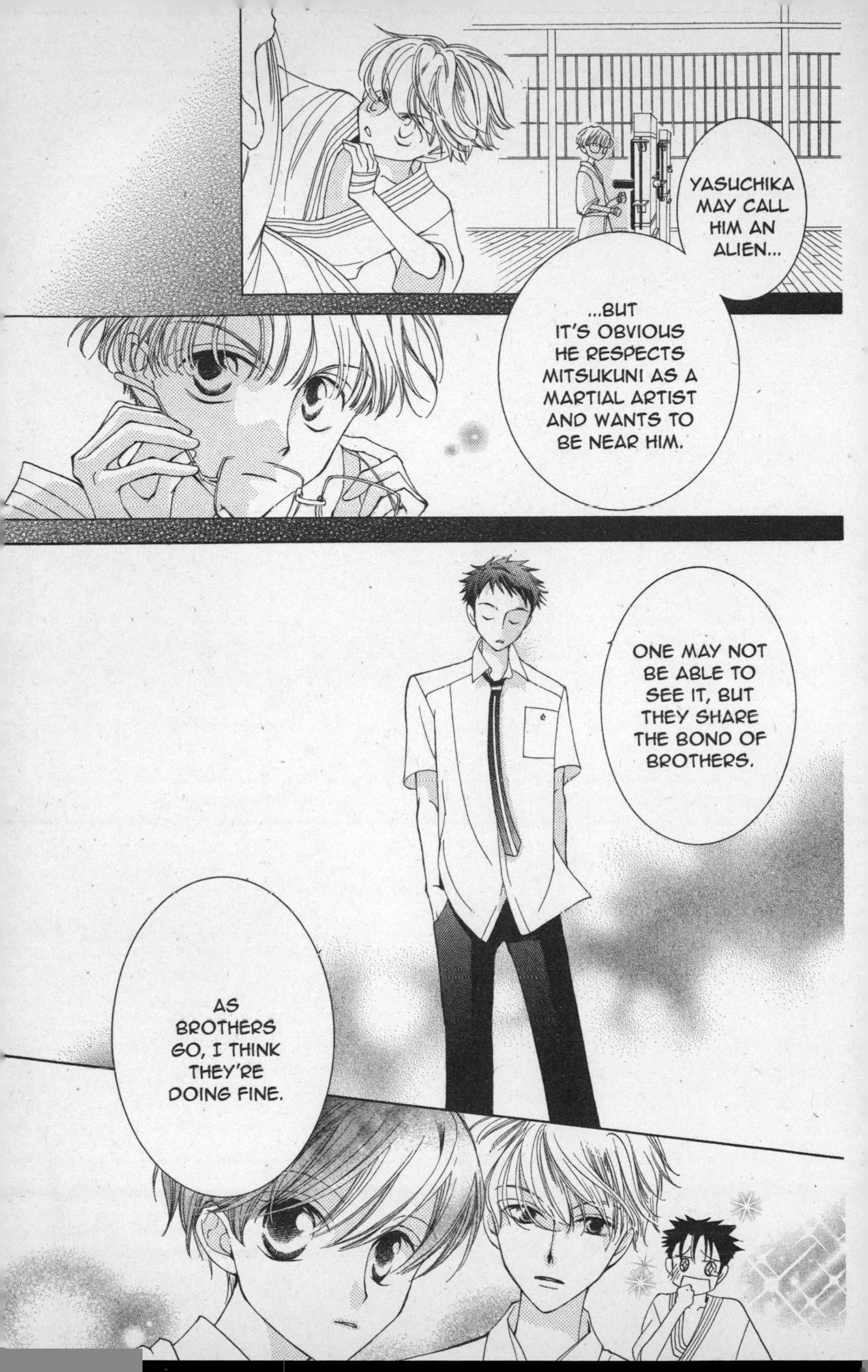
YASUCHIKA MAY CALL HIM AN ALIEN...
...BUT IT'S OBVIOUS HE RESPECTS MITSUKUNI AS A MARTIAL ARTIST AND WANTS TO BE NEAR HIM.
ONE MAY NOT BE ABLE TO SEE IT, BUT THEY SHARE THE BOND OF BROTHERS.
AS BROTHERS GO, I THINK THEY'RE DOING FINE.

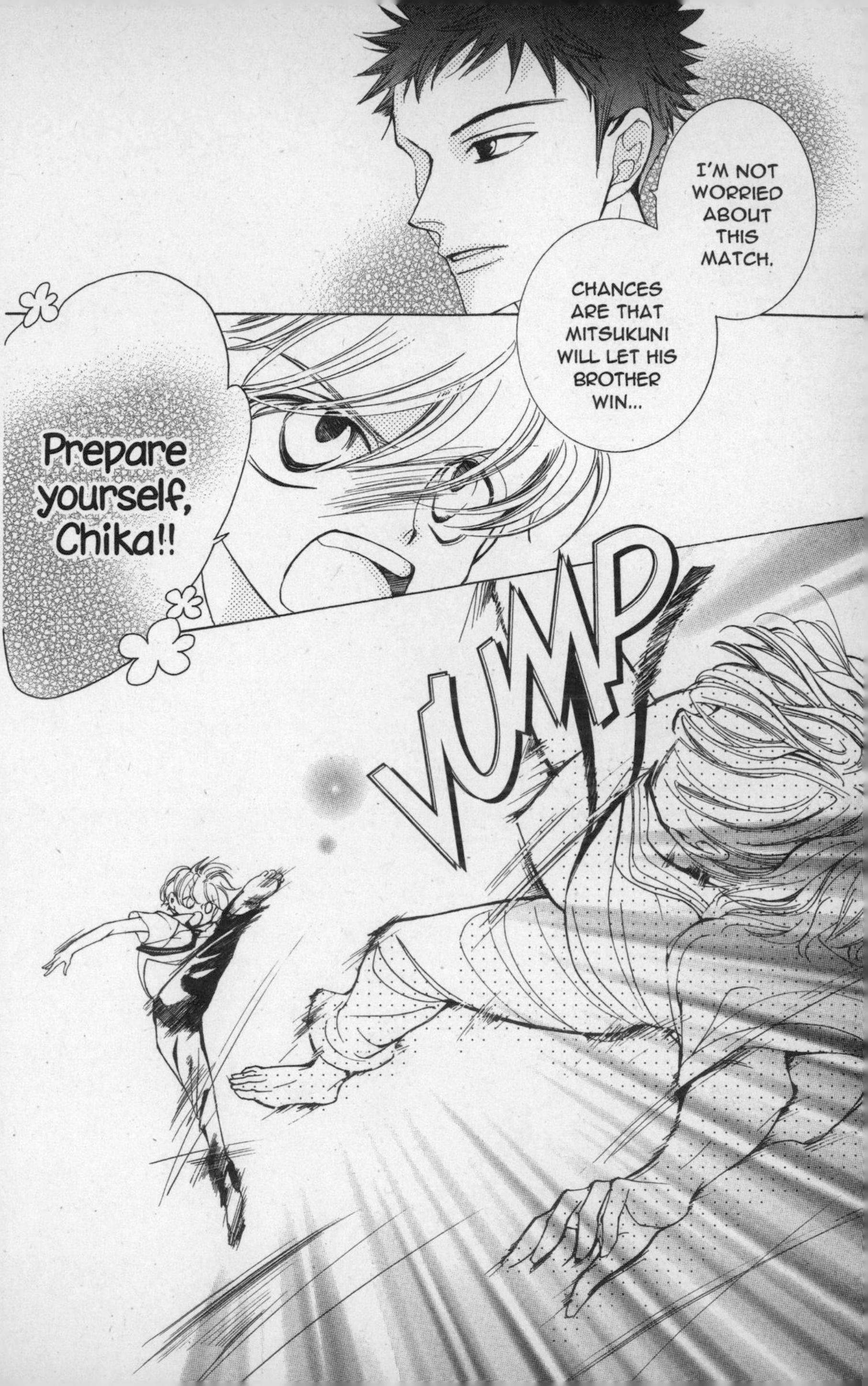
I'M NOT WORRIED ABOUT THIS MATCH.
CHANCES ARE THAT MITSUKUNI WILL LET HIS BROTHER WIN...
Prepare yourself, Chika!!
VUMP

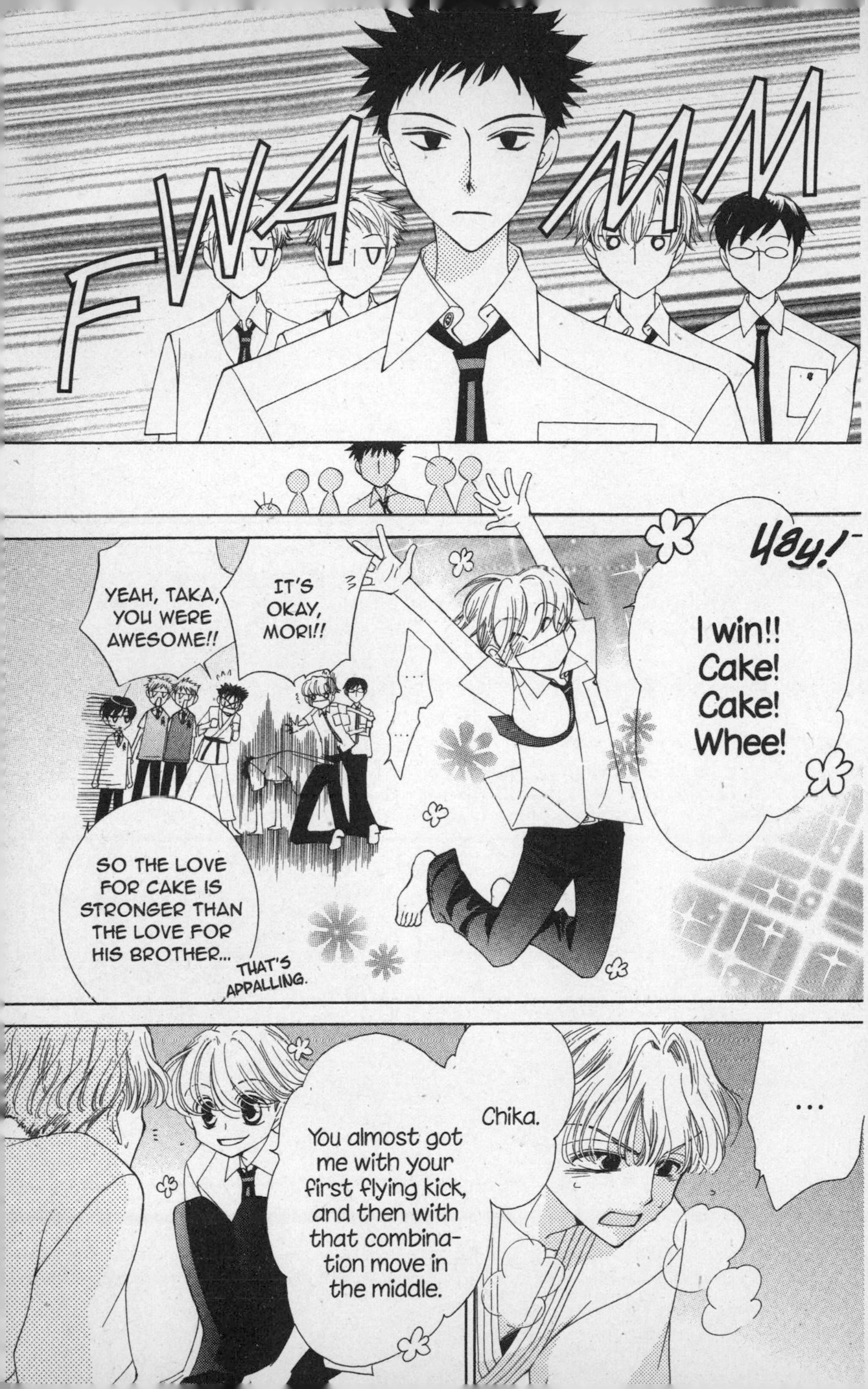
FWAMM
Yay!
I win!! Cake! Cake! Whee!
...
...
IT'S OKAY, MORI!!
YEAH, TAKA, YOU WERE AWESOME!!
SO THE LOVE FOR CAKE IS STRONGER THAN THE LOVE FOR HIS BROTHER...
THAT'S APPALLING.
...
Chika.
You almost got me with your first flying kick, and then with that combination move in the middle.

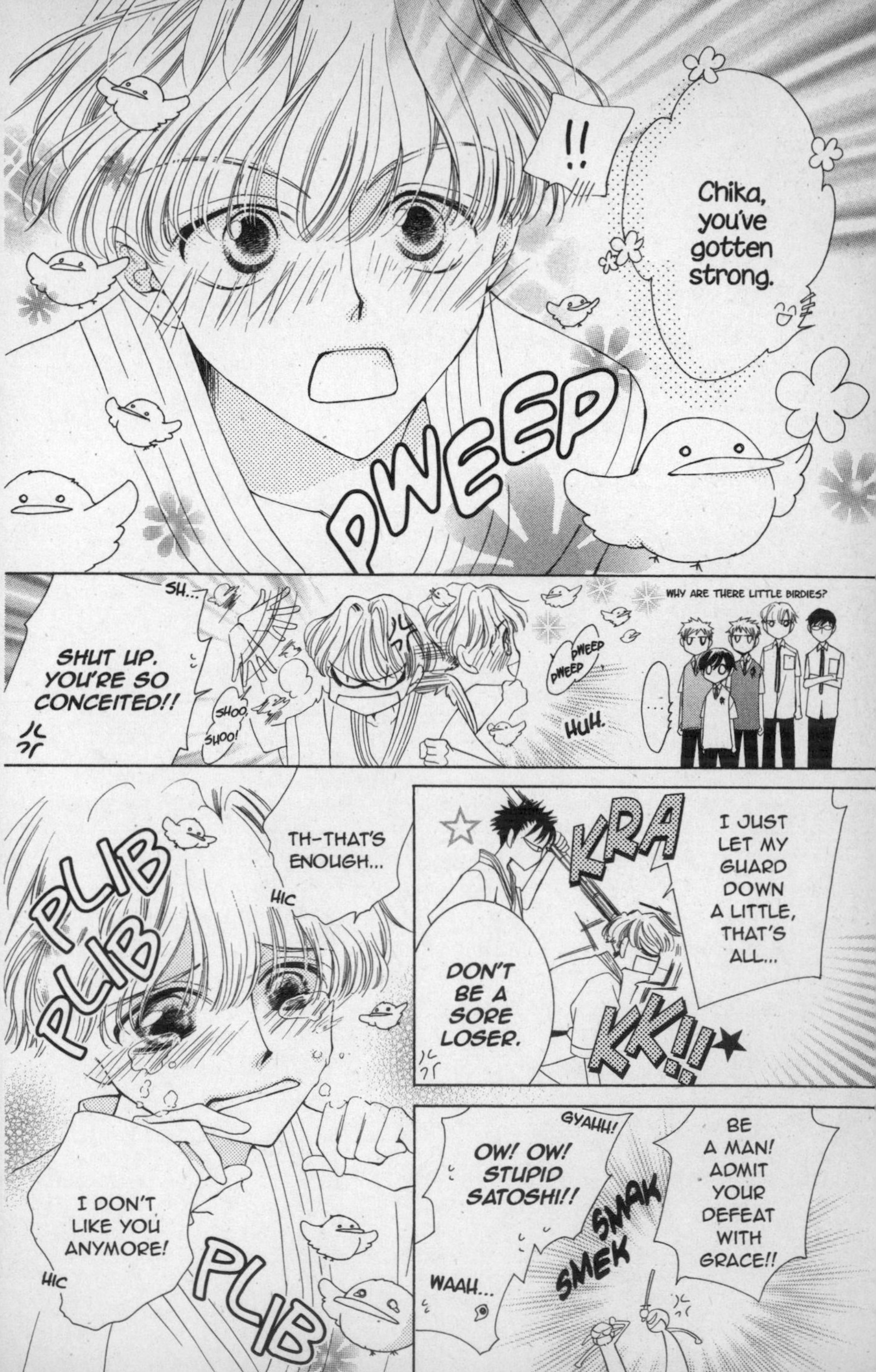
!!
Chika, you've gotten strong.
PWEEP
WHY ARE THERE LITTLE BIRDIES?
...
HUH.
PWEEP PWEEP
SHOO, SHOO!
SH...
SHUT UP. YOU'RE SO CONCEITED!!
I JUST LET MY GUARD DOWN A LITTLE, THAT'S ALL...
KRAKK!!
DON'T BE A SORE LOSER.
BE A MAN! ADMIT YOUR DEFEAT WITH GRACE!!
GYAHH!
OW! OW! STUPID SATOSHI!!
SMAK SMEK
WAAH...
TH-THAT'S ENOUGH...
HIC
PLIB PLIB
I DON'T LIKE YOU ANYMORE!
HIC
PLIB

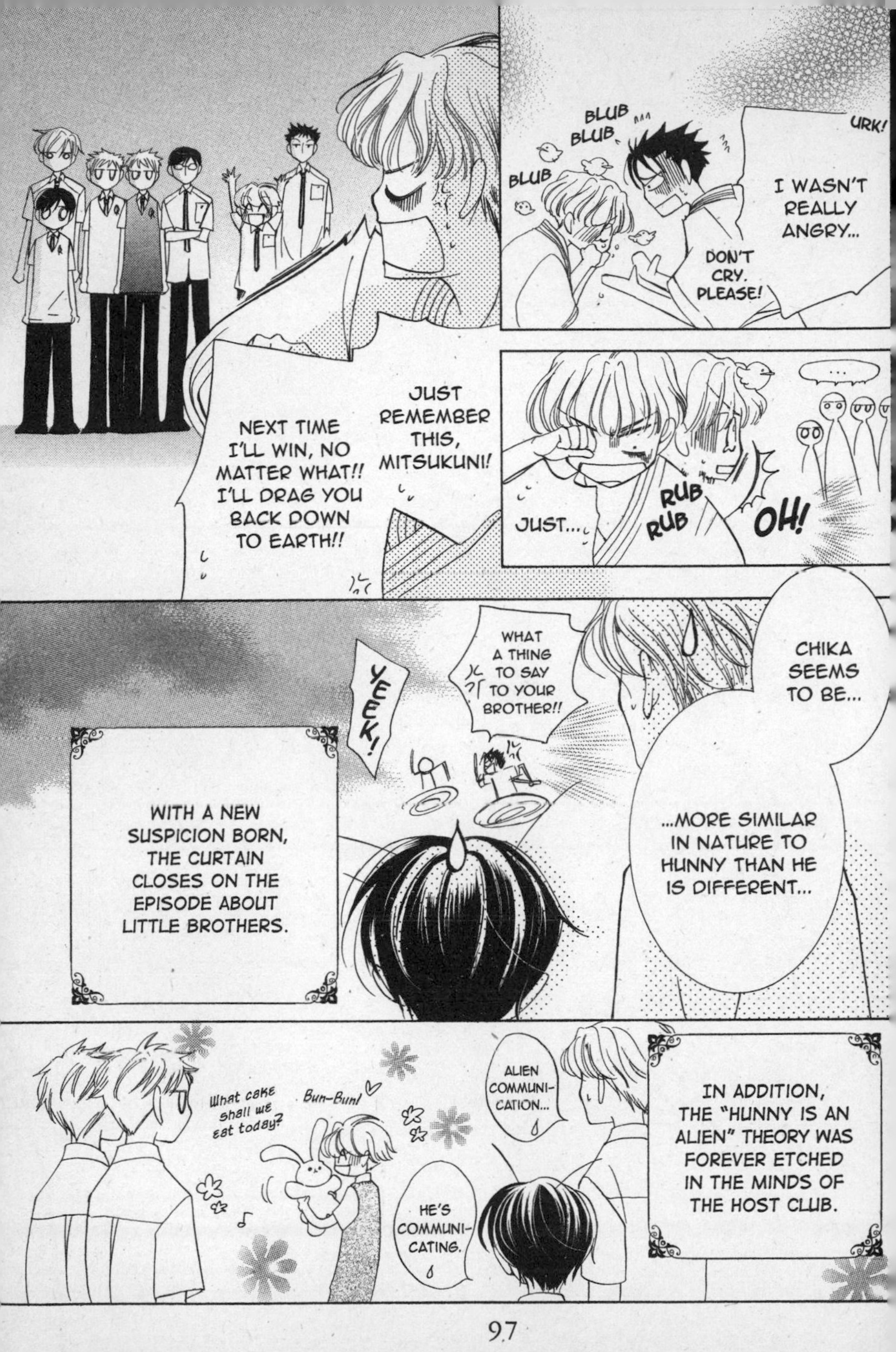
URK!
BLUB BLUB BLUB
I WASN'T REALLY ANGRY...
DON'T CRY. PLEASE!
...
OH!
RUB RUB
JUST...
JUST REMEMBER THIS, MITSUKUNI!
NEXT TIME I'LL WIN, NO MATTER WHAT!! I'LL DRAG YOU BACK DOWN TO EARTH!!
CHIKA SEEMS TO BE...
...MORE SIMILAR IN NATURE TO HUNNY THAN HE IS DIFFERENT...
WHAT A THING TO SAY TO YOUR BROTHER!!
YEEK!
WITH A NEW SUSPICION BORN, THE CURTAIN CLOSES ON THE EPISODE ABOUT LITTLE BROTHERS.
IN ADDITION, THE "HUNNY IS AN ALIEN" THEORY WAS FOREVER ETCHED IN THE MINDS OF THE HOST CLUB.
ALIEN COMMUNICATION...
HE'S COMMUNICATING.
Bun-Bun!
What cake shall we eat today?

✿ IT'S KIND OF LATE TO BRING IT UP NOW, BUT REGARDING THE THERMOTYPE LETTER FROM TAMAKI'S FATHER IN VOLUME 6--I HAD MY OLDER BROTHER WRITE IT FOR ME WHEN HE WAS HOME OVER NEW YEAR'S. HIS SPECIAL TALENT: JAPANESE CALLIGRAPHY AND ENGLISH.

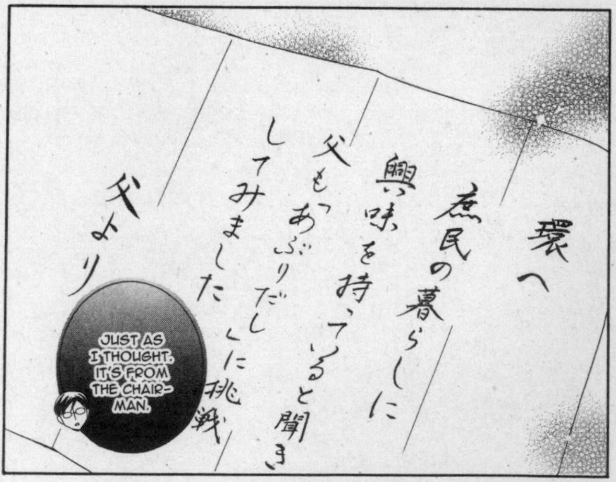
環へ
庶民の暮らしに
興味を持っていると聞き
父もあぶりだしに挑戦
してみました
父より
JUST AS I THOUGHT. IT'S FROM THE CHAIR-MAN.

SORRY ABOUT DRAGGING YOU ALL THE WAY OVER TO MY OFFICE ON NEW YEAR'S DAY (A FIVE-MINUTE WALK FROM HOME). THANK YOU, DEAR BROTHER!!!

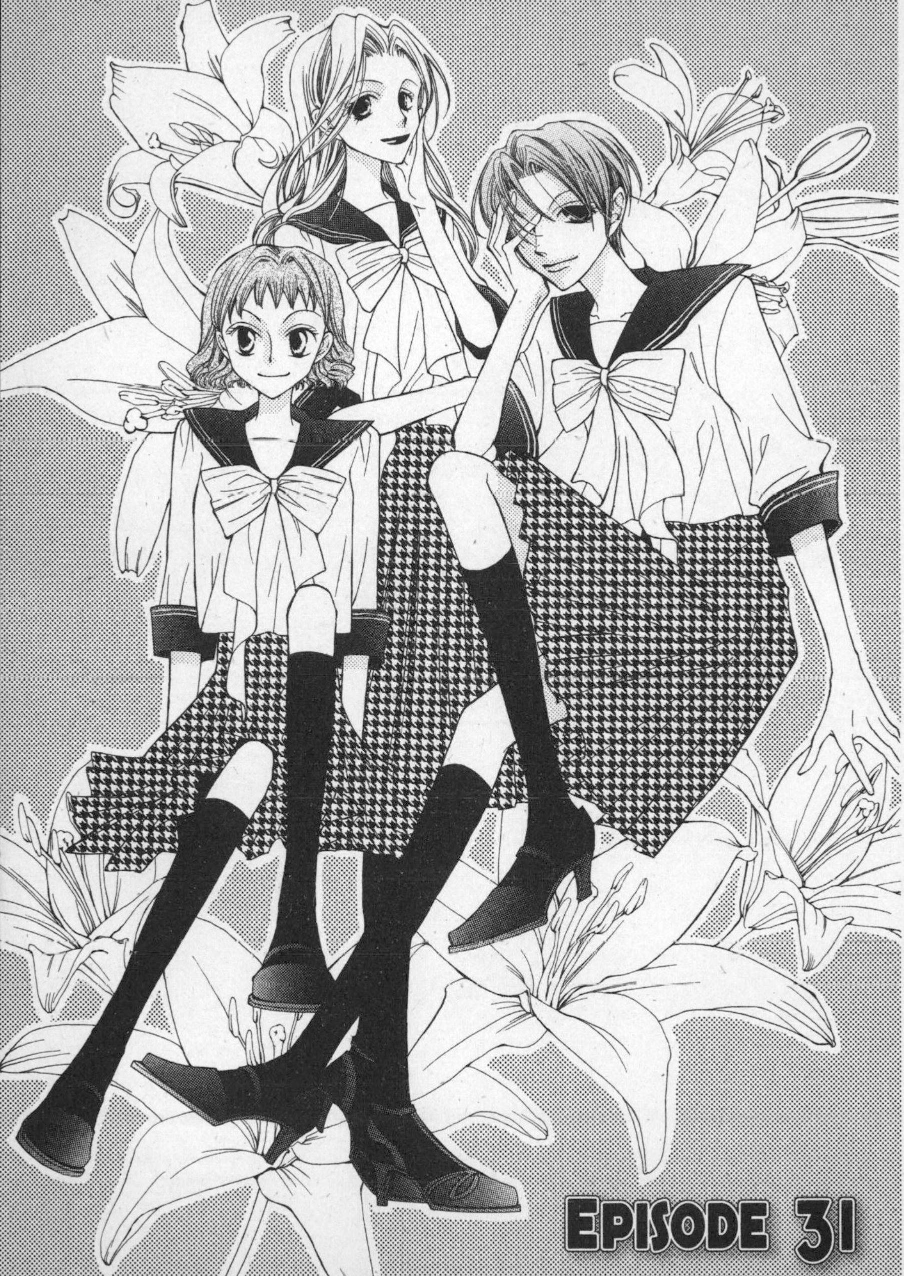

EPISODE 31

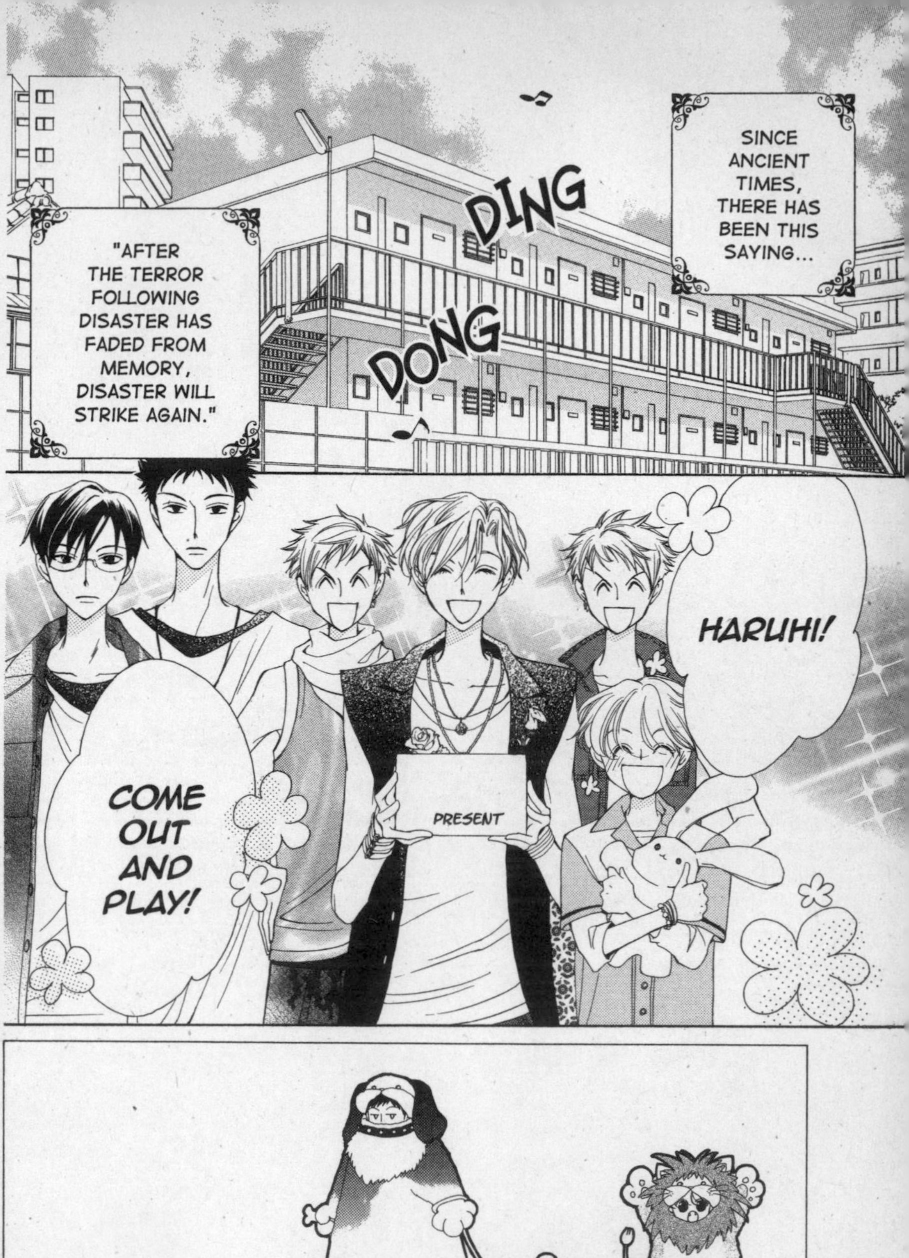
SINCE ANCIENT TIMES, THERE HAS BEEN THIS SAYING...
DING
DONG
"AFTER THE TERROR FOLLOWING DISASTER HAS FADED FROM MEMORY, DISASTER WILL STRIKE AGAIN."
HARUHI!
PRESENT
COME OUT AND PLAY!

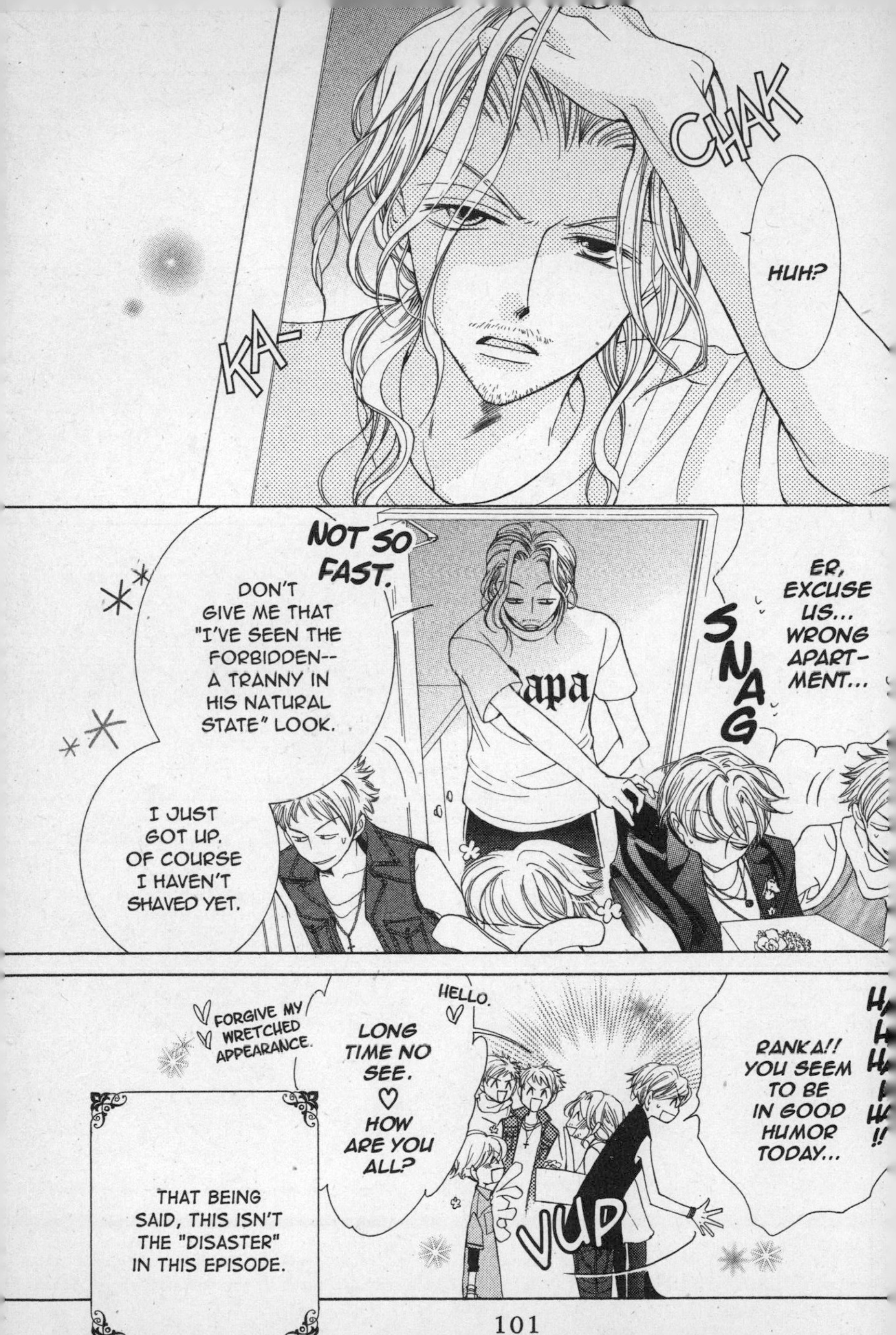
KA-
CHAK
HUH?
SNAG
ER, EXCUSE US... WRONG APART-MENT...
NOT SO FAST.
DON'T GIVE ME THAT "I'VE SEEN THE FORBIDDEN-- A TRANNY IN HIS NATURAL STATE" LOOK.
I JUST GOT UP. OF COURSE I HAVEN'T SHAVED YET.
HA HA HA HA!!
RANKA!! YOU SEEM TO BE IN GOOD HUMOR TODAY...
VUP
HELLO.
LONG TIME NO SEE. ♡ HOW ARE YOU ALL?
♡ FORGIVE MY ♡ WRETCHED APPEARANCE.
THAT BEING SAID, THIS ISN'T THE "DISASTER" IN THIS EPISODE.

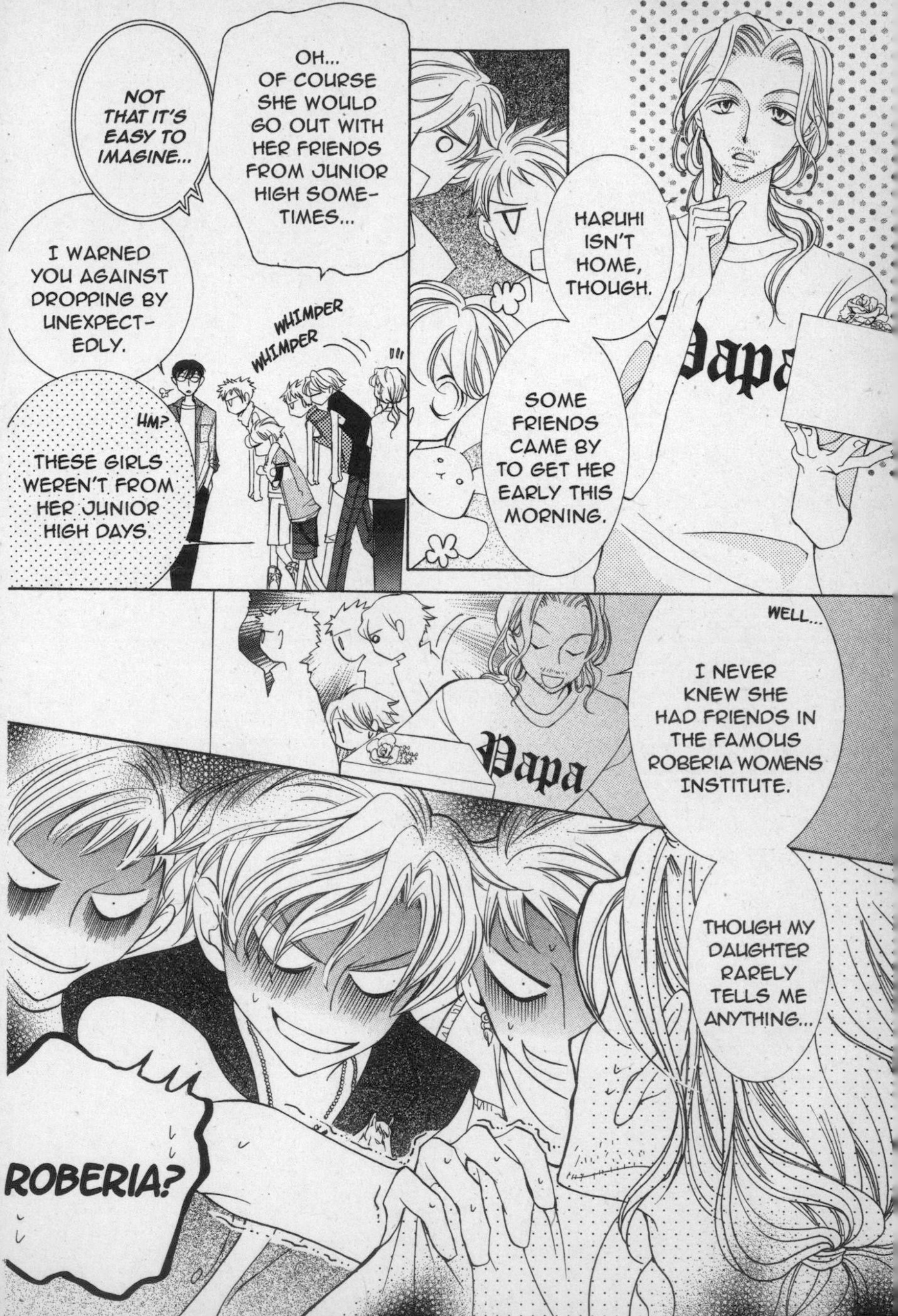
HARUHI ISN'T HOME, THOUGH.
SOME FRIENDS CAME BY TO GET HER EARLY THIS MORNING.
OH... OF COURSE SHE WOULD GO OUT WITH HER FRIENDS FROM JUNIOR HIGH SOME-TIMES...
NOT THAT IT'S EASY TO IMAGINE...
I WARNED YOU AGAINST DROPPING BY UNEXPECT-EDLY.
WHIMPER
WHIMPER
HM?
THESE GIRLS WEREN'T FROM HER JUNIOR HIGH DAYS.
WELL...
I NEVER KNEW SHE HAD FRIENDS IN THE FAMOUS ROBERIA WOMENS INSTITUTE.
THOUGH MY DAUGHTER RARELY TELLS ME ANYTHING...
ROBERIA?

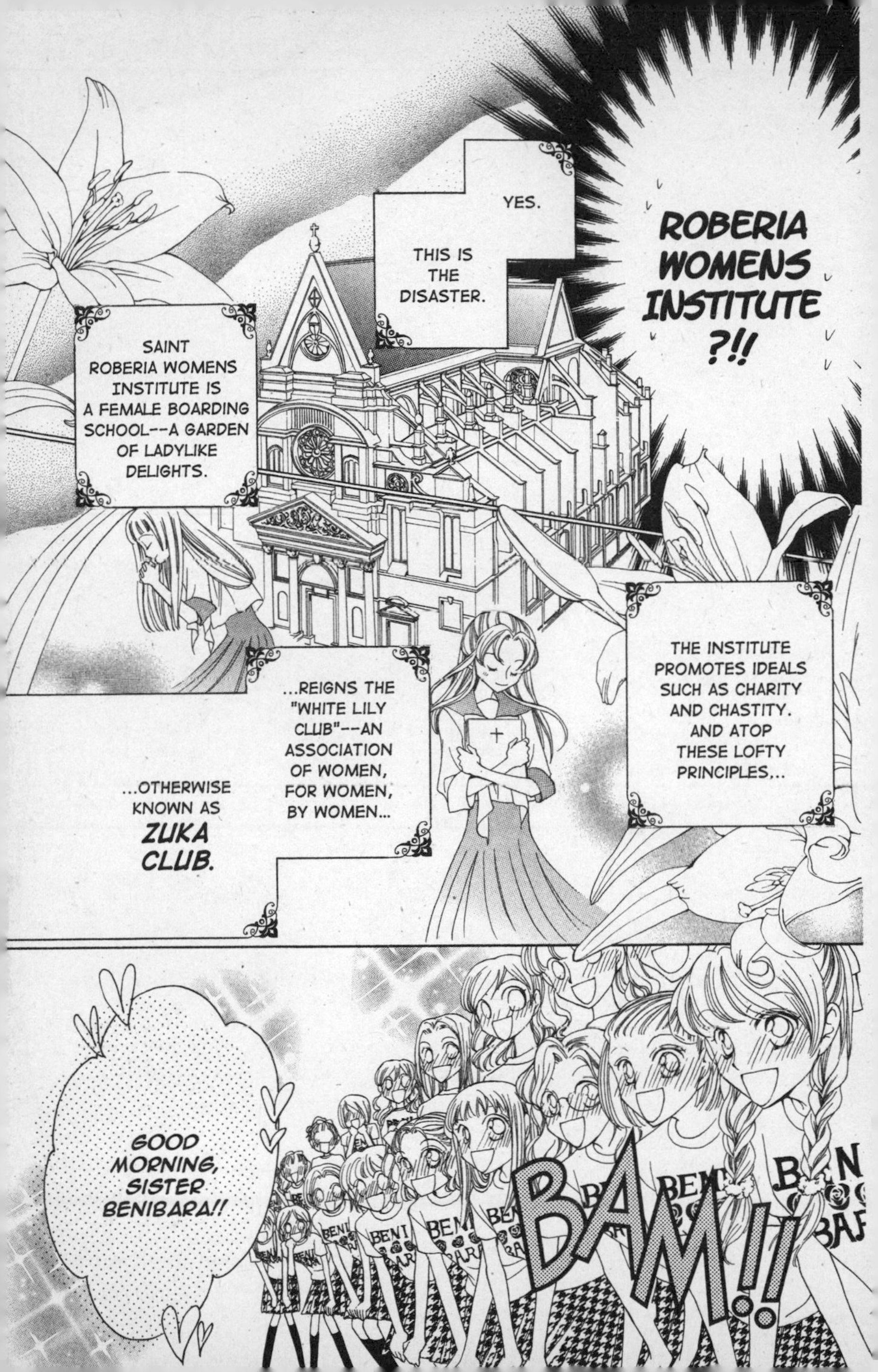
ROBERIA WOMENS INSTITUTE ?!!
YES.
THIS IS THE DISASTER.
SAINT ROBERIA WOMENS INSTITUTE IS A FEMALE BOARDING SCHOOL--A GARDEN OF LADYLIKE DELIGHTS.
THE INSTITUTE PROMOTES IDEALS SUCH AS CHARITY AND CHASTITY. AND ATOP THESE LOFTY PRINCIPLES...
...REIGNS THE "WHITE LILY CLUB"--AN ASSOCIATION OF WOMEN, FOR WOMEN, BY WOMEN...
...OTHERWISE KNOWN AS ZUKA CLUB.
GOOD MORNING, SISTER BENIBARA!!
BAM!!

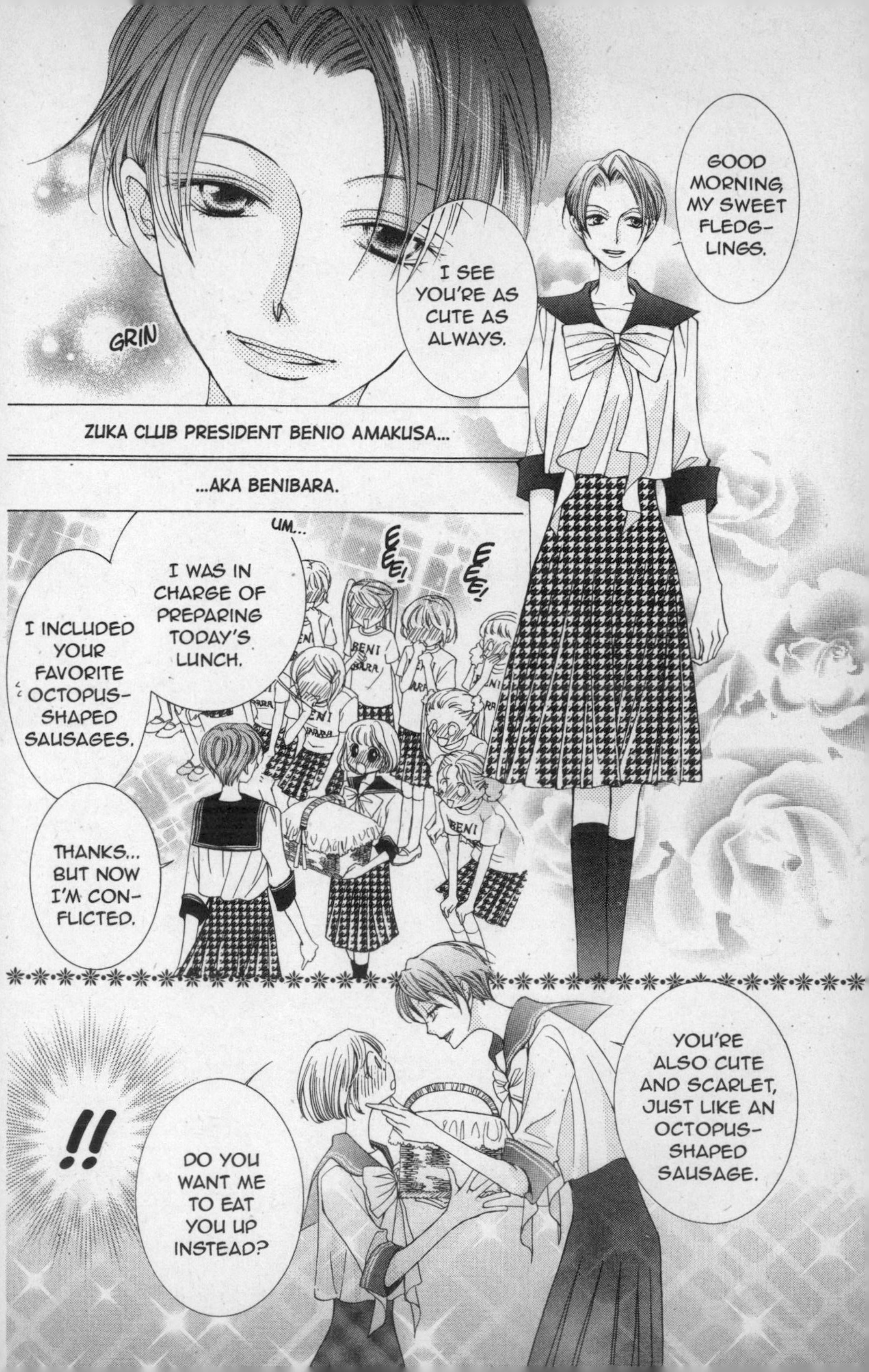
GOOD MORNING, MY SWEET FLEDG-LINGS.
I SEE YOU'RE AS CUTE AS ALWAYS.
GRIN
ZUKA CLUB PRESIDENT BENIO AMAKUSA...
...AKA BENIBARA.
EEE!
EEE!
UM...
I WAS IN CHARGE OF PREPARING TODAY'S LUNCH.
I INCLUDED YOUR FAVORITE OCTOPUS-SHAPED SAUSAGES.
THANKS... BUT NOW I'M CON-FLICTED.
YOU'RE ALSO CUTE AND SCARLET, JUST LIKE AN OCTOPUS-SHAPED SAUSAGE.
!!
DO YOU WANT ME TO EAT YOU UP INSTEAD?

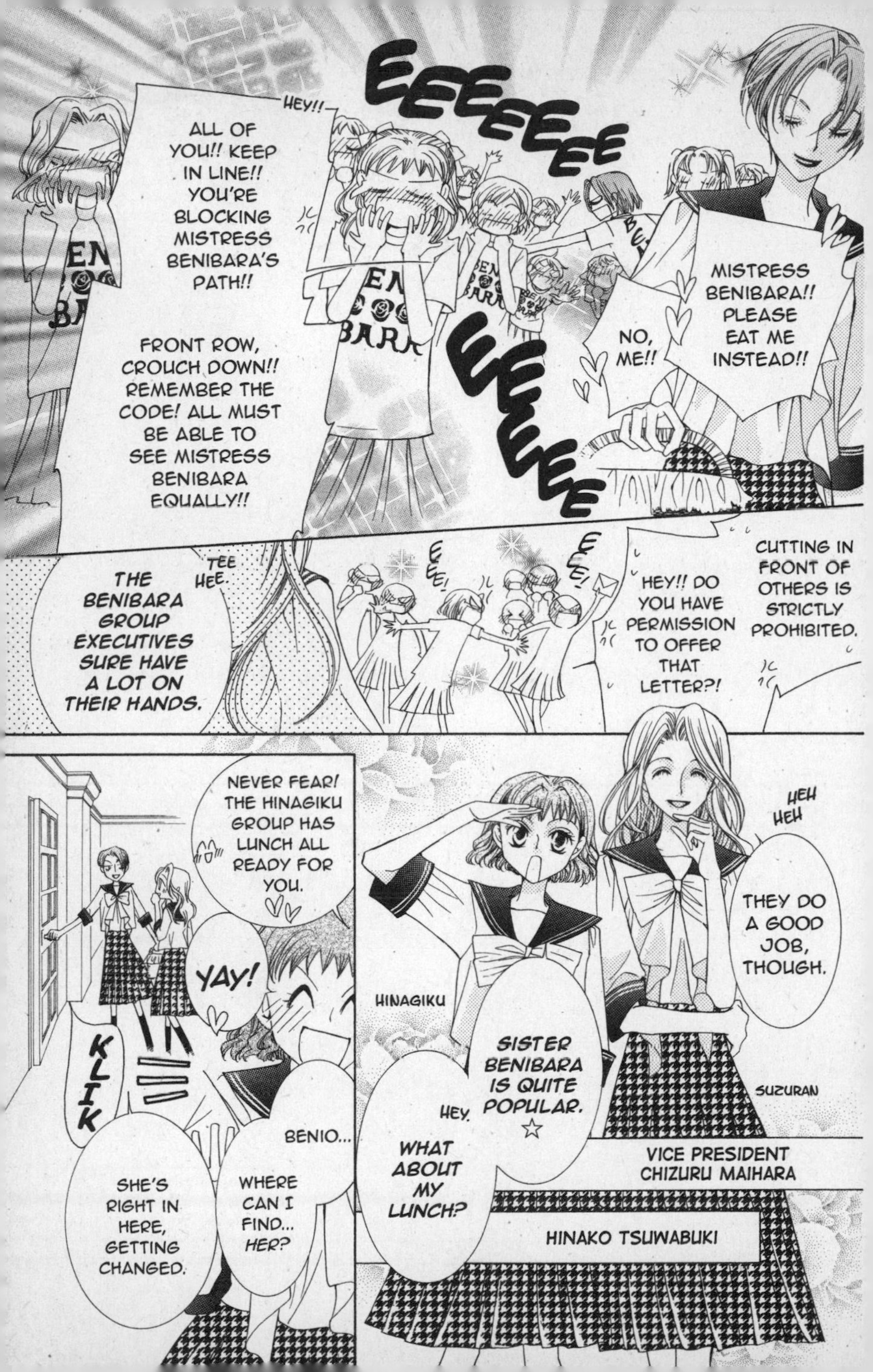
EEEEEEE
MISTRESS BENIBARA!! PLEASE EAT ME INSTEAD!!
NO, ME!!
HEY!!
ALL OF YOU!! KEEP IN LINE!! YOU'RE BLOCKING MISTRESS BENIBARA'S PATH!!
FRONT ROW, CROUCH DOWN!! REMEMBER THE CODE! ALL MUST BE ABLE TO SEE MISTRESS BENIBARA EQUALLY!!
EEEEEE
CUTTING IN FRONT OF OTHERS IS STRICTLY PROHIBITED.
HEY!! DO YOU HAVE PERMISSION TO OFFER THAT LETTER?!
EEE!
EEE!
TEE HEE.
THE BENIBARA GROUP EXECUTIVES SURE HAVE A LOT ON THEIR HANDS.
HEH HEH
THEY DO A GOOD JOB, THOUGH.
HINAGIKU
SUZURAN
SISTER BENIBARA IS QUITE POPULAR. ☆
VICE PRESIDENT CHIZURU MAIHARA
HINAKO TSUWABUKI
HEY.
WHAT ABOUT MY LUNCH?
NEVER FEAR! THE HINAGIKU GROUP HAS LUNCH ALL READY FOR YOU.
YAY!
KLIK
BENIO...
WHERE CAN I FIND... HER?
SHE'S RIGHT IN HERE, GETTING CHANGED.

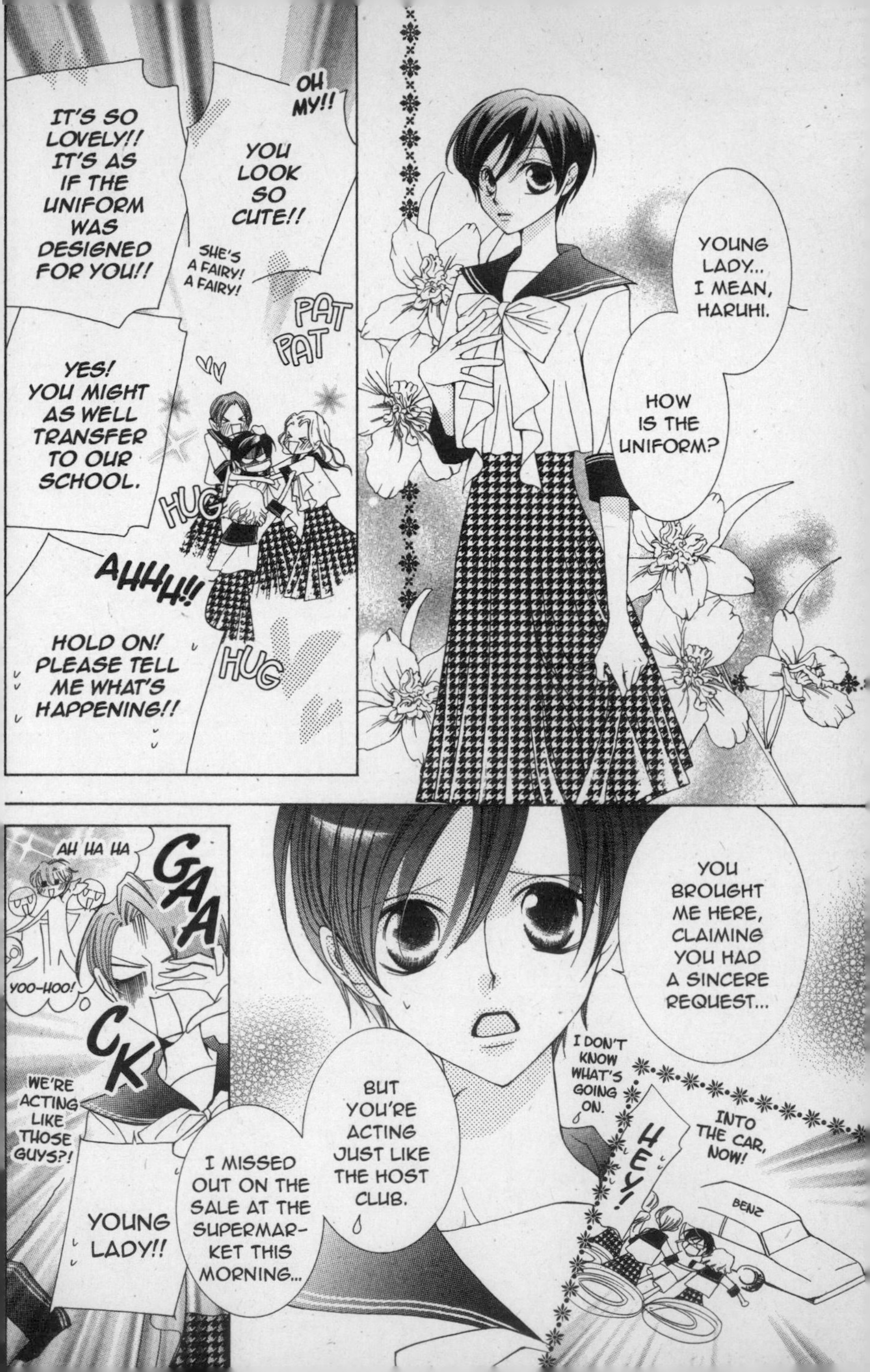
YOUNG LADY... I MEAN, HARUHI.
HOW IS THE UNIFORM?
OH MY!!
YOU LOOK SO CUTE!!
IT'S SO LOVELY!! IT'S AS IF THE UNIFORM WAS DESIGNED FOR YOU!!
SHE'S A FAIRY! A FAIRY!
PAT PAT
YES! YOU MIGHT AS WELL TRANSFER TO OUR SCHOOL.
HUG
AHHH!!
HOLD ON! PLEASE TELL ME WHAT'S HAPPENING!!
HUG
YOU BROUGHT ME HERE, CLAIMING YOU HAD A SINCERE REQUEST...
I DON'T KNOW WHAT'S GOING ON.
INTO THE CAR, NOW!
HEY!
BENZ
BUT YOU'RE ACTING JUST LIKE THE HOST CLUB.
I MISSED OUT ON THE SALE AT THE SUPERMARKET THIS MORNING...
GAACK
AH HA HA
YOO-HOO!
WE'RE ACTING LIKE THOSE GUYS?!
YOUNG LADY!!

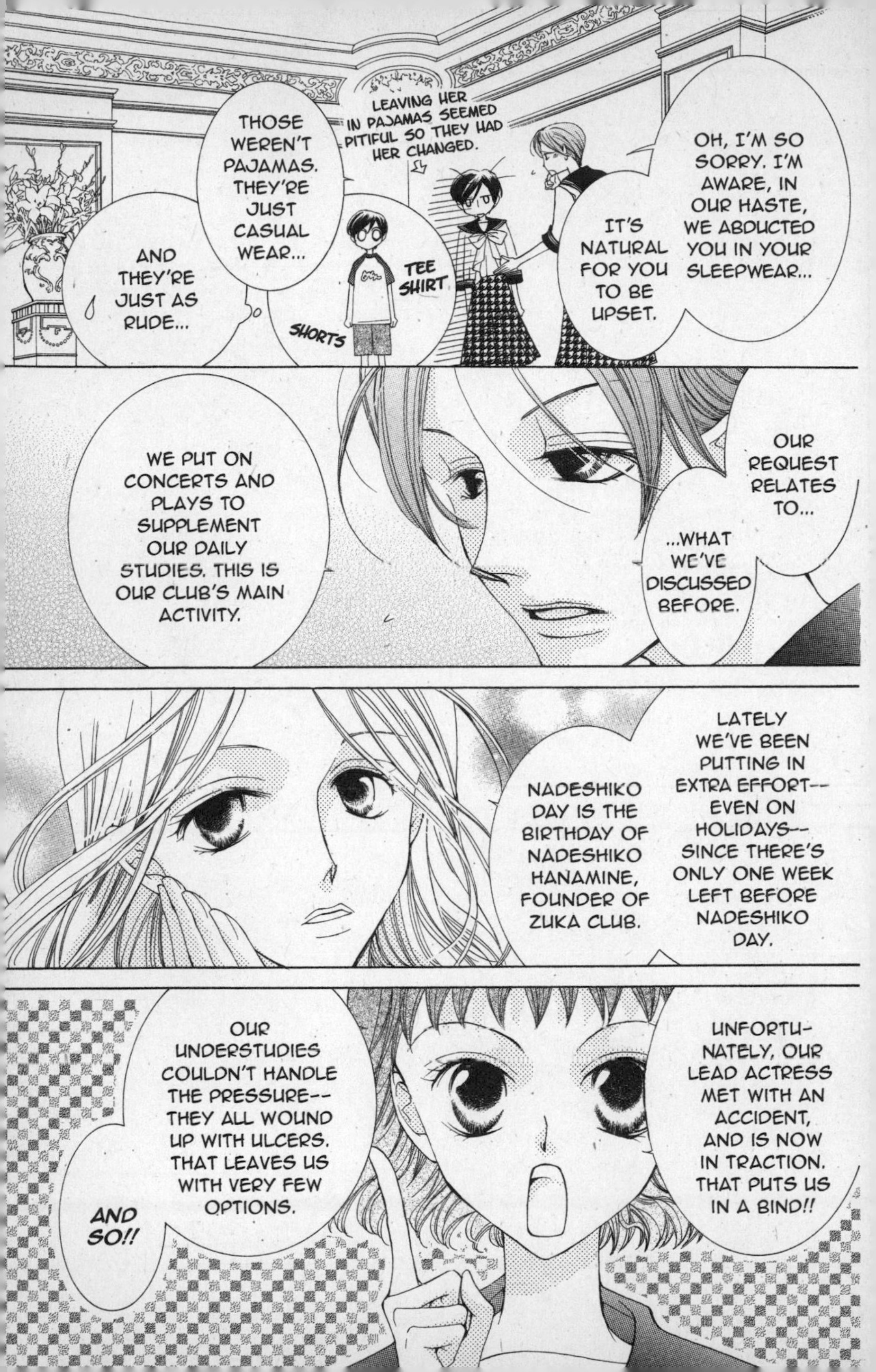
OH, I'M SO SORRY. I'M AWARE, IN OUR HASTE, WE ABDUCTED YOU IN YOUR SLEEPWEAR...
IT'S NATURAL FOR YOU TO BE UPSET.
LEAVING HER IN PAJAMAS SEEMED PITIFUL SO THEY HAD HER CHANGED.
TEE SHIRT
SHORTS
THOSE WEREN'T PAJAMAS. THEY'RE JUST CASUAL WEAR...
AND THEY'RE JUST AS RUDE...
OUR REQUEST RELATES TO...
...WHAT WE'VE DISCUSSED BEFORE.
WE PUT ON CONCERTS AND PLAYS TO SUPPLEMENT OUR DAILY STUDIES. THIS IS OUR CLUB'S MAIN ACTIVITY.
LATELY WE'VE BEEN PUTTING IN EXTRA EFFORT--EVEN ON HOLIDAYS--SINCE THERE'S ONLY ONE WEEK LEFT BEFORE NADESHIKO DAY.
NADESHIKO DAY IS THE BIRTHDAY OF NADESHIKO HANAMINE, FOUNDER OF ZUKA CLUB.
UNFORTU-NATELY, OUR LEAD ACTRESS MET WITH AN ACCIDENT, AND IS NOW IN TRACTION. THAT PUTS US IN A BIND!!
OUR UNDERSTUDIES COULDN'T HANDLE THE PRESSURE--THEY ALL WOUND UP WITH ULCERS. THAT LEAVES US WITH VERY FEW OPTIONS.
AND SO!!

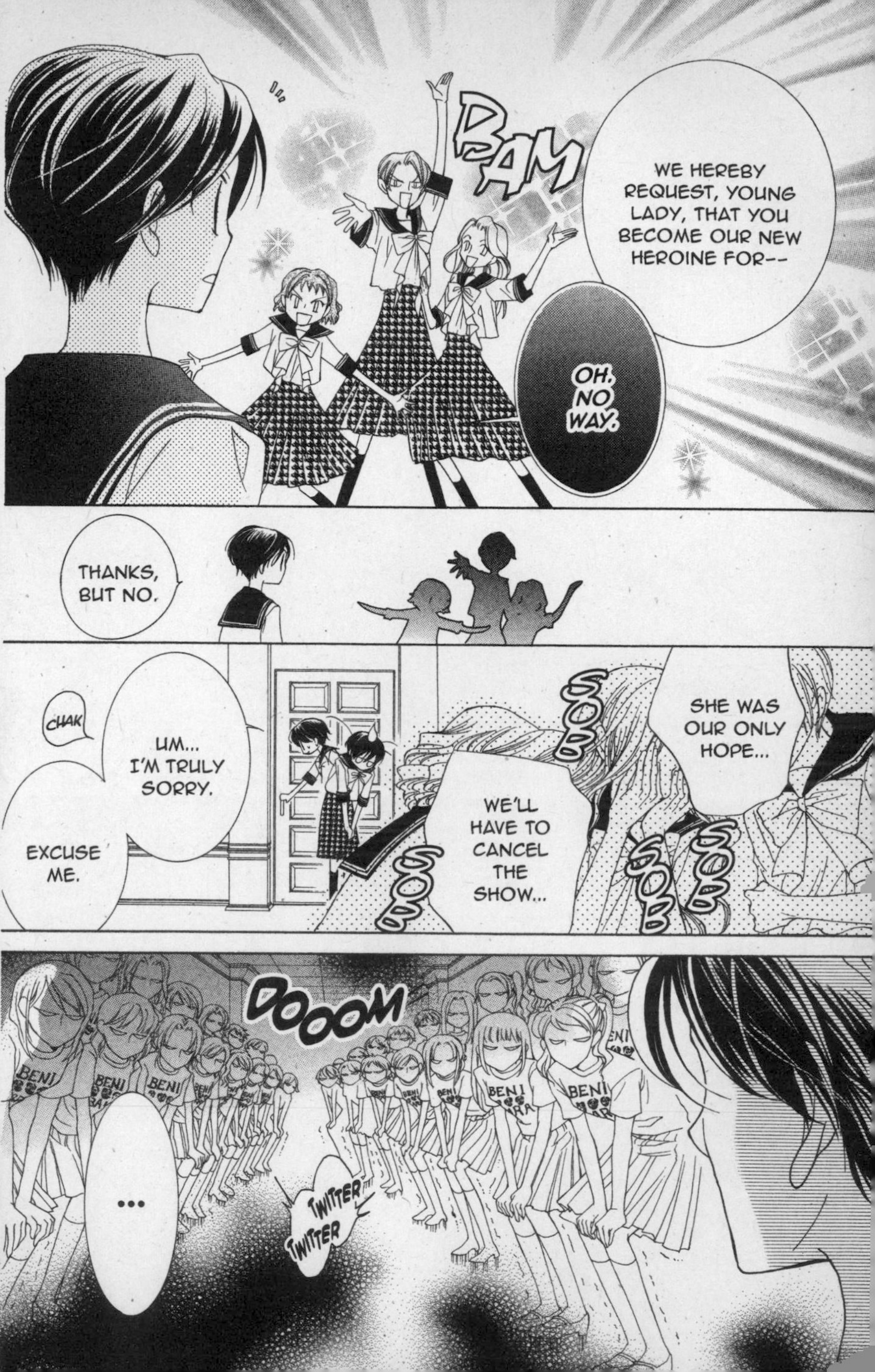

WE HEREBY REQUEST, YOUNG LADY, THAT YOU BECOME OUR NEW HEROINE FOR--
BAM
OH. NO WAY.
THANKS, BUT NO.
SHE WAS OUR ONLY HOPE...
SOB SOB
SOB
WE'LL HAVE TO CANCEL THE SHOW...
SOB
UM... I'M TRULY SORRY.
CHAK
EXCUSE ME.
DOOOM
TWITTER TWITTER
...

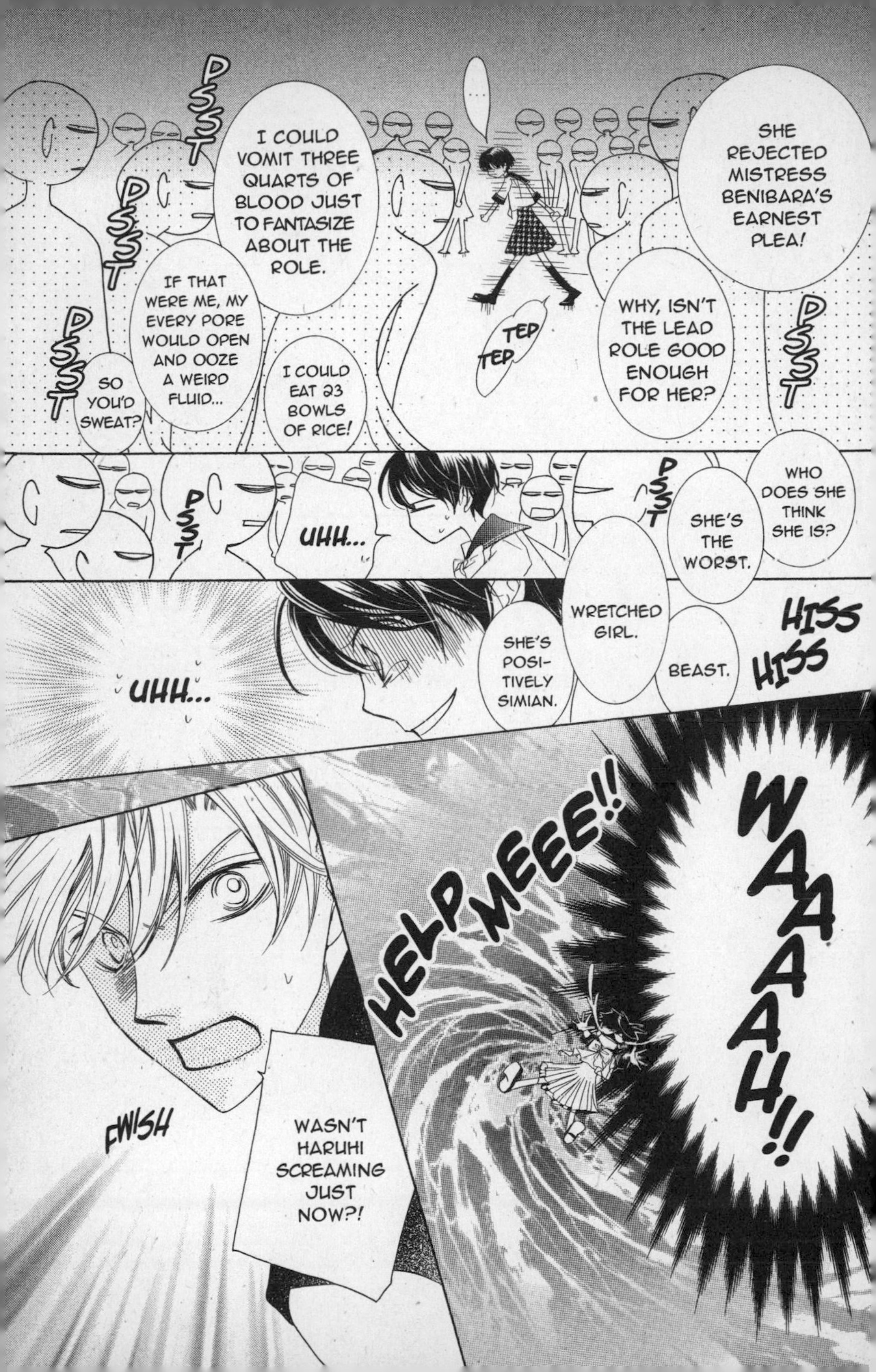
SHE REJECTED MISTRESS BENIBARA'S EARNEST PLEA!
PSST
WHY, ISN'T THE LEAD ROLE GOOD ENOUGH FOR HER?
...
TEP TEP
I COULD VOMIT THREE QUARTS OF BLOOD JUST TO FANTASIZE ABOUT THE ROLE.
PSST
I COULD EAT 23 BOWLS OF RICE!
IF THAT WERE ME, MY EVERY PORE WOULD OPEN AND OOZE A WEIRD FLUID...
PSST
SO YOU'D SWEAT?
WHO DOES SHE THINK SHE IS?
SHE'S THE WORST.
PSST
UHH...
PSST
HISS HISS
BEAST.
WRETCHED GIRL.
SHE'S POSITIVELY SIMIAN.
UHH...
WAAAAH!!
HELP MEEE!!
WASN'T HARUHI SCREAMING JUST NOW?!
FWISH

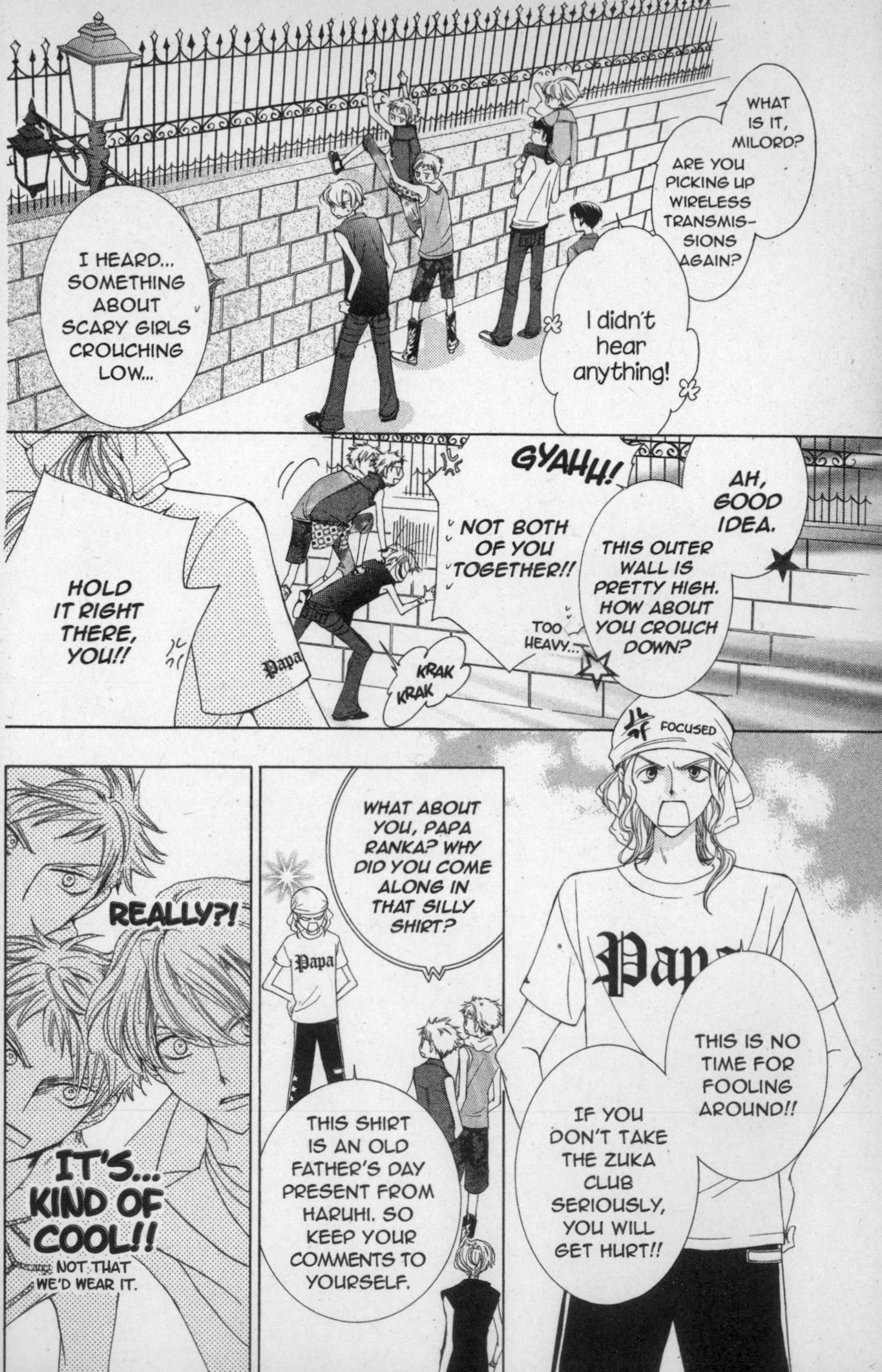
WHAT IS IT, MILORD? ARE YOU PICKING UP WIRELESS TRANSMISSIONS AGAIN?
I didn't hear anything!
I HEARD... SOMETHING ABOUT SCARY GIRLS CROUCHING LOW...
AH, GOOD IDEA.
THIS OUTER WALL IS PRETTY HIGH. HOW ABOUT YOU CROUCH DOWN?
GYAHH!
TOO HEAVY...
NOT BOTH OF YOU TOGETHER!!
KRAK KRAK
HOLD IT RIGHT THERE, YOU!!
FOCUSED
THIS IS NO TIME FOR FOOLING AROUND!!
IF YOU DON'T TAKE THE ZUKA CLUB SERIOUSLY, YOU WILL GET HURT!!
WHAT ABOUT YOU, PAPA RANKA? WHY DID YOU COME ALONG IN THAT SILLY SHIRT?
THIS SHIRT IS AN OLD FATHER'S DAY PRESENT FROM HARUHI. SO KEEP YOUR COMMENTS TO YOURSELF.
REALLY?!
IT'S... KIND OF COOL!!
NOT THAT WE'D WEAR IT.

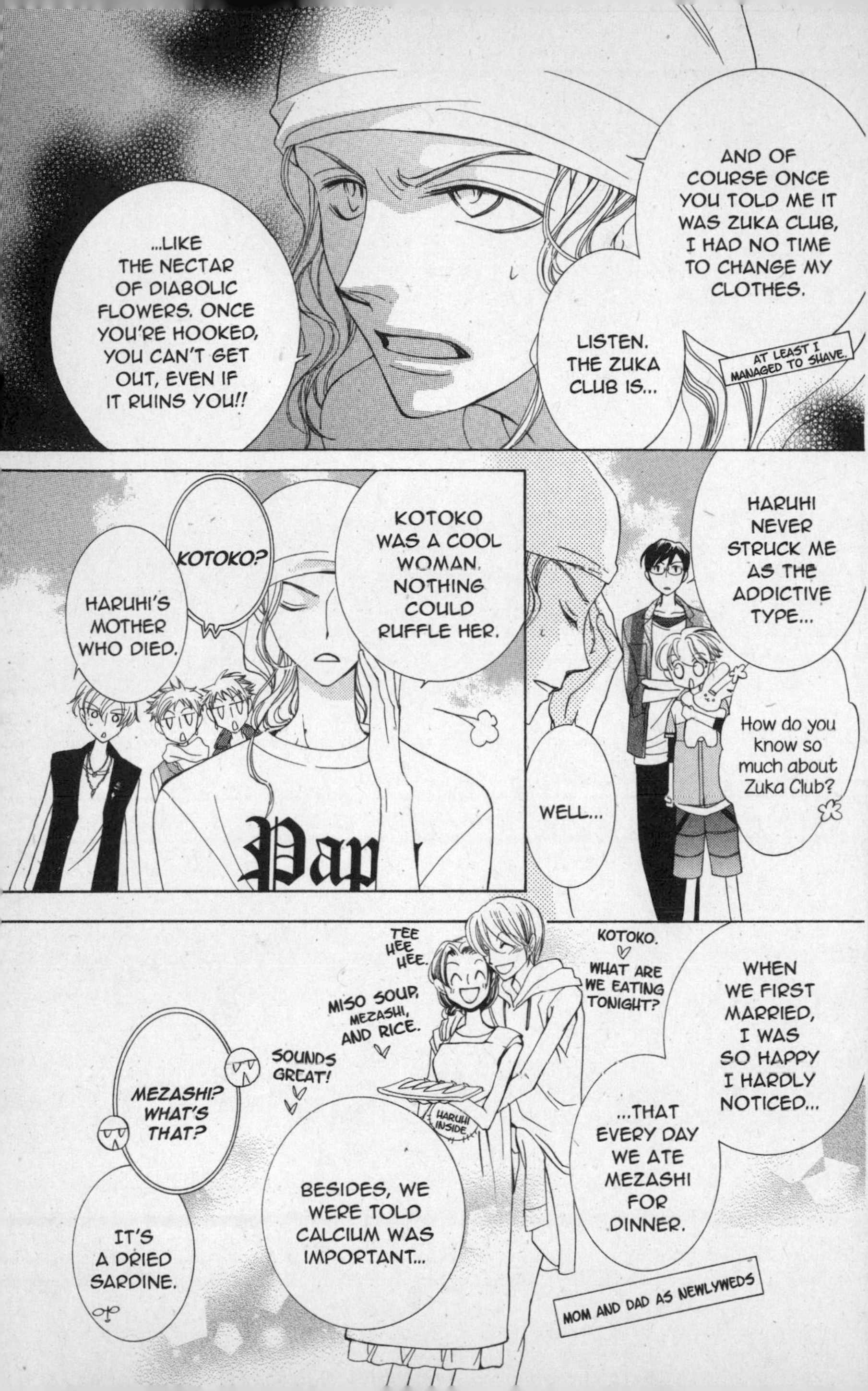
AND OF COURSE ONCE YOU TOLD ME IT WAS ZUKA CLUB, I HAD NO TIME TO CHANGE MY CLOTHES.
AT LEAST I MANAGED TO SHAVE.
LISTEN. THE ZUKA CLUB IS...
...LIKE THE NECTAR OF DIABOLIC FLOWERS. ONCE YOU'RE HOOKED, YOU CAN'T GET OUT, EVEN IF IT RUINS YOU!!
HARUHI NEVER STRUCK ME AS THE ADDICTIVE TYPE...
How do you know so much about Zuka Club?
WELL...
KOTOKO WAS A COOL WOMAN. NOTHING COULD RUFFLE HER.
KOTOKO?
HARUHI'S MOTHER WHO DIED.
Pap
WHEN WE FIRST MARRIED, I WAS SO HAPPY I HARDLY NOTICED...
...THAT EVERY DAY WE ATE MEZASHI FOR DINNER.
KOTOKO. WHAT ARE WE EATING TONIGHT?
TEE HEE HEE.
MISO SOUP, MEZASHI, AND RICE.
SOUNDS GREAT!
HARUHI INSIDE
MOM AND DAD AS NEWLYWEDS
BESIDES, WE WERE TOLD CALCIUM WAS IMPORTANT...
MEZASHI? WHAT'S THAT?
IT'S A DRIED SARDINE.

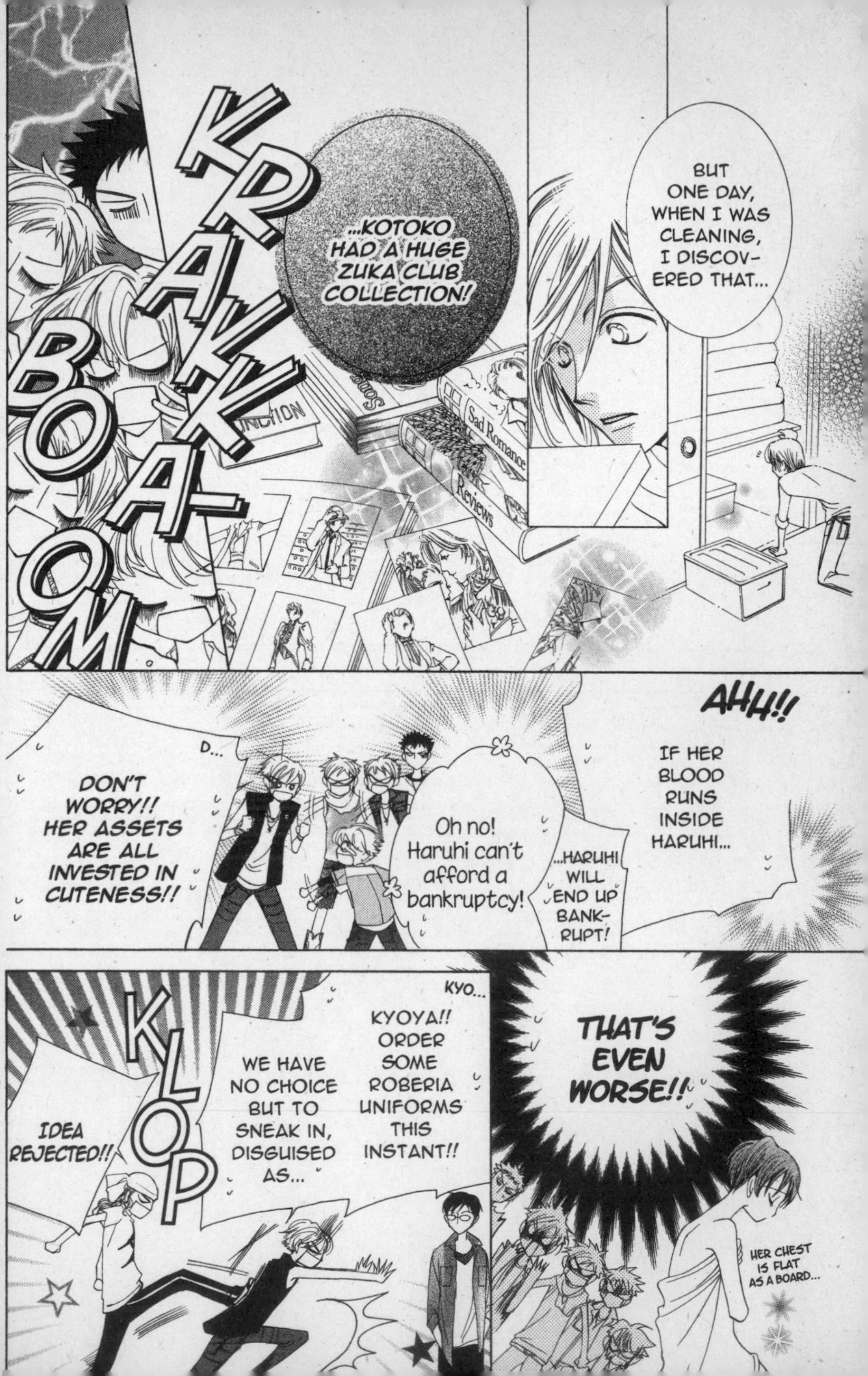
BUT ONE DAY, WHEN I WAS CLEANING, I DISCOVERED THAT...
...KOTOKO HAD A HUGE ZUKA CLUB COLLECTION!
Sad Romance
Reviews
AHH!!
IF HER BLOOD RUNS INSIDE HARUHI...
...HARUHI WILL END UP BANKRUPT!
Oh no! Haruhi can't afford a bankruptcy!
D...
DON'T WORRY!! HER ASSETS ARE ALL INVESTED IN CUTENESS!!
THAT'S EVEN WORSE!!
HER CHEST IS FLAT AS A BOARD...
KYO...
KYOYA!! ORDER SOME ROBERIA UNIFORMS THIS INSTANT!!
WE HAVE NO CHOICE BUT TO SNEAK IN, DISGUISED AS...
KLOP
IDEA REJECTED!!

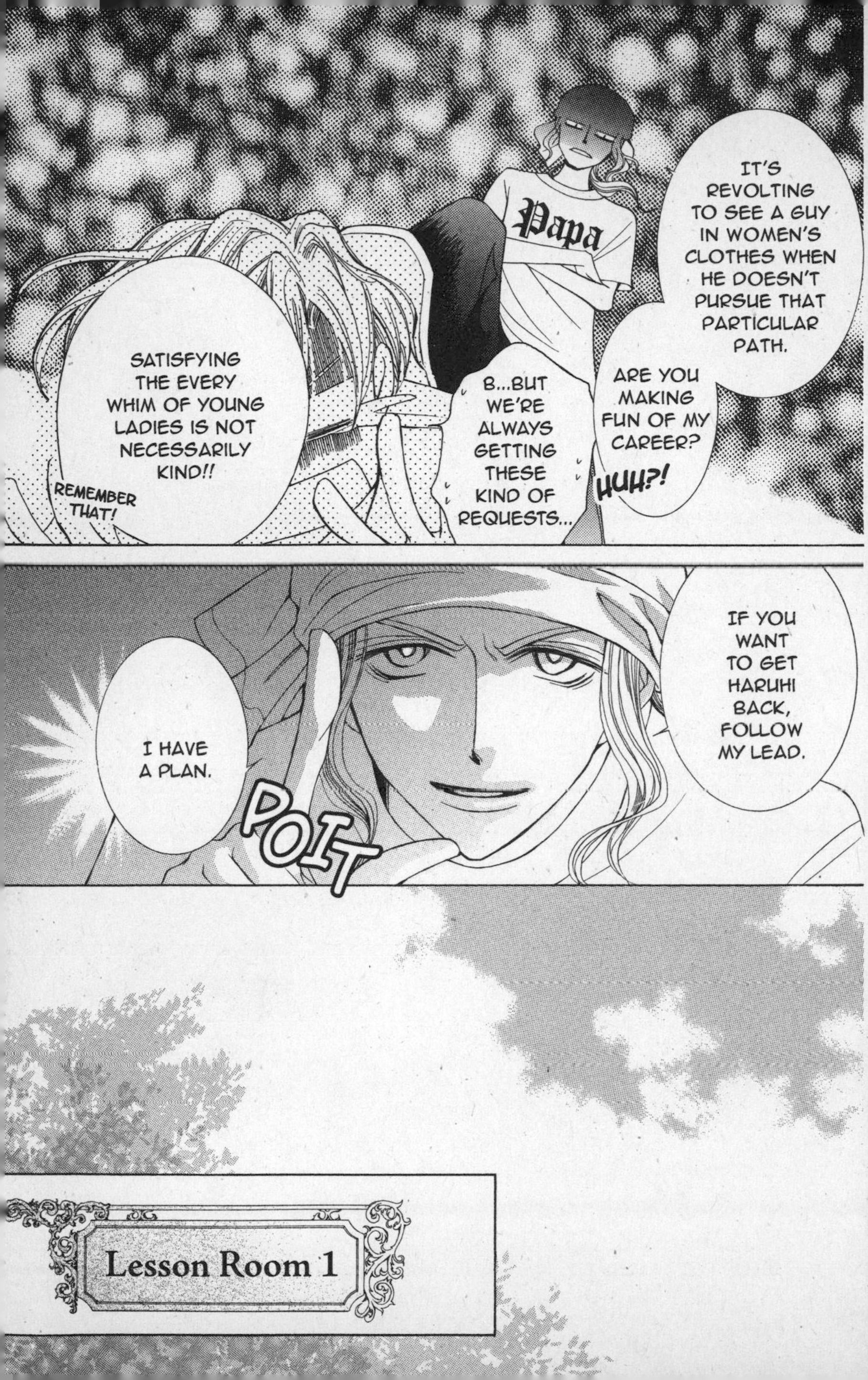
IT'S REVOLTING TO SEE A GUY IN WOMEN'S CLOTHES WHEN HE DOESN'T PURSUE THAT PARTICULAR PATH.
ARE YOU MAKING FUN OF MY CAREER?
HUH?!
B...BUT WE'RE ALWAYS GETTING THESE KIND OF REQUESTS...
SATISFYING THE EVERY WHIM OF YOUNG LADIES IS NOT NECESSARILY KIND!!
REMEMBER THAT!
IF YOU WANT TO GET HARUHI BACK, FOLLOW MY LEAD.
I HAVE A PLAN.
POIT
Lesson Room 1

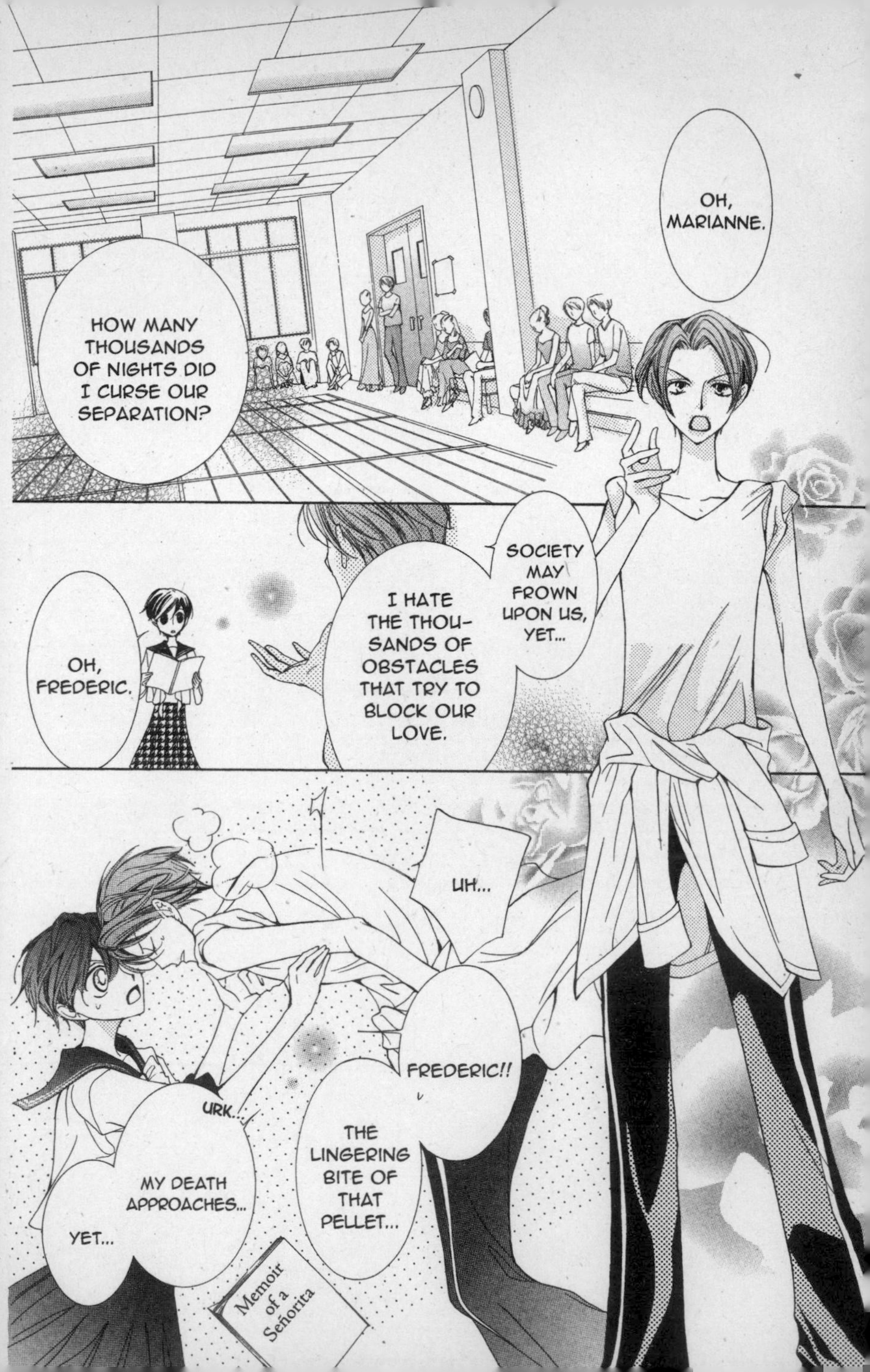
OH, MARIANNE.
HOW MANY THOUSANDS OF NIGHTS DID I CURSE OUR SEPARATION?
SOCIETY MAY FROWN UPON US, YET...
I HATE THE THOU-SANDS OF OBSTACLES THAT TRY TO BLOCK OUR LOVE.
OH, FREDERIC.
UH...
FREDERIC!!
THE LINGERING BITE OF THAT PELLET...
URK...
MY DEATH APPROACHES...
YET...
Memoir of a Señorita

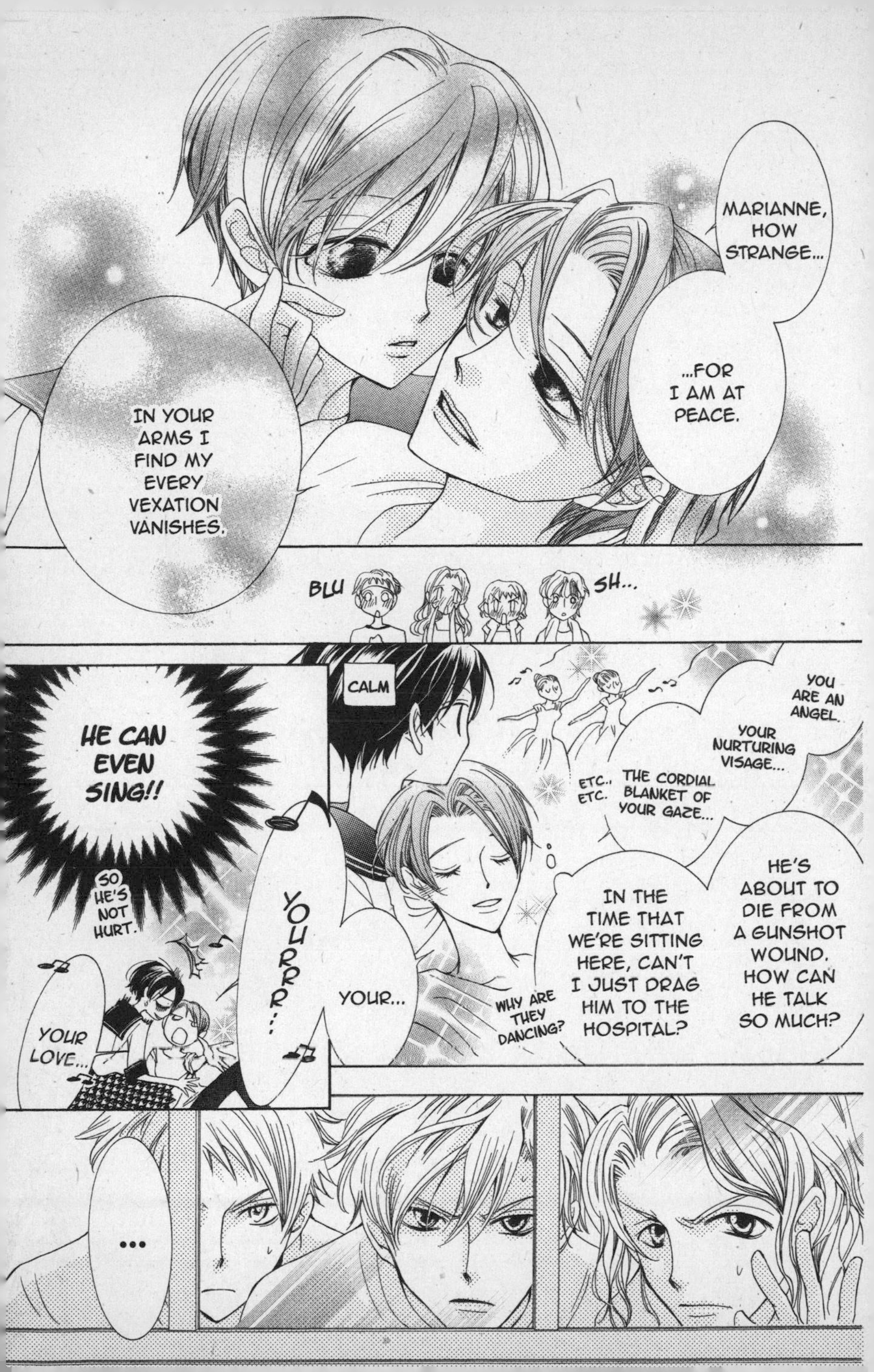
MARIANNE, HOW STRANGE...
...FOR I AM AT PEACE.
IN YOUR ARMS I FIND MY EVERY VEXATION VANISHES.
BLU SH...
YOU ARE AN ANGEL.
YOUR NURTURING VISAGE...
THE CORDIAL BLANKET OF YOUR GAZE...
ETC., ETC.
CALM
HE'S ABOUT TO DIE FROM A GUNSHOT WOUND. HOW CAN HE TALK SO MUCH?
IN THE TIME THAT WE'RE SITTING HERE, CAN'T I JUST DRAG HIM TO THE HOSPITAL?
WHY ARE THEY DANCING?
YOUR...
YOURRR...
HE CAN EVEN SING!!
SO HE'S NOT HURT.
YOUR LOVE...
...

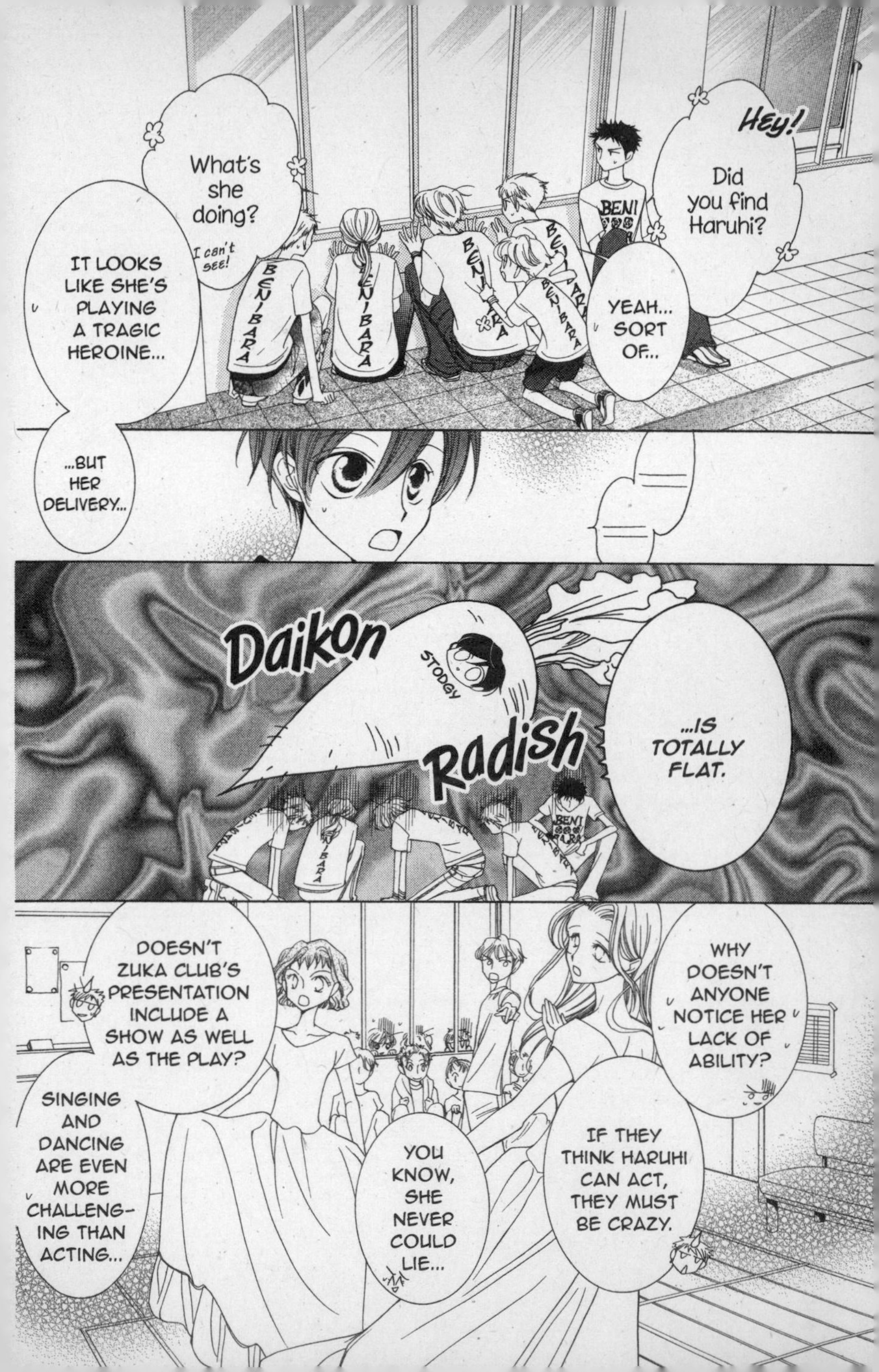
HEY!
Did you find Haruhi?
What's she doing?
I can't see!
YEAH... SORT OF...
IT LOOKS LIKE SHE'S PLAYING A TRAGIC HEROINE...
...BUT HER DELIVERY...
...IS TOTALLY FLAT.
STODGY
Daikon
Radish
WHY DOESN'T ANYONE NOTICE HER LACK OF ABILITY?
DOESN'T ZUKA CLUB'S PRESENTATION INCLUDE A SHOW AS WELL AS THE PLAY?
IF THEY THINK HARUHI CAN ACT, THEY MUST BE CRAZY.
YOU KNOW, SHE NEVER COULD LIE...
SINGING AND DANCING ARE EVEN MORE CHALLENG-ING THAN ACTING...

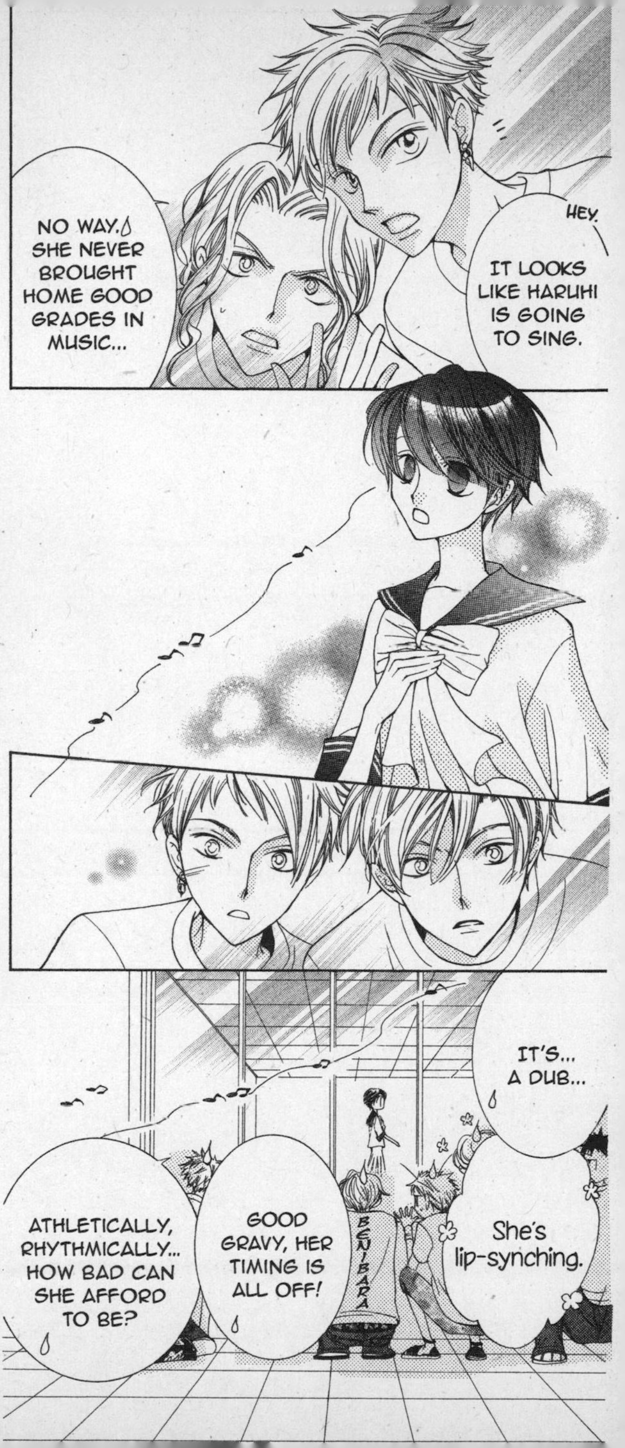
HEY.
IT LOOKS LIKE HARUHI IS GOING TO SING.
NO WAY. SHE NEVER BROUGHT HOME GOOD GRADES IN MUSIC...
IT'S... A DUB...
She's lip-synching.
BENIBARA
GOOD GRAVY, HER TIMING IS ALL OFF!
ATHLETICALLY, RHYTHMICALLY... HOW BAD CAN SHE AFFORD TO BE?

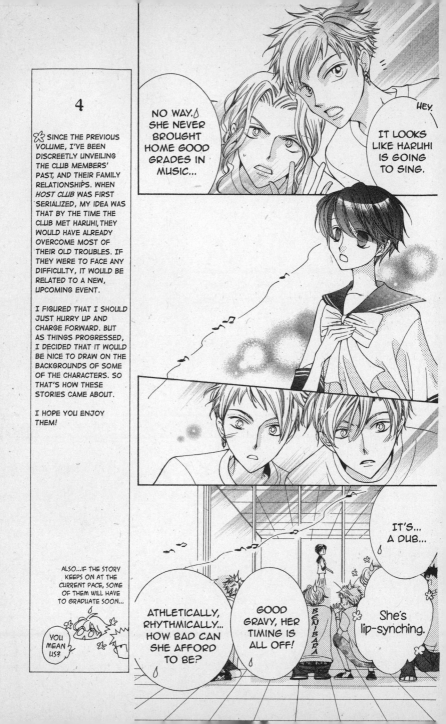

4

SINCE THE PREVIOUS VOLUME, I'VE BEEN DISCREETLY UNVEILING THE CLUB MEMBERS' PAST, AND THEIR FAMILY RELATIONSHIPS. WHEN *HOST CLUB* WAS FIRST SERIALIZED, MY IDEA WAS THAT BY THE TIME THE CLUB MET HARUHI, THEY WOULD HAVE ALREADY OVERCOME MOST OF THEIR OLD TROUBLES. IF THEY WERE TO FACE ANY DIFFICULTY, IT WOULD BE RELATED TO A NEW, UPCOMING EVENT.

I FIGURED THAT I SHOULD JUST HURRY UP AND CHARGE FORWARD. BUT AS THINGS PROGRESSED, I DECIDED THAT IT WOULD BE NICE TO DRAW ON THE BACKGROUNDS OF SOME OF THE CHARACTERS. SO THAT'S HOW THESE STORIES CAME ABOUT.

I HOPE YOU ENJOY THEM!

ALSO...IF THE STORY KEEPS ON AT THE CURRENT PACE, SOME OF THEM WILL HAVE TO GRADUATE SOON...

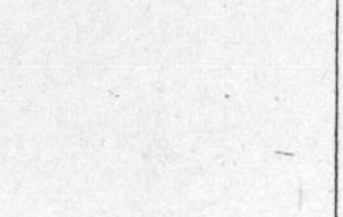
YOU MEAN US?

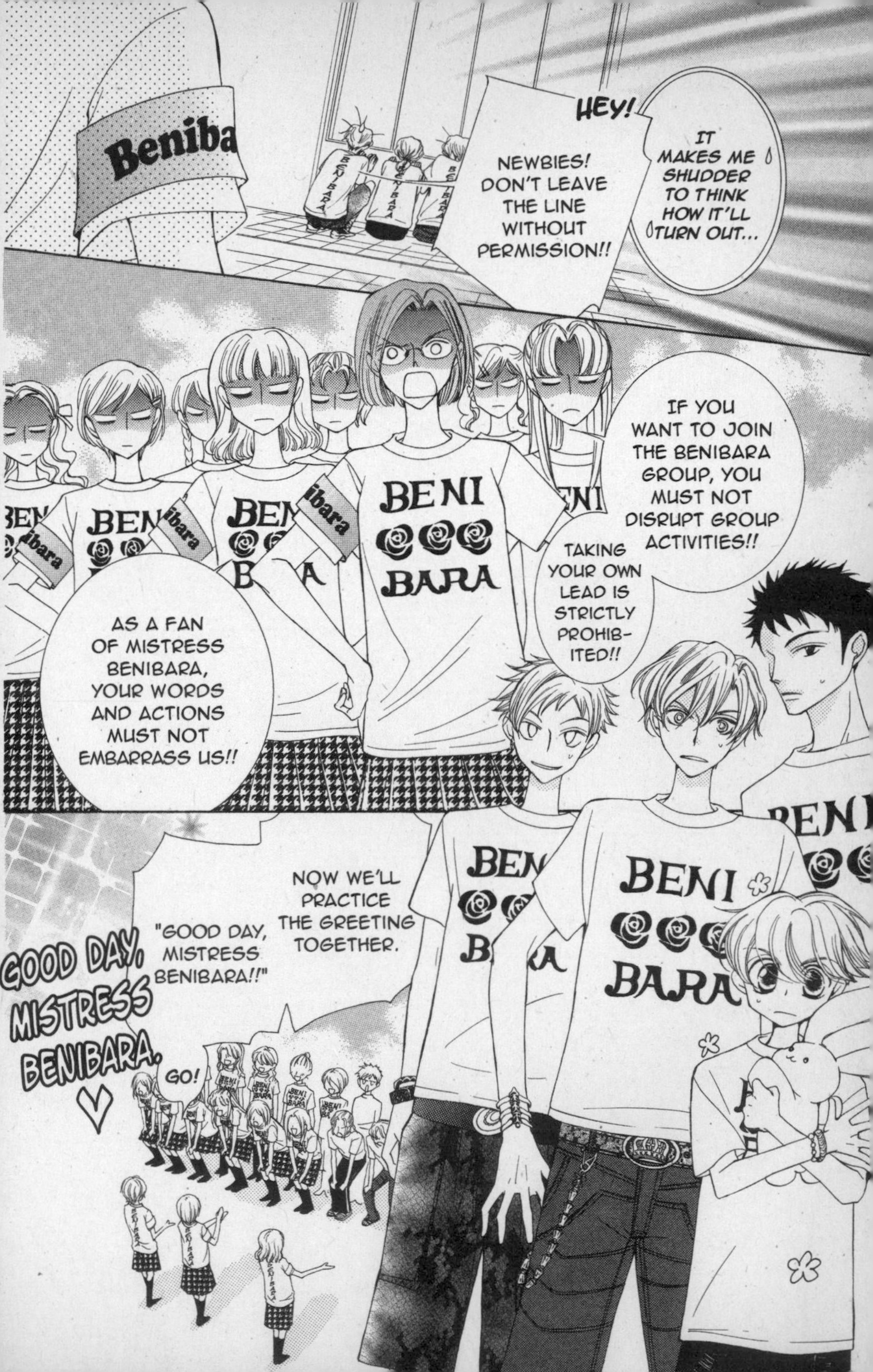
Beniba
IT MAKES ME SHUDDER TO THINK HOW IT'LL TURN OUT...
HEY! NEWBIES! DON'T LEAVE THE LINE WITHOUT PERMISSION!!
IF YOU WANT TO JOIN THE BENIBARA GROUP, YOU MUST NOT DISRUPT GROUP ACTIVITIES!!
TAKING YOUR OWN LEAD IS STRICTLY PROHIBITED!!
BENI BARA
AS A FAN OF MISTRESS BENIBARA, YOUR WORDS AND ACTIONS MUST NOT EMBARRASS US!!
NOW WE'LL PRACTICE THE GREETING TOGETHER.
"GOOD DAY, MISTRESS BENIBARA!!"
GO!
GOOD DAY, MISTRESS BENIBARA. ♥

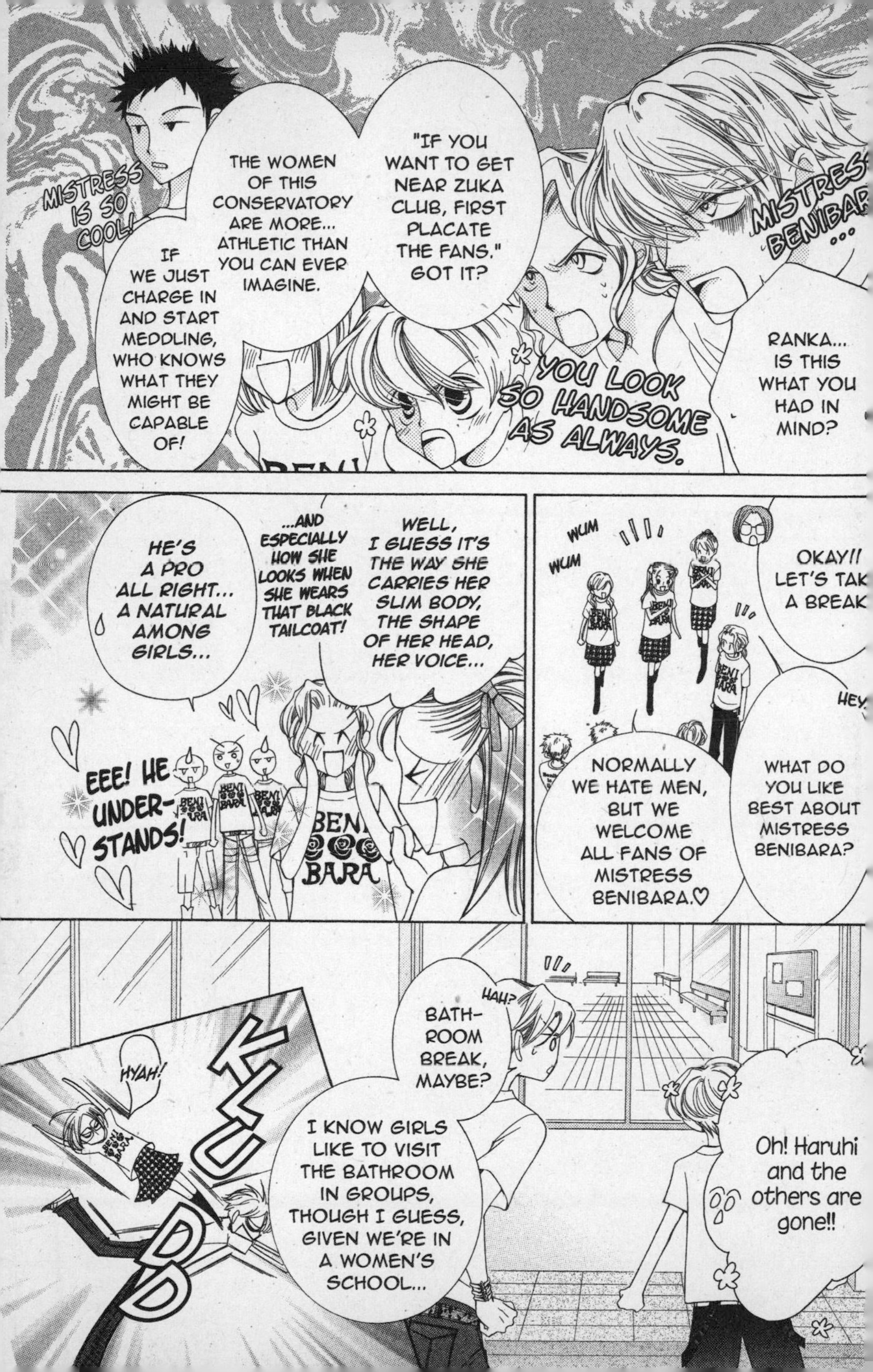
MISTRES BENIBAR...
RANKA... IS THIS WHAT YOU HAD IN MIND?
YOU LOOK SO HANDSOME AS ALWAYS.
"IF YOU WANT TO GET NEAR ZUKA CLUB, FIRST PLACATE THE FANS." GOT IT?
THE WOMEN OF THIS CONSERVATORY ARE MORE... ATHLETIC THAN YOU CAN EVER IMAGINE.
IF WE JUST CHARGE IN AND START MEDDLING, WHO KNOWS WHAT THEY MIGHT BE CAPABLE OF!
MISTRESS IS SO COOL!
OKAY!! LET'S TAK A BREAK
WUM
WUM
HEY,
WHAT DO YOU LIKE BEST ABOUT MISTRESS BENIBARA?
NORMALLY WE HATE MEN, BUT WE WELCOME ALL FANS OF MISTRESS BENIBARA.♡
WELL, I GUESS IT'S THE WAY SHE CARRIES HER SLIM BODY, THE SHAPE OF HER HEAD, HER VOICE...
...AND ESPECIALLY HOW SHE LOOKS WHEN SHE WEARS THAT BLACK TAILCOAT!
HE'S A PRO ALL RIGHT... A NATURAL AMONG GIRLS...
EEE! HE UNDER-STANDS!
Oh! Haruhi and the others are gone!!
HAH?
BATH-ROOM BREAK, MAYBE?
I KNOW GIRLS LIKE TO VISIT THE BATHROOM IN GROUPS, THOUGH I GUESS, GIVEN WE'RE IN A WOMEN'S SCHOOL...
KLUDD
HYAH!

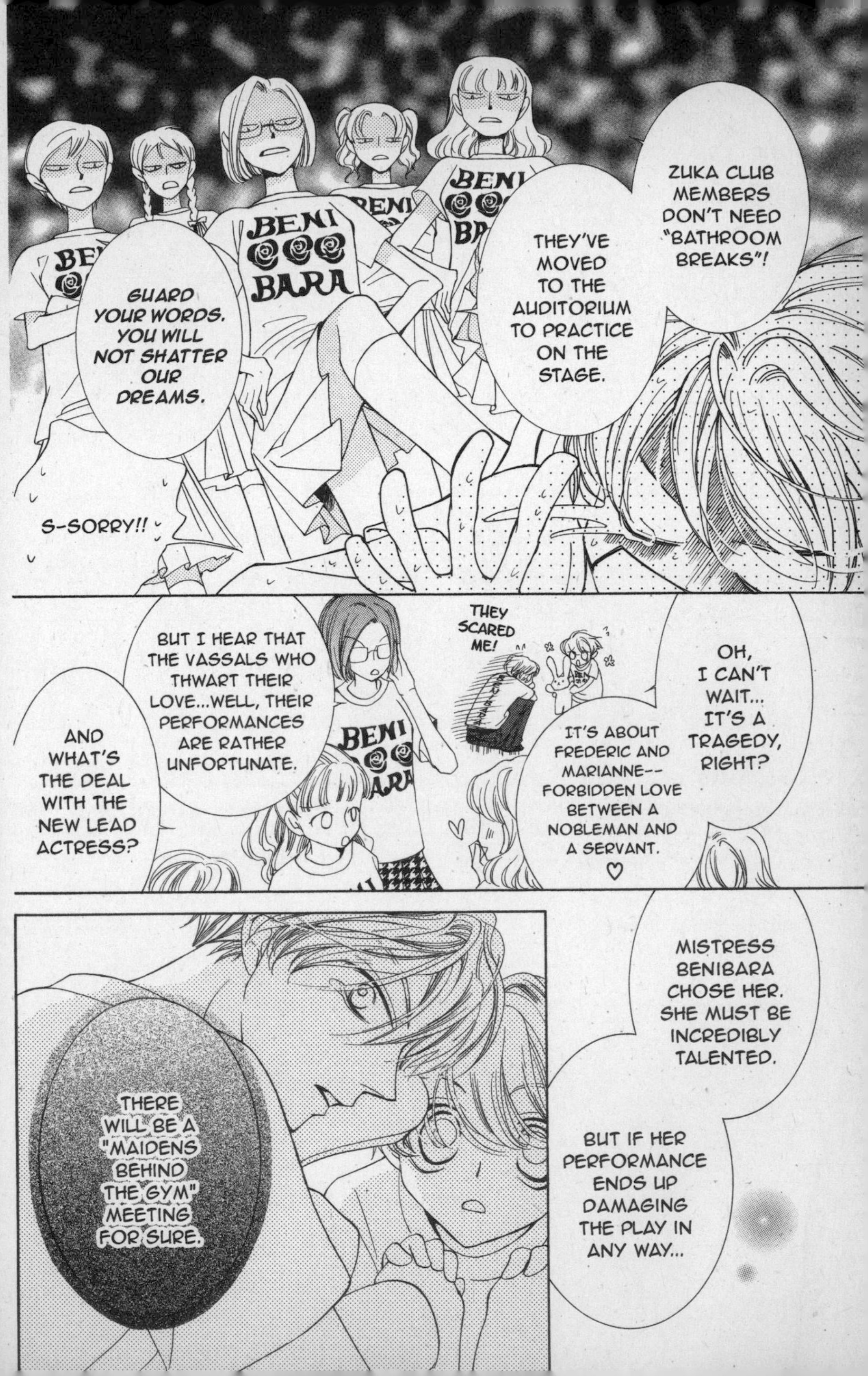
ZUKA CLUB MEMBERS DON'T NEED "BATHROOM BREAKS"!
THEY'VE MOVED TO THE AUDITORIUM TO PRACTICE ON THE STAGE.
GUARD YOUR WORDS. YOU WILL NOT SHATTER OUR DREAMS.
S-SORRY!!
OH, I CAN'T WAIT... IT'S A TRAGEDY, RIGHT?
IT'S ABOUT FREDERIC AND MARIANNE-- FORBIDDEN LOVE BETWEEN A NOBLEMAN AND A SERVANT. ♡
THEY SCARED ME!
BUT I HEAR THAT THE VASSALS WHO THWART THEIR LOVE...WELL, THEIR PERFORMANCES ARE RATHER UNFORTUNATE.
AND WHAT'S THE DEAL WITH THE NEW LEAD ACTRESS?
MISTRESS BENIBARA CHOSE HER. SHE MUST BE INCREDIBLY TALENTED.
BUT IF HER PERFORMANCE ENDS UP DAMAGING THE PLAY IN ANY WAY...
THERE WILL BE A "MAIDENS BEHIND THE GYM" MEETING FOR SURE.

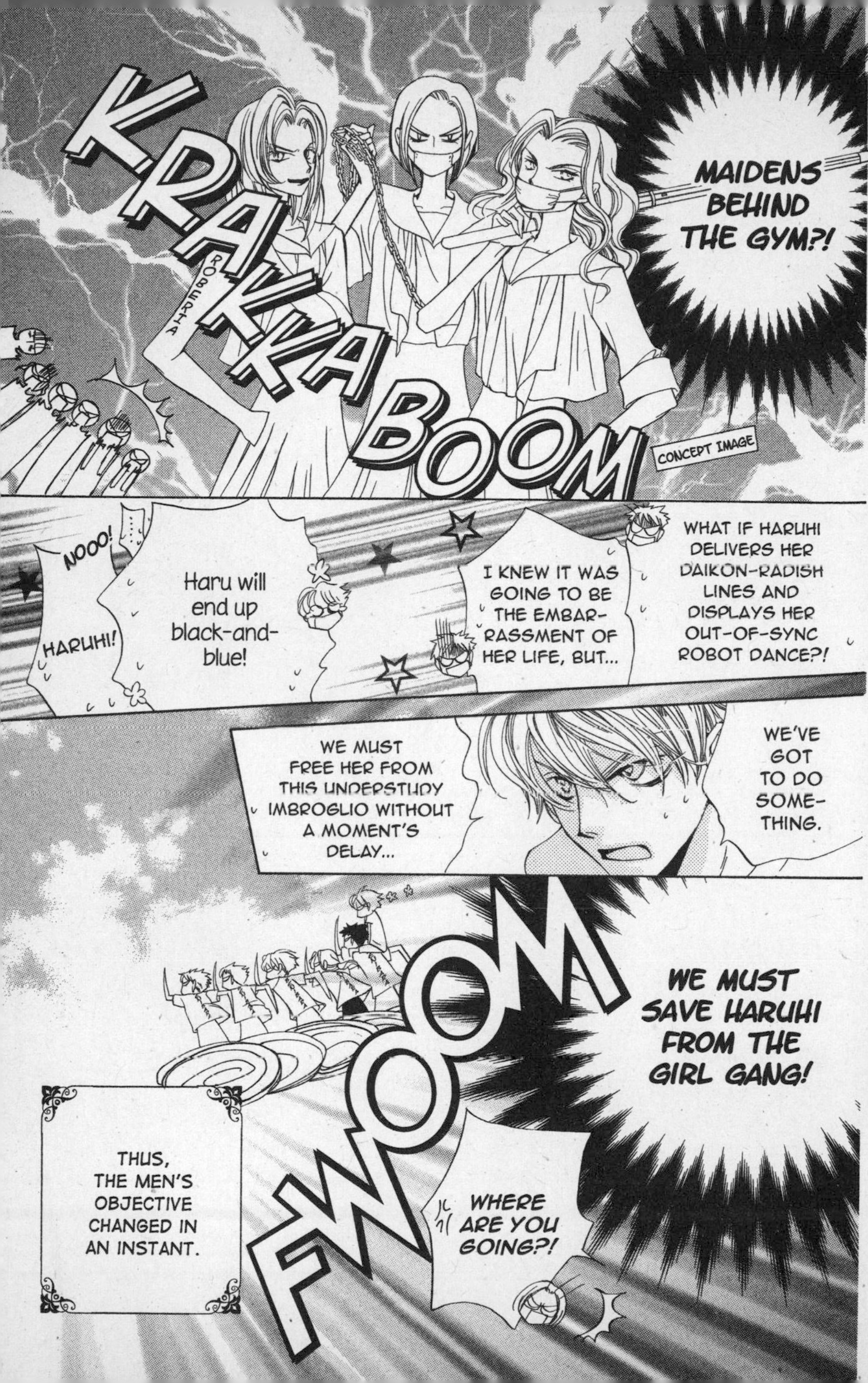
MAIDENS BEHIND THE GYM?!
KRAKKABOOM
ROBERTA
CONCEPT IMAGE
WHAT IF HARUHI DELIVERS HER DAIKON-RADISH LINES AND DISPLAYS HER OUT-OF-SYNC ROBOT DANCE?!
I KNEW IT WAS GOING TO BE THE EMBARRASSMENT OF HER LIFE, BUT...
Haru will end up black-and-blue!
NOOO!
HARUHI!
WE'VE GOT TO DO SOMETHING.
WE MUST FREE HER FROM THIS UNDERSTUDY IMBROGLIO WITHOUT A MOMENT'S DELAY...
WE MUST SAVE HARUHI FROM THE GIRL GANG!
FWOOOM
WHERE ARE YOU GOING?!
THUS, THE MEN'S OBJECTIVE CHANGED IN AN INSTANT.

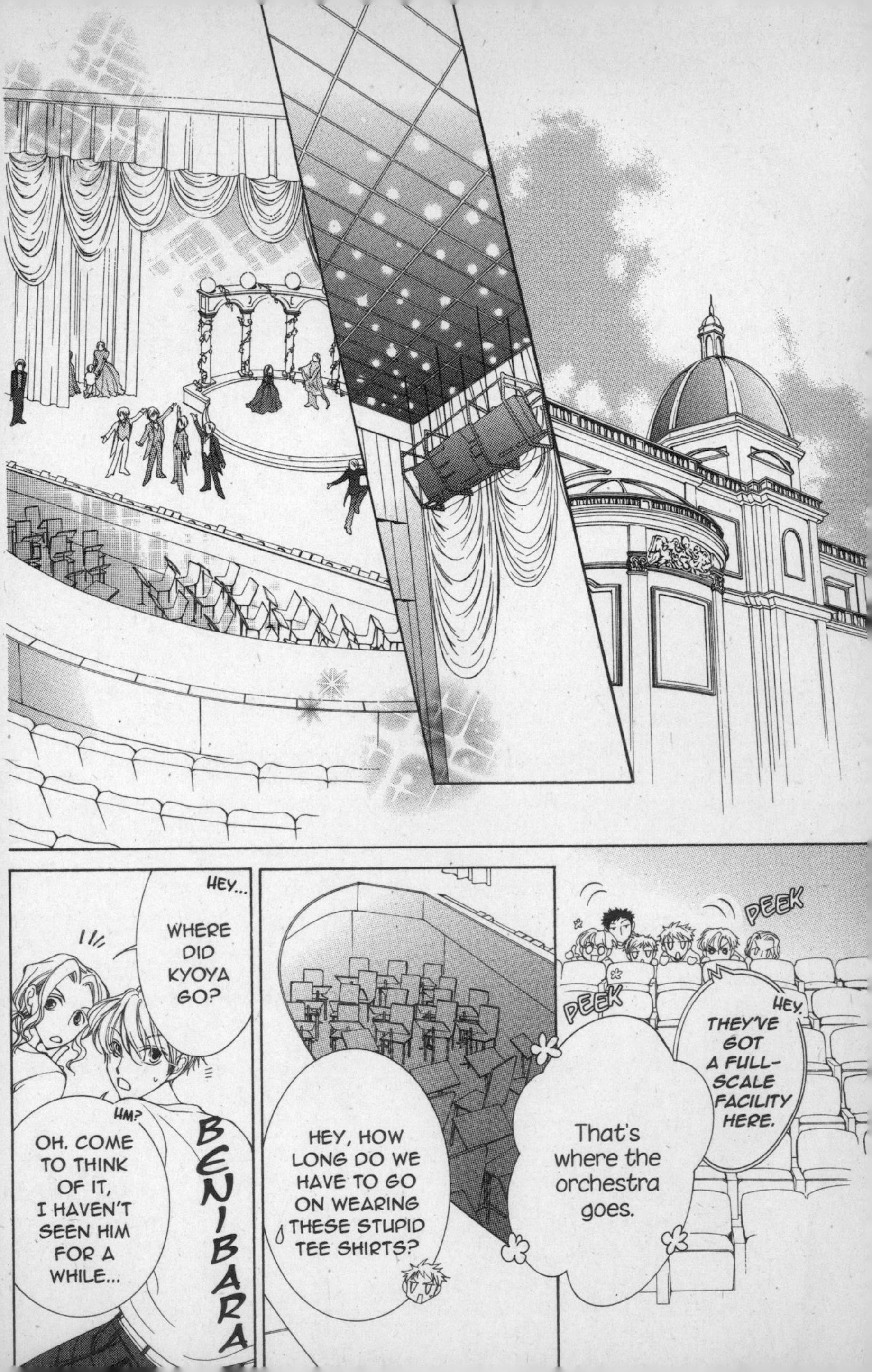
PEEK
HEY. THEY'VE GOT A FULL-SCALE FACILITY HERE.
PEEK
That's where the orchestra goes.
HEY, HOW LONG DO WE HAVE TO GO ON WEARING THESE STUPID TEE SHIRTS?
HEY... WHERE DID KYOYA GO?
HM? OH. COME TO THINK OF IT, I HAVEN'T SEEN HIM FOR A WHILE...
BENIBARA

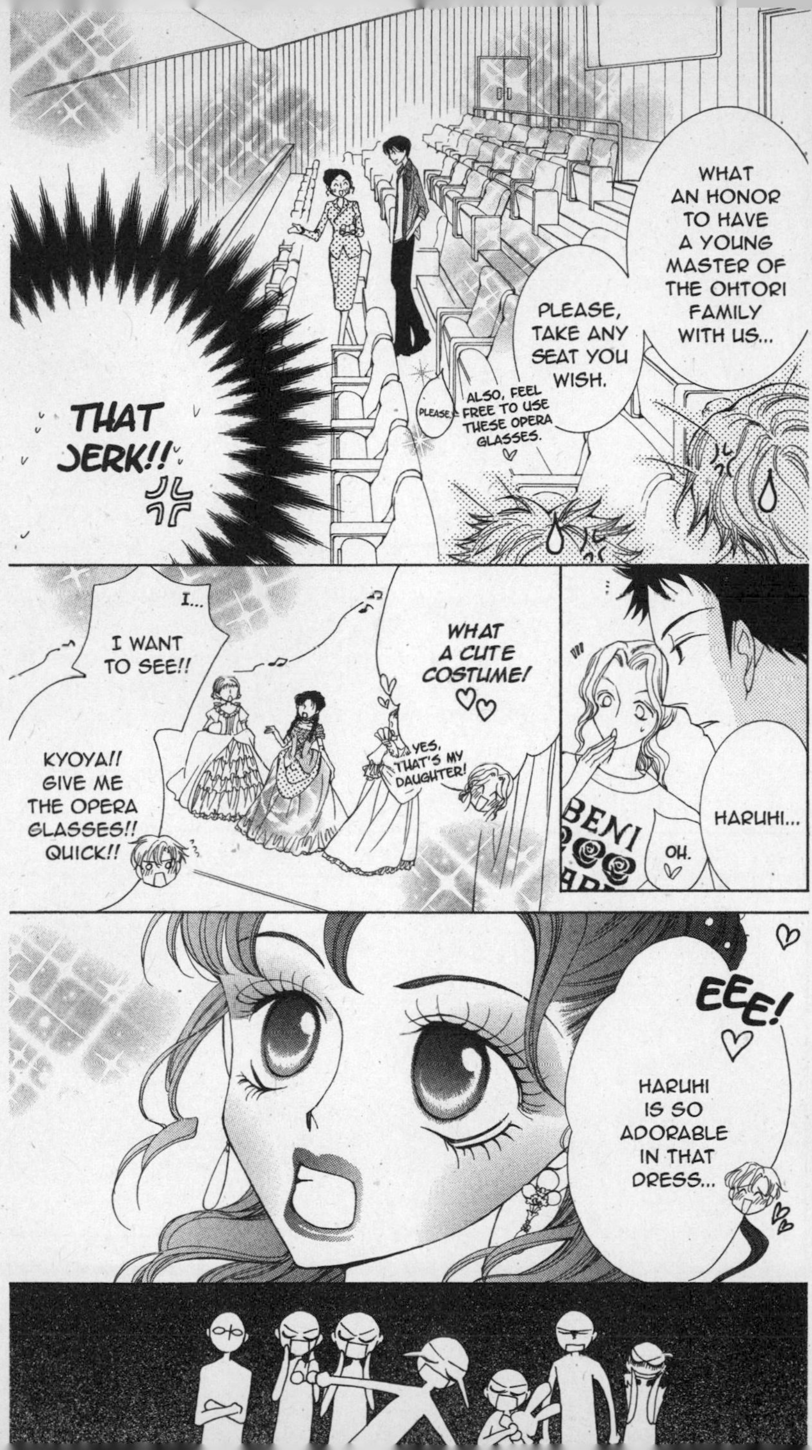
WHAT AN HONOR TO HAVE A YOUNG MASTER OF THE OHTORI FAMILY WITH US...
PLEASE, TAKE ANY SEAT YOU WISH.
PLEASE.
ALSO, FEEL FREE TO USE THESE OPERA GLASSES.
THAT JERK!!
HARUHI...
OH.
WHAT A CUTE COSTUME!
YES, THAT'S MY DAUGHTER!
I...
I WANT TO SEE!!
KYOYA!! GIVE ME THE OPERA GLASSES!! QUICK!!
EEE!
HARUHI IS SO ADORABLE IN THAT DRESS...
BENI

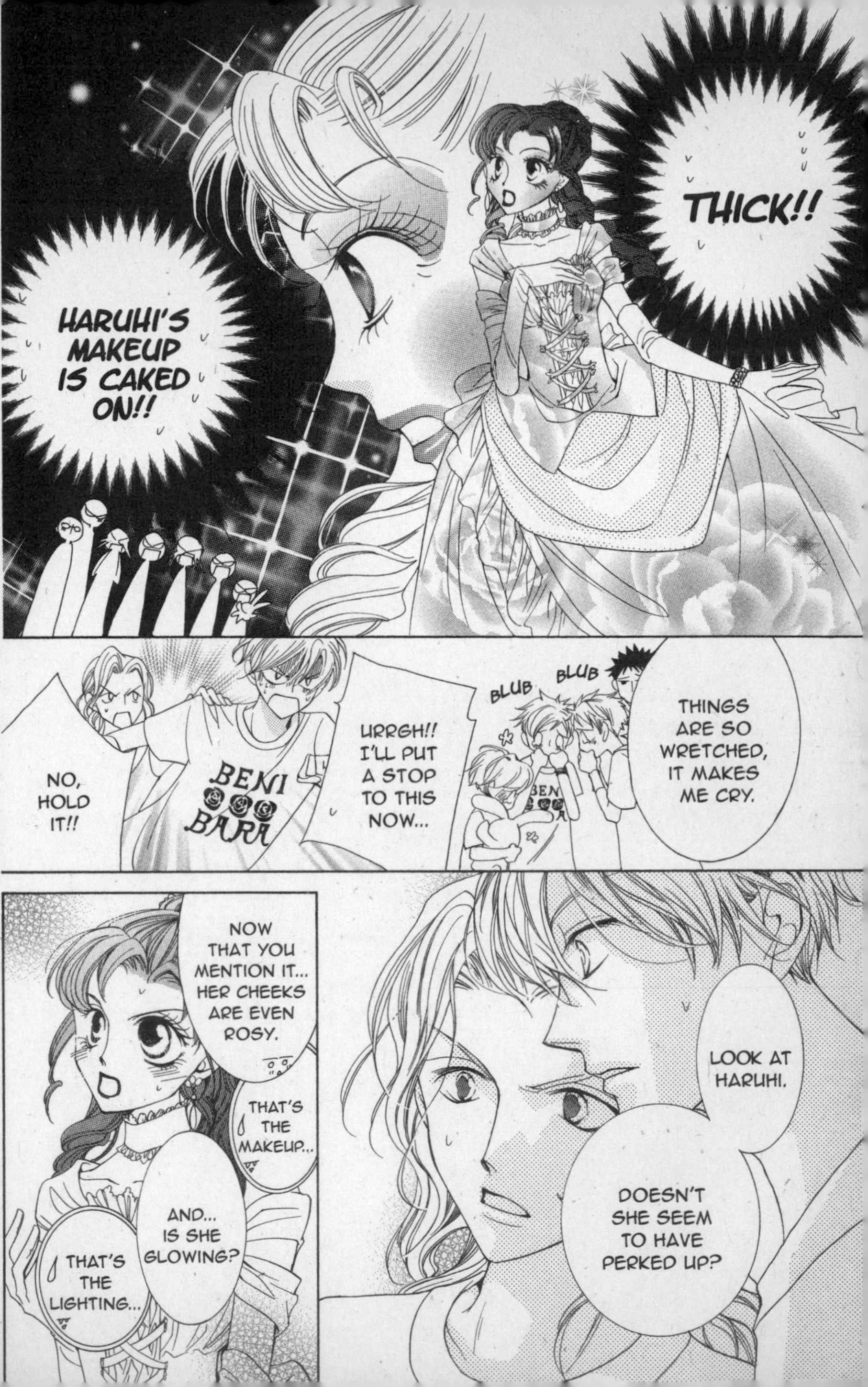
THICK!!
HARUHI'S MAKEUP IS CAKED ON!!
BLUB
BLUB
THINGS ARE SO WRETCHED, IT MAKES ME CRY.
URRGH!! I'LL PUT A STOP TO THIS NOW...
BENI BARA
NO, HOLD IT!!
LOOK AT HARUHI.
DOESN'T SHE SEEM TO HAVE PERKED UP?
NOW THAT YOU MENTION IT... HER CHEEKS ARE EVEN ROSY.
THAT'S THE MAKEUP...
AND... IS SHE GLOWING?
THAT'S THE LIGHTING...

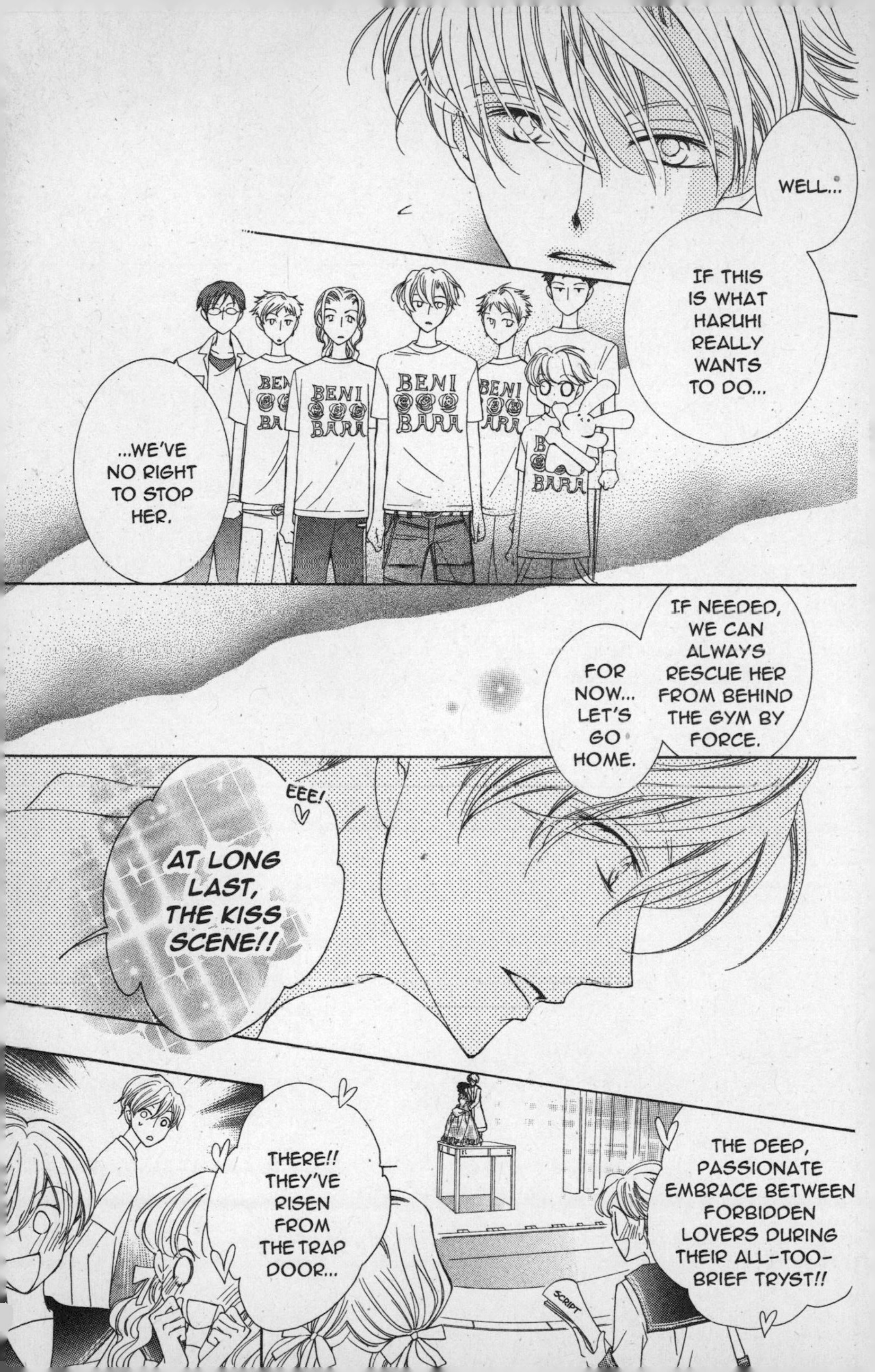
WELL...
IF THIS IS WHAT HARUHI REALLY WANTS TO DO...
...WE'VE NO RIGHT TO STOP HER.
IF NEEDED, WE CAN ALWAYS RESCUE HER FROM BEHIND THE GYM BY FORCE.
FOR NOW... LET'S GO HOME.
EEE!
AT LONG LAST, THE KISS SCENE!!
THE DEEP, PASSIONATE EMBRACE BETWEEN FORBIDDEN LOVERS DURING THEIR ALL-TOO-BRIEF TRYST!!
SCRIPT
THERE!! THEY'VE RISEN FROM THE TRAP DOOR...

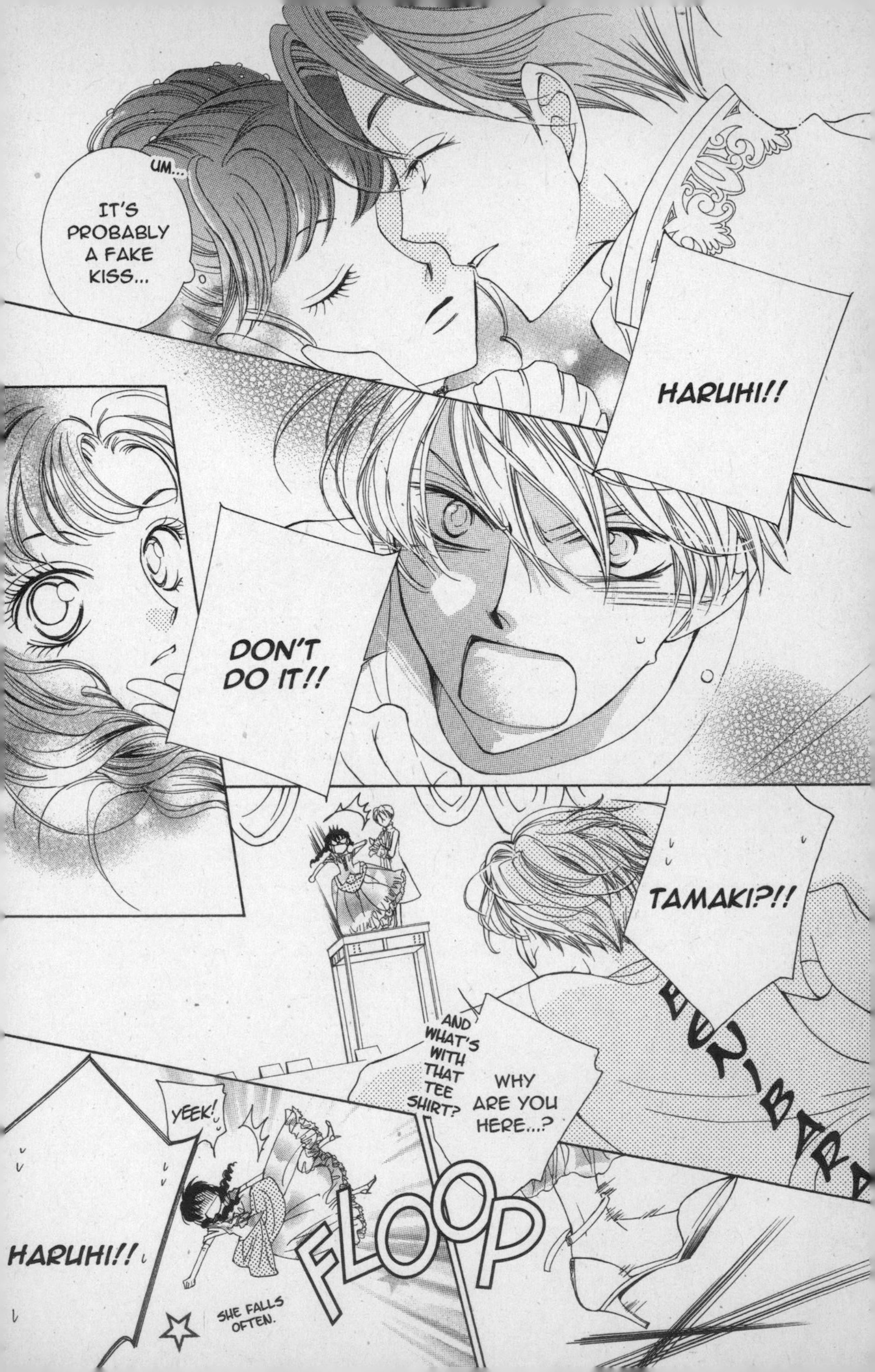
UM...
IT'S PROBABLY A FAKE KISS...
HARUHI!!
DON'T DO IT!!
TAMAKI?!!
WHY ARE YOU HERE...?
AND WHAT'S WITH THAT TEE SHIRT?
YEEK!
FLOOP
HARUHI!!
SHE FALLS OFTEN.

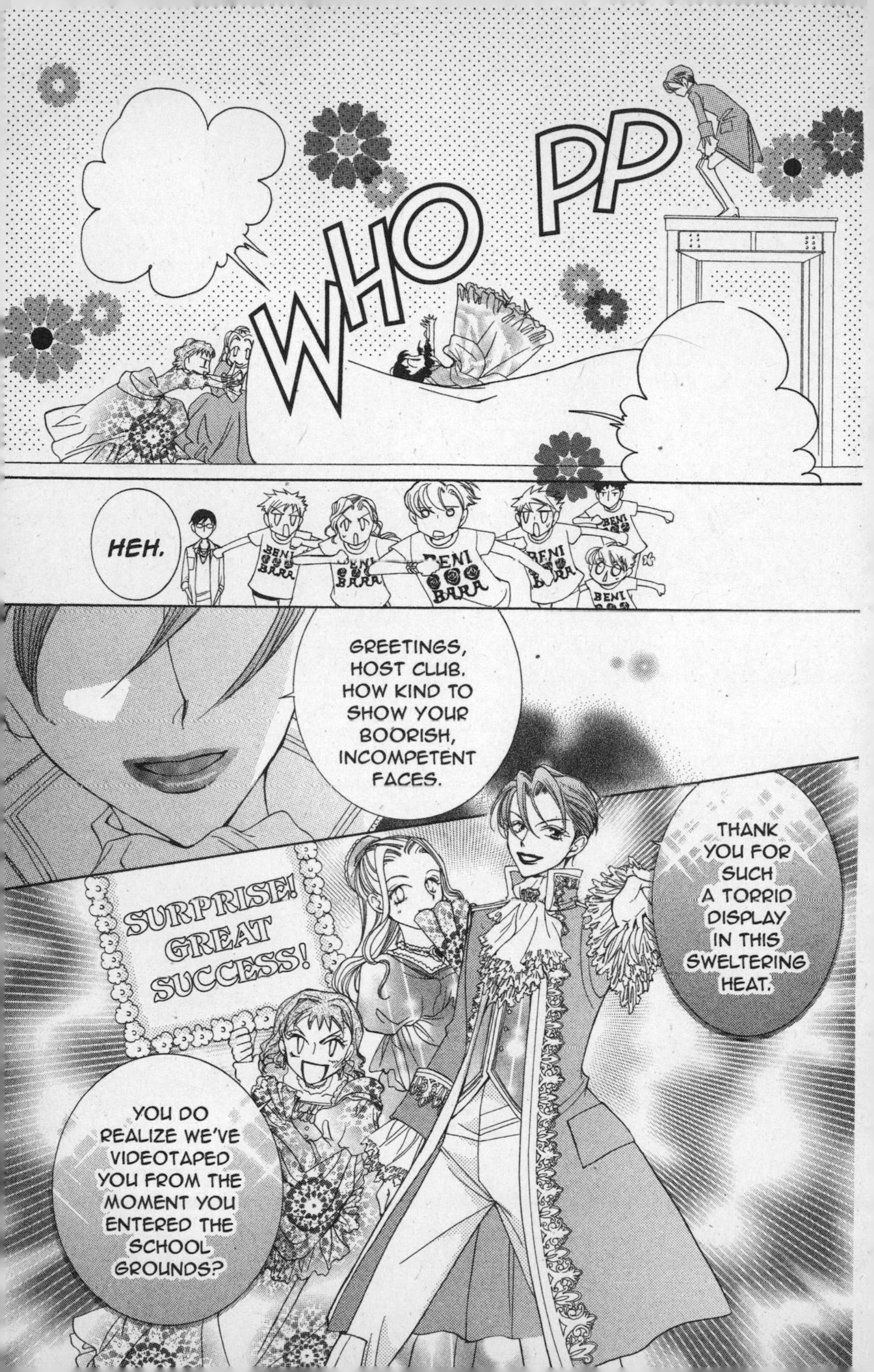
WHOOPP
HEH.
GREETINGS, HOST CLUB. HOW KIND TO SHOW YOUR BOORISH, INCOMPETENT FACES.
THANK YOU FOR SUCH A TORRID DISPLAY IN THIS SWELTERING HEAT.
SURPRISE! GREAT SUCCESS!
BENI BARA
YOU DO REALIZE WE'VE VIDEOTAPED YOU FROM THE MOMENT YOU ENTERED THE SCHOOL GROUNDS?

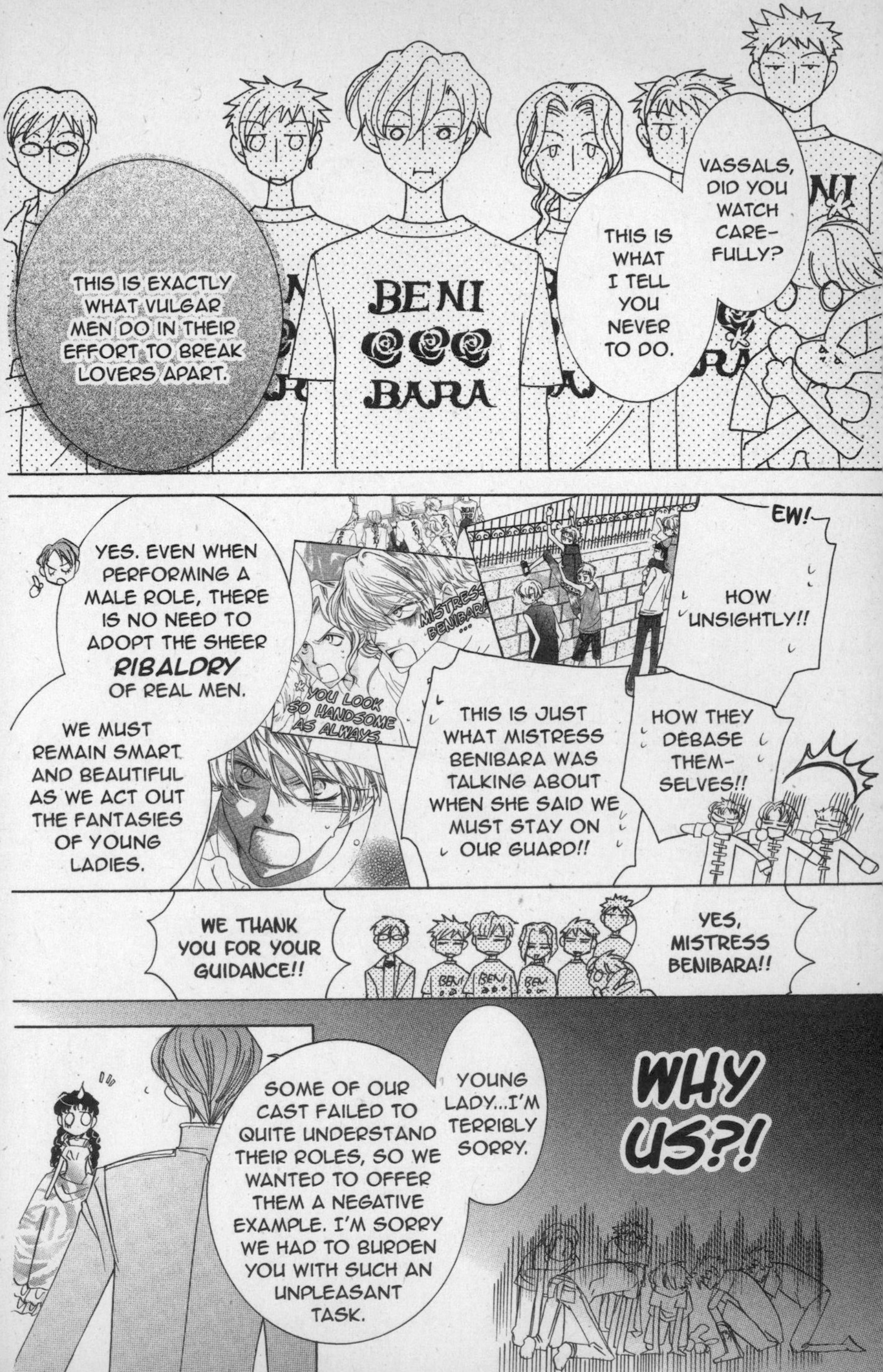
VASSALS, DID YOU WATCH CAREFULLY?
THIS IS WHAT I TELL YOU NEVER TO DO.
BENI BARA
THIS IS EXACTLY WHAT VULGAR MEN DO IN THEIR EFFORT TO BREAK LOVERS APART.
EW!
HOW UNSIGHTLY!!
HOW THEY DEBASE THEMSELVES!!
THIS IS JUST WHAT MISTRESS BENIBARA WAS TALKING ABOUT WHEN SHE SAID WE MUST STAY ON OUR GUARD!!
MISTRESS BENIBARA...
YOU LOOK SO HANDSOME AS ALWAYS.
YES. EVEN WHEN PERFORMING A MALE ROLE, THERE IS NO NEED TO ADOPT THE SHEER RIBALDRY OF REAL MEN.
WE MUST REMAIN SMART AND BEAUTIFUL AS WE ACT OUT THE FANTASIES OF YOUNG LADIES.
YES, MISTRESS BENIBARA!!
WE THANK YOU FOR YOUR GUIDANCE!!
WHY US?!
YOUNG LADY...I'M TERRIBLY SORRY.
SOME OF OUR CAST FAILED TO QUITE UNDERSTAND THEIR ROLES, SO WE WANTED TO OFFER THEM A NEGATIVE EXAMPLE. I'M SORRY WE HAD TO BURDEN YOU WITH SUCH AN UNPLEASANT TASK.

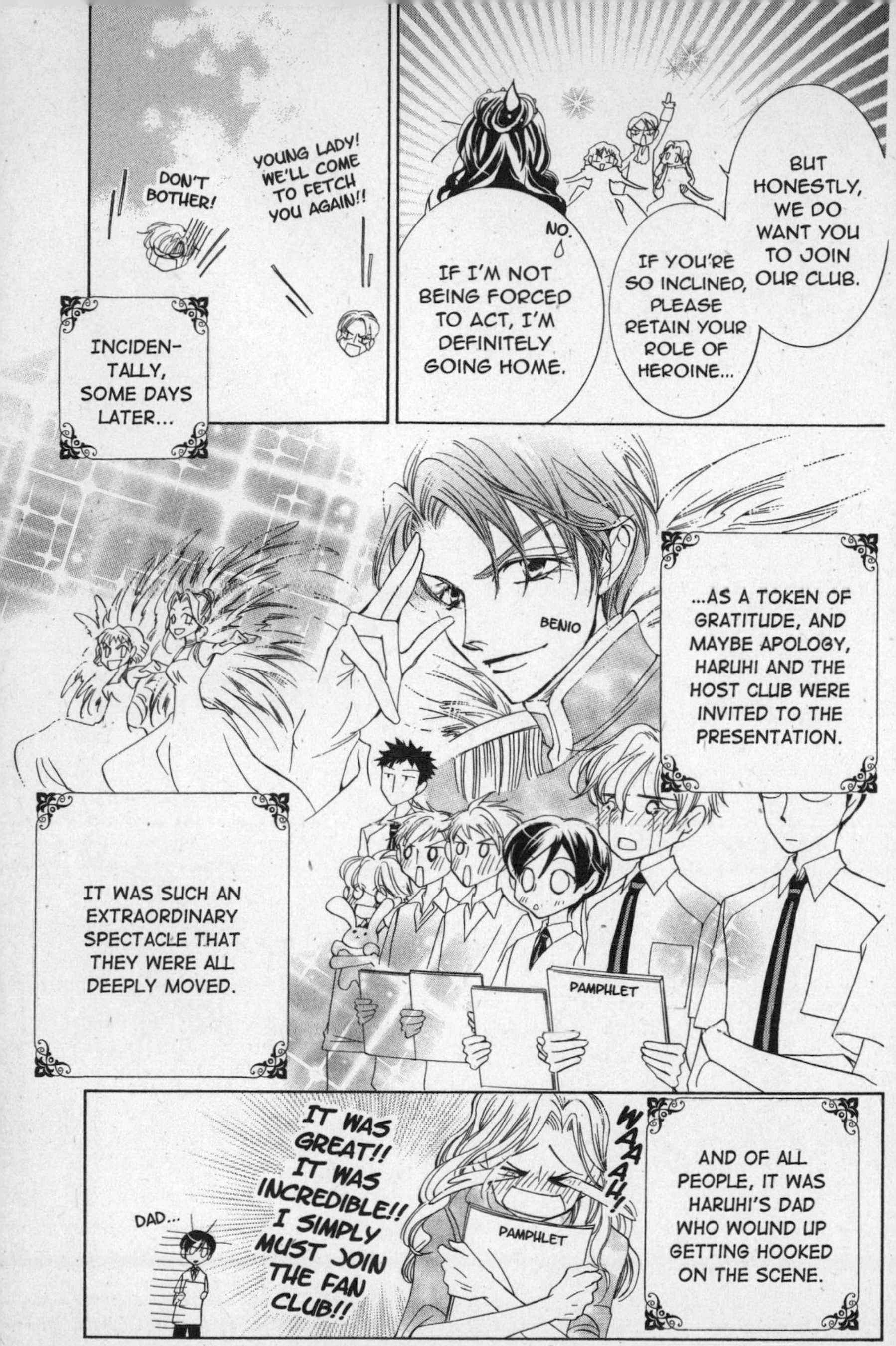
BUT HONESTLY, WE DO WANT YOU TO JOIN OUR CLUB.
IF YOU'RE SO INCLINED, PLEASE RETAIN YOUR ROLE OF HEROINE...
NO.
IF I'M NOT BEING FORCED TO ACT, I'M DEFINITELY GOING HOME.
YOUNG LADY! WE'LL COME TO FETCH YOU AGAIN!!
DON'T BOTHER!
INCIDEN-TALLY, SOME DAYS LATER...
...AS A TOKEN OF GRATITUDE, AND MAYBE APOLOGY, HARUHI AND THE HOST CLUB WERE INVITED TO THE PRESENTATION.
BENIO
PAMPHLET
IT WAS SUCH AN EXTRAORDINARY SPECTACLE THAT THEY WERE ALL DEEPLY MOVED.
AND OF ALL PEOPLE, IT WAS HARUHI'S DAD WHO WOUND UP GETTING HOOKED ON THE SCENE.
WAAAH!
PAMPHLET
IT WAS GREAT!! IT WAS INCREDIBLE!! I SIMPLY MUST JOIN THE FAN CLUB!!
DAD...

OURAN HIGH SCHOOL HOST CLUB, VOL. 7/THE END

TAKE US TO THE AMUSEMENT PARK, STUPID KING!

THIS IS AN IMAGE SHOWING HOW BOTH SHIRO AND KIRIMI VISIT THE HOST CLUB EVERY NOW AND THEN.

THOUGH KIRIMI INSISTS TAMAKI ISN'T HER REAL BROTHER, SHE STILL REFERS TO HIM AS HER "DEAR BROTHER TAMAKI." I THINK.

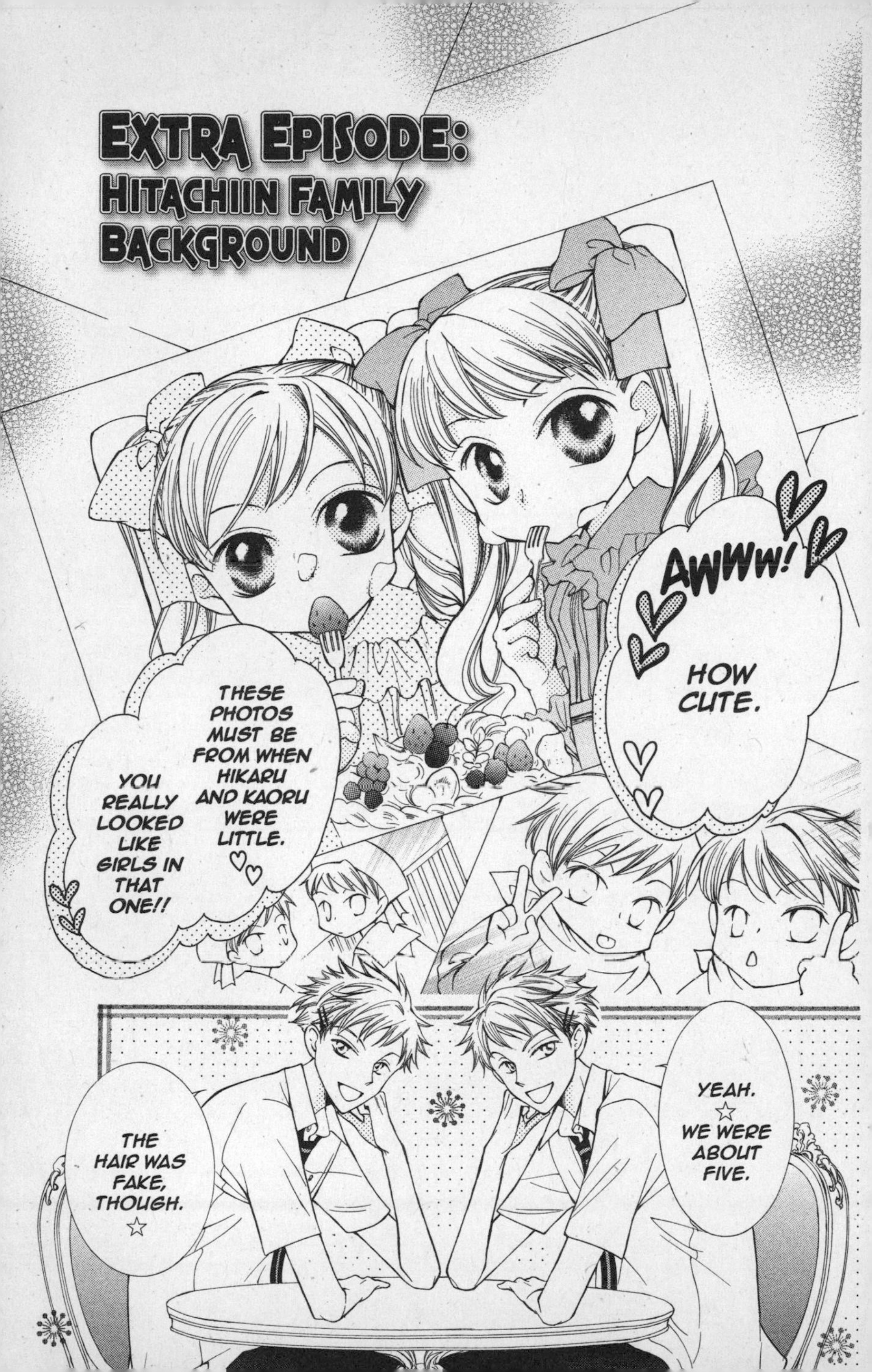
EXTRA EPISODE: HITACHIIN FAMILY BACKGROUND
AWWW! HOW CUTE.
THESE PHOTOS MUST BE FROM WHEN HIKARU AND KAORU WERE LITTLE.
YOU REALLY LOOKED LIKE GIRLS IN THAT ONE!!
YEAH. ☆ WE WERE ABOUT FIVE.
THE HAIR WAS FAKE, THOUGH. ☆

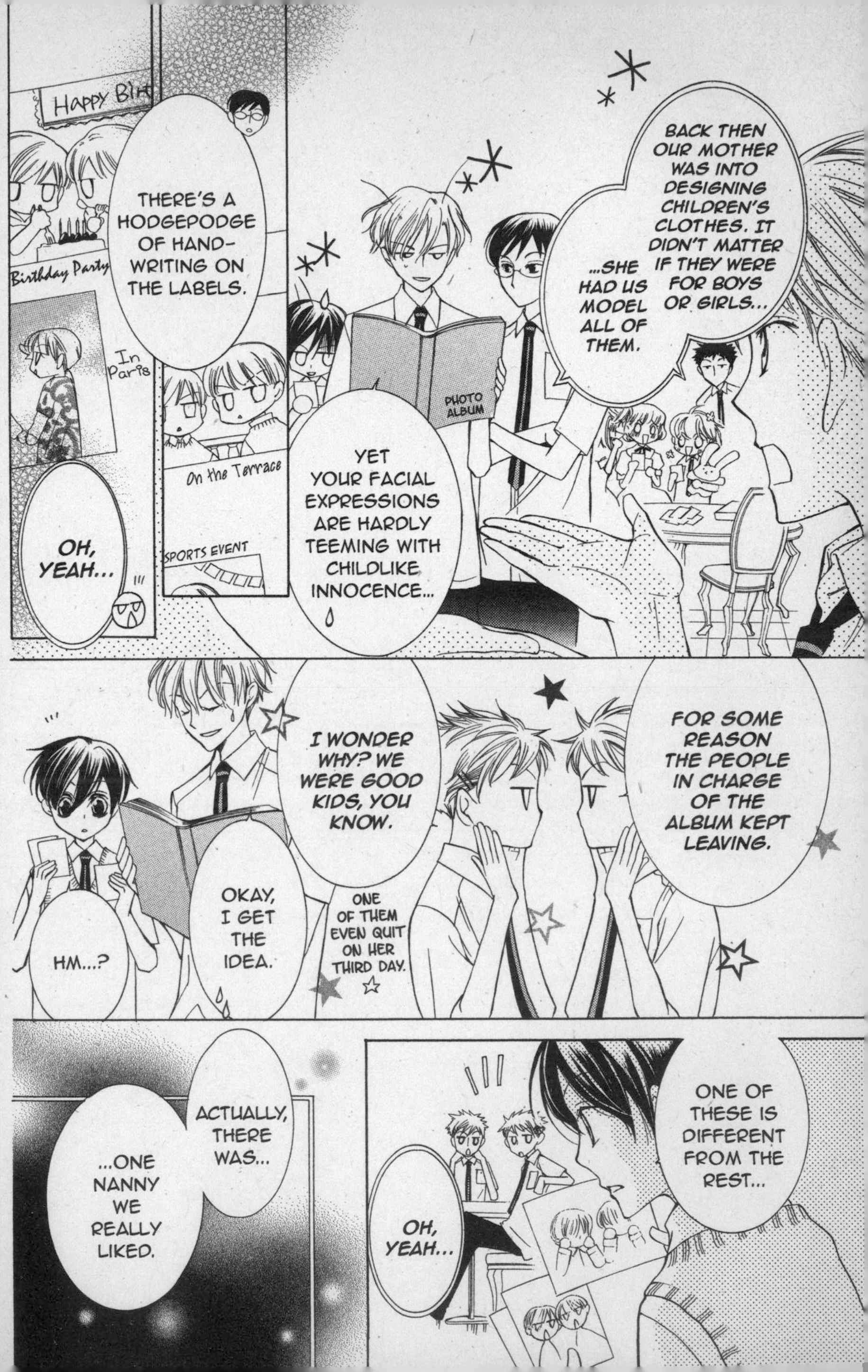
BACK THEN OUR MOTHER WAS INTO DESIGNING CHILDREN'S CLOTHES. IT DIDN'T MATTER IF THEY WERE FOR BOYS OR GIRLS...
...SHE HAD US MODEL ALL OF THEM.
PHOTO ALBUM
YET YOUR FACIAL EXPRESSIONS ARE HARDLY TEEMING WITH CHILDLIKE INNOCENCE...
Happy Birt
THERE'S A HODGEPODGE OF HAND-WRITING ON THE LABELS.
Birthday Party
In Paris
On the Terrace
SPORTS EVENT
OH, YEAH...
FOR SOME REASON THE PEOPLE IN CHARGE OF THE ALBUM KEPT LEAVING.
I WONDER WHY? WE WERE GOOD KIDS, YOU KNOW.
ONE OF THEM EVEN QUIT ON HER THIRD DAY.
OKAY, I GET THE IDEA.
HM...?
ONE OF THESE IS DIFFERENT FROM THE REST...
OH, YEAH...
ACTUALLY, THERE WAS...
...ONE NANNY WE REALLY LIKED.

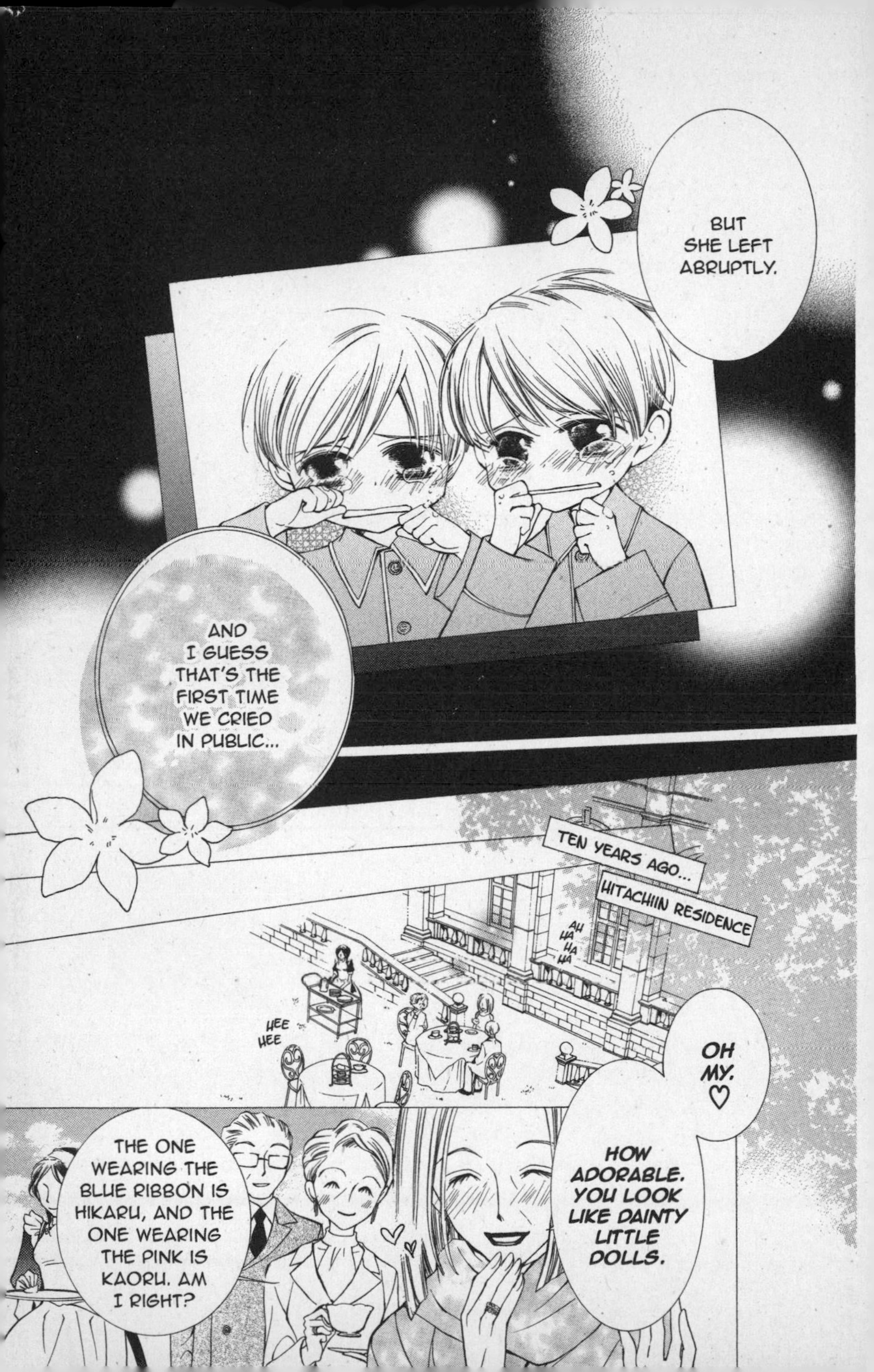
BUT SHE LEFT ABRUPTLY.
AND I GUESS THAT'S THE FIRST TIME WE CRIED IN PUBLIC...
TEN YEARS AGO...
HITACHIIN RESIDENCE
AH HA HA HA
HEE HEE
OH MY. ♡
HOW ADORABLE. YOU LOOK LIKE DAINTY LITTLE DOLLS.
THE ONE WEARING THE BLUE RIBBON IS HIKARU, AND THE ONE WEARING THE PINK IS KAORU. AM I RIGHT?

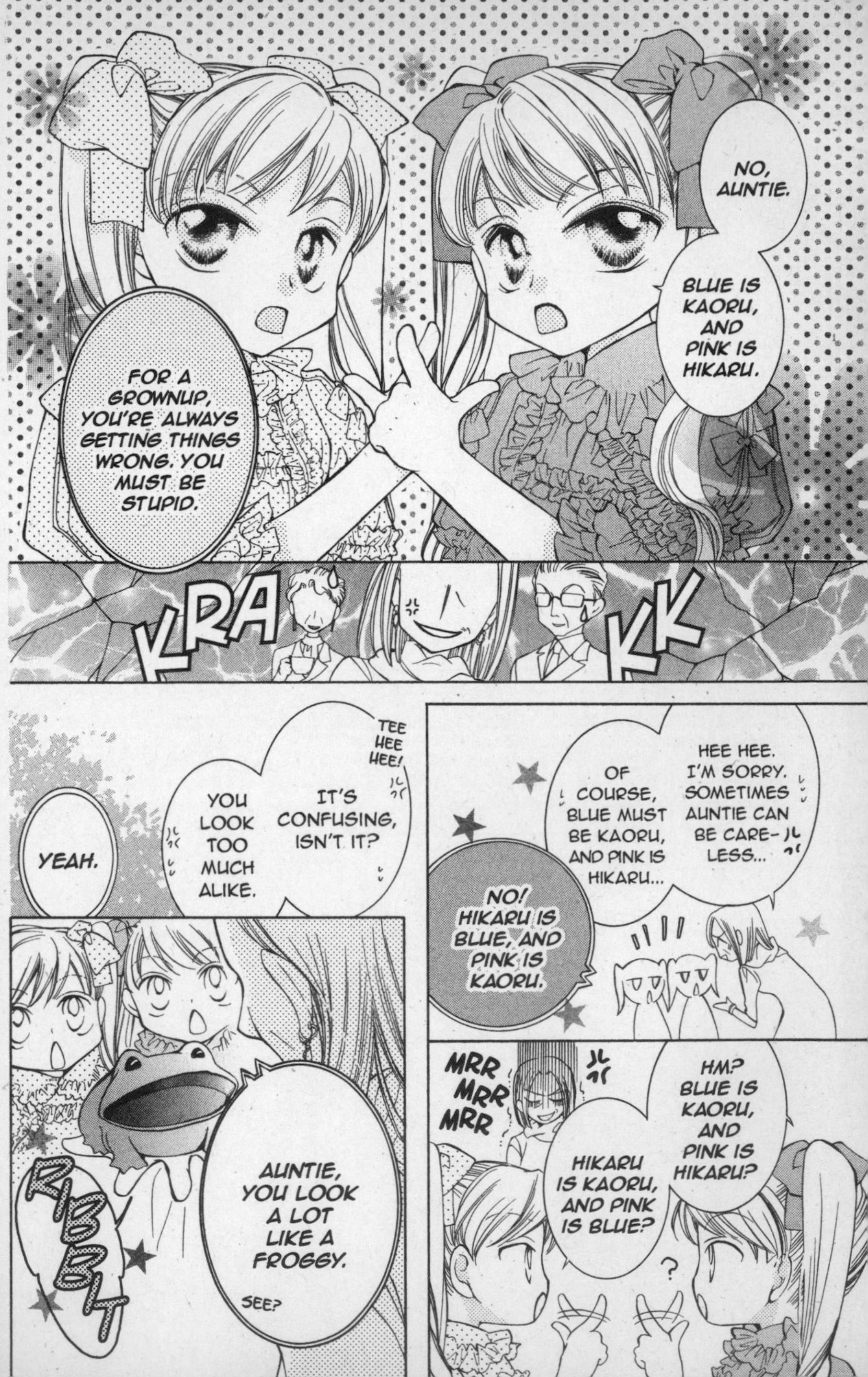
NO, AUNTIE.
BLUE IS KAORU, AND PINK IS HIKARU.
FOR A GROWNUP, YOU'RE ALWAYS GETTING THINGS WRONG. YOU MUST BE STUPID.
KRAKK
HEE HEE. I'M SORRY. SOMETIMES AUNTIE CAN BE CARE-LESS...
OF COURSE, BLUE MUST BE KAORU, AND PINK IS HIKARU...
NO! HIKARU IS BLUE, AND PINK IS KAORU.
MRR MRR MRR
HM? BLUE IS KAORU, AND PINK IS HIKARU?
HIKARU IS KAORU, AND PINK IS BLUE?
?
TEE HEE HEE!
IT'S CONFUSING, ISN'T IT?
YOU LOOK TOO MUCH ALIKE.
YEAH.
AUNTIE, YOU LOOK A LOT LIKE A FROGGY.
SEE?
RIBBIT

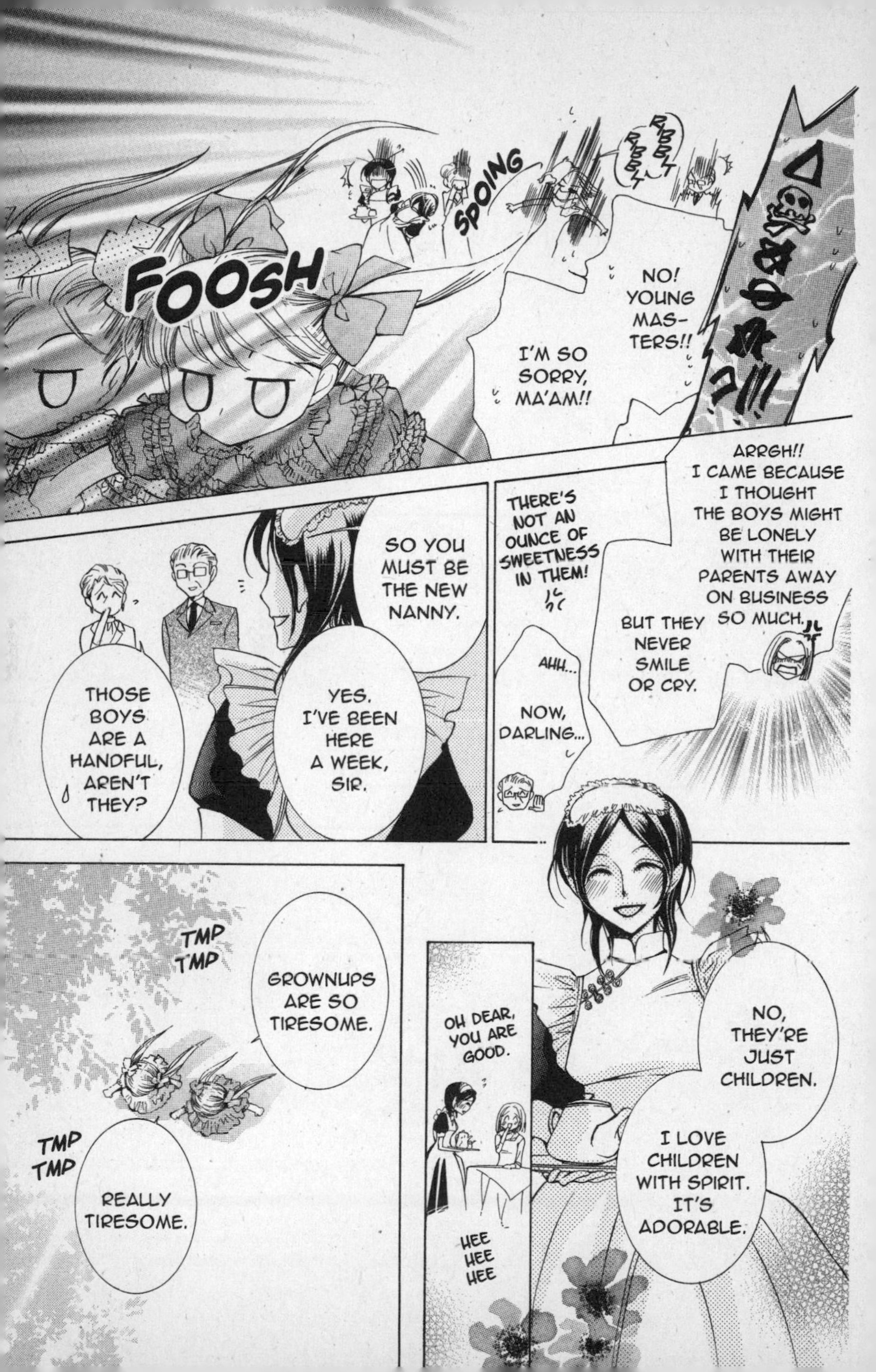
RIBBIT RIBBIT
SPOING
NO! YOUNG MAS-TERS!!
I'M SO SORRY, MA'AM!!
FOOSH
ARRGH!! I CAME BECAUSE I THOUGHT THE BOYS MIGHT BE LONELY WITH THEIR PARENTS AWAY ON BUSINESS SO MUCH.
BUT THEY NEVER SMILE OR CRY.
THERE'S NOT AN OUNCE OF SWEETNESS IN THEM!
AHH...
NOW, DARLING...
SO YOU MUST BE THE NEW NANNY.
YES. I'VE BEEN HERE A WEEK, SIR.
THOSE BOYS ARE A HANDFUL, AREN'T THEY?
NO, THEY'RE JUST CHILDREN.
I LOVE CHILDREN WITH SPIRIT. IT'S ADORABLE.
OH DEAR, YOU ARE GOOD.
HEE HEE HEE
GROWNUPS ARE SO TIRESOME.
TMP TMP
TMP TMP
REALLY TIRESOME.

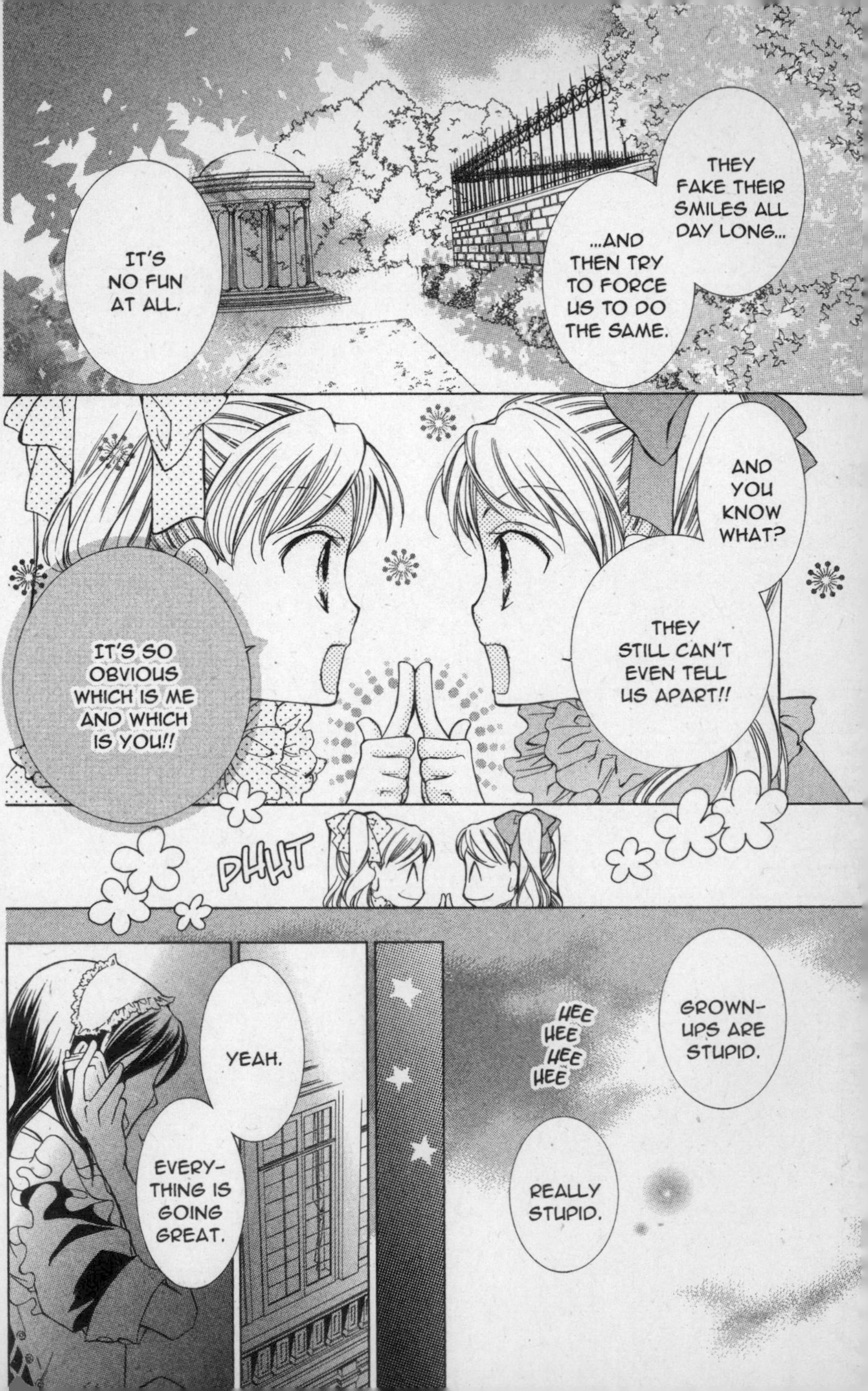

THEY FAKE THEIR SMILES ALL DAY LONG...
...AND THEN TRY TO FORCE US TO DO THE SAME.
IT'S NO FUN AT ALL.
AND YOU KNOW WHAT?
THEY STILL CAN'T EVEN TELL US APART!!
IT'S SO OBVIOUS WHICH IS ME AND WHICH IS YOU!!
PHHT
GROWN-UPS ARE STUPID.
HEE HEE HEE HEE
REALLY STUPID.
YEAH.
EVERY-THING IS GOING GREAT.

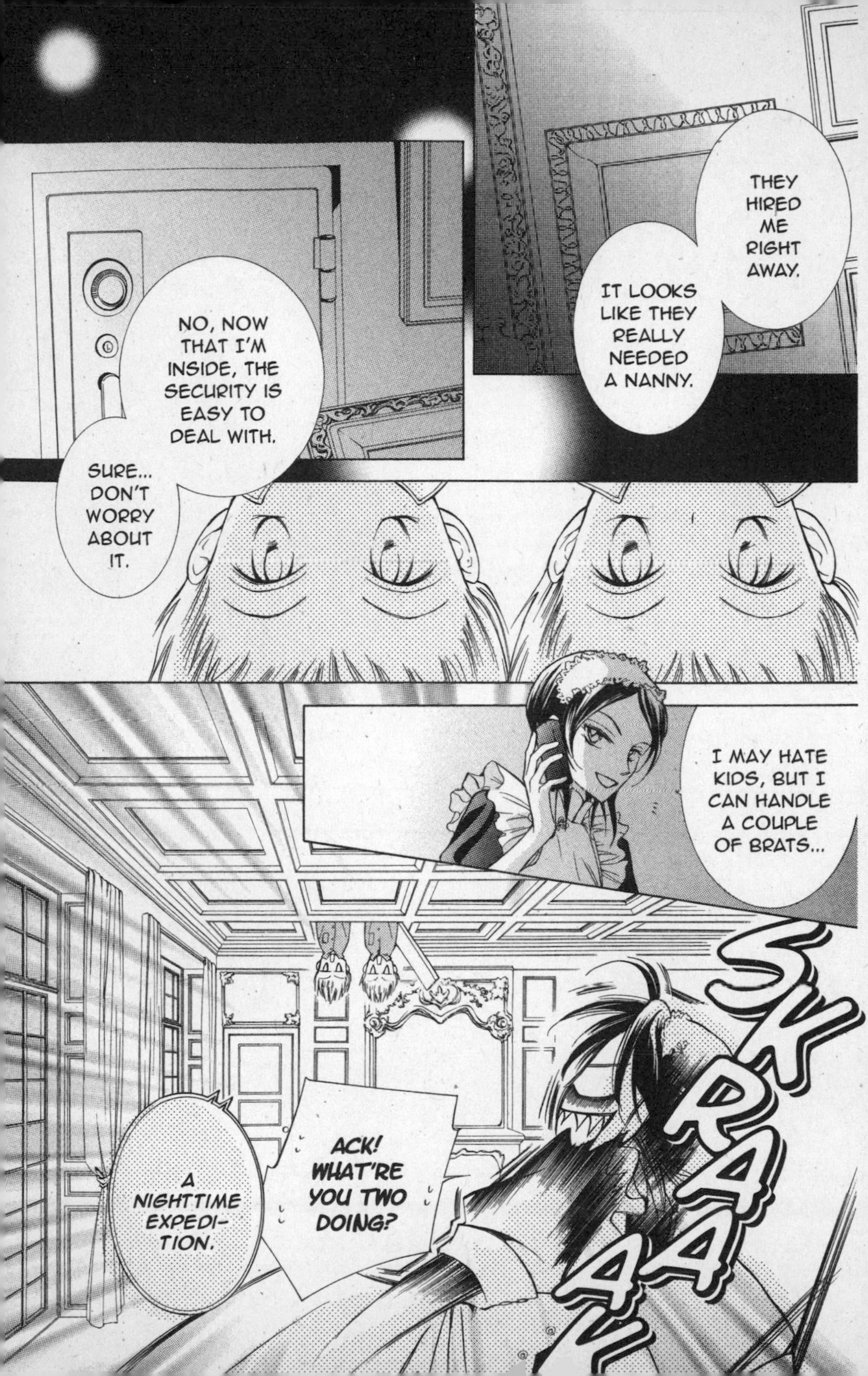
THEY HIRED ME RIGHT AWAY.
IT LOOKS LIKE THEY REALLY NEEDED A NANNY.
NO, NOW THAT I'M INSIDE, THE SECURITY IS EASY TO DEAL WITH.
SURE... DON'T WORRY ABOUT IT.
I MAY HATE KIDS, BUT I CAN HANDLE A COUPLE OF BRATS...
SKRAAAA
ACK! WHAT'RE YOU TWO DOING?
A NIGHTTIME EXPEDITION.

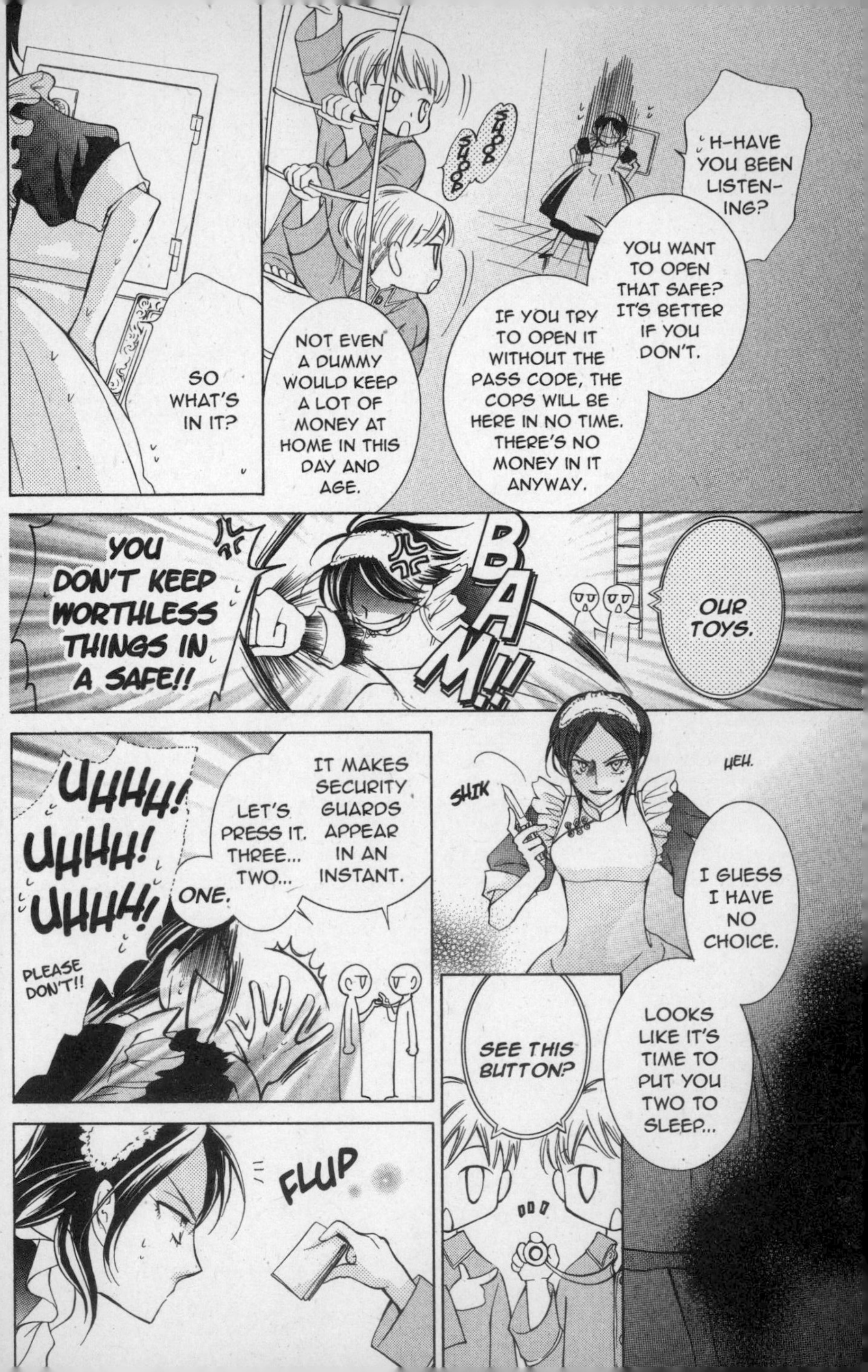
H-HAVE YOU BEEN LISTENING?
YOU WANT TO OPEN THAT SAFE? IT'S BETTER IF YOU DON'T.
IF YOU TRY TO OPEN IT WITHOUT THE PASS CODE, THE COPS WILL BE HERE IN NO TIME. THERE'S NO MONEY IN IT ANYWAY.
SHOOP SHOOP
NOT EVEN A DUMMY WOULD KEEP A LOT OF MONEY AT HOME IN THIS DAY AND AGE.
SO WHAT'S IN IT?
OUR TOYS.
BAM!!
YOU DON'T KEEP WORTHLESS THINGS IN A SAFE!!
HEH.
I GUESS I HAVE NO CHOICE.
SHIK
LOOKS LIKE IT'S TIME TO PUT YOU TWO TO SLEEP...
SEE THIS BUTTON?
IT MAKES SECURITY GUARDS APPEAR IN AN INSTANT.
LET'S PRESS IT. THREE... TWO...
ONE.
UHHH! UHHH! UHHH!
PLEASE DON'T!!
FLUP

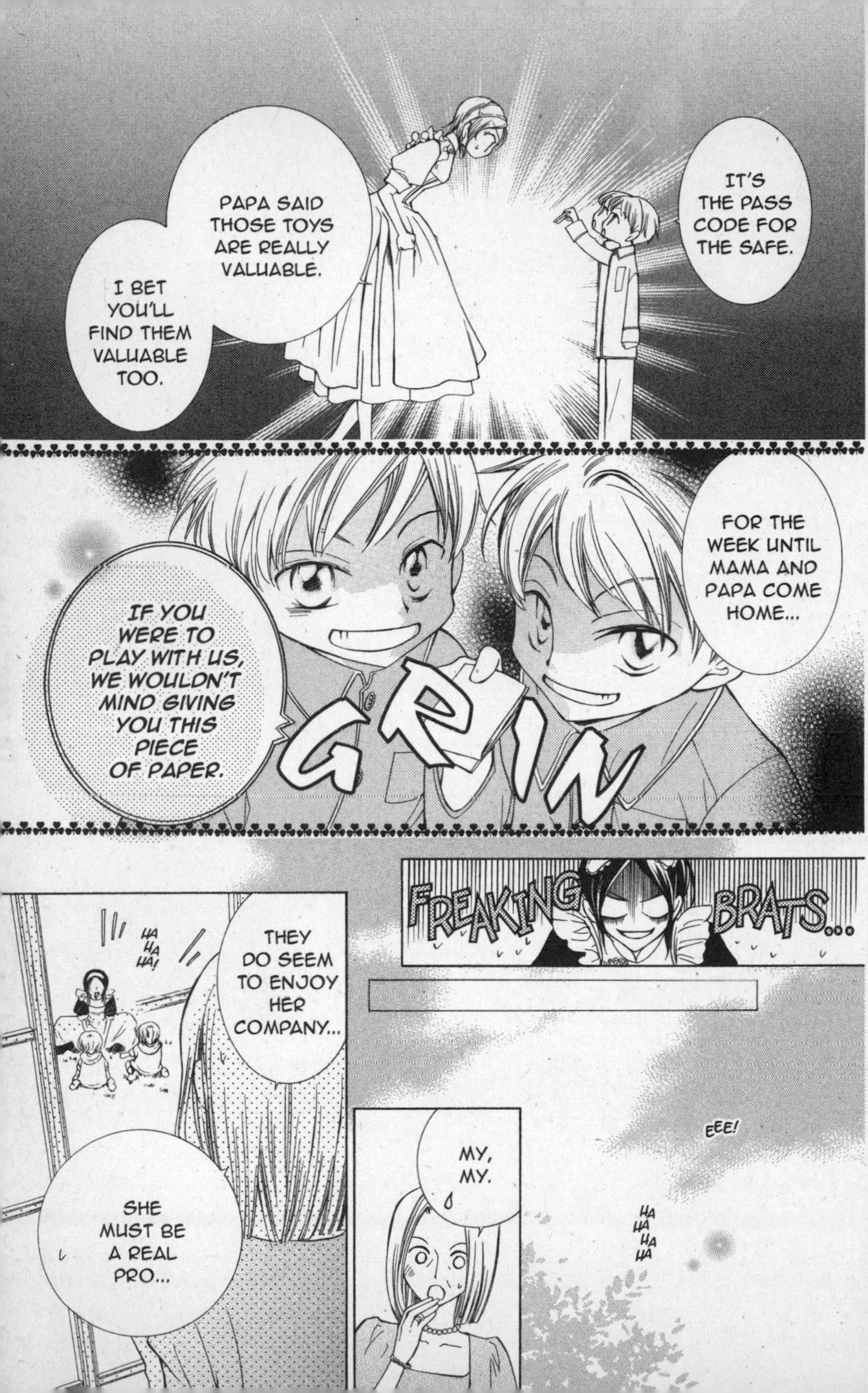
IT'S THE PASS CODE FOR THE SAFE.
PAPA SAID THOSE TOYS ARE REALLY VALUABLE.
I BET YOU'LL FIND THEM VALUABLE TOO.
FOR THE WEEK UNTIL MAMA AND PAPA COME HOME...
GRIN
IF YOU WERE TO PLAY WITH US, WE WOULDN'T MIND GIVING YOU THIS PIECE OF PAPER.
FREAKING BRATS...
EEE!
HA HA HA HA
MY, MY.
HA HA HA!
THEY DO SEEM TO ENJOY HER COMPANY...
SHE MUST BE A REAL PRO...

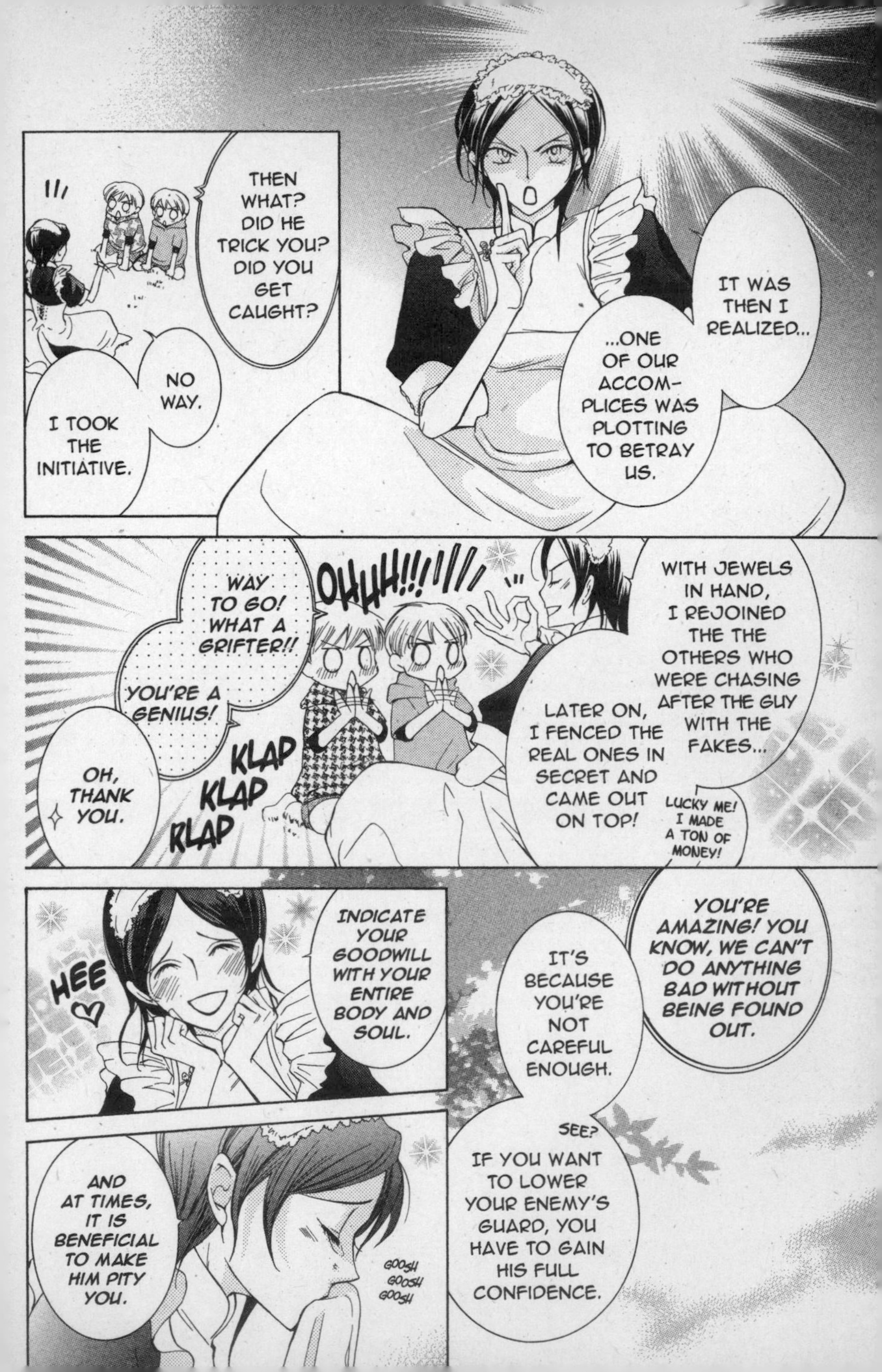
IT WAS THEN I REALIZED...
...ONE OF OUR ACCOM-PLICES WAS PLOTTING TO BETRAY US.
THEN WHAT? DID HE TRICK YOU? DID YOU GET CAUGHT?
NO WAY.
I TOOK THE INITIATIVE.
WITH JEWELS IN HAND, I REJOINED THE THE OTHERS WHO WERE CHASING AFTER THE GUY WITH THE FAKES...
LATER ON, I FENCED THE REAL ONES IN SECRET AND CAME OUT ON TOP!
LUCKY ME! I MADE A TON OF MONEY!
OHHH!!!!
WAY TO GO! WHAT A GRIFTER!!
YOU'RE A GENIUS!
KLAP KLAP KLAP
OH, THANK YOU.
YOU'RE AMAZING! YOU KNOW, WE CAN'T DO ANYTHING BAD WITHOUT BEING FOUND OUT.
IT'S BECAUSE YOU'RE NOT CAREFUL ENOUGH.
SEE?
IF YOU WANT TO LOWER YOUR ENEMY'S GUARD, YOU HAVE TO GAIN HIS FULL CONFIDENCE.
INDICATE YOUR GOODWILL WITH YOUR ENTIRE BODY AND SOUL.
HEE ♡
GOOSH GOOSH GOOSH
AND AT TIMES, IT IS BENEFICIAL TO MAKE HIM PITY YOU.

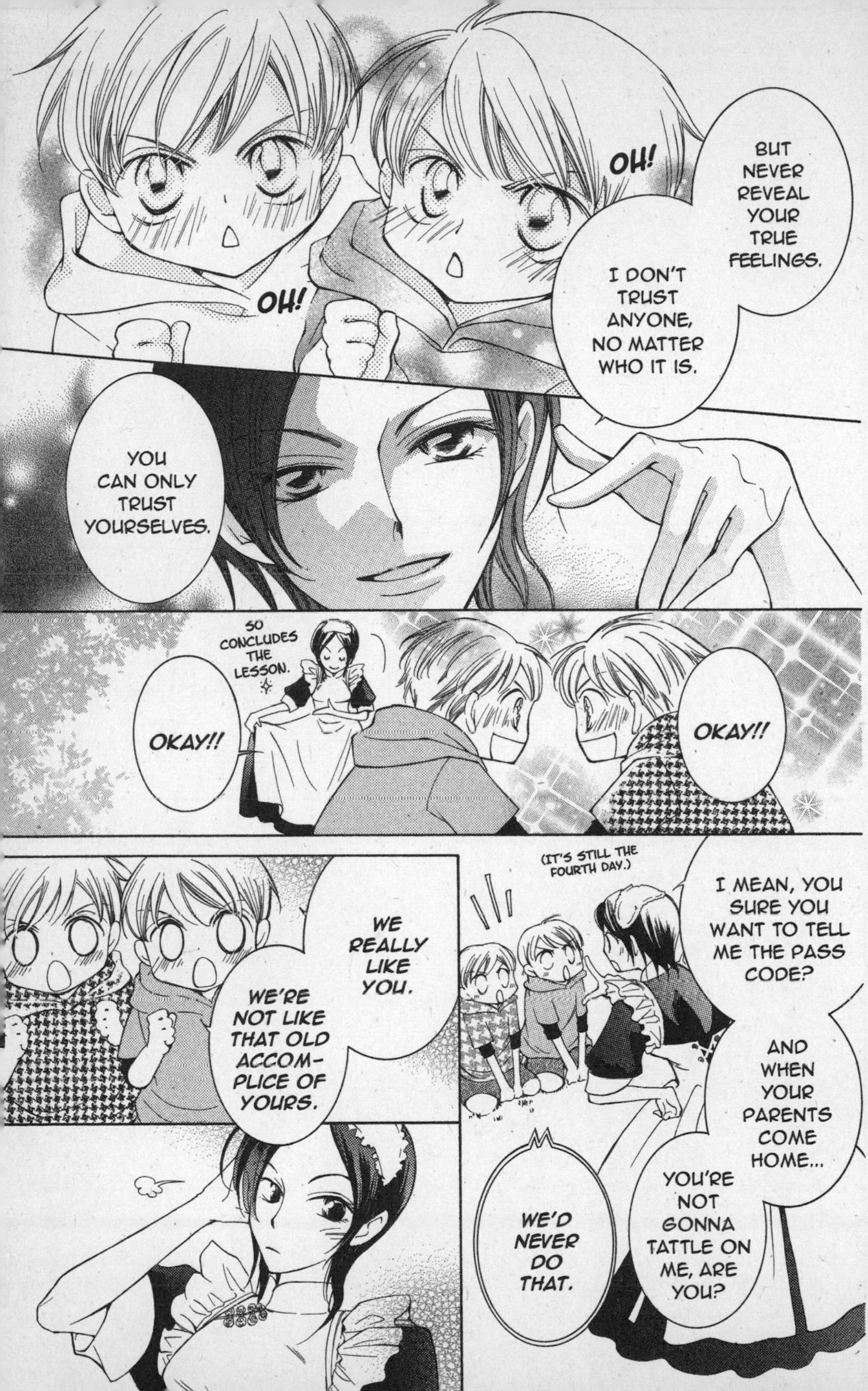
BUT NEVER REVEAL YOUR TRUE FEELINGS.
I DON'T TRUST ANYONE, NO MATTER WHO IT IS.
OH!
OH!
YOU CAN ONLY TRUST YOURSELVES.
OKAY!!
SO CONCLUDES THE LESSON.
OKAY!!
(IT'S STILL THE FOURTH DAY.)
I MEAN, YOU SURE YOU WANT TO TELL ME THE PASS CODE?
AND WHEN YOUR PARENTS COME HOME...
YOU'RE NOT GONNA TATTLE ON ME, ARE YOU?
WE'D NEVER DO THAT.
WE REALLY LIKE YOU.
WE'RE NOT LIKE THAT OLD ACCOM-PLICE OF YOURS.

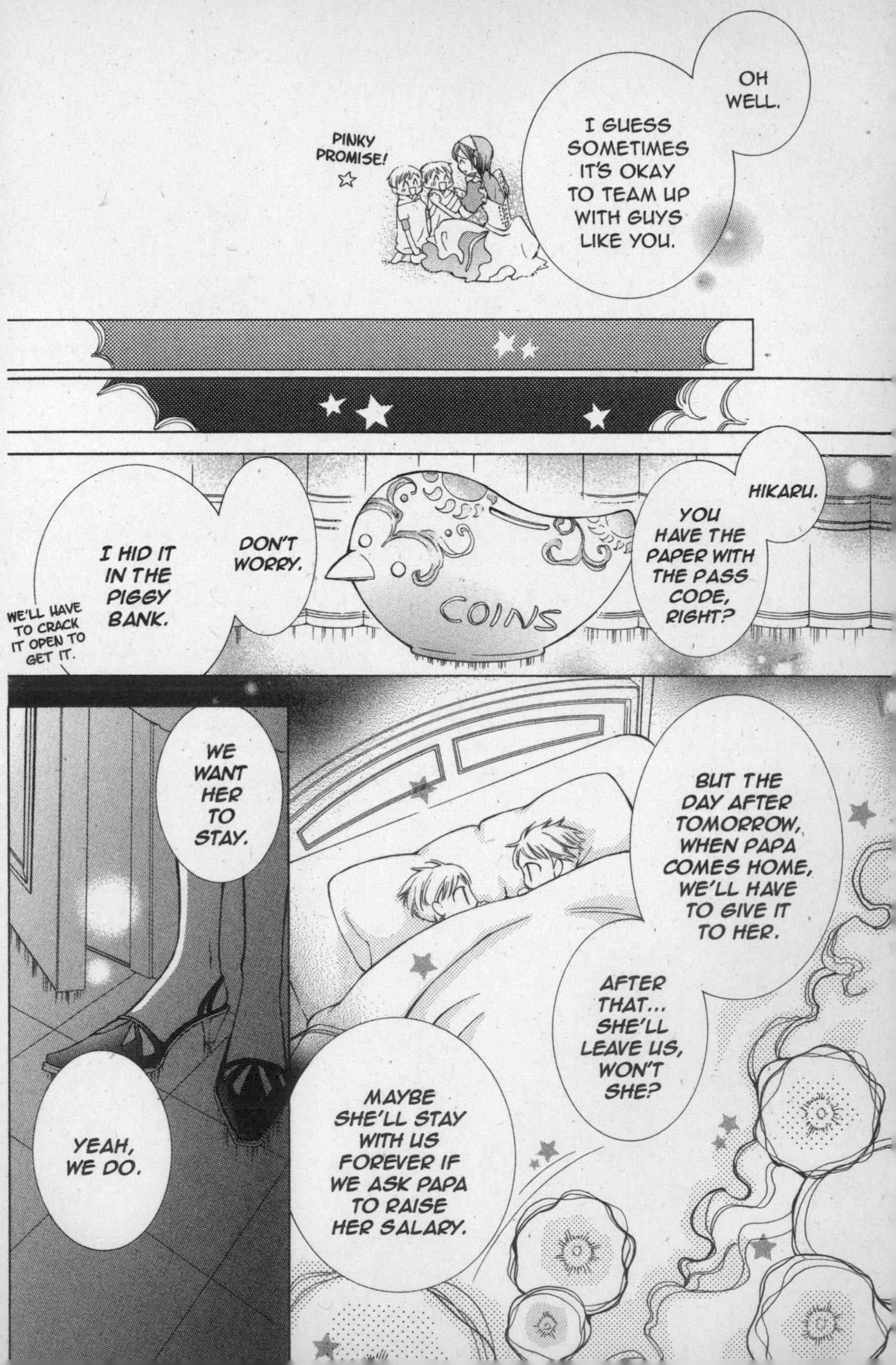
OH WELL.
I GUESS SOMETIMES IT'S OKAY TO TEAM UP WITH GUYS LIKE YOU.
PINKY PROMISE!
HIKARU.
YOU HAVE THE PAPER WITH THE PASS CODE, RIGHT?
COINS
DON'T WORRY.
I HID IT IN THE PIGGY BANK.
WE'LL HAVE TO CRACK IT OPEN TO GET IT.
BUT THE DAY AFTER TOMORROW, WHEN PAPA COMES HOME, WE'LL HAVE TO GIVE IT TO HER.
AFTER THAT... SHE'LL LEAVE US, WON'T SHE?
MAYBE SHE'LL STAY WITH US FOREVER IF WE ASK PAPA TO RAISE HER SALARY.
WE WANT HER TO STAY.
YEAH, WE DO.

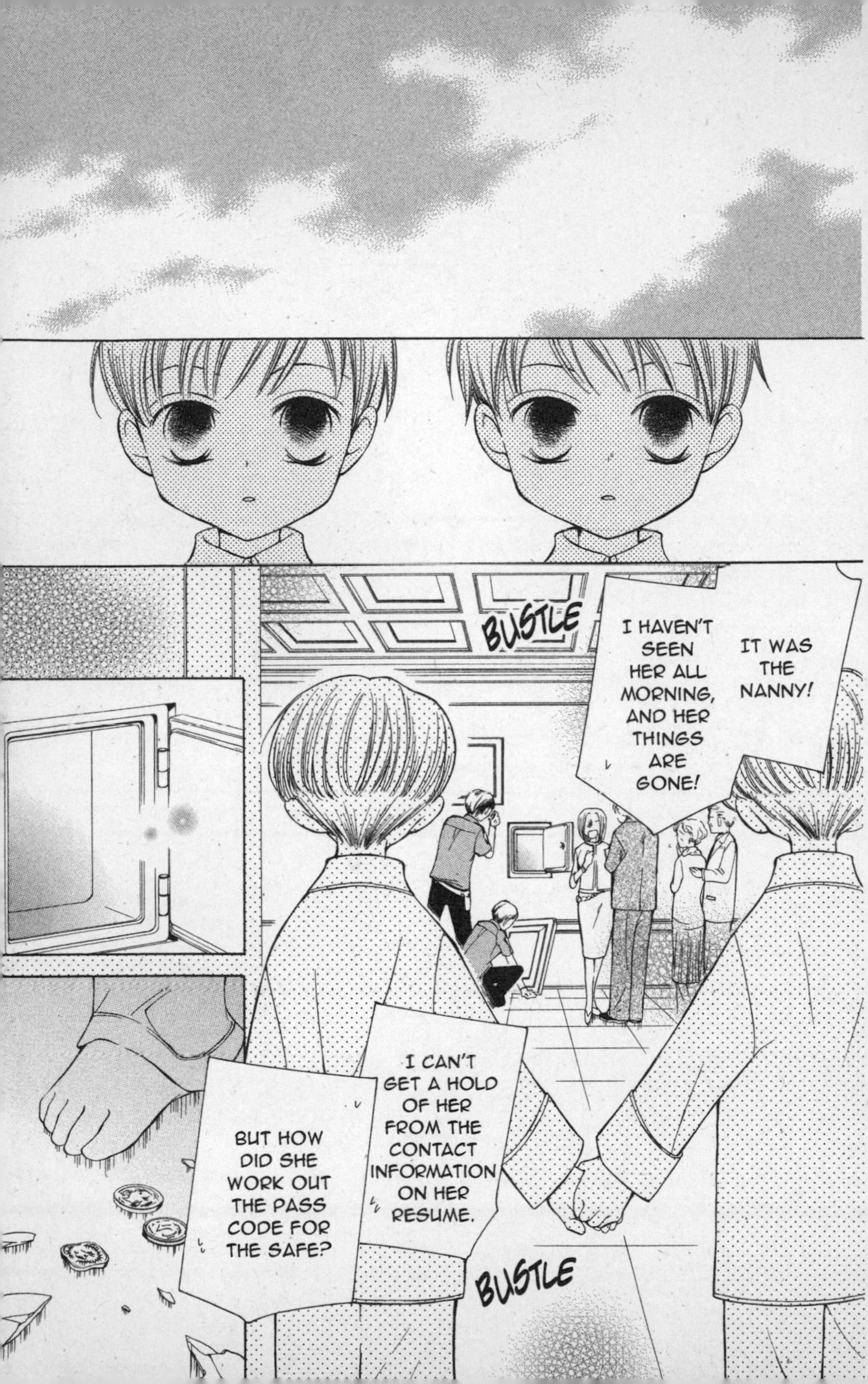
IT WAS THE NANNY!
I HAVEN'T SEEN HER ALL MORNING, AND HER THINGS ARE GONE!
BUSTLE
I CAN'T GET A HOLD OF HER FROM THE CONTACT INFORMATION ON HER RESUME.
BUT HOW DID SHE WORK OUT THE PASS CODE FOR THE SAFE?
BUSTLE

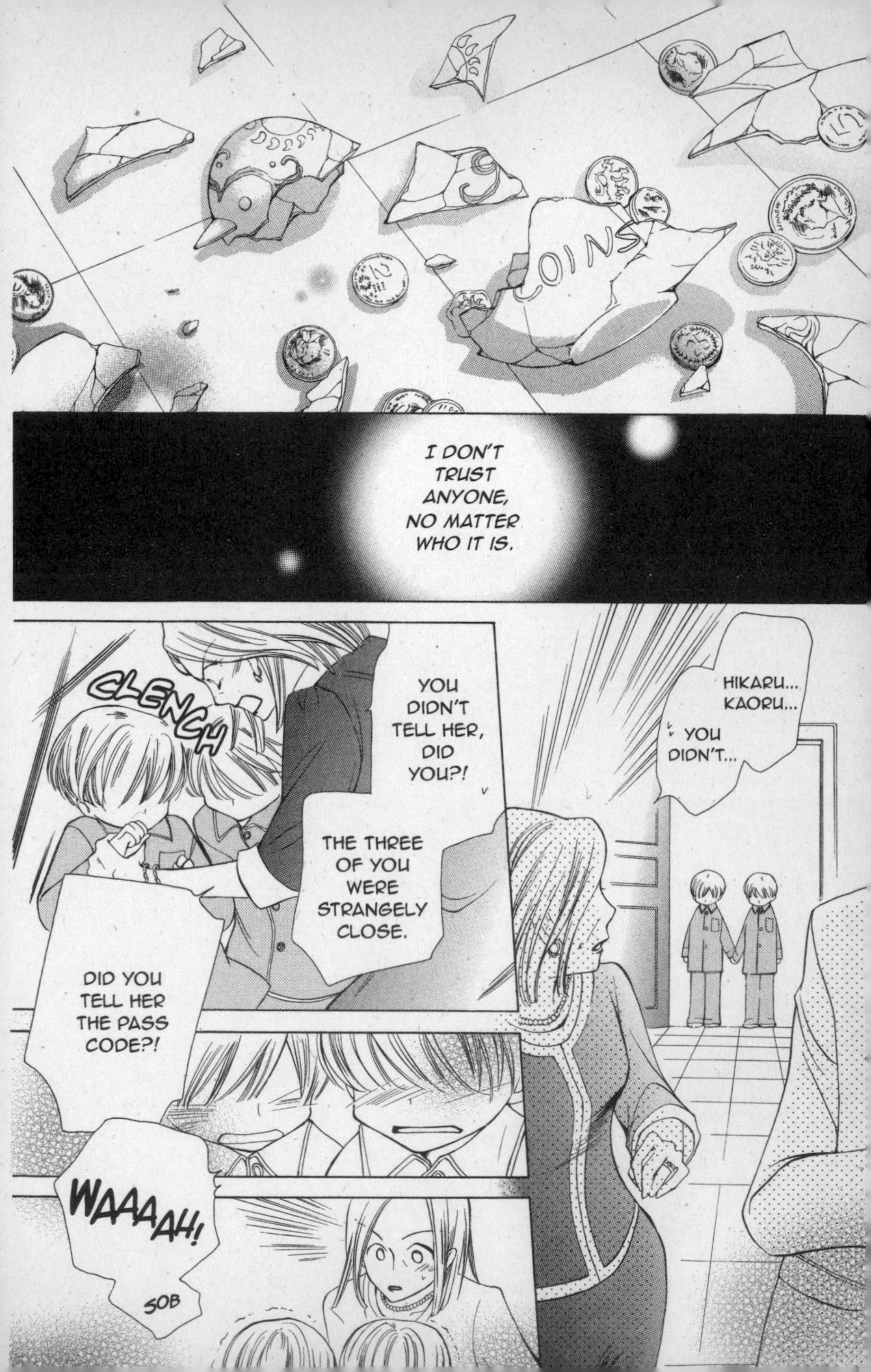
COINS
I DON'T TRUST ANYONE, NO MATTER WHO IT IS.
HIKARU... KAORU...
YOU DIDN'T...
CLENCH
YOU DIDN'T TELL HER, DID YOU?!
THE THREE OF YOU WERE STRANGELY CLOSE.
DID YOU TELL HER THE PASS CODE?!
WAAAAH!
SOB

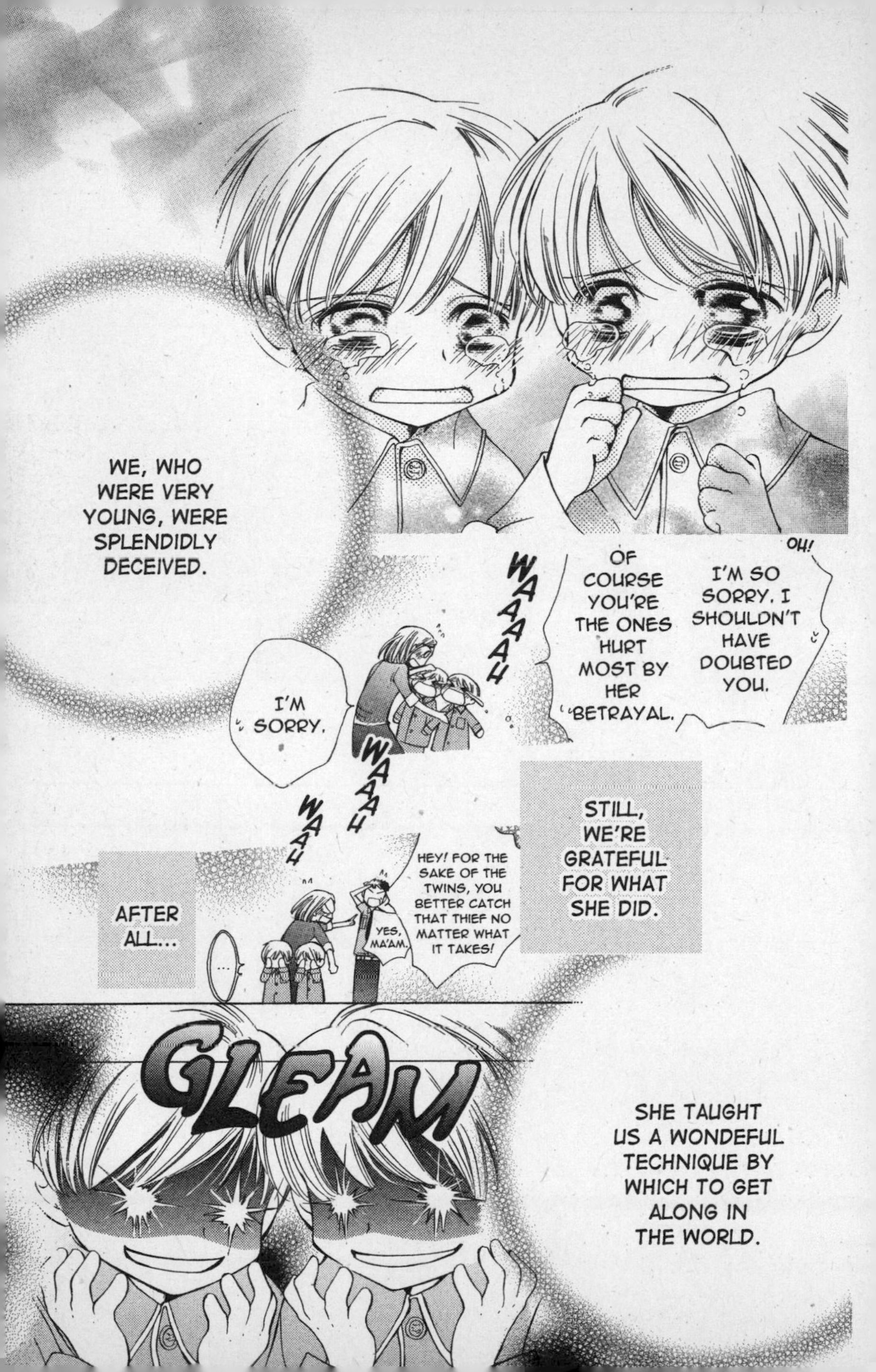
WE, WHO WERE VERY YOUNG, WERE SPLENDIDLY DECEIVED.
OH!
I'M SO SORRY. I SHOULDN'T HAVE DOUBTED YOU.
OF COURSE YOU'RE THE ONES HURT MOST BY HER BETRAYAL.
WAAAAH
I'M SORRY.
WAAAAH
WAAH
STILL, WE'RE GRATEFUL FOR WHAT SHE DID.
HEY! FOR THE SAKE OF THE TWINS, YOU BETTER CATCH THAT THIEF NO MATTER WHAT IT TAKES!
YES, MA'AM.
...
AFTER ALL...
SHE TAUGHT US A WONDEFUL TECHNIQUE BY WHICH TO GET ALONG IN THE WORLD.
GLEAM

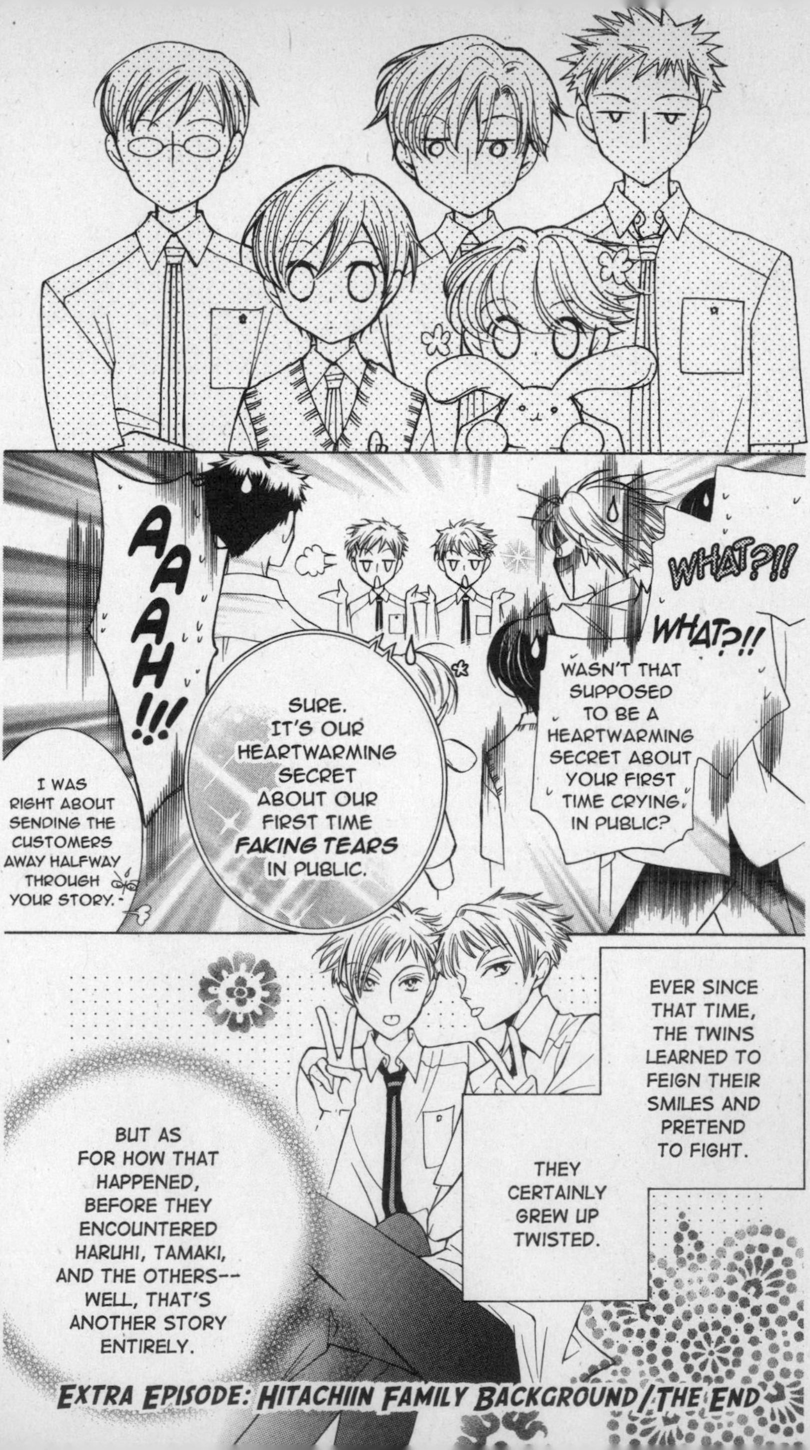
WHAT?!!
WHAT?!!
WASN'T THAT SUPPOSED TO BE A HEARTWARMING SECRET ABOUT YOUR FIRST TIME CRYING IN PUBLIC?
SURE. IT'S OUR HEARTWARMING SECRET ABOUT OUR FIRST TIME FAKING TEARS IN PUBLIC.
AAAH!!!
I WAS RIGHT ABOUT SENDING THE CUSTOMERS AWAY HALFWAY THROUGH YOUR STORY.
EVER SINCE THAT TIME, THE TWINS LEARNED TO FEIGN THEIR SMILES AND PRETEND TO FIGHT.
THEY CERTAINLY GREW UP TWISTED.
BUT AS FOR HOW THAT HAPPENED, BEFORE THEY ENCOUNTERED HARUHI, TAMAKI, AND THE OTHERS--WELL, THAT'S ANOTHER STORY ENTIRELY.
EXTRA EPISODE: HITACHIIN FAMILY BACKGROUND / THE END

FOR
COLORING
IN

IT'S TOO
LATE NOW, BUT
HIKARU'S FOOT
IS IN AN ODD
POSITION...

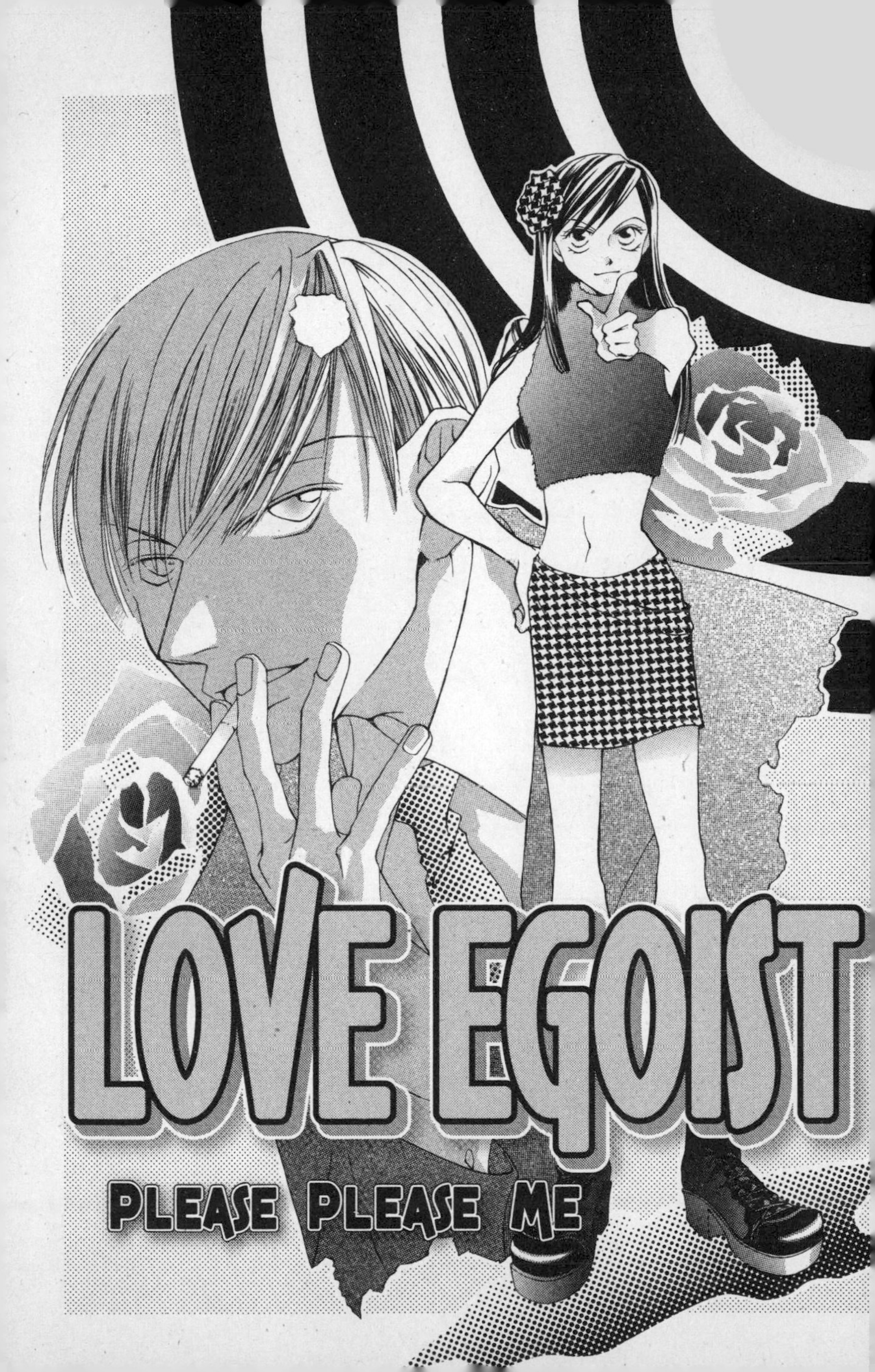
LOVE EGOIST
PLEASE PLEASE ME

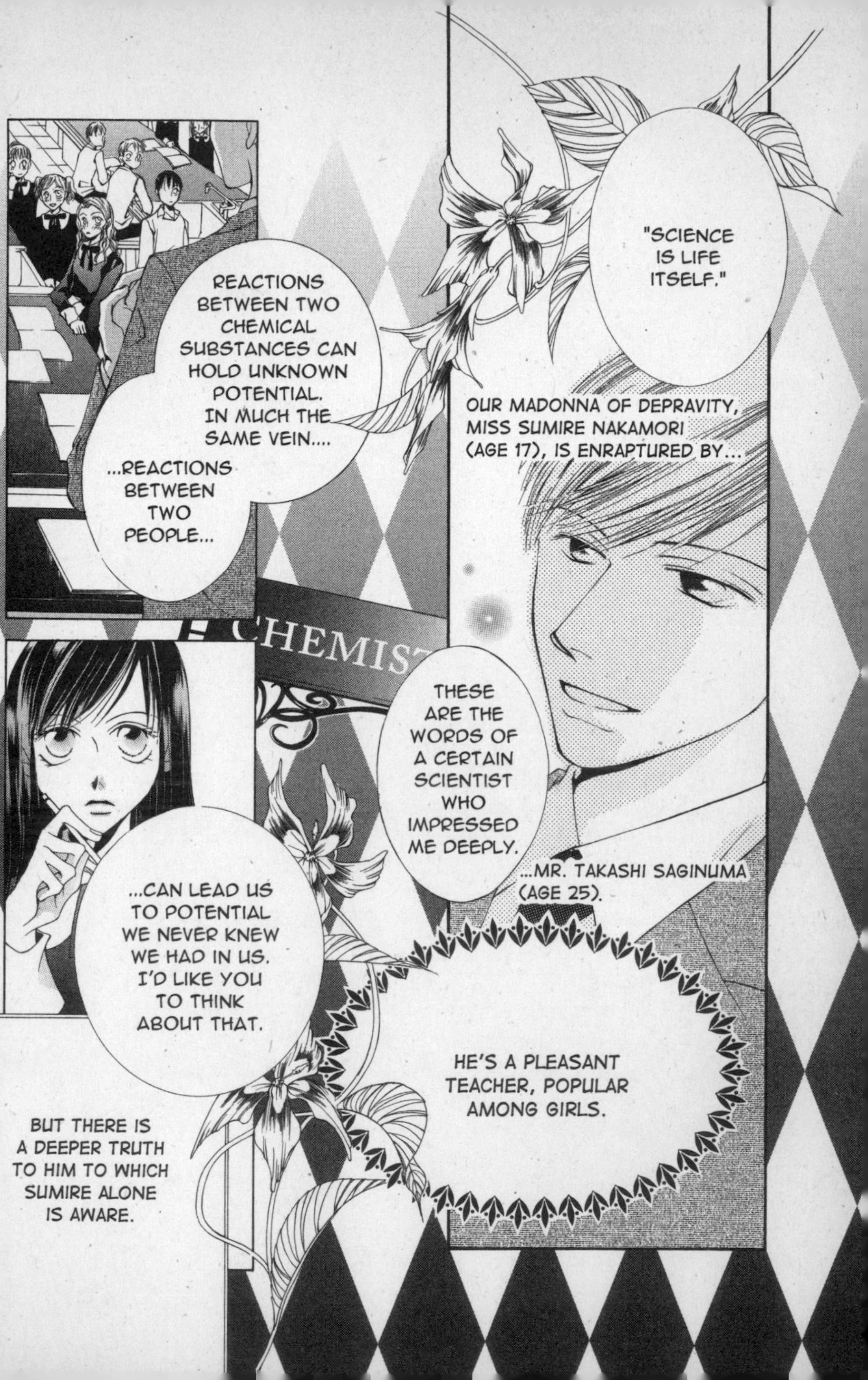
"SCIENCE IS LIFE ITSELF."
OUR MADONNA OF DEPRAVITY, MISS SUMIRE NAKAMORI (AGE 17), IS ENRAPTURED BY...
THESE ARE THE WORDS OF A CERTAIN SCIENTIST WHO IMPRESSED ME DEEPLY.
...MR. TAKASHI SAGINUMA (AGE 25).
HE'S A PLEASANT TEACHER, POPULAR AMONG GIRLS.
REACTIONS BETWEEN TWO CHEMICAL SUBSTANCES CAN HOLD UNKNOWN POTENTIAL. IN MUCH THE SAME VEIN....
...REACTIONS BETWEEN TWO PEOPLE...
...CAN LEAD US TO POTENTIAL WE NEVER KNEW WE HAD IN US. I'D LIKE YOU TO THINK ABOUT THAT.
BUT THERE IS A DEEPER TRUTH TO HIM TO WHICH SUMIRE ALONE IS AWARE.

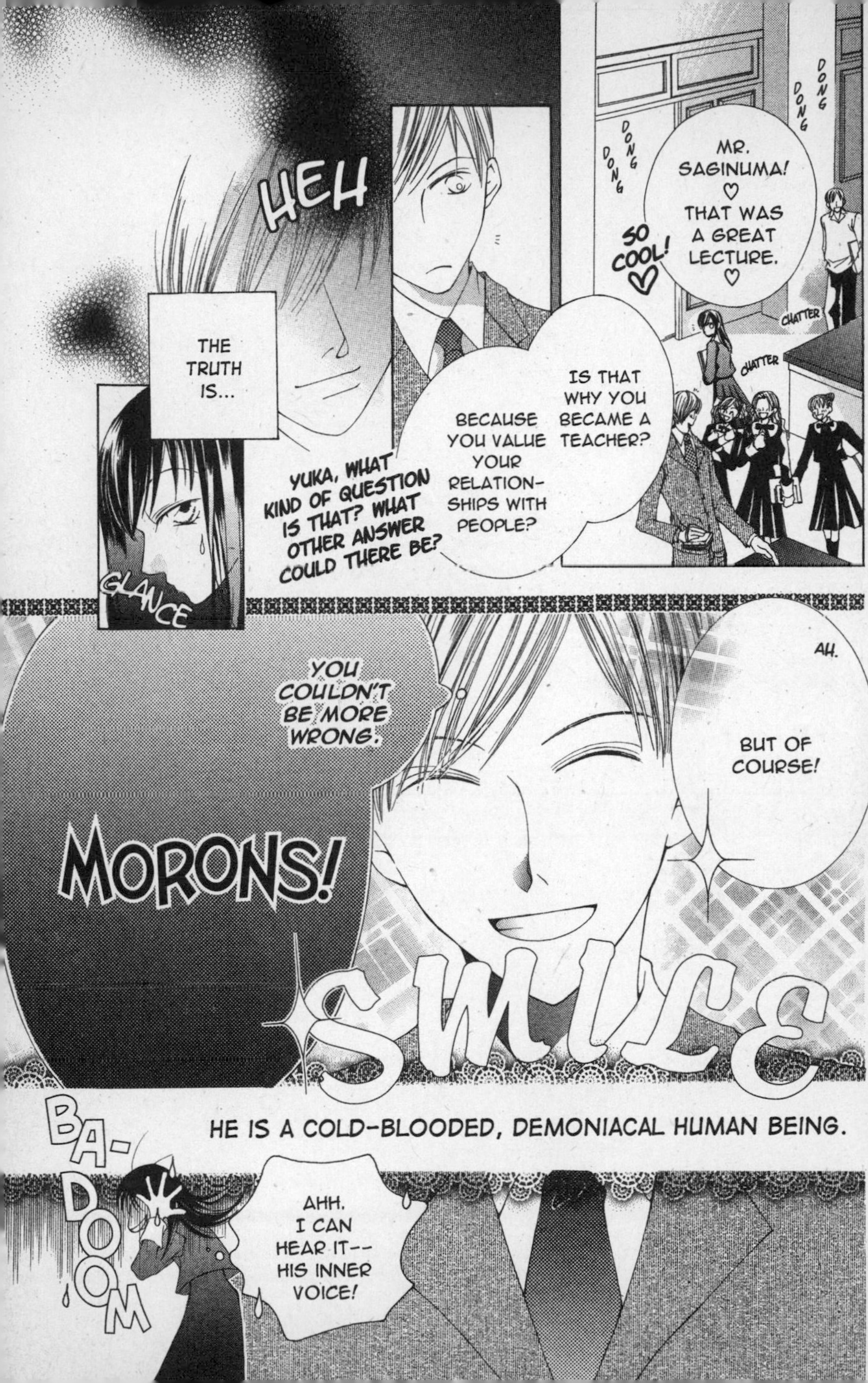
DONG DONG
DONG DONG
MR. SAGINUMA! ♡ THAT WAS A GREAT LECTURE. ♡
SO COOL! ♡
CHATTER
CHATTER
IS THAT WHY YOU BECAME A TEACHER?
BECAUSE YOU VALUE YOUR RELATION-SHIPS WITH PEOPLE?
HEH
THE TRUTH IS...
YUKA, WHAT KIND OF QUESTION IS THAT? WHAT OTHER ANSWER COULD THERE BE?
GLANCE
AH.
BUT OF COURSE!
YOU COULDN'T BE MORE WRONG.
MORONS!
SMILE
HE IS A COLD-BLOODED, DEMONIACAL HUMAN BEING.
AHH. I CAN HEAR IT-- HIS INNER VOICE!
BA-DOOM

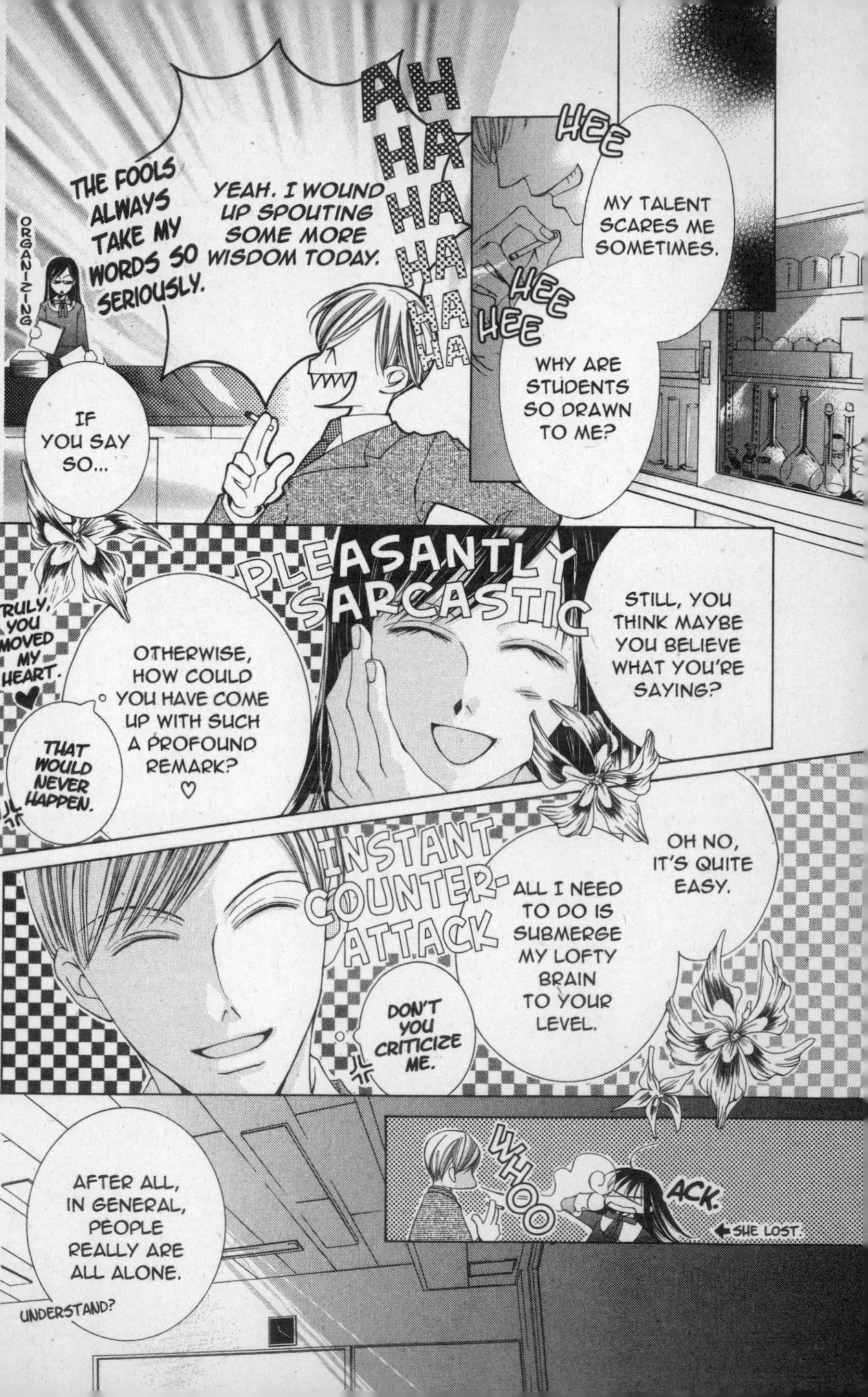
HEE
MY TALENT SCARES ME SOMETIMES.
HEE HEE
WHY ARE STUDENTS SO DRAWN TO ME?
AH HA HA HA HA HA
YEAH. I WOUND UP SPOUTING SOME MORE WISDOM TODAY.
THE FOOLS ALWAYS TAKE MY WORDS SO SERIOUSLY.
ORGANIZING
IF YOU SAY SO...
STILL, YOU THINK MAYBE YOU BELIEVE WHAT YOU'RE SAYING?
PLEASANTLY SARCASTIC
OTHERWISE, HOW COULD YOU HAVE COME UP WITH SUCH A PROFOUND REMARK? ♡
TRULY, YOU MOVED MY HEART. ♥
THAT WOULD NEVER HAPPEN.
OH NO, IT'S QUITE EASY.
ALL I NEED TO DO IS SUBMERGE MY LOFTY BRAIN TO YOUR LEVEL.
INSTANT COUNTER-ATTACK
DON'T YOU CRITICIZE ME.
WHOO
ACK.
SHE LOST.
AFTER ALL, IN GENERAL, PEOPLE REALLY ARE ALL ALONE.
UNDERSTAND?

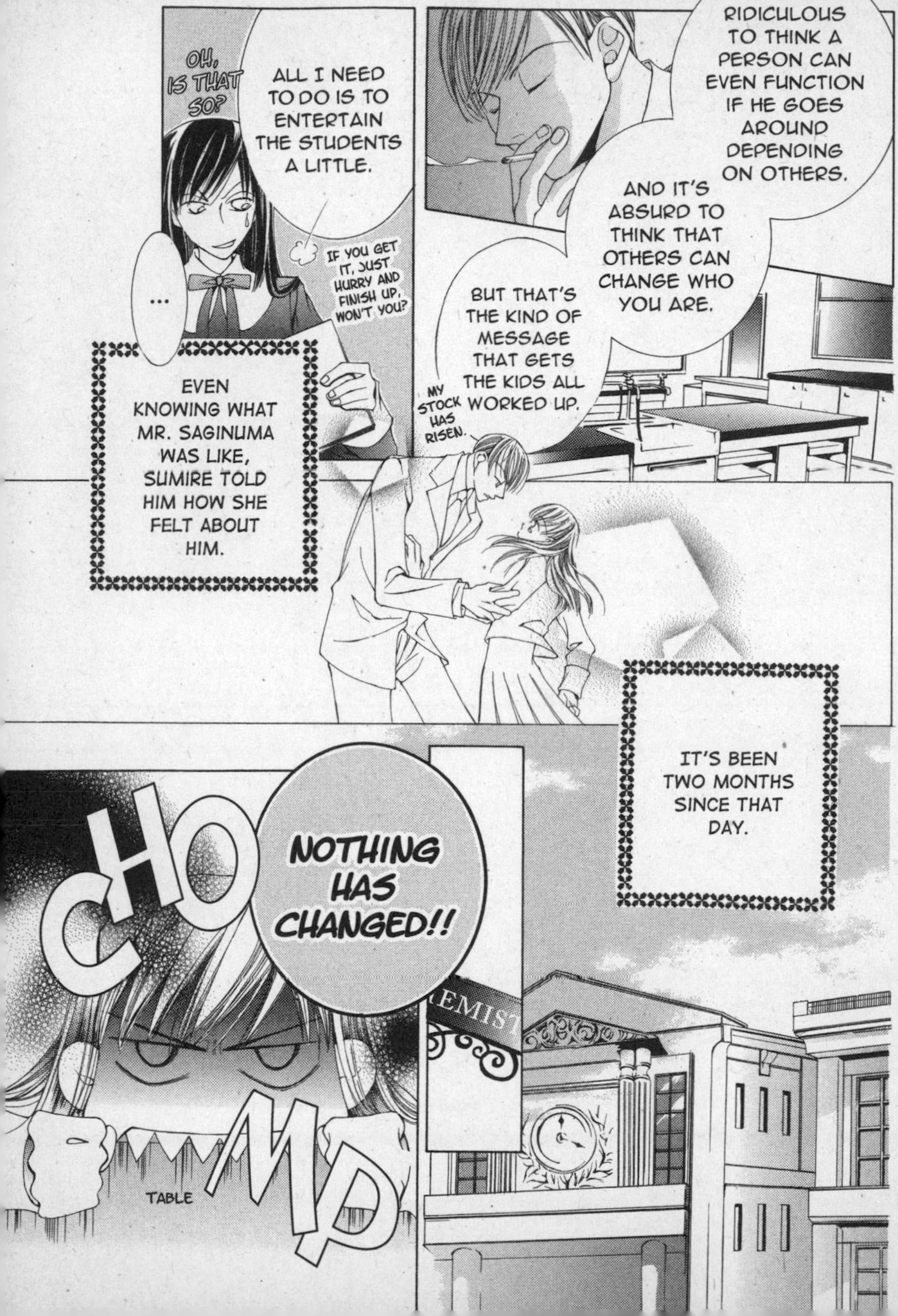
IT'S RIDICULOUS TO THINK A PERSON CAN EVEN FUNCTION IF HE GOES AROUND DEPENDING ON OTHERS.
AND IT'S ABSURD TO THINK THAT OTHERS CAN CHANGE WHO YOU ARE.
BUT THAT'S THE KIND OF MESSAGE THAT GETS THE KIDS ALL WORKED UP.
MY STOCK HAS RISEN.
ALL I NEED TO DO IS TO ENTERTAIN THE STUDENTS A LITTLE.
OH, IS THAT SO?
IF YOU GET IT, JUST HURRY AND FINISH UP, WON'T YOU?
...
EVEN KNOWING WHAT MR. SAGINUMA WAS LIKE, SUMIRE TOLD HIM HOW SHE FELT ABOUT HIM.
IT'S BEEN TWO MONTHS SINCE THAT DAY.
NOTHING HAS CHANGED!!
CHOMP
TABLE

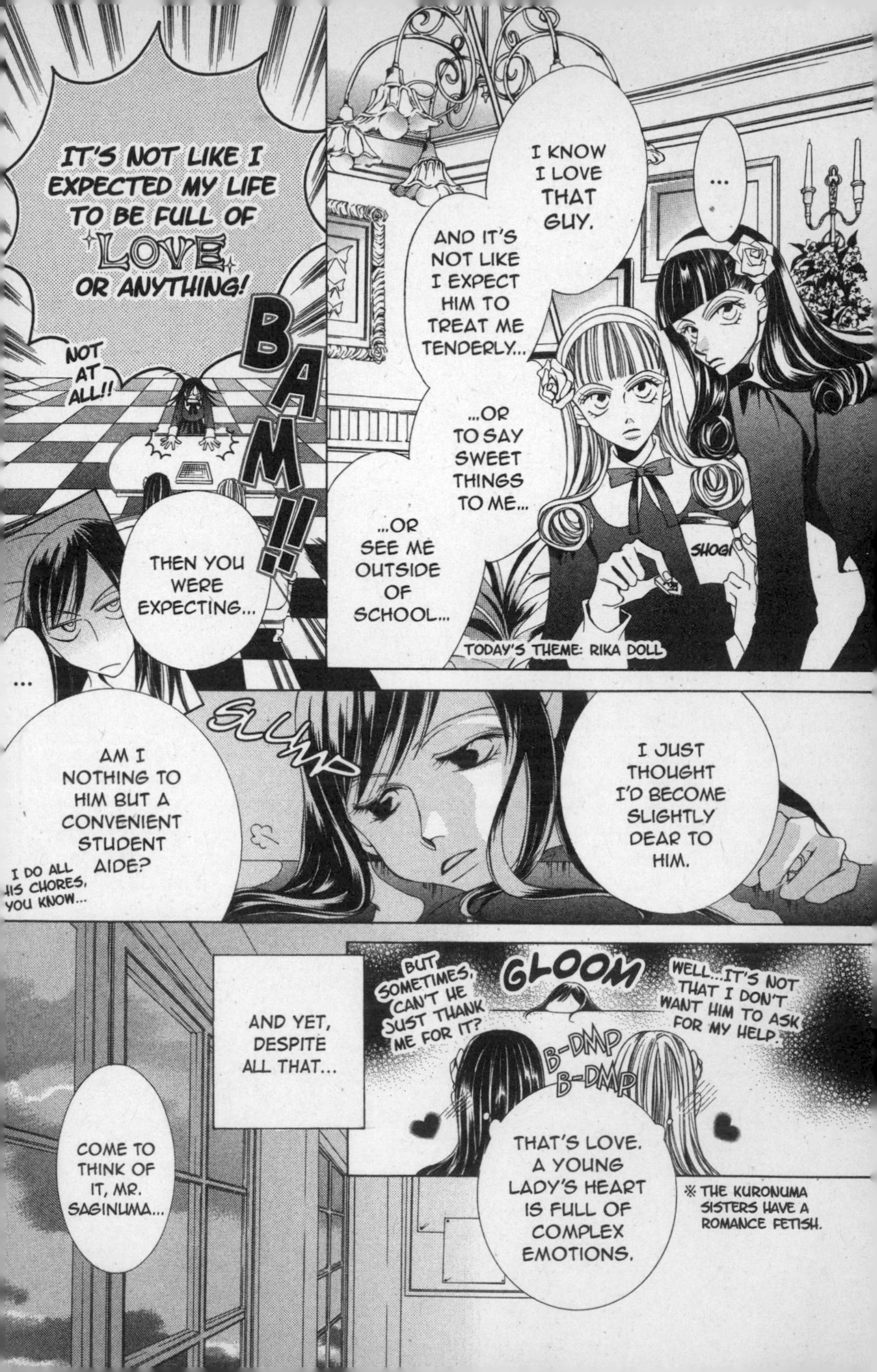
...
I KNOW I LOVE THAT GUY.
AND IT'S NOT LIKE I EXPECT HIM TO TREAT ME TENDERLY...
...OR TO SAY SWEET THINGS TO ME...
...OR SEE ME OUTSIDE OF SCHOOL...
SHOGI
TODAY'S THEME: RIKA DOLL
IT'S NOT LIKE I EXPECTED MY LIFE TO BE FULL OF LOVE OR ANYTHING!
NOT AT ALL!!
BAM!!
THEN YOU WERE EXPECTING...
...
I JUST THOUGHT I'D BECOME SLIGHTLY DEAR TO HIM.
SLUMP
AM I NOTHING TO HIM BUT A CONVENIENT STUDENT AIDE?
I DO ALL HIS CHORES, YOU KNOW...
WELL...IT'S NOT THAT I DON'T WANT HIM TO ASK FOR MY HELP.
GLOOM
BUT SOMETIMES, CAN'T HE JUST THANK ME FOR IT?
B-DMP B-DMP
THAT'S LOVE. A YOUNG LADY'S HEART IS FULL OF COMPLEX EMOTIONS.
※ THE KURONUMA SISTERS HAVE A ROMANCE FETISH.
AND YET, DESPITE ALL THAT...
COME TO THINK OF IT, MR. SAGINUMA...

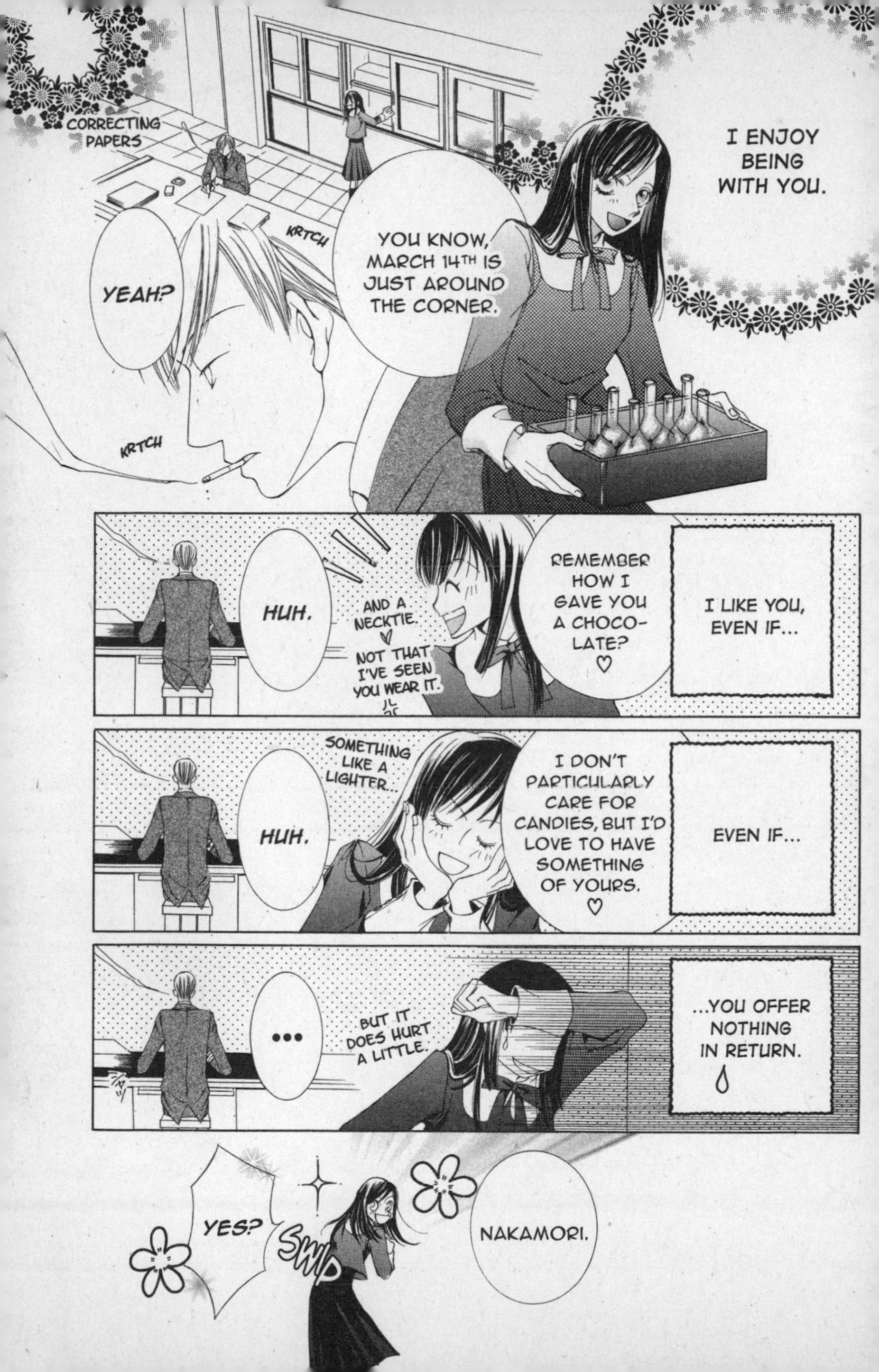
I ENJOY BEING WITH YOU.
YOU KNOW, MARCH 14TH IS JUST AROUND THE CORNER.
CORRECTING PAPERS
KRTCH
YEAH?
KRTCH
I LIKE YOU, EVEN IF...
REMEMBER HOW I GAVE YOU A CHOCOLATE? ♡
AND A NECKTIE. ♡
NOT THAT I'VE SEEN YOU WEAR IT.
HUH.
EVEN IF...
I DON'T PARTICULARLY CARE FOR CANDIES, BUT I'D LOVE TO HAVE SOMETHING OF YOURS. ♡
SOMETHING LIKE A LIGHTER...
HUH.
...YOU OFFER NOTHING IN RETURN.
BUT IT DOES HURT A LITTLE.
...
NAKAMORI.
SWP
YES?

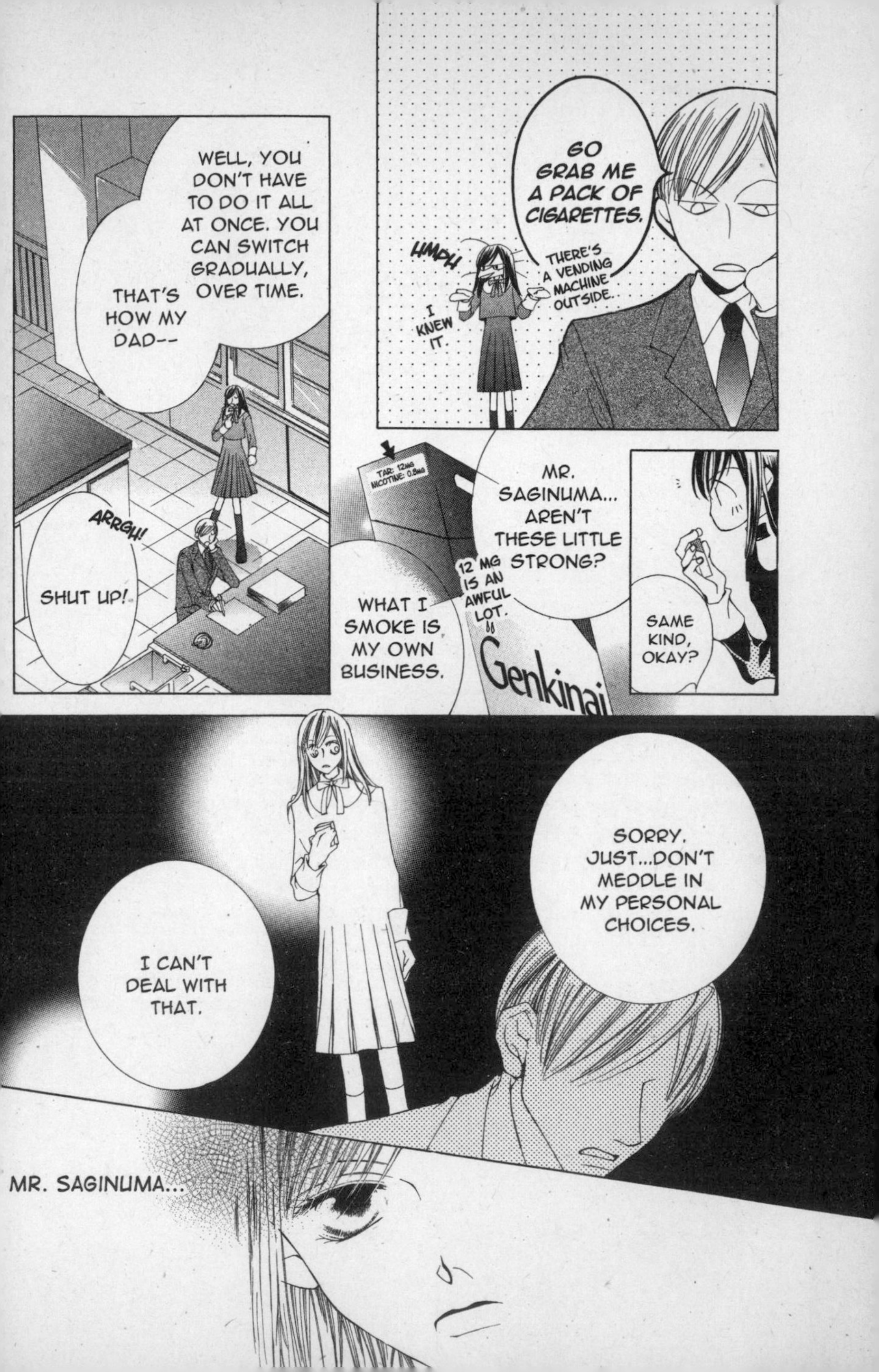
GO GRAB ME A PACK OF CIGARETTES.
THERE'S A VENDING MACHINE OUTSIDE.
HMPH
I KNEW IT.
SAME KIND, OKAY?
MR. SAGINUMA... AREN'T THESE LITTLE STRONG?
TAR: 12MG NICOTINE: 0.8MG
12 MG IS AN AWFUL LOT.
WHAT I SMOKE IS MY OWN BUSINESS.
Genkinai
WELL, YOU DON'T HAVE TO DO IT ALL AT ONCE. YOU CAN SWITCH GRADUALLY, OVER TIME.
THAT'S HOW MY DAD--
ARRGH!
SHUT UP!
SORRY. JUST...DON'T MEDDLE IN MY PERSONAL CHOICES.
I CAN'T DEAL WITH THAT.
MR. SAGINUMA...

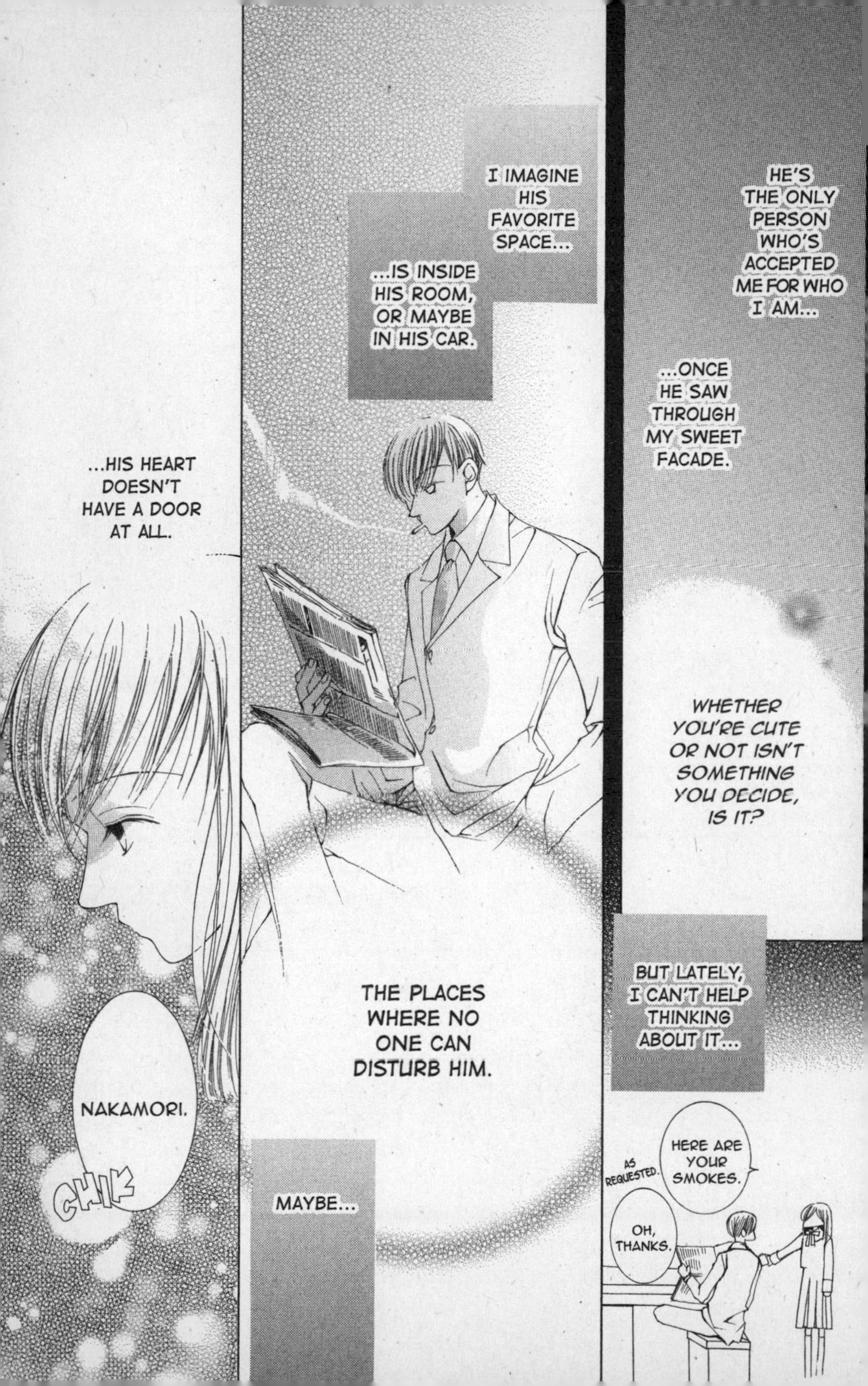
HE'S THE ONLY PERSON WHO'S ACCEPTED ME FOR WHO I AM...
...ONCE HE SAW THROUGH MY SWEET FACADE.
WHETHER YOU'RE CUTE OR NOT ISN'T SOMETHING YOU DECIDE, IS IT?
BUT LATELY, I CAN'T HELP THINKING ABOUT IT...
HERE ARE YOUR SMOKES.
AS REQUESTED.
OH, THANKS.
I IMAGINE HIS FAVORITE SPACE...
...IS INSIDE HIS ROOM, OR MAYBE IN HIS CAR.
THE PLACES WHERE NO ONE CAN DISTURB HIM.
MAYBE...
...HIS HEART DOESN'T HAVE A DOOR AT ALL.
NAKAMORI.
CHIK

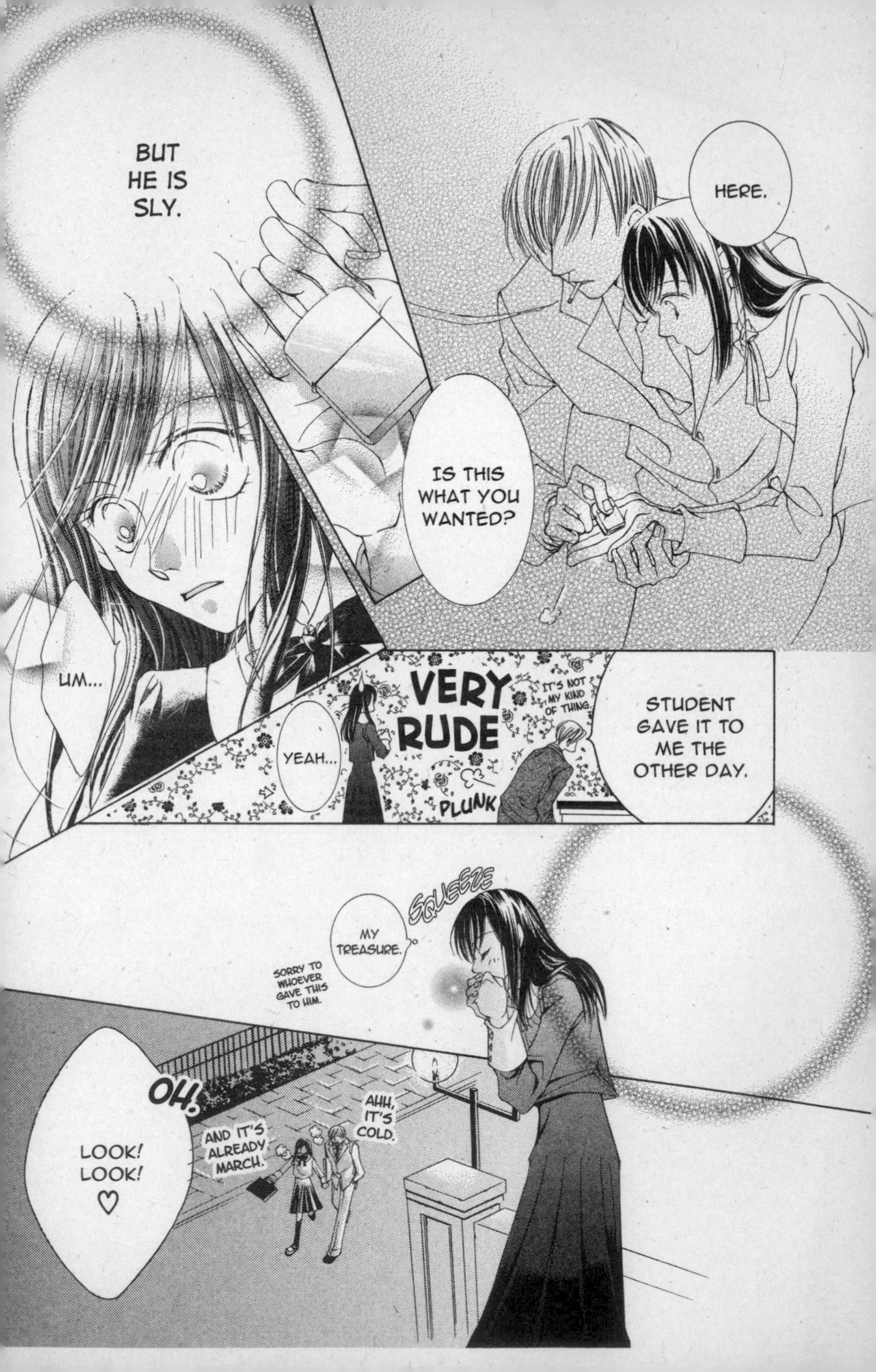
HERE.
IS THIS WHAT YOU WANTED?
BUT HE IS SLY.
UM...
STUDENT GAVE IT TO ME THE OTHER DAY.
IT'S NOT MY KIND OF THING.
VERY RUDE
PLUNK
YEAH...
SQUEEZE
MY TREASURE.
SORRY TO WHOEVER GAVE THIS TO HIM.
AHH, IT'S COLD.
AND IT'S ALREADY MARCH.
OH.
LOOK! LOOK! ♡

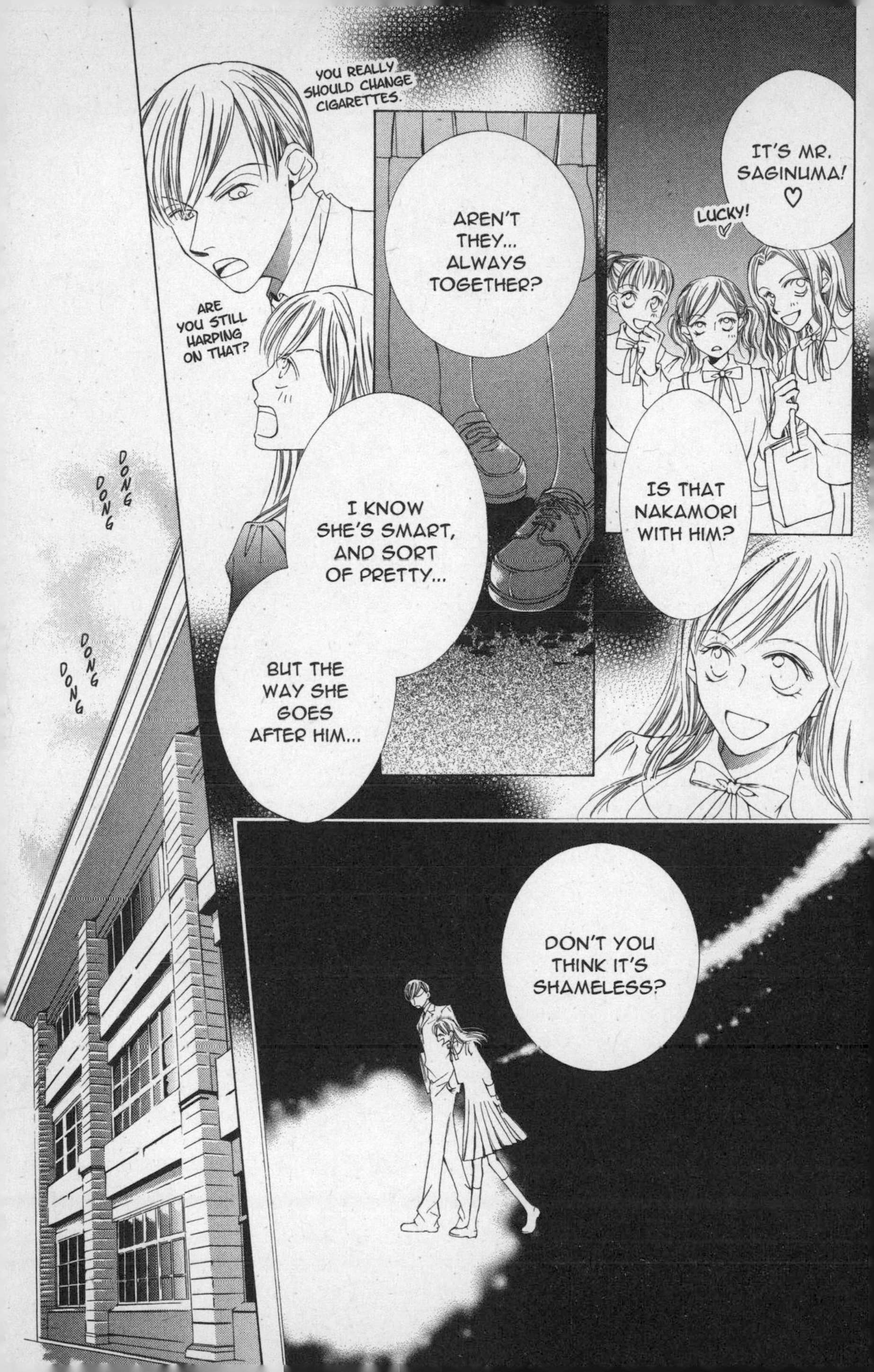
IT'S MR. SAGINUMA! ♡
LUCKY! ♡
IS THAT NAKAMORI WITH HIM?
AREN'T THEY... ALWAYS TOGETHER?
YOU REALLY SHOULD CHANGE CIGARETTES.
ARE YOU STILL HARPING ON THAT?
I KNOW SHE'S SMART, AND SORT OF PRETTY...
BUT THE WAY SHE GOES AFTER HIM...
DON'T YOU THINK IT'S SHAMELESS?
DONG DONG
DONG DONG

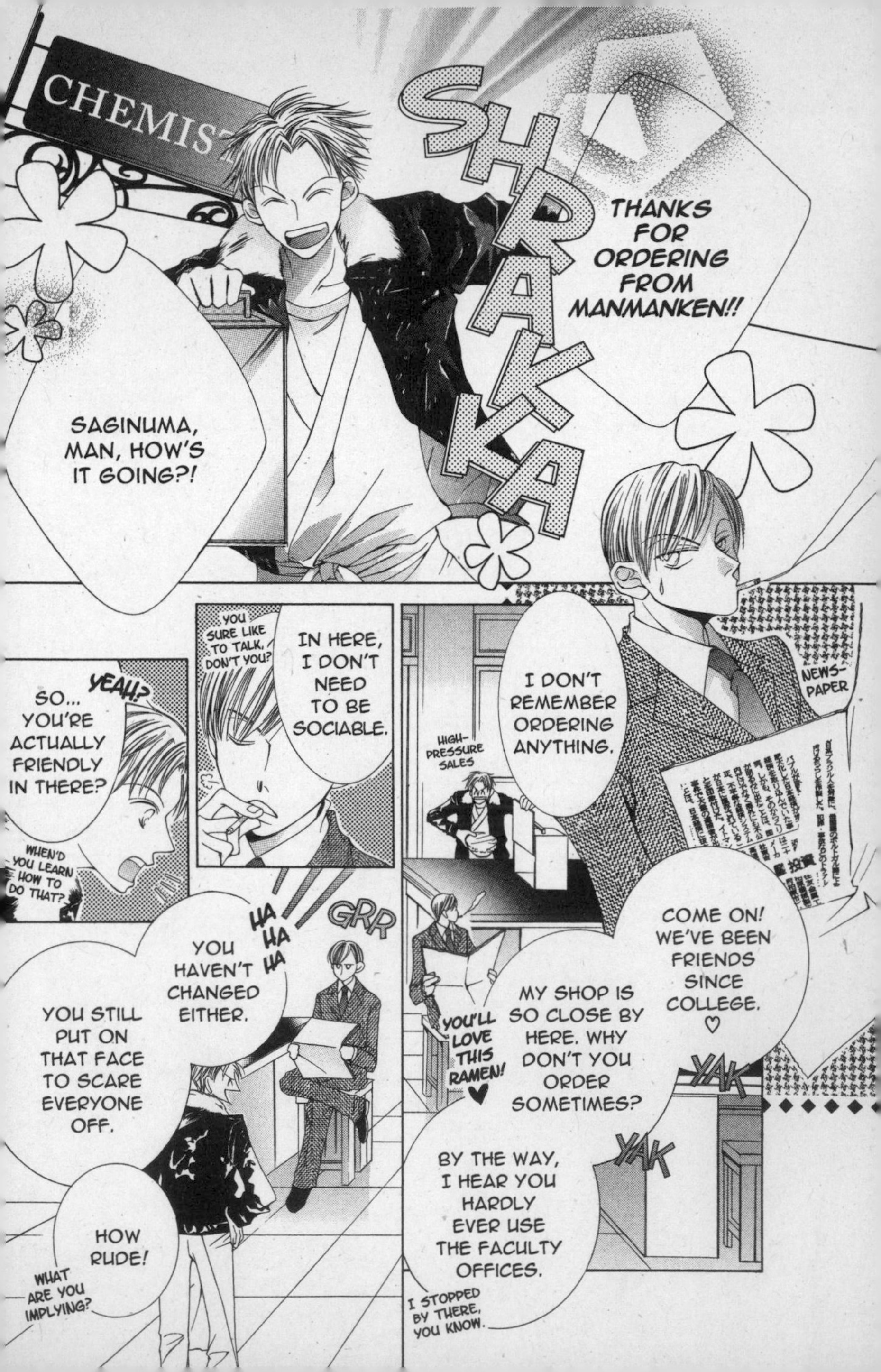
CHEMIS
SHRAKKA
THANKS FOR ORDERING FROM MANMANKEN!!
SAGINUMA, MAN, HOW'S IT GOING?!
NEWS-PAPER
I DON'T REMEMBER ORDERING ANYTHING.
HIGH-PRESSURE SALES
IN HERE, I DON'T NEED TO BE SOCIABLE.
YOU SURE LIKE TO TALK, DON'T YOU?
YEAH?
SO... YOU'RE ACTUALLY FRIENDLY IN THERE?
WHEN'D YOU LEARN HOW TO DO THAT?
COME ON! WE'VE BEEN FRIENDS SINCE COLLEGE. ♡
YAK
MY SHOP IS SO CLOSE BY HERE. WHY DON'T YOU ORDER SOMETIMES?
YOU'LL LOVE THIS RAMEN! ♥
YAK
BY THE WAY, I HEAR YOU HARDLY EVER USE THE FACULTY OFFICES.
I STOPPED BY THERE, YOU KNOW.
GRR
HA HA HA
YOU HAVEN'T CHANGED EITHER.
YOU STILL PUT ON THAT FACE TO SCARE EVERYONE OFF.
HOW RUDE!
WHAT ARE YOU IMPLYING?

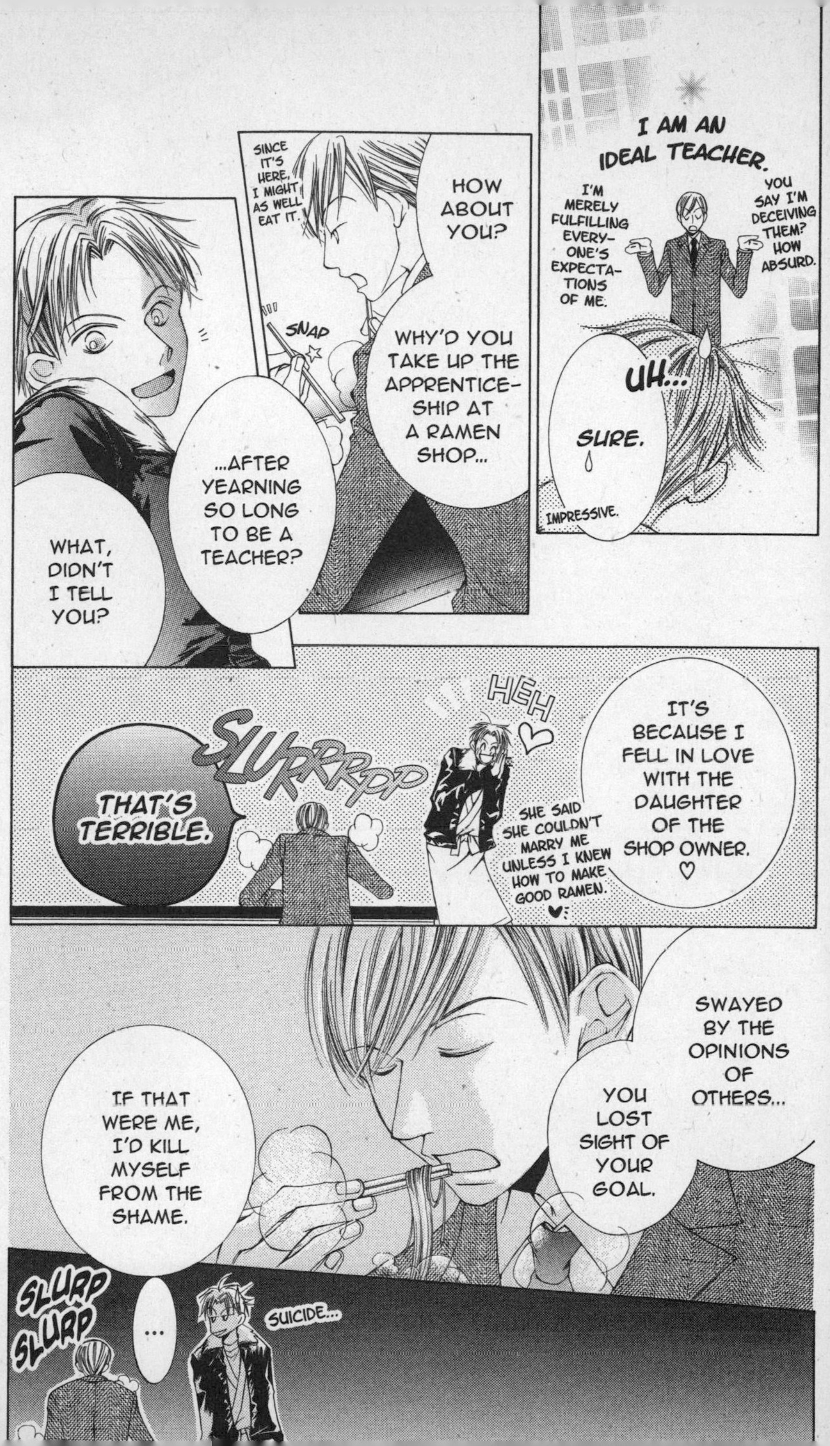
I AM AN IDEAL TEACHER.
YOU SAY I'M DECEIVING THEM? HOW ABSURD.
I'M MERELY FULFILLING EVERYONE'S EXPECTATIONS OF ME.
UH... SURE.
IMPRESSIVE.
HOW ABOUT YOU?
SINCE IT'S HERE, I MIGHT AS WELL EAT IT.
SNAP
WHY'D YOU TAKE UP THE APPRENTICESHIP AT A RAMEN SHOP...
...AFTER YEARNING SO LONG TO BE A TEACHER?
WHAT, DIDN'T I TELL YOU?
IT'S BECAUSE I FELL IN LOVE WITH THE DAUGHTER OF THE SHOP OWNER. ♡
HEH ♡
SHE SAID SHE COULDN'T MARRY ME UNLESS I KNEW HOW TO MAKE GOOD RAMEN. ♥
SLURRRPP
THAT'S TERRIBLE.
SWAYED BY THE OPINIONS OF OTHERS...
YOU LOST SIGHT OF YOUR GOAL.
IF THAT WERE ME, I'D KILL MYSELF FROM THE SHAME.
SUICIDE...
...
SLURP SLURP

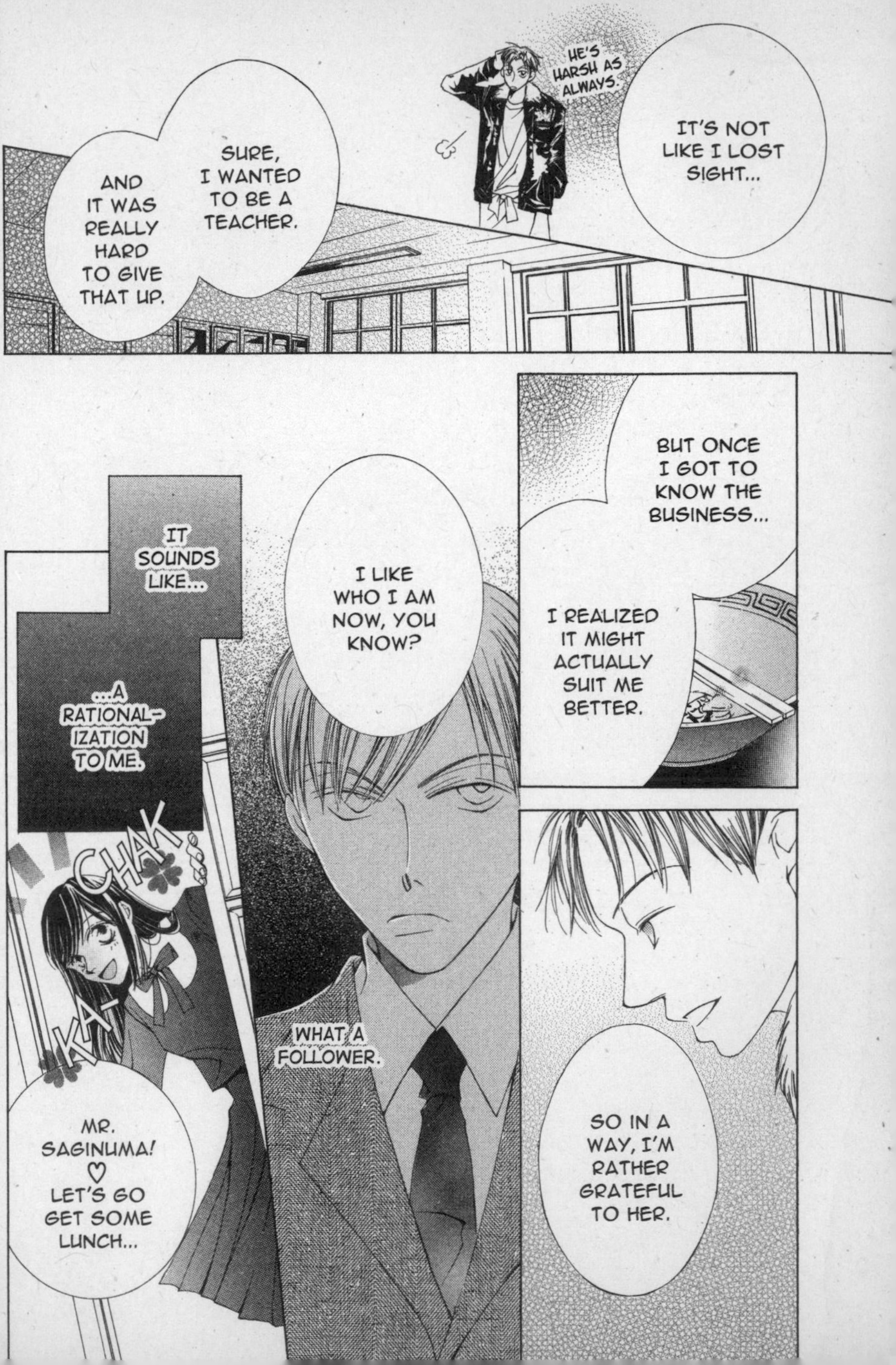
HE'S HARSH AS ALWAYS.
IT'S NOT LIKE I LOST SIGHT...
SURE, I WANTED TO BE A TEACHER.
AND IT WAS REALLY HARD TO GIVE THAT UP.
BUT ONCE I GOT TO KNOW THE BUSINESS...
I REALIZED IT MIGHT ACTUALLY SUIT ME BETTER.
SO IN A WAY, I'M RATHER GRATEFUL TO HER.
I LIKE WHO I AM NOW, YOU KNOW?
WHAT A FOLLOWER.
IT SOUNDS LIKE...
...A RATIONALIZATION TO ME.
KA-CHAK
MR. SAGINUMA! ♡ LET'S GO GET SOME LUNCH...

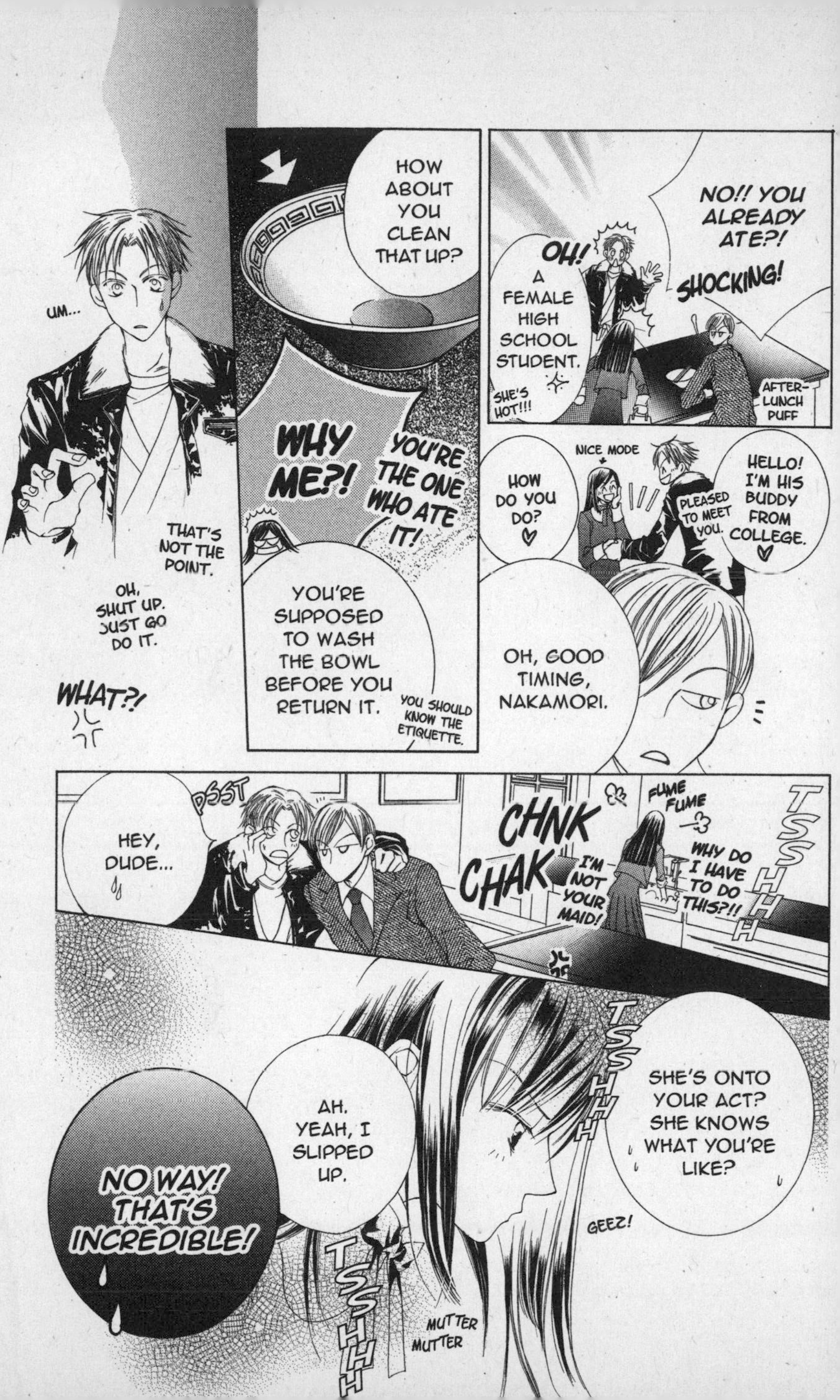
NO!! YOU ALREADY ATE?!
SHOCKING!
OH!
A FEMALE HIGH SCHOOL STUDENT.
SHE'S HOT!!!
AFTER-LUNCH PUFF
HELLO! I'M HIS BUDDY FROM COLLEGE.
PLEASED TO MEET YOU.
NICE MODE
HOW DO YOU DO?
OH, GOOD TIMING, NAKAMORI.
HOW ABOUT YOU CLEAN THAT UP?
WHY ME?!
YOU'RE THE ONE WHO ATE IT!
YOU'RE SUPPOSED TO WASH THE BOWL BEFORE YOU RETURN IT.
YOU SHOULD KNOW THE ETIQUETTE.
UM...
THAT'S NOT THE POINT.
OH, SHUT UP. JUST GO DO IT.
WHAT?!
TSSHHHH
WHY DO I HAVE TO DO THIS?!!
FUME FUME
I'M NOT YOUR MAID!
CHNK CHAK
PSST
HEY, DUDE...
SHE'S ONTO YOUR ACT? SHE KNOWS WHAT YOU'RE LIKE?
TSSHHHH
GEEZ!
AH. YEAH, I SLIPPED UP.
NO WAY! THAT'S INCREDIBLE!
TSSHHHH
MUTTER MUTTER

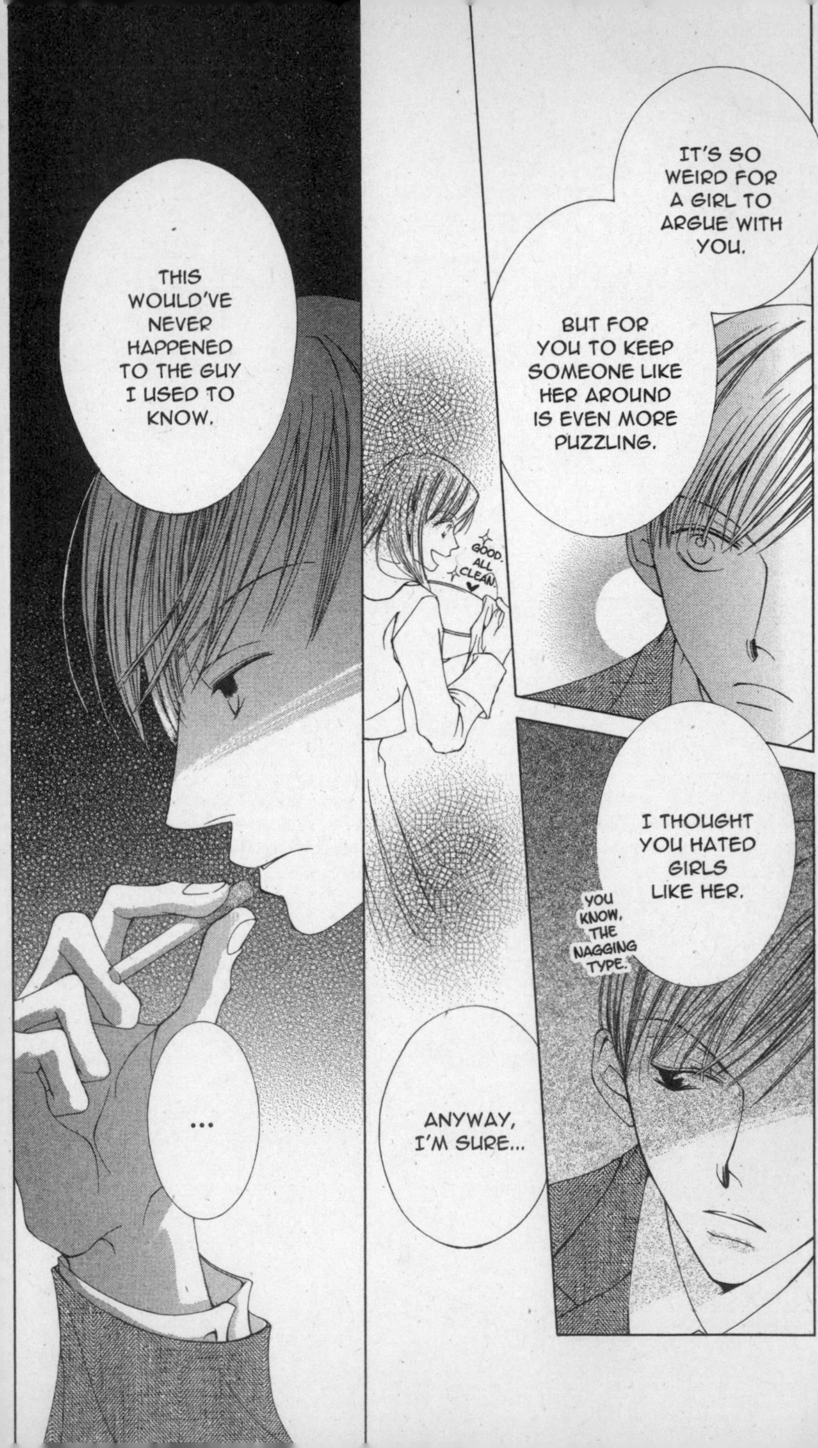
IT'S SO WEIRD FOR A GIRL TO ARGUE WITH YOU.
BUT FOR YOU TO KEEP SOMEONE LIKE HER AROUND IS EVEN MORE PUZZLING.
GOOD. ALL CLEAN.
I THOUGHT YOU HATED GIRLS LIKE HER.
YOU KNOW, THE NAGGING TYPE.
ANYWAY, I'M SURE...
THIS WOULD'VE NEVER HAPPENED TO THE GUY I USED TO KNOW.
...

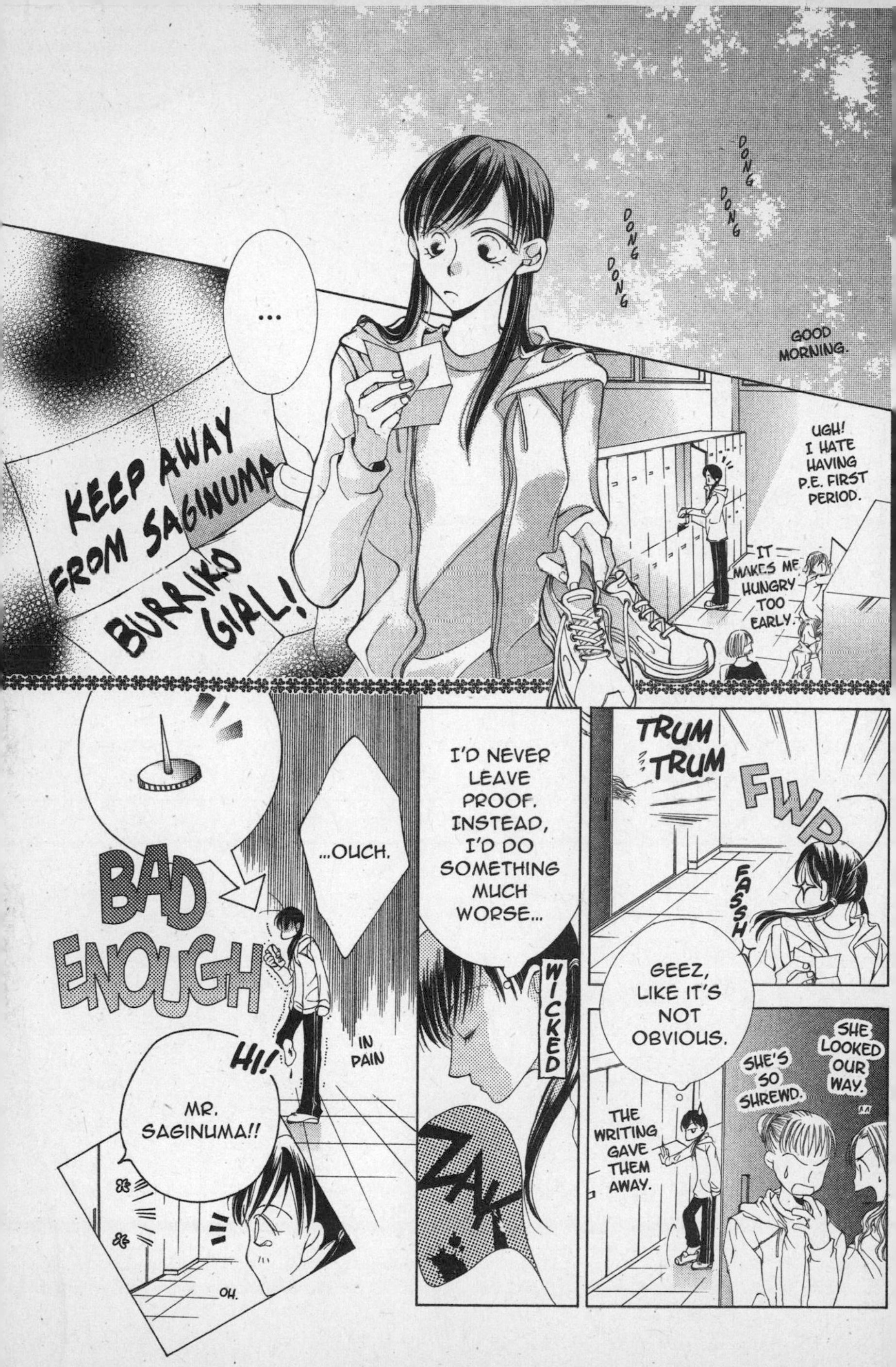
DONG DONG
DONG DONG
GOOD MORNING.
UGH! I HATE HAVING P.E. FIRST PERIOD.
IT MAKES ME HUNGRY TOO EARLY.
...
KEEP AWAY FROM SAGINUMA
BURRIKO GIRL!
TRUM TRUM
FWP
FASSH
GEEZ, LIKE IT'S NOT OBVIOUS.
SHE LOOKED OUR WAY.
SHE'S SO SHREWD.
THE WRITING GAVE THEM AWAY.
I'D NEVER LEAVE PROOF. INSTEAD, I'D DO SOMETHING MUCH WORSE...
WICKED
ZAP
BAD ENOUGH
...OUCH.
IN PAIN
HI!
MR. SAGINUMA!!
OH.

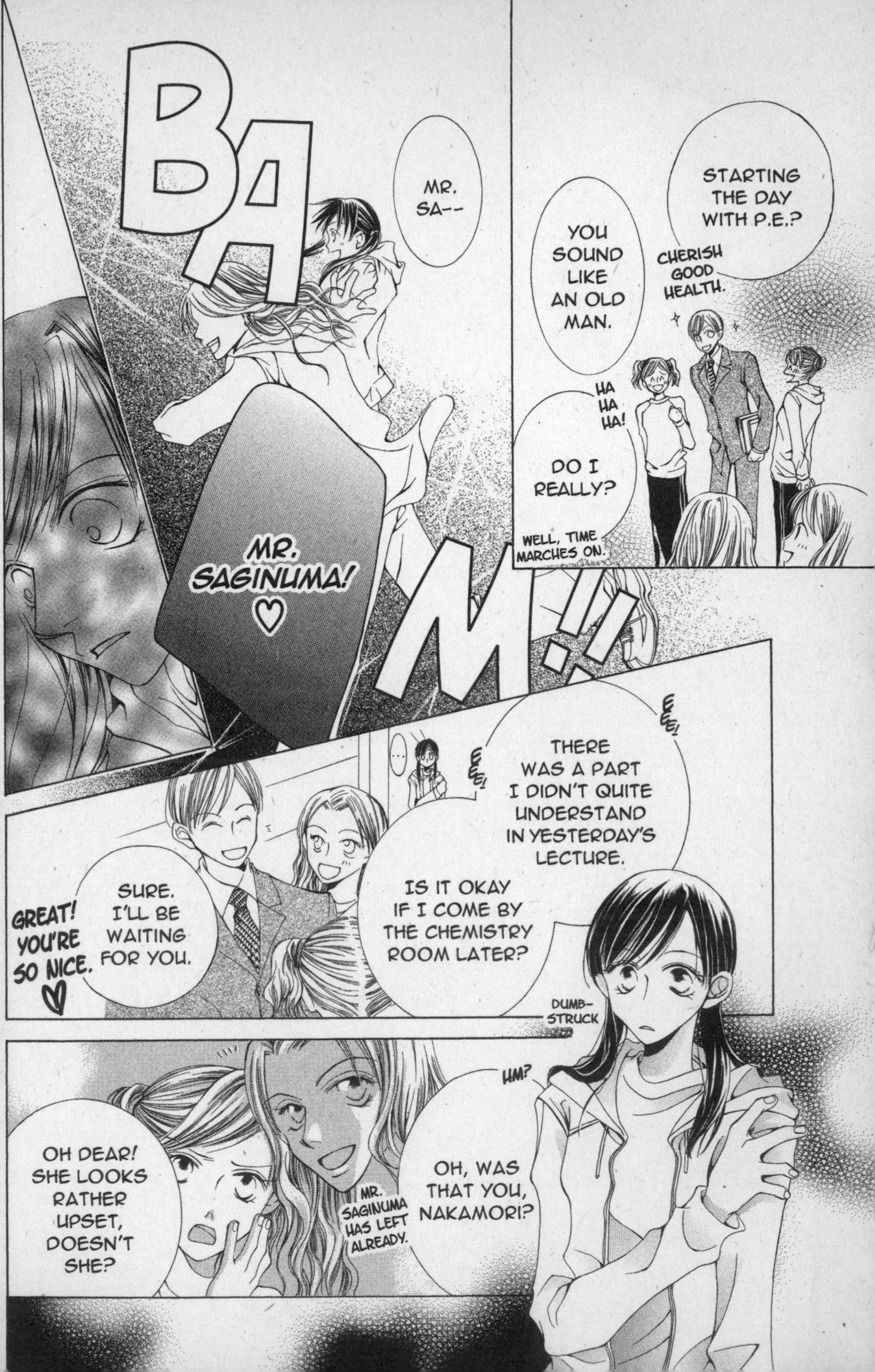
STARTING THE DAY WITH P.E.?
CHERISH GOOD HEALTH.
YOU SOUND LIKE AN OLD MAN.
HA HA HA!
DO I REALLY?
WELL, TIME MARCHES ON.
MR. SA--
BA
M!!
MR. SAGINUMA! ♡
EEE!
EEE!
...
THERE WAS A PART I DIDN'T QUITE UNDERSTAND IN YESTERDAY'S LECTURE.
IS IT OKAY IF I COME BY THE CHEMISTRY ROOM LATER?
SURE. I'LL BE WAITING FOR YOU.
GREAT! YOU'RE SO NICE. ♡
DUMB-STRUCK
HM?
OH, WAS THAT YOU, NAKAMORI?
MR. SAGINUMA HAS LEFT ALREADY.
OH DEAR! SHE LOOKS RATHER UPSET, DOESN'T SHE?

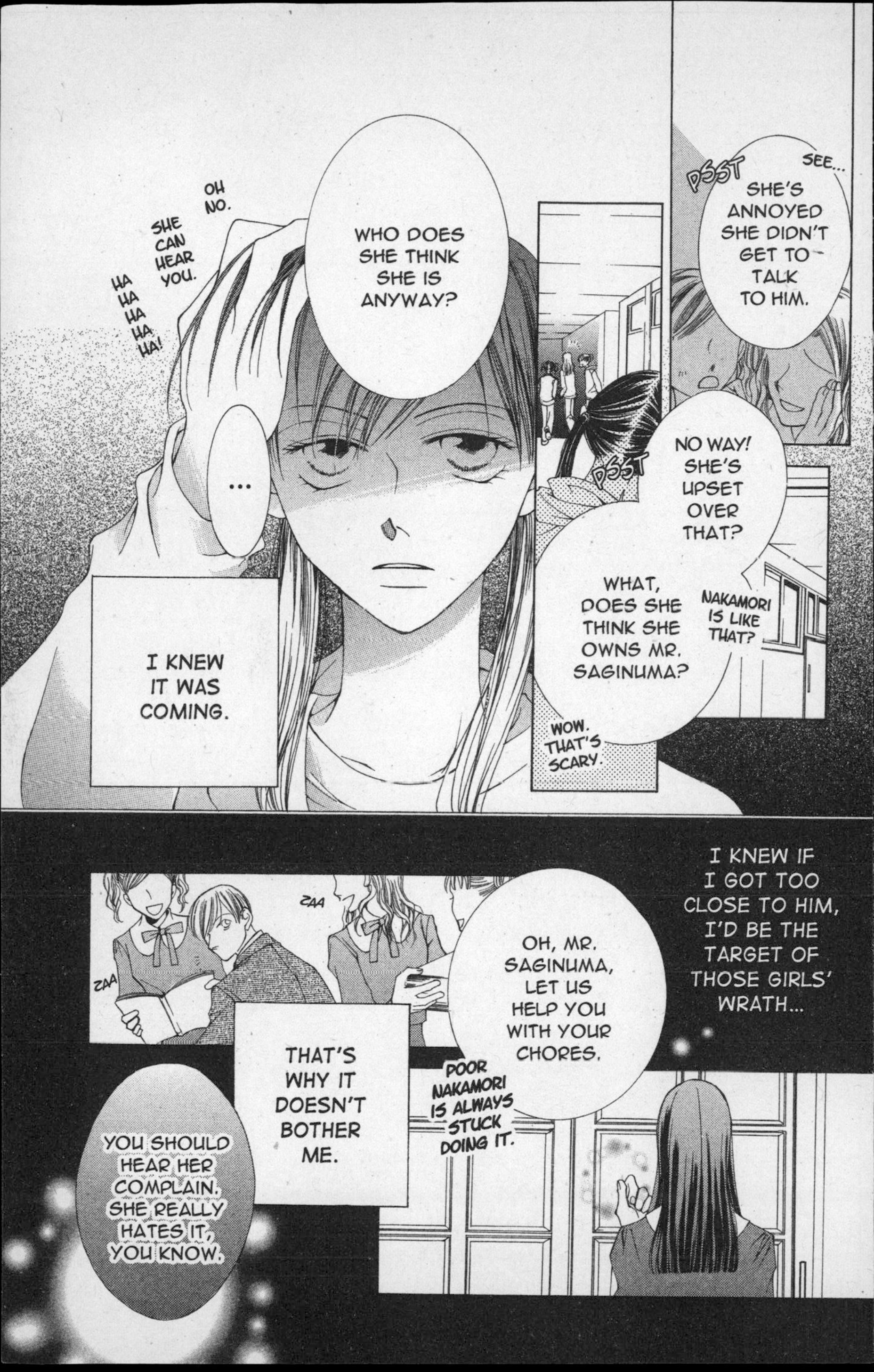
PSST
SEE...
SHE'S ANNOYED SHE DIDN'T GET TO TALK TO HIM.
PSST
NO WAY! SHE'S UPSET OVER THAT?
NAKAMORI IS LIKE THAT?
WHAT, DOES SHE THINK SHE OWNS MR. SAGINUMA?
WOW. THAT'S SCARY.
WHO DOES SHE THINK SHE IS ANYWAY?
OH NO.
SHE CAN HEAR YOU.
HA HA HA HA HA!
...
I KNEW IT WAS COMING.
I KNEW IF I GOT TOO CLOSE TO HIM, I'D BE THE TARGET OF THOSE GIRLS' WRATH...
OH, MR. SAGINUMA, LET US HELP YOU WITH YOUR CHORES.
ZAA
ZAA
THAT'S WHY IT DOESN'T BOTHER ME.
POOR NAKAMORI IS ALWAYS STUCK DOING IT.
YOU SHOULD HEAR HER COMPLAIN. SHE REALLY HATES IT, YOU KNOW.

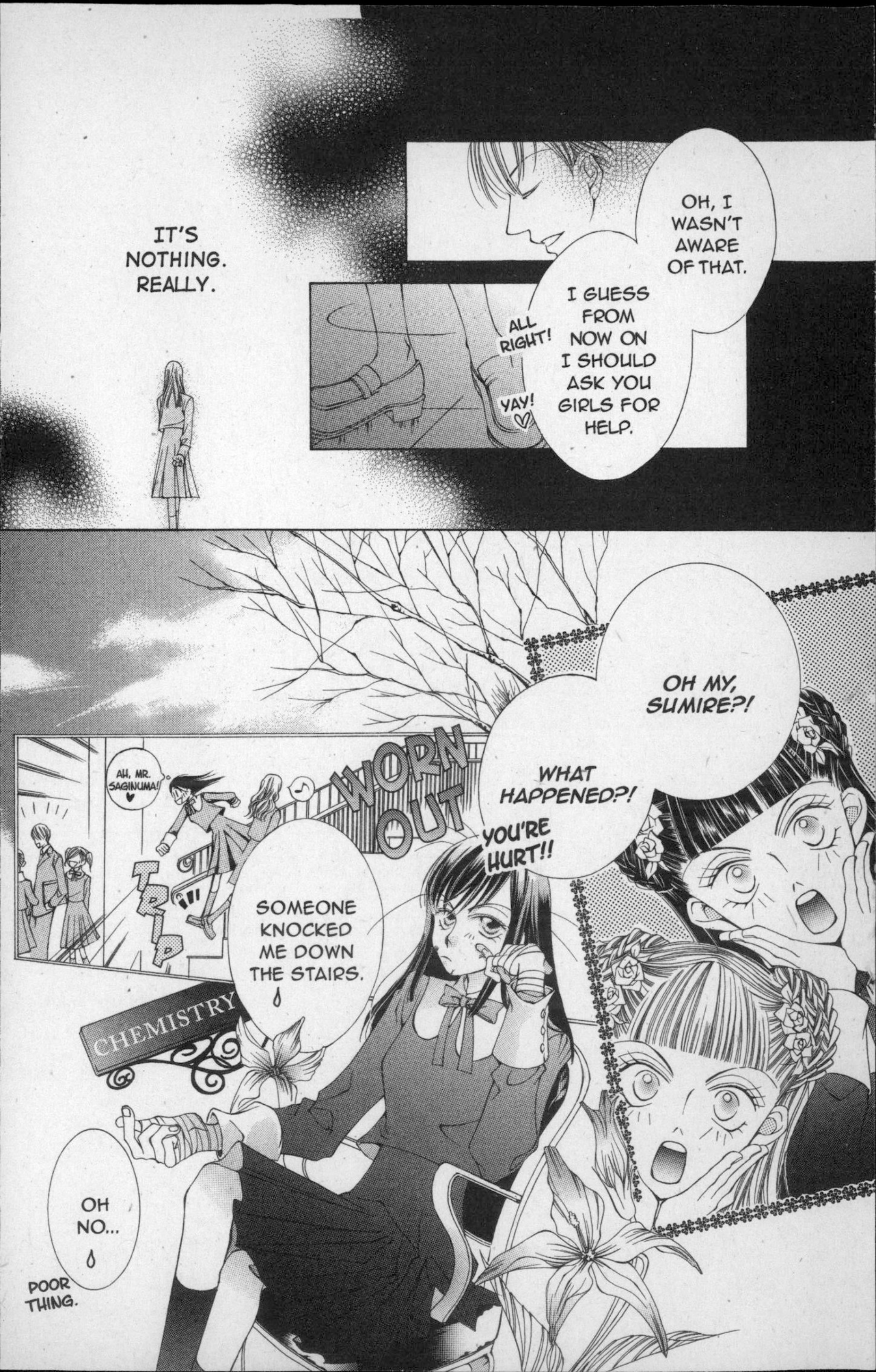
OH, I WASN'T AWARE OF THAT.
I GUESS FROM NOW ON I SHOULD ASK YOU GIRLS FOR HELP.
ALL RIGHT!
YAY! ♥
IT'S NOTHING. REALLY.
OH MY, SUMIRE?!
WHAT HAPPENED?!
YOU'RE HURT!!
SOMEONE KNOCKED ME DOWN THE STAIRS.
WORN OUT
AH, MR. SAGINUMA! ♥
TRIP
CHEMISTRY
OH NO...
POOR THING.

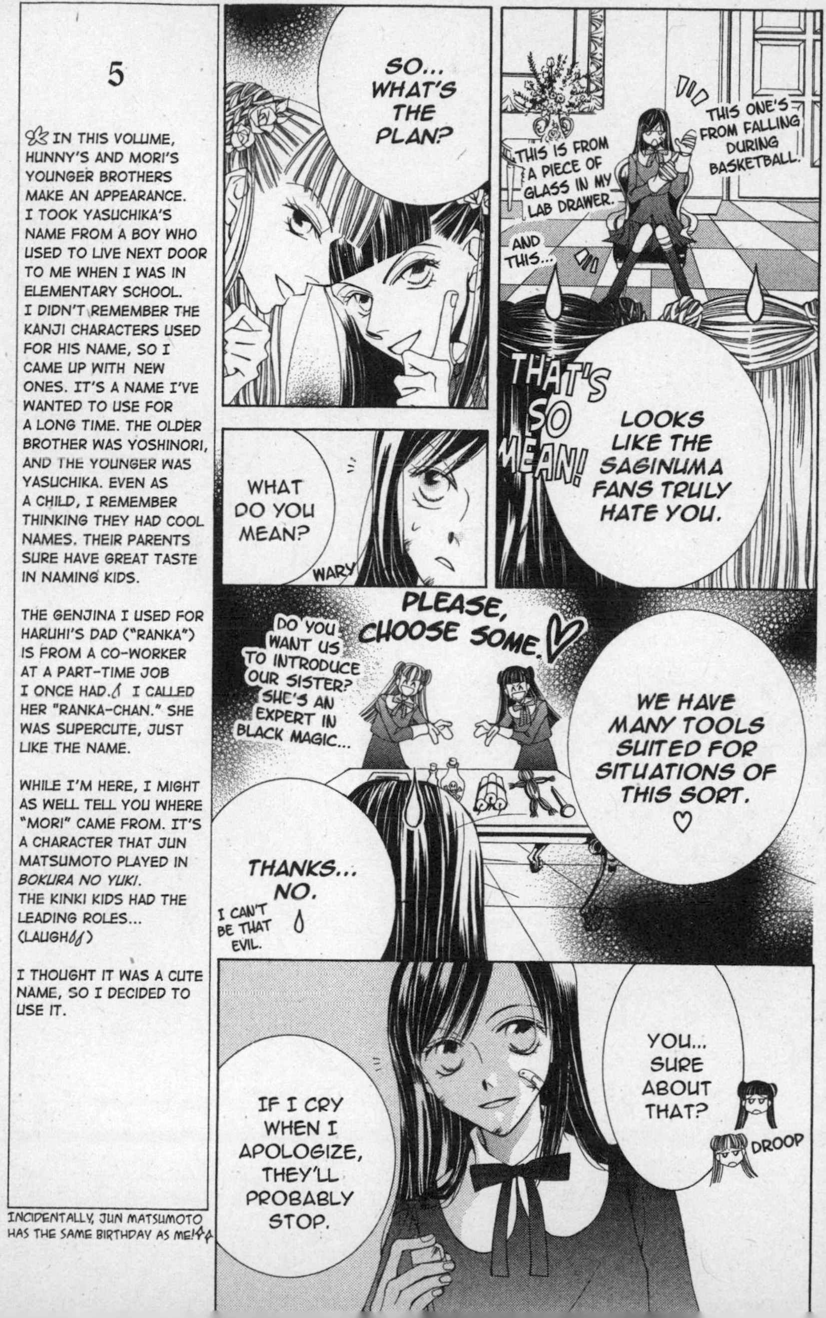
THIS ONE'S FROM FALLING DURING BASKETBALL.
THIS IS FROM A PIECE OF GLASS IN MY LAB DRAWER.
AND THIS...
THAT'S SO MEAN!
LOOKS LIKE THE SAGINUMA FANS TRULY HATE YOU.
SO... WHAT'S THE PLAN?
WHAT DO YOU MEAN?
WARY
WE HAVE MANY TOOLS SUITED FOR SITUATIONS OF THIS SORT. ♡
PLEASE, CHOOSE SOME. ♡
DO YOU WANT US TO INTRODUCE OUR SISTER? SHE'S AN EXPERT IN BLACK MAGIC...
THANKS... NO.
I CAN'T BE THAT EVIL.
YOU... SURE ABOUT THAT?
DROOP
IF I CRY WHEN I APOLOGIZE, THEY'LL PROBABLY STOP.

5

IN THIS VOLUME, HUNNY'S AND MORI'S YOUNGER BROTHERS MAKE AN APPEARANCE. I TOOK YASUCHIKA'S NAME FROM A BOY WHO USED TO LIVE NEXT DOOR TO ME WHEN I WAS IN ELEMENTARY SCHOOL. I DIDN'T REMEMBER THE KANJI CHARACTERS USED FOR HIS NAME, SO I CAME UP WITH NEW ONES. IT'S A NAME I'VE WANTED TO USE FOR A LONG TIME. THE OLDER BROTHER WAS YOSHINORI, AND THE YOUNGER WAS YASUCHIKA. EVEN AS A CHILD, I REMEMBER THINKING THEY HAD COOL NAMES. THEIR PARENTS SURE HAVE GREAT TASTE IN NAMING KIDS.

THE GENJINA I USED FOR HARUHI'S DAD ("RANKA") IS FROM A CO-WORKER AT A PART-TIME JOB I ONCE HAD. I CALLED HER "RANKA-CHAN." SHE WAS SUPERCUTE, JUST LIKE THE NAME.

WHILE I'M HERE, I MIGHT AS WELL TELL YOU WHERE "MORI" CAME FROM. IT'S A CHARACTER THAT JUN MATSUMOTO PLAYED IN *BOKURA NO YUKI*. THE KINKI KIDS HAD THE LEADING ROLES... (LAUGH)

I THOUGHT IT WAS A CUTE NAME, SO I DECIDED TO USE IT.

INCIDENTALLY, JUN MATSUMOTO HAS THE SAME BIRTHDAY AS ME!

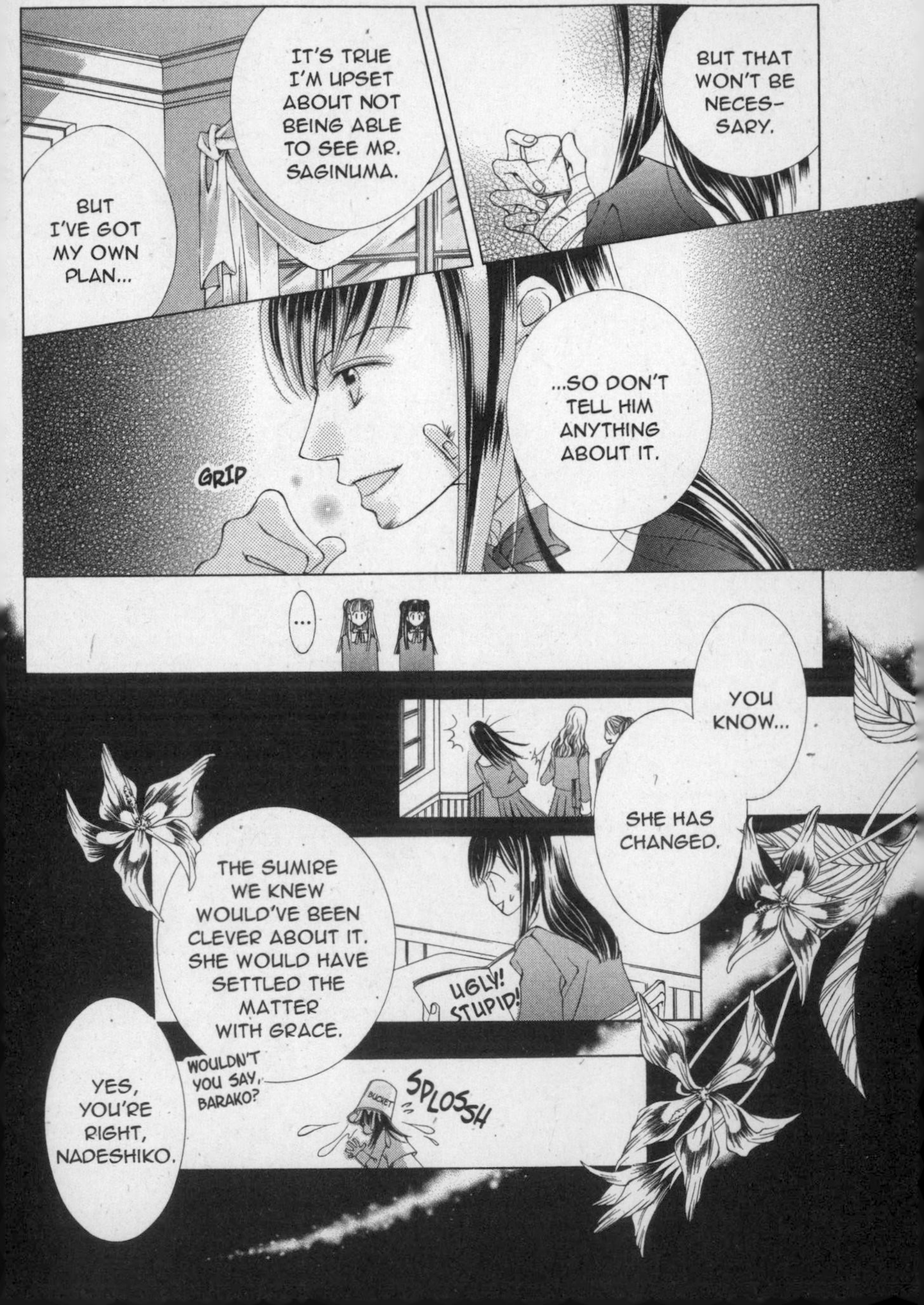
BUT THAT WON'T BE NECES-SARY.
IT'S TRUE I'M UPSET ABOUT NOT BEING ABLE TO SEE MR. SAGINUMA.
BUT I'VE GOT MY OWN PLAN...
...SO DON'T TELL HIM ANYTHING ABOUT IT.
GRIP
...
YOU KNOW...
SHE HAS CHANGED.
THE SUMIRE WE KNEW WOULD'VE BEEN CLEVER ABOUT IT. SHE WOULD HAVE SETTLED THE MATTER WITH GRACE.
UGLY! STUPID!
WOULDN'T YOU SAY, BARAKO?
SPLOSSH
BUCKET
YES, YOU'RE RIGHT, NADESHIKO.

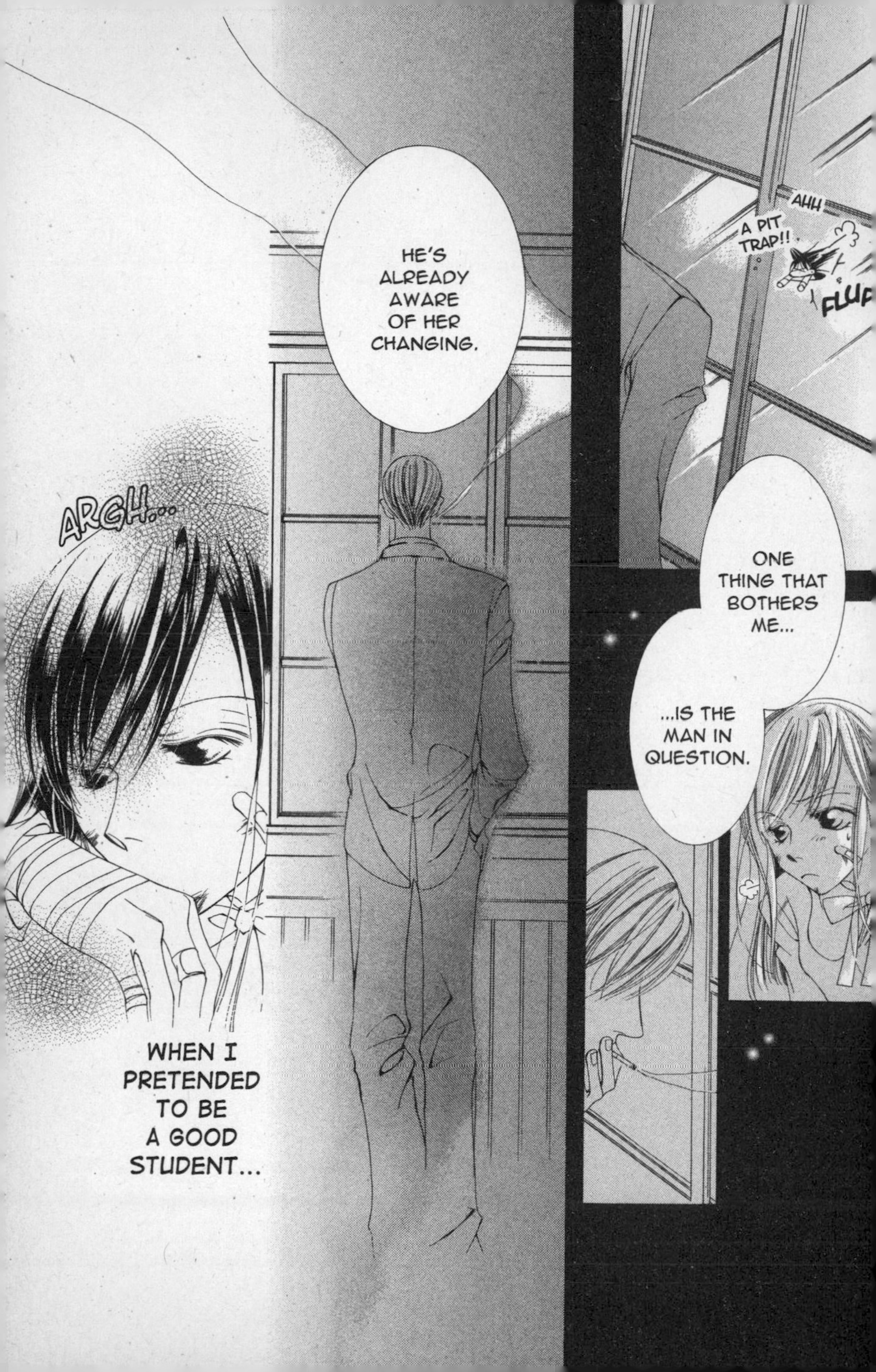
AHH
A PIT TRAP!!
FLUP
ONE THING THAT BOTHERS ME...
...IS THE MAN IN QUESTION.
HE'S ALREADY AWARE OF HER CHANGING.
ARGH...
WHEN I PRETENDED TO BE A GOOD STUDENT...

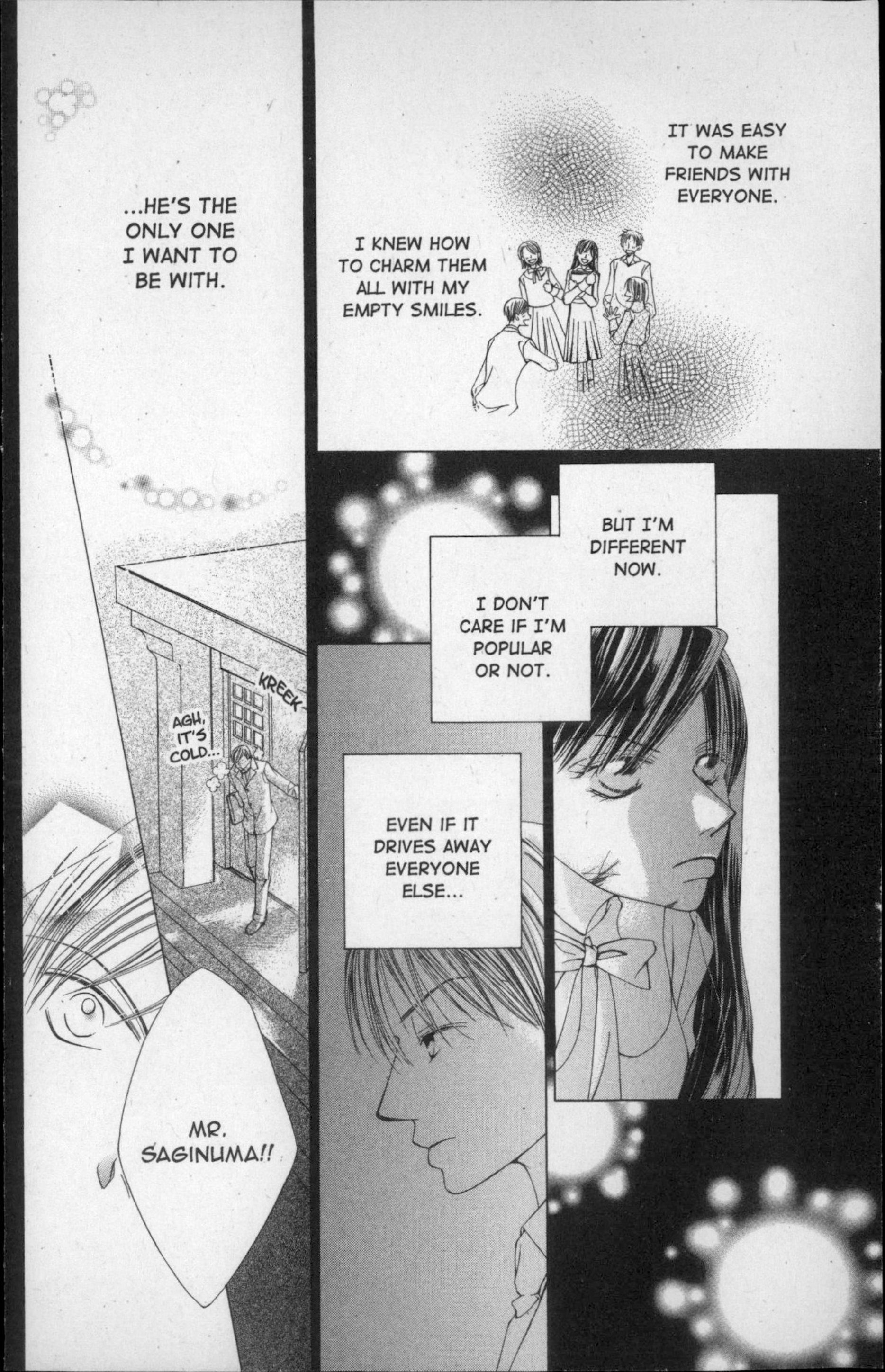
IT WAS EASY TO MAKE FRIENDS WITH EVERYONE.
I KNEW HOW TO CHARM THEM ALL WITH MY EMPTY SMILES.
BUT I'M DIFFERENT NOW.
I DON'T CARE IF I'M POPULAR OR NOT.
EVEN IF IT DRIVES AWAY EVERYONE ELSE...
...HE'S THE ONLY ONE I WANT TO BE WITH.
KREEK
AGH, IT'S COLD...
MR. SAGINUMA!!

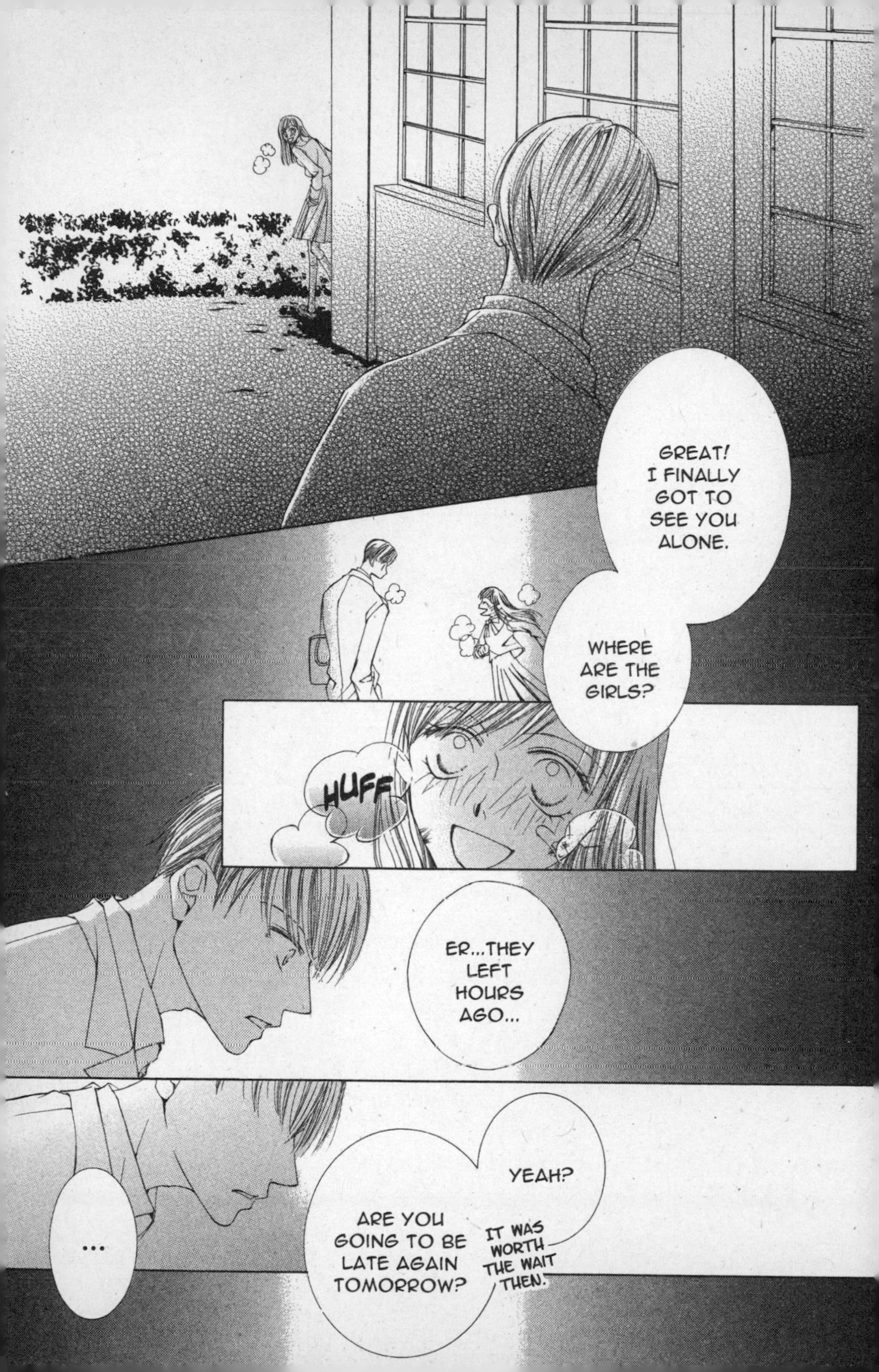
GREAT! I FINALLY GOT TO SEE YOU ALONE.
WHERE ARE THE GIRLS?
HUFF
ER...THEY LEFT HOURS AGO...
YEAH?
IT WAS WORTH THE WAIT THEN.
ARE YOU GOING TO BE LATE AGAIN TOMORROW?
...

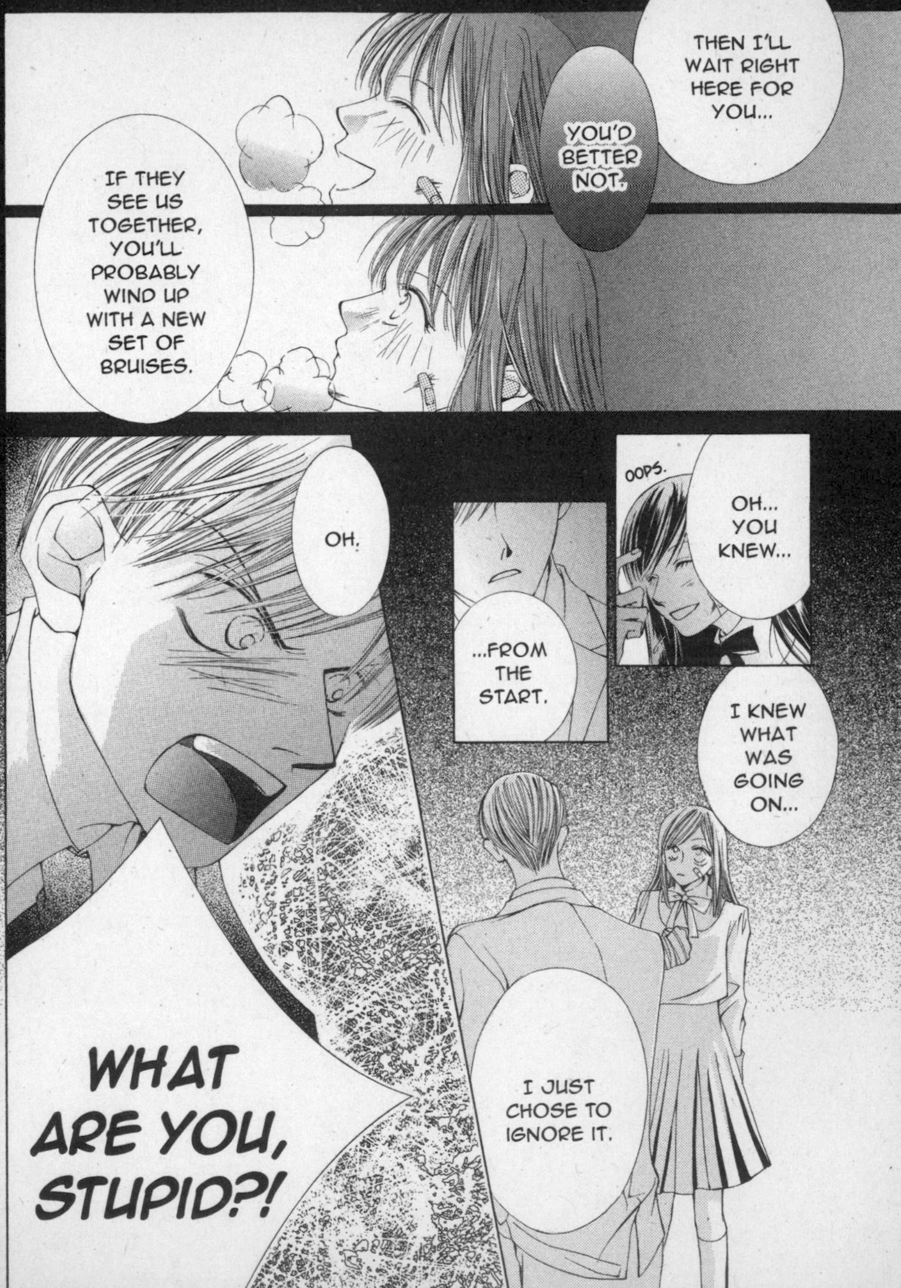
THEN I'LL WAIT RIGHT HERE FOR YOU...
YOU'D BETTER NOT.
IF THEY SEE US TOGETHER, YOU'LL PROBABLY WIND UP WITH A NEW SET OF BRUISES.
OOPS.
OH... YOU KNEW...
...FROM THE START.
I KNEW WHAT WAS GOING ON...
I JUST CHOSE TO IGNORE IT.
OH.
WHAT ARE YOU, STUPID?!

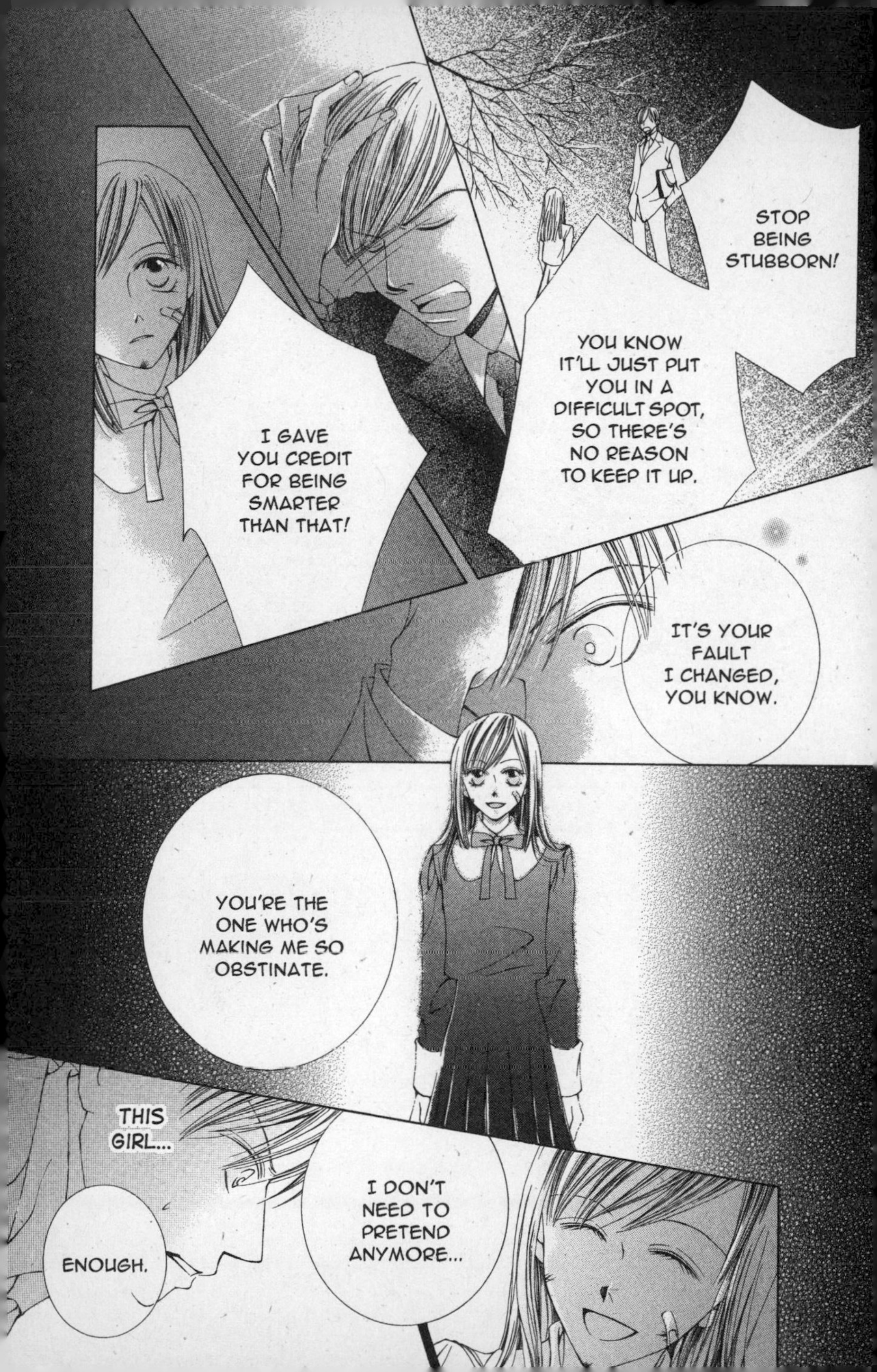
STOP BEING STUBBORN!
YOU KNOW IT'LL JUST PUT YOU IN A DIFFICULT SPOT, SO THERE'S NO REASON TO KEEP IT UP.
I GAVE YOU CREDIT FOR BEING SMARTER THAN THAT!
IT'S YOUR FAULT I CHANGED, YOU KNOW.
YOU'RE THE ONE WHO'S MAKING ME SO OBSTINATE.
I DON'T NEED TO PRETEND ANYMORE...
THIS GIRL...
ENOUGH.

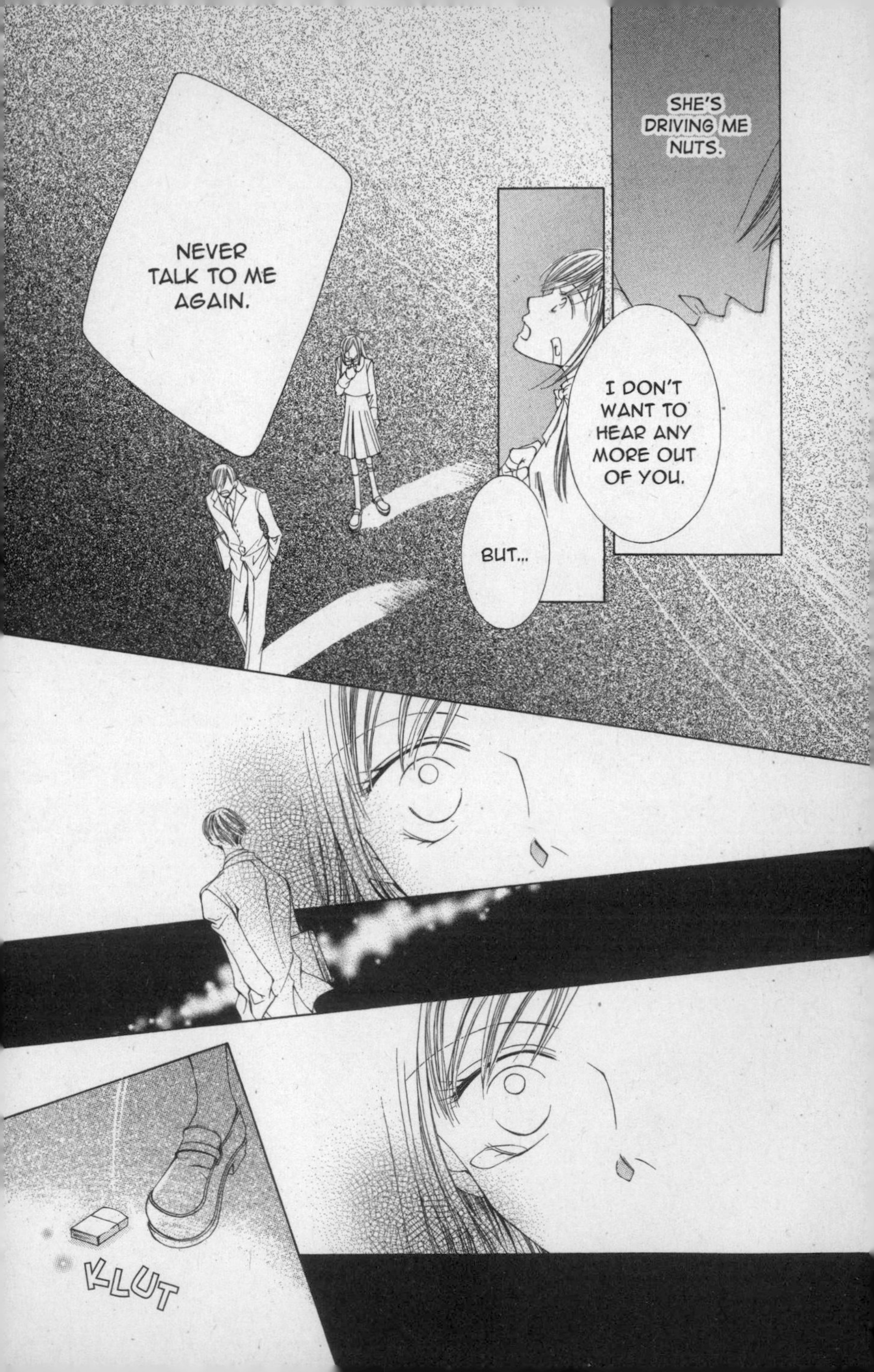
SHE'S DRIVING ME NUTS.
I DON'T WANT TO HEAR ANY MORE OUT OF YOU.
BUT...
NEVER TALK TO ME AGAIN.
KLUT

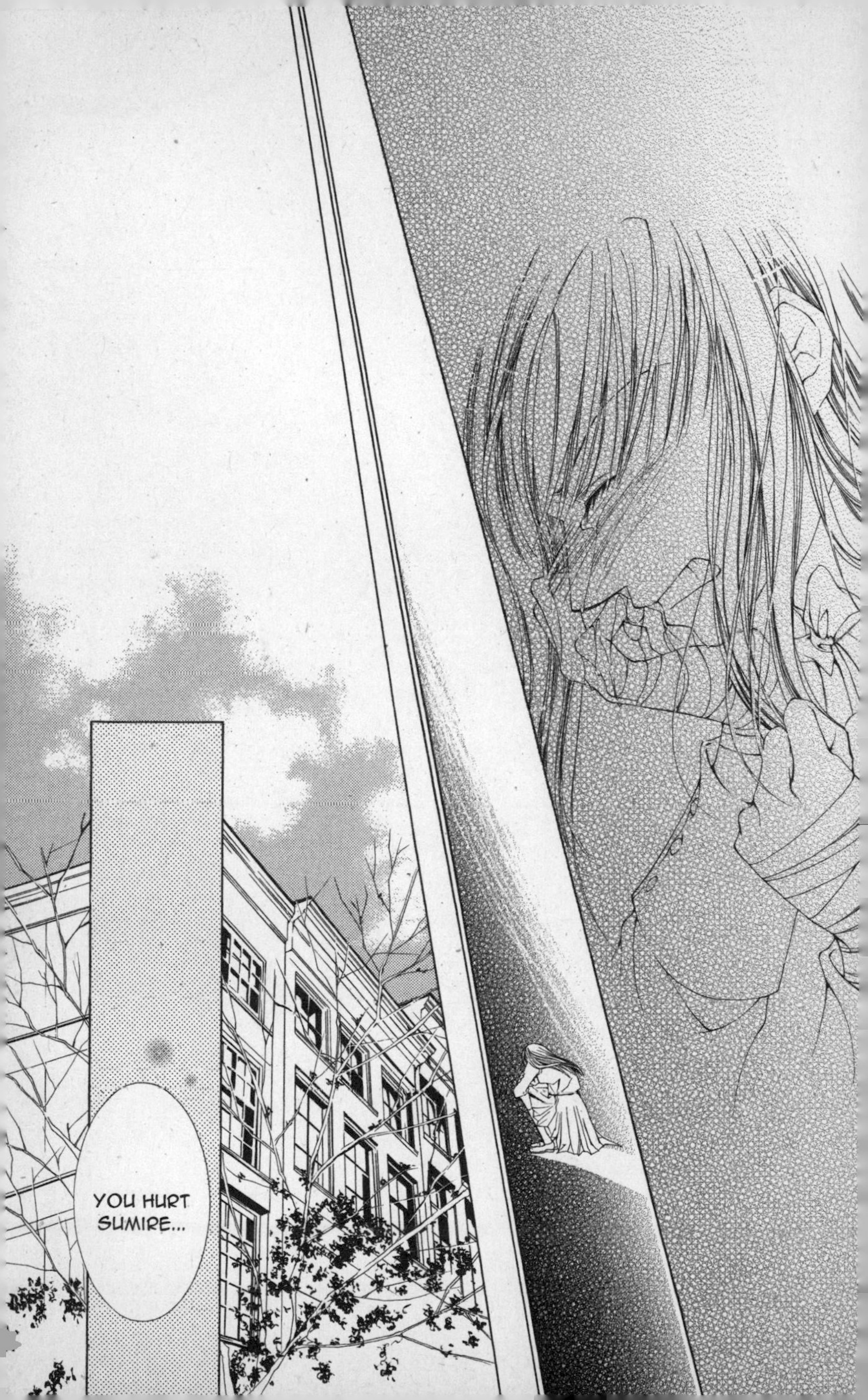
YOU HURT SUMIRE...

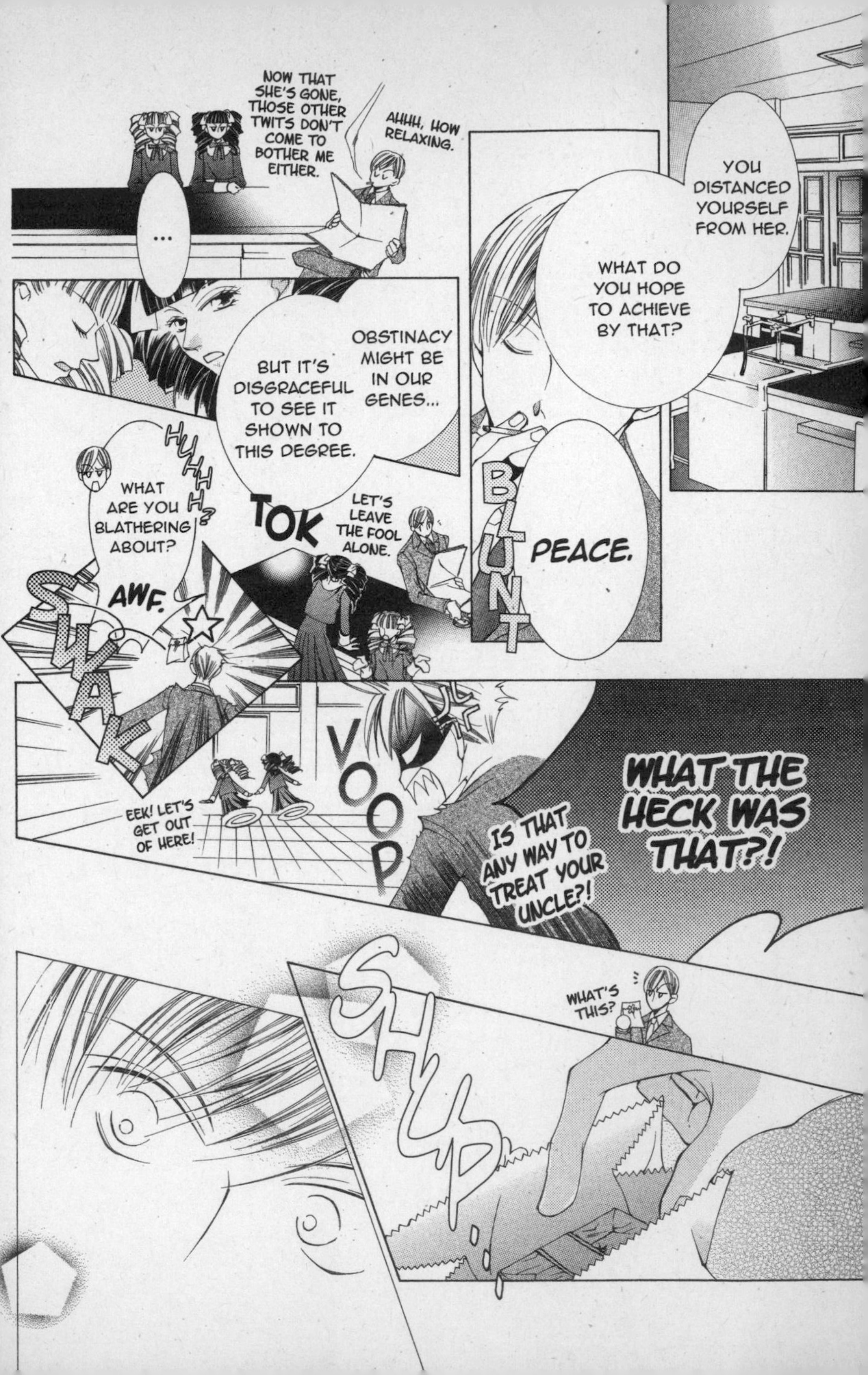

YOU DISTANCED YOURSELF FROM HER.
WHAT DO YOU HOPE TO ACHIEVE BY THAT?
BLUNT
PEACE.
AHHH, HOW RELAXING.
NOW THAT SHE'S GONE, THOSE OTHER TWITS DON'T COME TO BOTHER ME EITHER.
...
OBSTINACY MIGHT BE IN OUR GENES...
BUT IT'S DISGRACEFUL TO SEE IT SHOWN TO THIS DEGREE.
HUHHH?
WHAT ARE YOU BLATHERING ABOUT?
TOK
LET'S LEAVE THE FOOL ALONE.
AWF.
SWAK
WHAT THE HECK WAS THAT?!
IS THAT ANY WAY TO TREAT YOUR UNCLE?!
VOOP
EEK! LET'S GET OUT OF HERE!
WHAT'S THIS?
SHUP

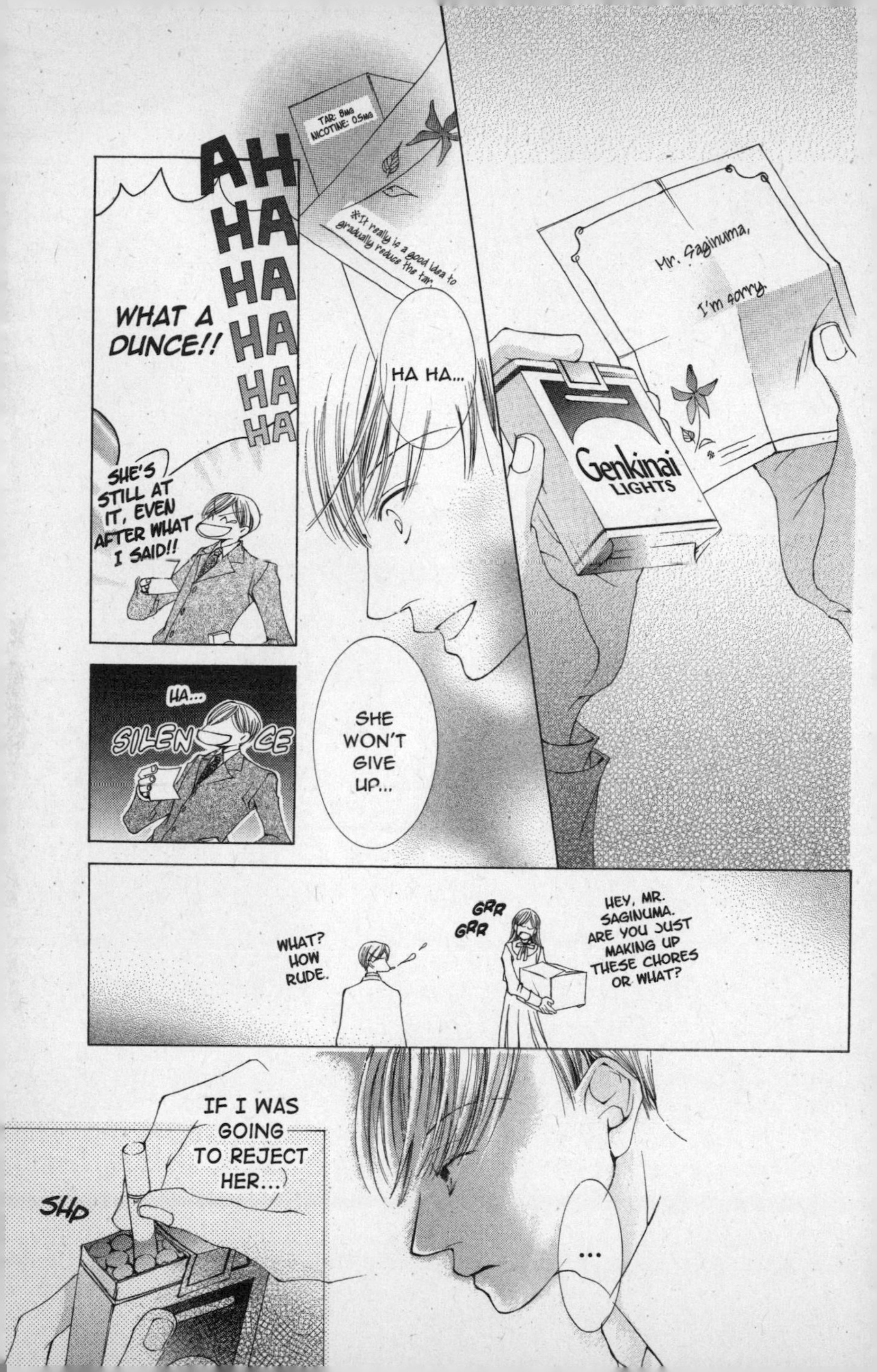
Mr. Saginuma,
I'm sorry.
Genkinai
LIGHTS
TAR: 8MG
NICOTINE: 0.5MG
※It really is a good idea to gradually reduce the tar.
HA HA...
SHE WON'T GIVE UP...
AH HA HA HA HA HA HA
WHAT A DUNCE!!
SHE'S STILL AT IT, EVEN AFTER WHAT I SAID!!
HA...
SILENCE
HEY, MR. SAGINUMA. ARE YOU JUST MAKING UP THESE CHORES OR WHAT?
GRR GRR
WHAT? HOW RUDE.
...
IF I WAS GOING TO REJECT HER...
SHp

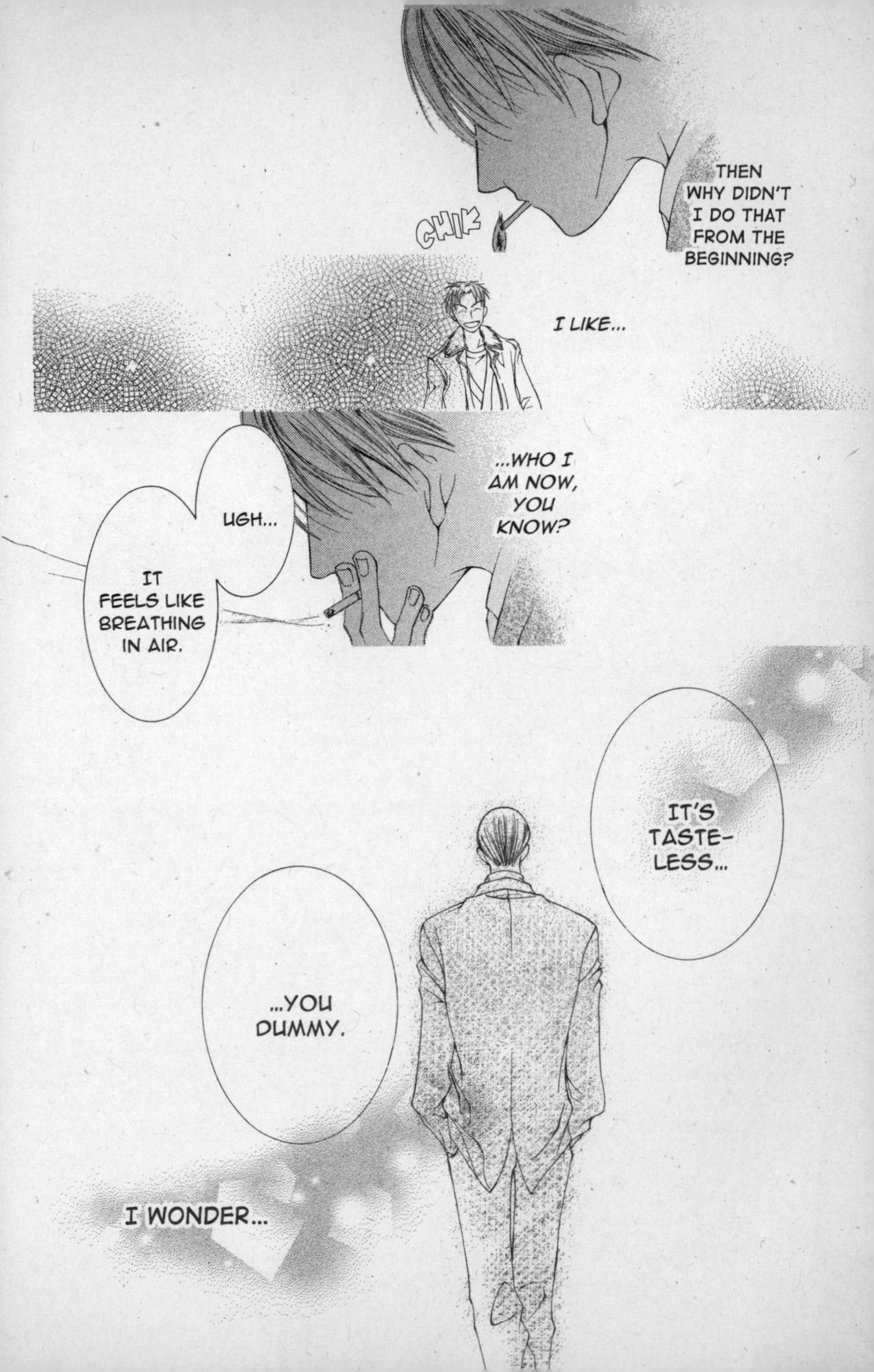
THEN WHY DIDN'T I DO THAT FROM THE BEGINNING?
CHIK
I LIKE...
...WHO I AM NOW, YOU KNOW?
UGH...
IT FEELS LIKE BREATHING IN AIR.
IT'S TASTE-LESS...
...YOU DUMMY.
I WONDER...

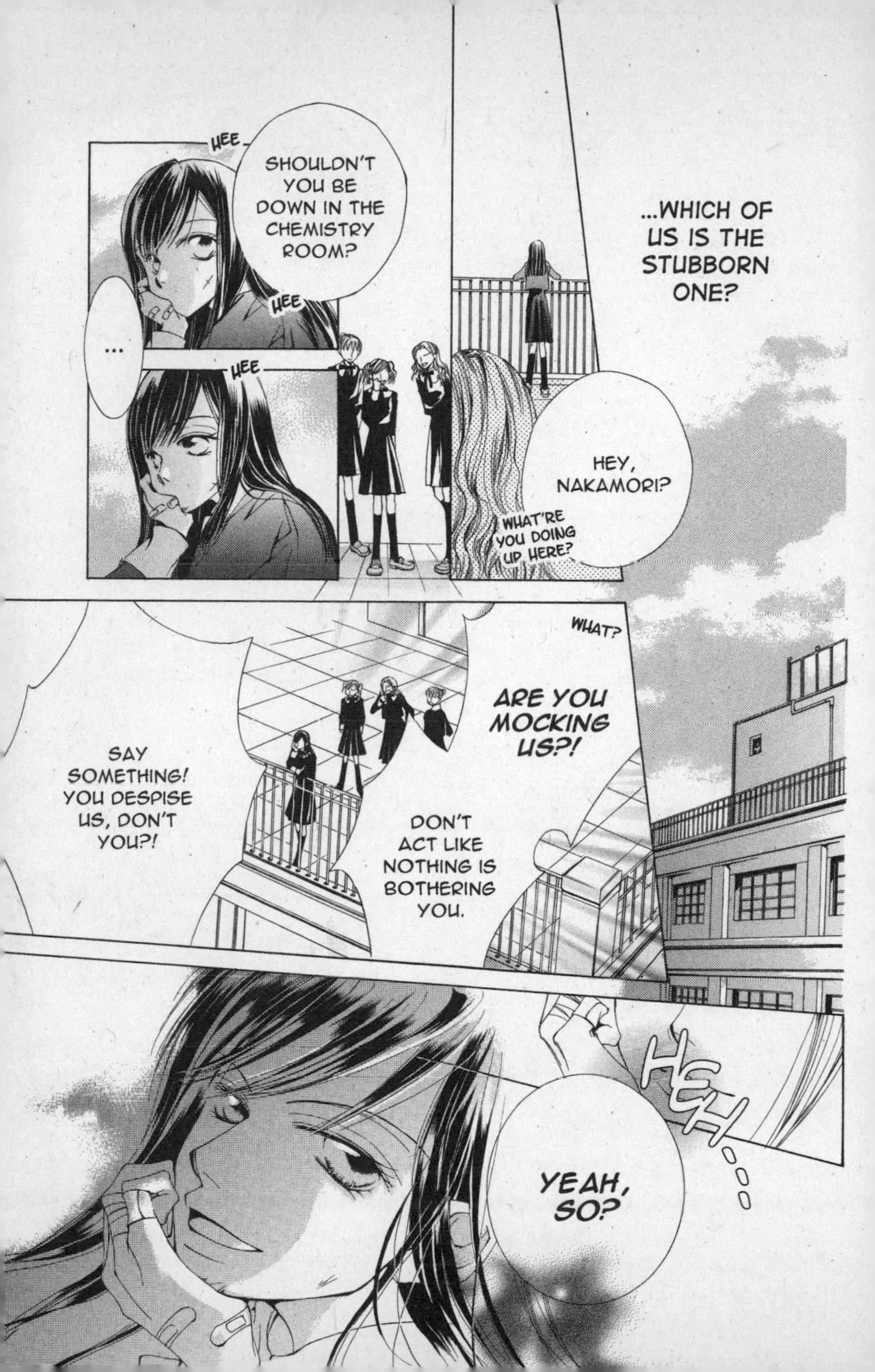
...WHICH OF US IS THE STUBBORN ONE?
HEY, NAKAMORI?
WHAT'RE YOU DOING UP HERE?
HEE
SHOULDN'T YOU BE DOWN IN THE CHEMISTRY ROOM?
HEE
...
HEE
WHAT?
ARE YOU MOCKING US?!
DON'T ACT LIKE NOTHING IS BOTHERING YOU.
SAY SOMETHING! YOU DESPISE US, DON'T YOU?!
HEH...
YEAH, SO?

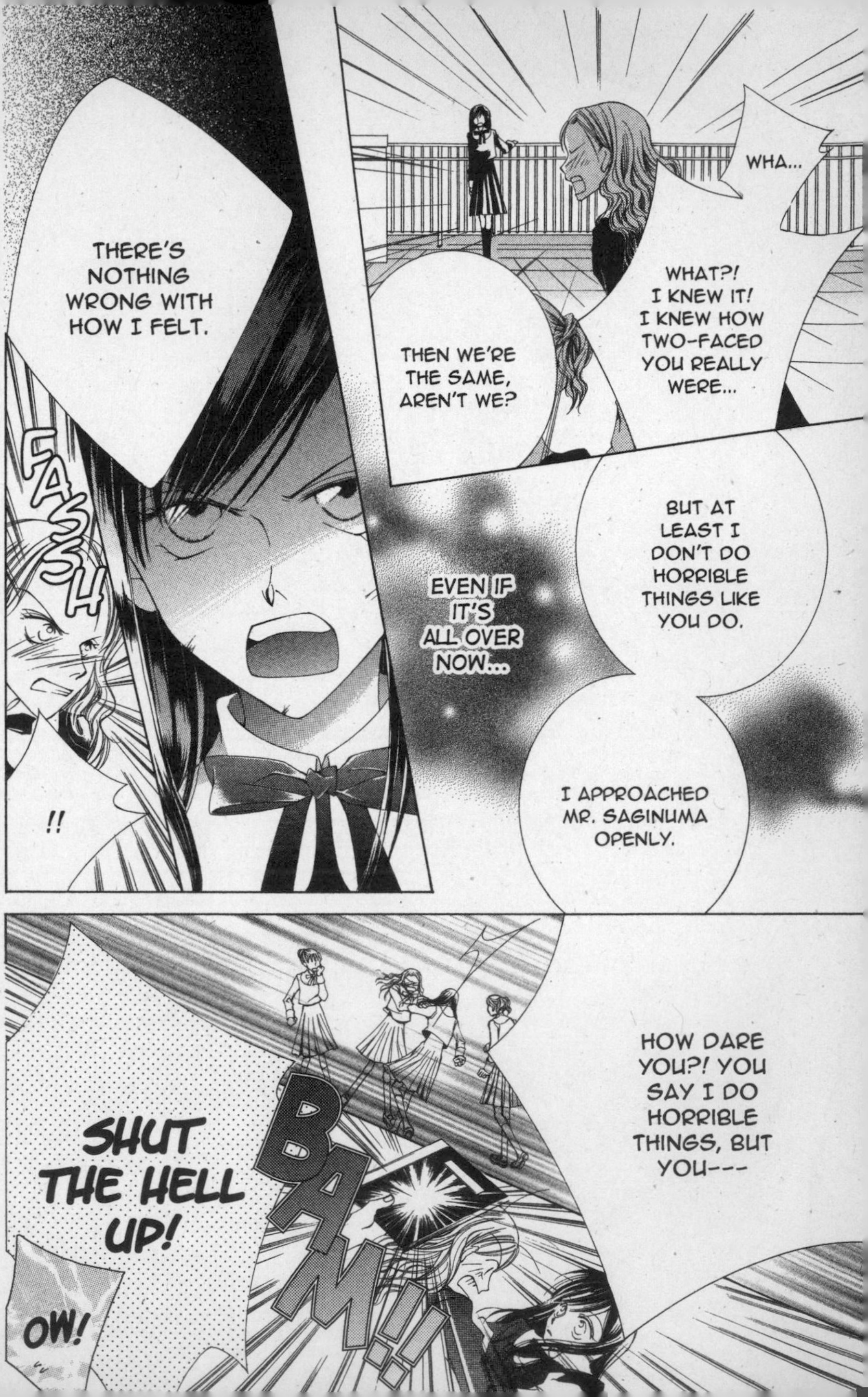
WHA...
WHAT?! I KNEW IT! I KNEW HOW TWO-FACED YOU REALLY WERE...
THEN WE'RE THE SAME, AREN'T WE?
BUT AT LEAST I DON'T DO HORRIBLE THINGS LIKE YOU DO.
EVEN IF IT'S ALL OVER NOW...
I APPROACHED MR. SAGINUMA OPENLY.
THERE'S NOTHING WRONG WITH HOW I FELT.
FASSH
!!
HOW DARE YOU?! YOU SAY I DO HORRIBLE THINGS, BUT YOU---
SHUT THE HELL UP!
BAM!!
OW!

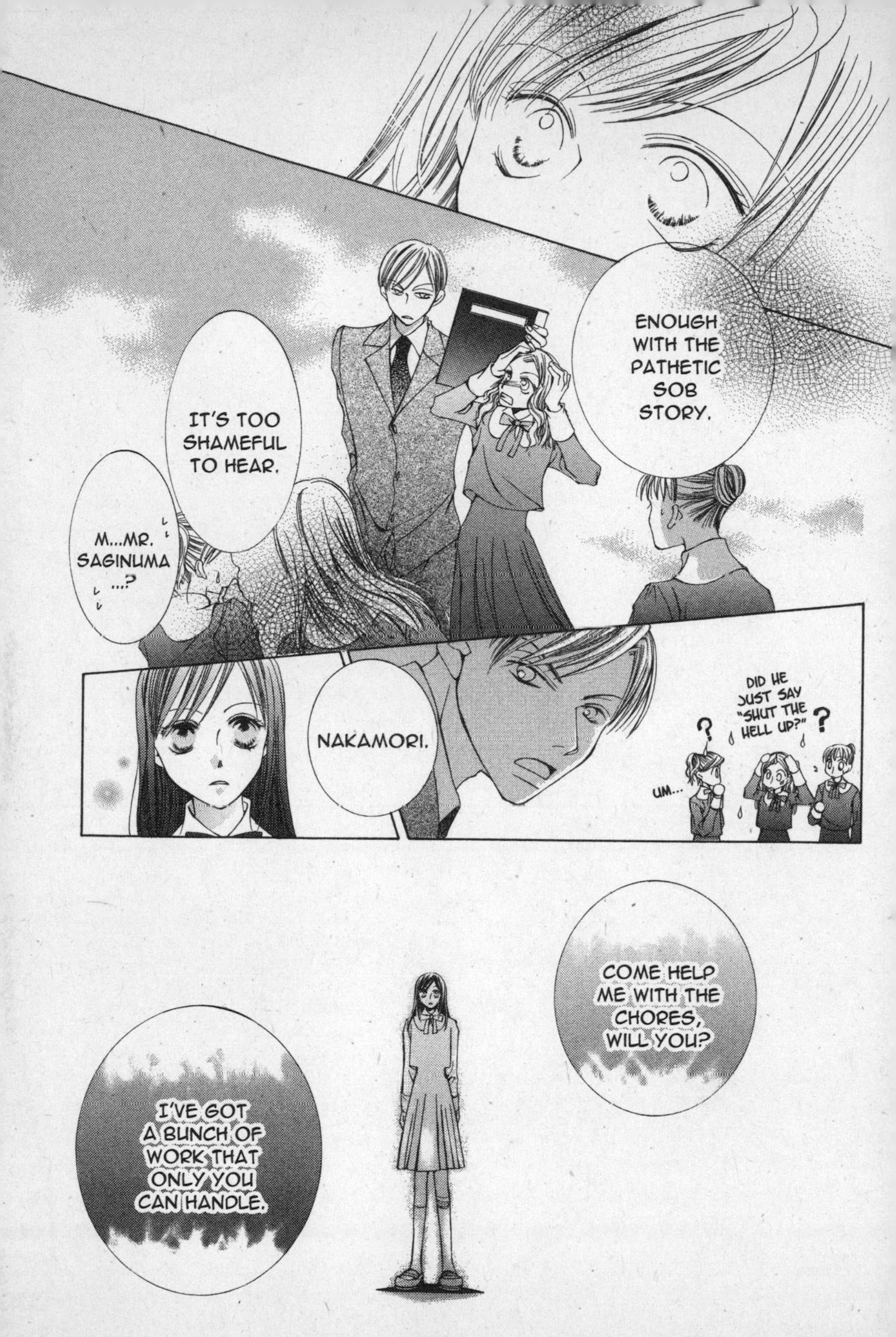
ENOUGH WITH THE PATHETIC SOB STORY.
IT'S TOO SHAMEFUL TO HEAR.
M...MR. SAGINUMA ...?
DID HE JUST SAY "SHUT THE HELL UP?"
UM...
NAKAMORI.
COME HELP ME WITH THE CHORES, WILL YOU?
I'VE GOT A BUNCH OF WORK THAT ONLY YOU CAN HANDLE.

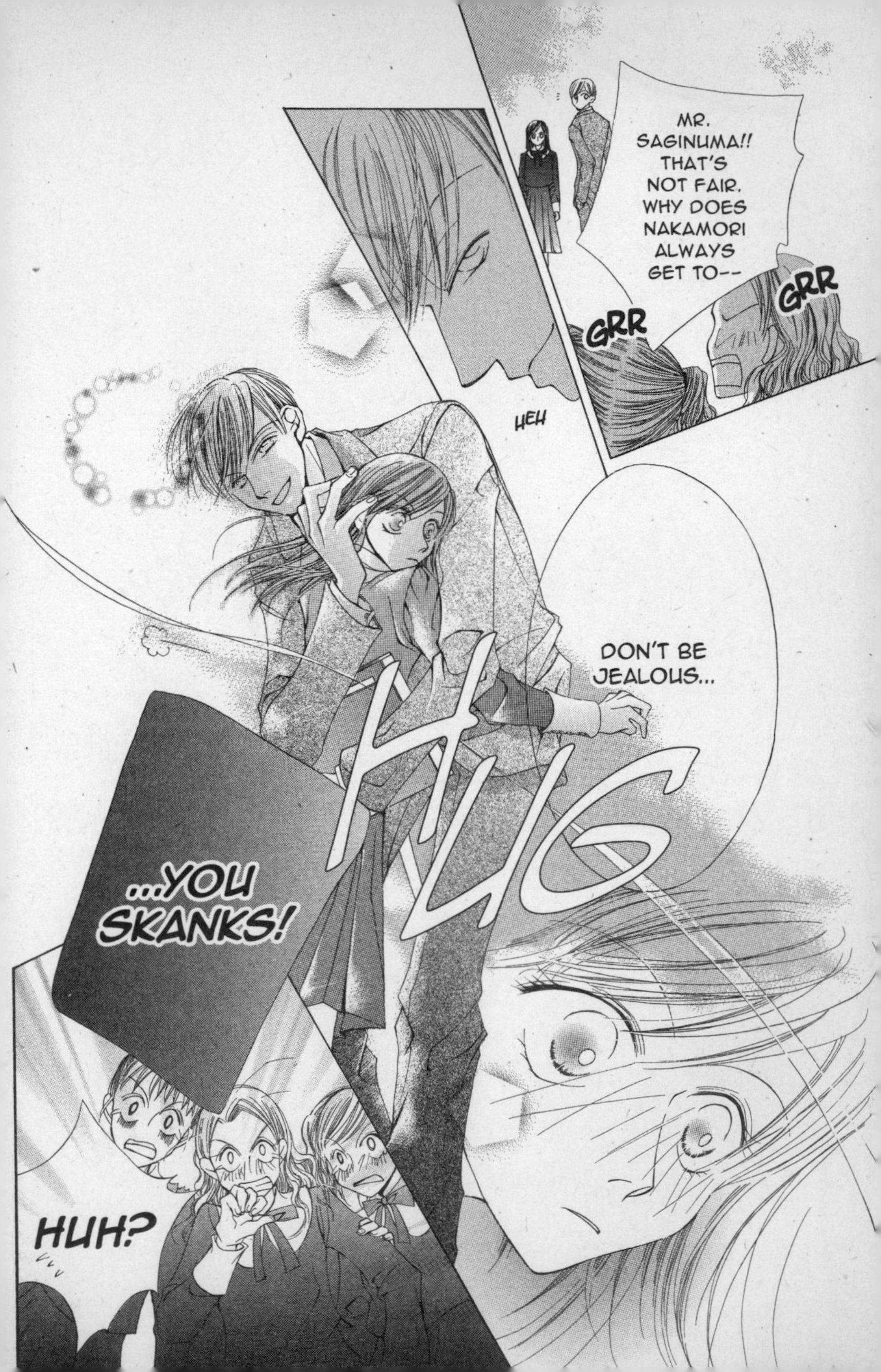
MR. SAGINUMA!! THAT'S NOT FAIR. WHY DOES NAKAMORI ALWAYS GET TO--
GRR
GRR
HEH
DON'T BE JEALOUS...
HUG
...YOU SKANKS!
HUH?

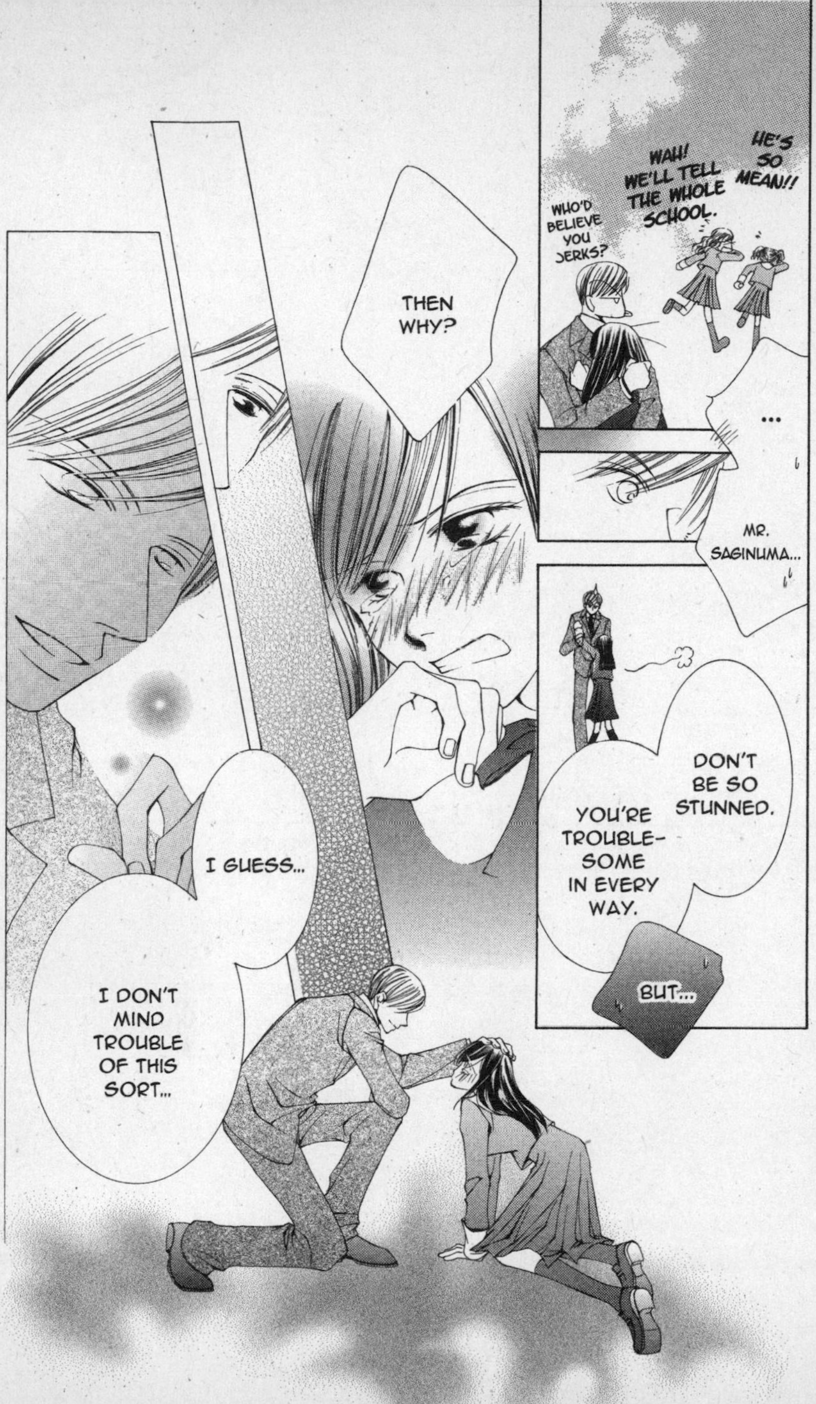
HE'S SO MEAN!!
WAH! WE'LL TELL THE WHOLE SCHOOL.
WHO'D BELIEVE YOU JERKS?
...
MR. SAGINUMA...
DON'T BE SO STUNNED.
YOU'RE TROUBLE-SOME IN EVERY WAY.
BUT...
THEN WHY?
I GUESS...
I DON'T MIND TROUBLE OF THIS SORT...

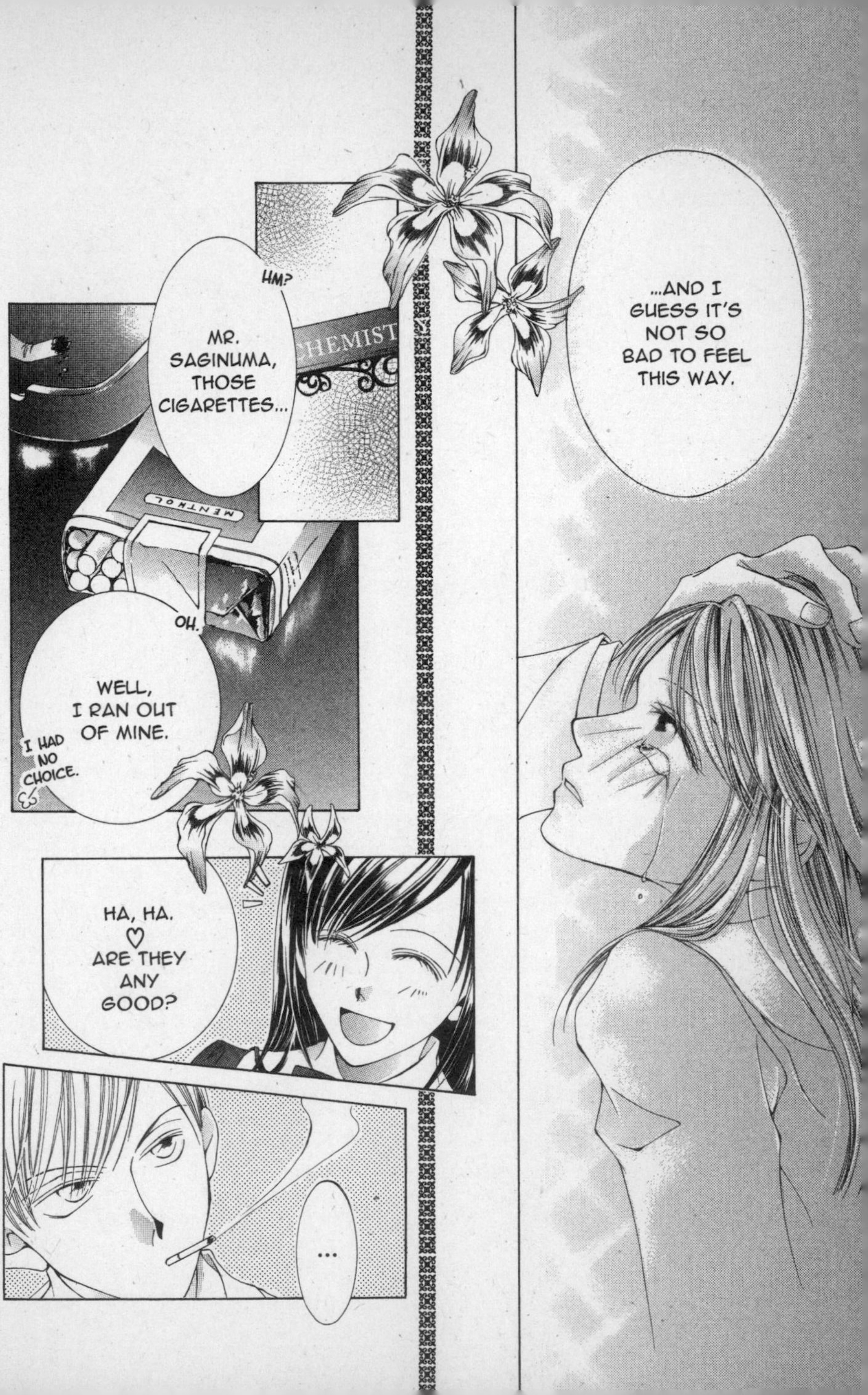
...AND I GUESS IT'S NOT SO BAD TO FEEL THIS WAY.
HM?
MR. SAGINUMA, THOSE CIGARETTES...
MENTHOL
OH.
WELL, I RAN OUT OF MINE.
I HAD NO CHOICE.
HA, HA. ♡ ARE THEY ANY GOOD?
...

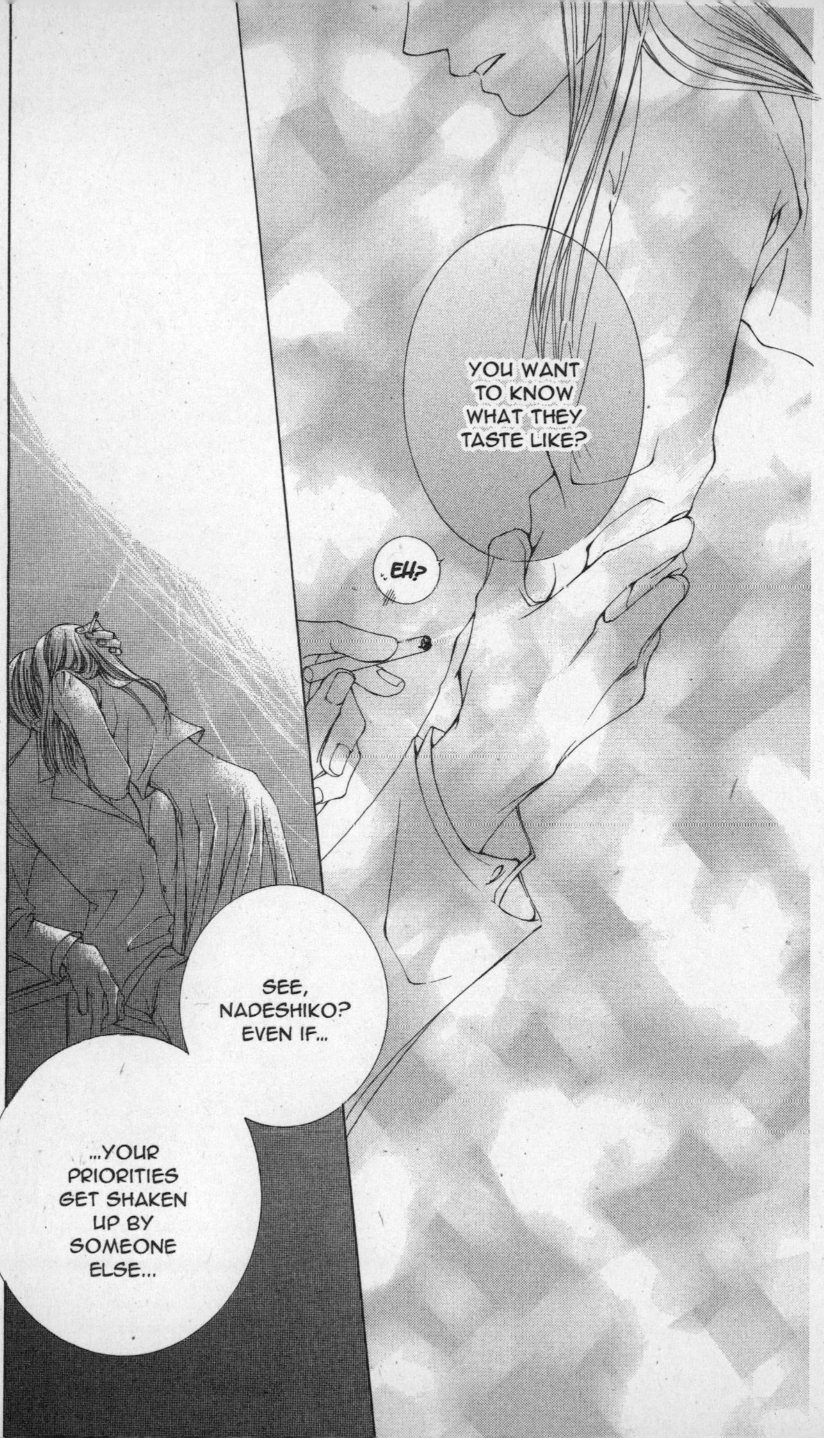
YOU WANT TO KNOW WHAT THEY TASTE LIKE?
EH?
SEE, NADESHIKO? EVEN IF...
...YOUR PRIORITIES GET SHAKEN UP BY SOMEONE ELSE...

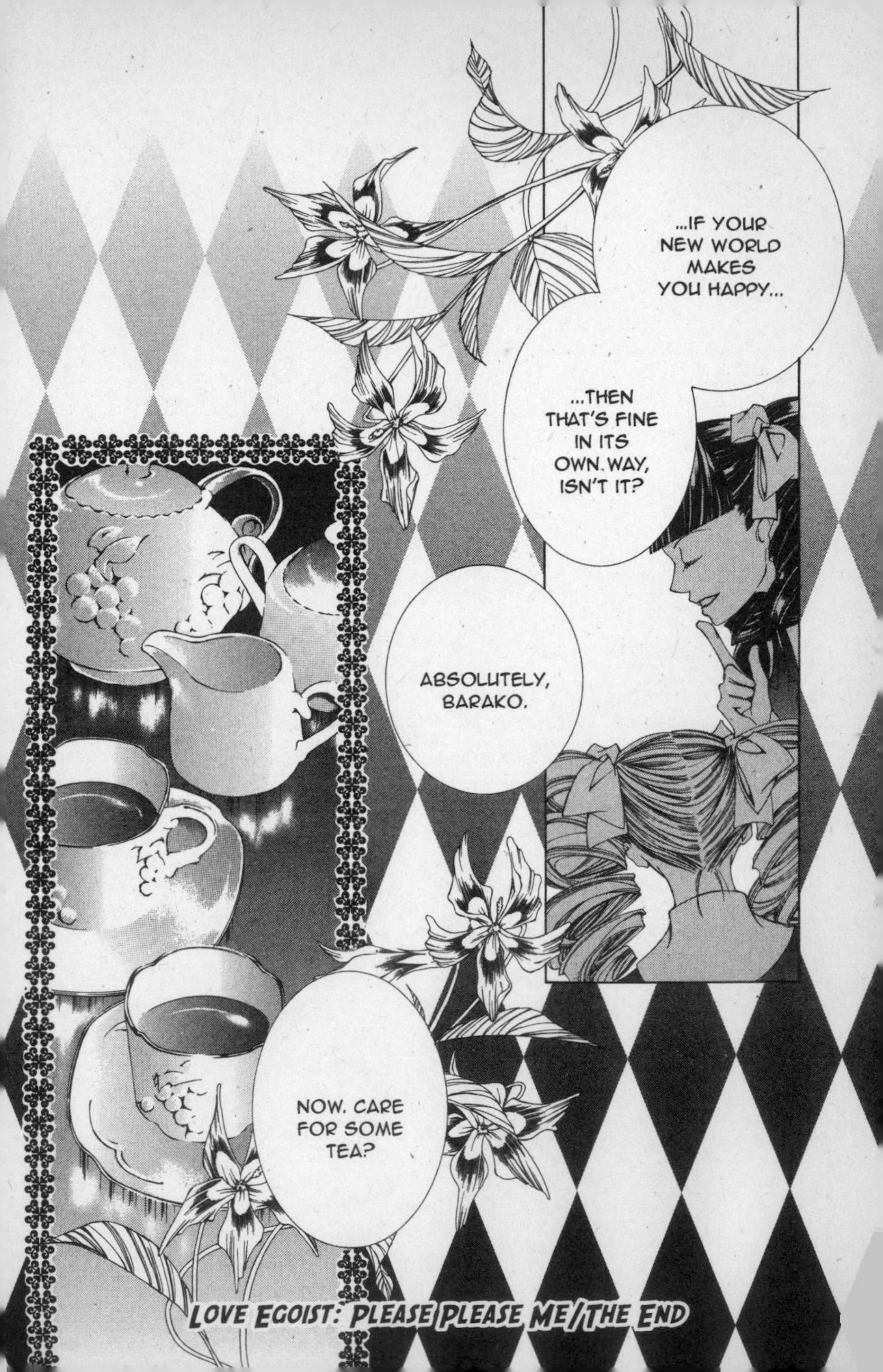
...IF YOUR NEW WORLD MAKES YOU HAPPY...
...THEN THAT'S FINE IN ITS OWN. WAY, ISN'T IT?
ABSOLUTELY, BARAKO.
NOW. CARE FOR SOME TEA?
LOVE EGOIST: PLEASE PLEASE ME/THE END

EGOISTIC CLUB

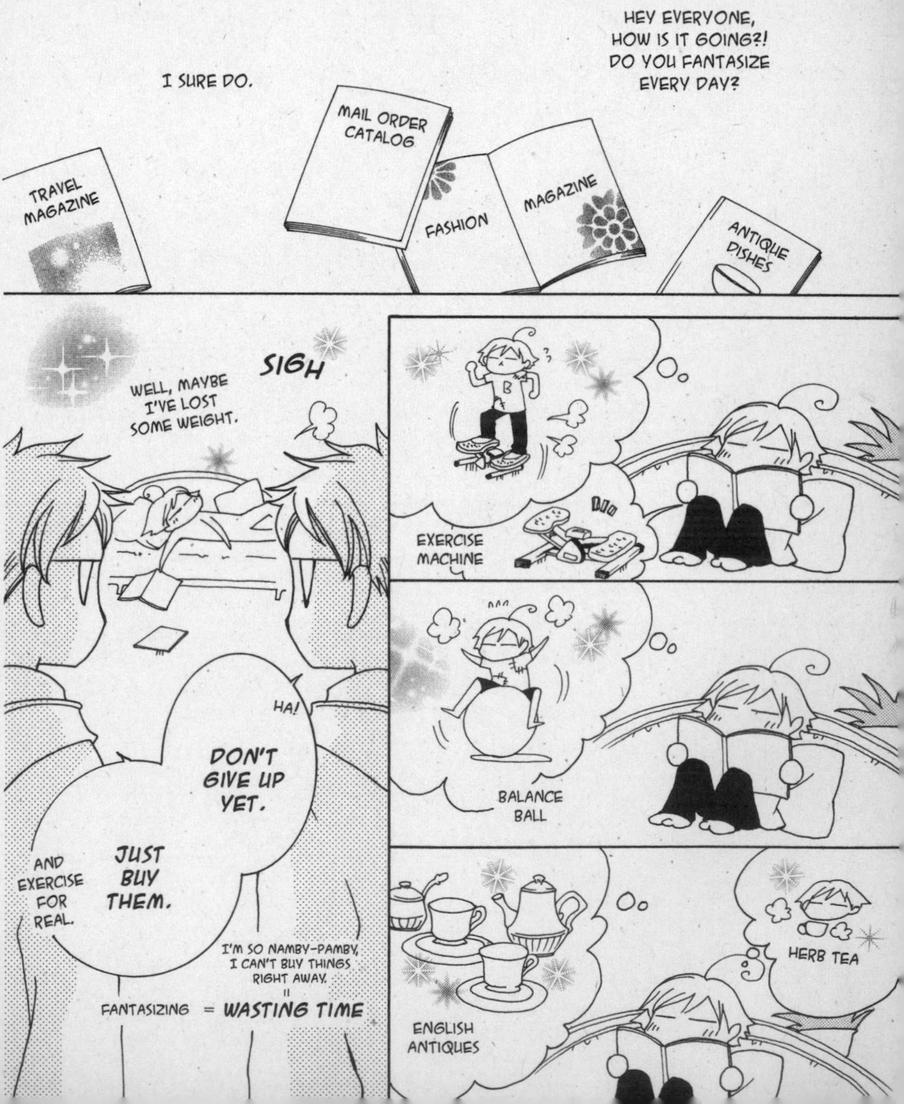
HEY EVERYONE, HOW IS IT GOING?! DO YOU FANTASIZE EVERY DAY?
I SURE DO.
ANTIQUE DISHES
FASHION MAGAZINE
MAIL ORDER CATALOG
TRAVEL MAGAZINE
EXERCISE MACHINE
BALANCE BALL
HERB TEA
ENGLISH ANTIQUES
SIGH
WELL, MAYBE I'VE LOST SOME WEIGHT.
HA!
DON'T GIVE UP YET.
JUST BUY THEM.
AND EXERCISE FOR REAL.
I'M SO NAMBY-PAMBY, I CAN'T BUY THINGS RIGHT AWAY.
II
FANTASIZING = WASTING TIME

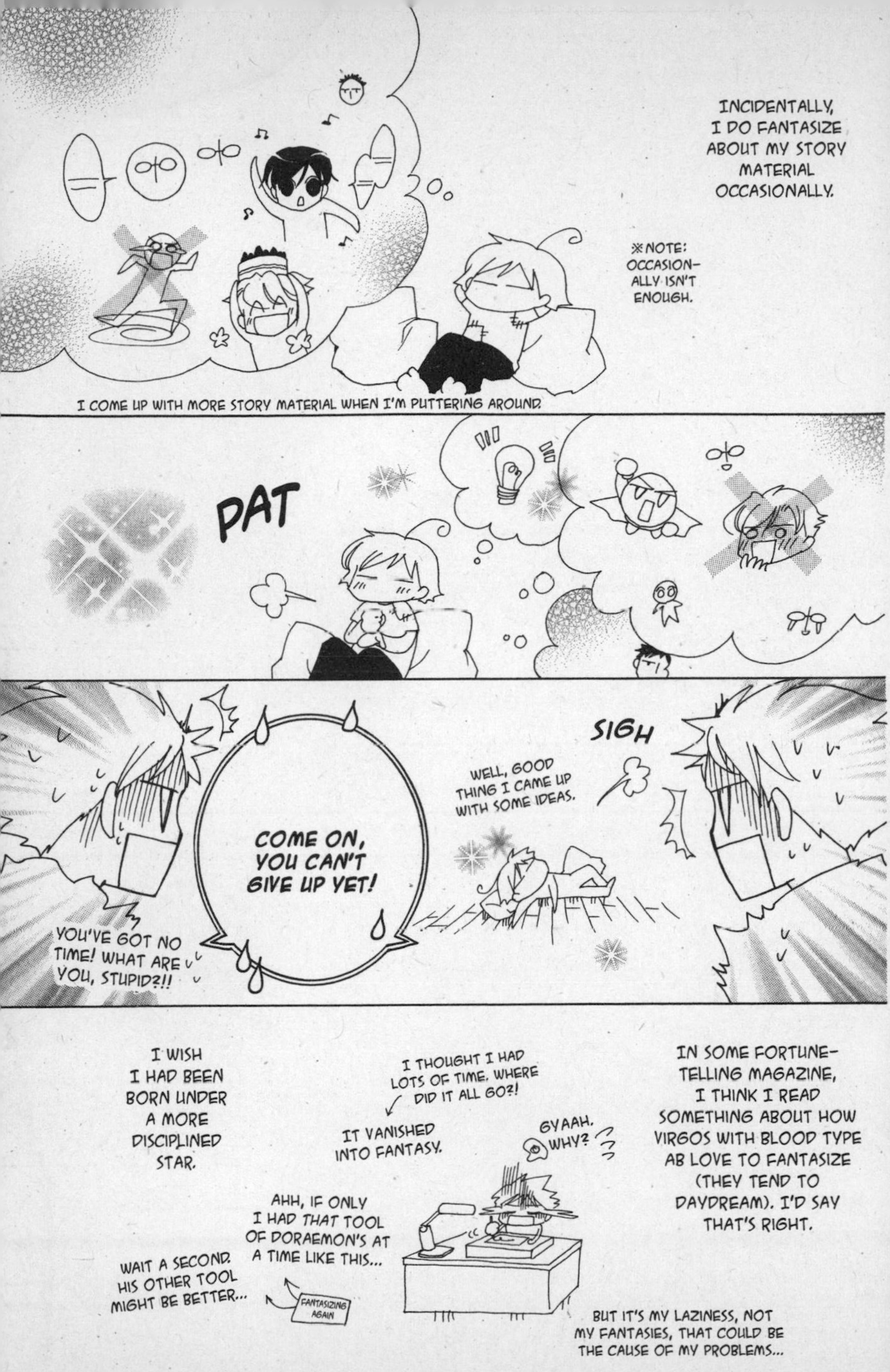
INCIDENTALLY, I DO FANTASIZE ABOUT MY STORY MATERIAL OCCASIONALLY.
※NOTE: OCCASION-ALLY ISN'T ENOUGH.
I COME UP WITH MORE STORY MATERIAL WHEN I'M PUTTERING AROUND.
PAT
SIGH
WELL, GOOD THING I CAME UP WITH SOME IDEAS.
COME ON, YOU CAN'T GIVE UP YET!
YOU'VE GOT NO TIME! WHAT ARE YOU, STUPID?!!
IN SOME FORTUNE-TELLING MAGAZINE, I THINK I READ SOMETHING ABOUT HOW VIRGOS WITH BLOOD TYPE AB LOVE TO FANTASIZE (THEY TEND TO DAYDREAM). I'D SAY THAT'S RIGHT.
BUT IT'S MY LAZINESS, NOT MY FANTASIES, THAT COULD BE THE CAUSE OF MY PROBLEMS...
GYAAH. WHY?
I THOUGHT I HAD LOTS OF TIME. WHERE DID IT ALL GO?!
IT VANISHED INTO FANTASY.
I WISH I HAD BEEN BORN UNDER A MORE DISCIPLINED STAR.
AHH, IF ONLY I HAD THAT TOOL OF DORAEMON'S AT A TIME LIKE THIS...
FANTASIZING AGAIN
WAIT A SECOND. HIS OTHER TOOL MIGHT BE BETTER...

FLIRTATIOUS DRAWING

SINCE THE NORMAL VERSION OF HARUHI AND HUNNY APPEARS ON PAGE 1, THIS ONE IS AN IMAGE OF DARK HUNNY ACCOSTING THE PRINCESS AS SHE SLUMBERS.

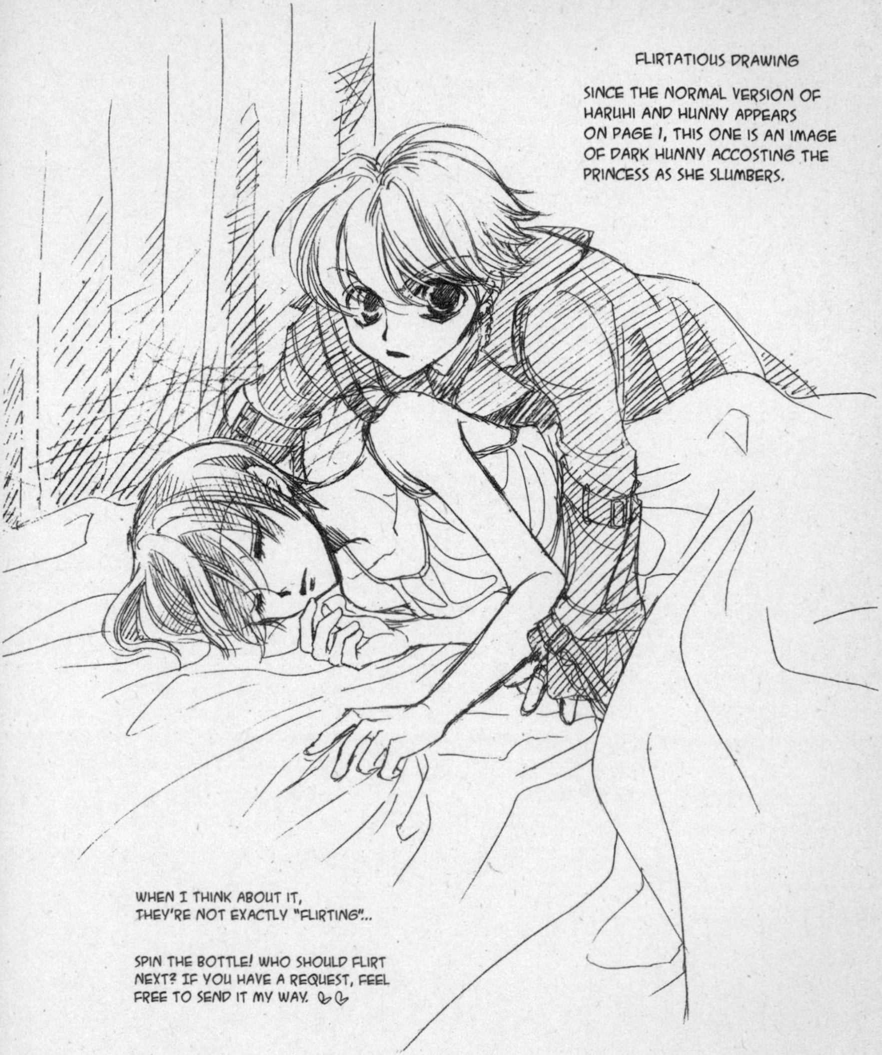

WHEN I THINK ABOUT IT, THEY'RE NOT EXACTLY "FLIRTING"...

SPIN THE BOTTLE! WHO SHOULD FLIRT NEXT? IF YOU HAVE A REQUEST, FEEL FREE TO SEND IT MY WAY. ♡♡

Special Thanks!!

AMASHITA✿, ALL THE EDITORS, ND EVERYONE INVOLVED IN PUBLISHING HIS BOOK. AND OF COURSE YOU, HE READERS!!

STAFF

YUI NATSUKI ✿ RIKU
AYA AOMURA ✿ YUTORI HIZAKURA
RIICHI HIGASHIMOTO ✿ HATORI'S MOM (IN CHARGE OF COOKING)

EGOISTIC CLUB / THE END

EDITOR'S NOTES

EPISODE 28
Page 11: *Namahage* are imaginary demons involved in a ritual for the New Year on the Oga peninsula of Japan. The townsfolk dress up as these scary demons and go house to house, asking if the children have been good.

EPISODE 29
Page 39: Usiwakamaru, aka Yoshitsune, was a general in the late Heian period who was well versed in martial arts. He was small in stature, like Hunny, and had a hostile relationship with his half brother, Yoritomo, after the Gempai War (1180-1185).

Page 42: When the Host Club members are cheering for Hunny, "3292" was used for his name in the Japanese version. These numbers represent "Mitsukuni": 3 is "mi"; the English word for 2 is close to the pronunciation of "tsu"; 9 is "ku"; and 2 is "ni." Using numbers for words is popular in text messaging in Japan.

EPISODE 30
Page 73: A *shinai* is a practice sword made out of bamboo.

LOVE EGOIST
Page 154: *Shogi* is Japanese chess. A Rika doll, or *Rika-chan ningyo*, is a doll similar to Barbie.

Page 155: March 14 is White Day in Japan, the day that men give presents to the women who gave them chocolate on February 14.

Page 165: A *burriko* is a female who puts on a false front to attract men and who is rude or unfriendly to other females. The term is short for *kawaiko burriko*, or "pretentious cutie." Although the singer Seiko Matsuda, famous for wearing frilly "little girl" dresses, was associated with the phrase, the term does not mean girls who dress younger than they are or "loli"--however, a female who dresses that way to attract men would fit in the burriko category.

EGOISTIC CLUB
Page 191: Doraemon is a cat in a manga and anime of the same name. He is known for having all sorts of useful gadgets.

Author Bio

Bisco Hatori made her manga debut with *Isshun kan no Romance* (A Moment of Romance) in *LaLa DX* magazine. The comedy *Ouran High School Host Club* is her breakout hit. When she's stuck thinking up characters' names, she gets inspired by loud, upbeat music (her radio is set to NACK5 FM). She enjoys reading all kinds of manga, but she's especially fond of the sci-fi drama *Please Save My Earth* and *Slam Dunk*, a basketball classic.

OURAN HIGH SCHOOL HOST CLUB
Vol. 7
The Shojo Beat Manga Edition

STORY AND ART BY BISCO HATORI

Translation & English Adaptation/Naomi Kokubo & Eric-Jon Rössel Waugh
Touch-up Art & Lettering/George Caltsoudas
Graphic Design/Izumi Evers
Editor/Nancy Thistlethwaite

Managing Editor/Megan Bates
Editorial Director/Elizabeth Kawasaki
VP & Editor in Chief/Yumi Hoashi
Sr. Director of Acquisitions/Rika Inouye
Sr. VP of Marketing/Liza Coppola
Exec. VP of Sales & Marketing/John Easum
Publisher/Hyoe Narita

Printed in Canada

Published by VIZ Media, LLC
P.O. Box 77010
San Francisco, CA 94107

Shojo Beat Manga Edition
10 9 8 7 6 5 4 3 2
First printing, September 2006
Second printing, September 2006

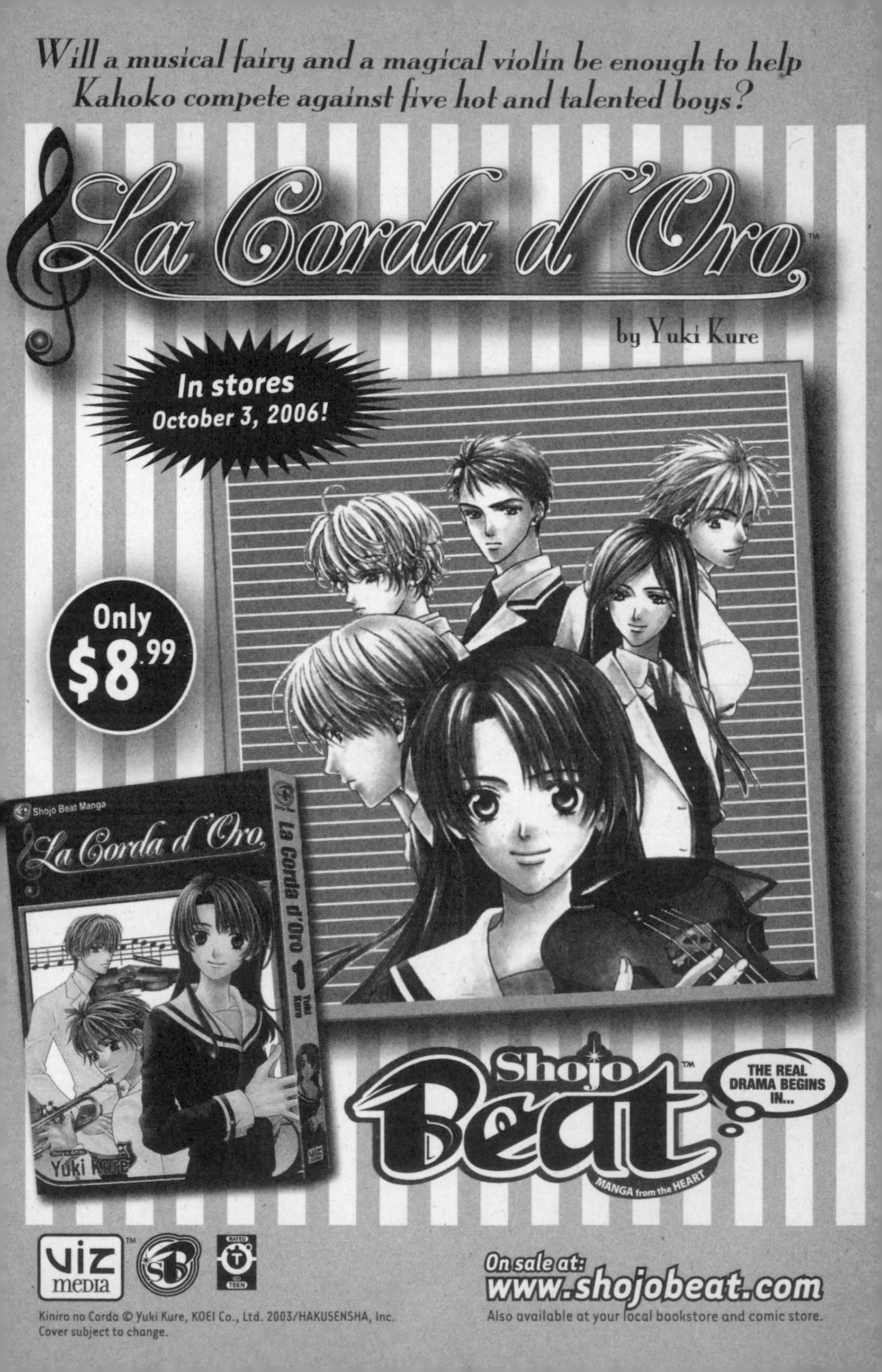